ISADORA

Dramatic pose by Arnold Genthe *(New York Public Library and the Museum of the City of New York)*.

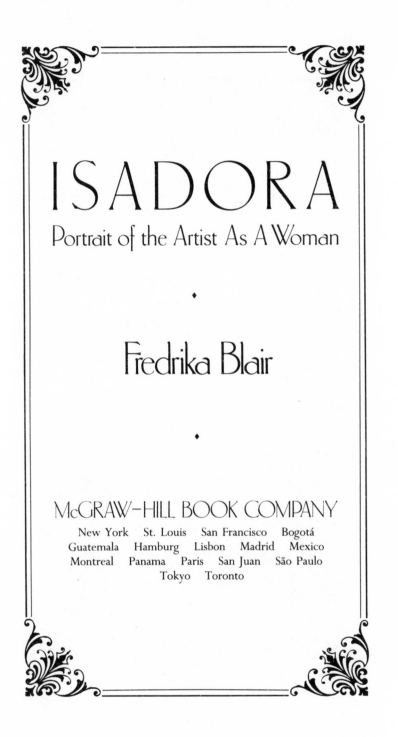

ISADORA

Portrait of the Artist As A Woman

◆

Fredrika Blair

◆

McGRAW-HILL BOOK COMPANY

New York   St. Louis   San Francisco   Bogotá
Guatemala   Hamburg   Lisbon   Madrid   Mexico
Montreal   Panama   Paris   San Juan   São Paulo
Tokyo   Toronto

Dedicated with love and gratitude to the memory of my parents,
Fredericka Staats Tuttle Callaway
and
Frank Tuttle,
who inspired me to start this book, and to my husband,
Jerome Hastings,
whose help and devotion have enabled me to finish it.

23456789 DOHDOH 8765

ISBN 0-07-005598-X

LIBRARY OF CONGRESS CATALOGING IN PUBLICATION DATA
Blair, Fredrika.
  Isadora.
  Bibliography: p.
  Includes index.
  1. Duncan, Isadora, 1878-1927.   2. Dancers—United
States—Biography.   3. Modern dance.   I. Title.
GV1785.D8B56 1985   793.3'2'0924[B]   85-12808
ISBN 0-07-005598-X

BOOK DESIGN BY KATHRYN PARISE

In an ermine hat (*Mme. Mario Meunier–Christine Dalliès Collection*).

Contents

Contents

Preface

EOPLE who had never seen Isadora Duncan dance used to be interested in Isadora the woman. They read her memoir, *My Life,* and they became captured by Isadora. And indeed Isadora—the innovator, the revolutionary of the dance, the rebel against society, the witty, the liberated, the extravagant, the tragic, the self-destructive, the healing, and the creative woman—is a fascinating person. Curiosity about Isadora has always been so great that Genevieve Oswald, curator of the Dance Collection in the Library of the Performing Arts at Lincoln Center, noted that there are ten times as many requests for books and other material about Isadora as there are for any other dancer.

But it was hitherto supposed that her dance had vanished forever, and that even if it were resurrected, it would be found too simple and naive to interest audiences accustomed to technical feats in both the modern dance and ballet.

Yet now we suddenly see a renewed interest in her dance. There have been, on the one hand, those works inspired by Isadora: *Isadora,* by Kenneth MacMillan; *Five Brahms Waltzes in the Manner of Isadora Duncan,* by Frederick Ashton; *Dances for Isadora,* by José Limon; and Maurice Béjart's *Isadora* (which critic Tobi Tobias characterized as an "unintentional travesty . . . danced with magnificent kitsch by the Bolshoi Ballet's Maya Plisetskaya . . .").[1] On the other hand, there have been Isadora's works themselves, re-created in solo recital by Annabelle Gamson (a pupil of Julia Levien and thus a fourth-generation Duncanite) and in group and solo works presented by the Isadora Duncan Centenary Dance Company, headed by Julia Levien, Gemze de Lappe (pupils of Anna and Irma Duncan), Hortense Kooluris (who studied with Maria-Theresa Duncan as well as Anna and Irma), and Sylvia Gold (of the New England Conservatory). Two other groups, Dancers for Isadora and the Quinlan-Kritchels Ensemble, have performed her dances and new works created in Duncan technique. WNET's "Dance in America" television series, *Trailblazers of the Modern Dance,* featured Lynne Seymour performing Ashton's *Five Brahms Waltzes in the Manner of Isadora Duncan* and Gamson interpreting two Duncan solos to Scriabin études. The Council for the Arts in Westchester County, New York, is filming Maria-Theresa (the Thérèse Duncan of Isadora's six original pupils) in the dances of Isadora. On the west coast there have been performances by The Dionysian Duncan Dancers (of the Paris-based Isadora Duncan International Institute of Classical Dance, directed by Ligoa Duncan), while in San Francisco, the Isadora Duncan Heritage Society, headed by Mignon Garland, celebrated Isadora's birthday with a program of her dances. An important book of dance notation, *The Dances of Isadora Duncan,* by Najda Chilkowsky, has been published.

Many of these dance events were, of course, prompted by the centennial of Isadora's birth, as were the various plays, "musical collages," poems, sculptures, and the like suggested by her life or personality. However, the critical reevaluation of Isadora's work and the public's enjoyment of it indicate that there is beginning to be a new understanding of her dance. People have begun to understand the historical significance of it and to appreciate it on its own terms.

They want to see more of it, and they wonder how it can be preserved for posterity. (The irony is that for years the remaining members of Isadora's band had tried in vain to interest various companies and foundations in filming Isadora's work.)

Of the original "Isadorables" (as Isadora's grown-up pupils were christened by the poet and critic Fernand Divoire) only two are still alive. Lisa Duncan, whose later career took place in Europe, died on January 24, 1976, in Dresden, Germany. Irma Duncan (Mrs. Sherman Rogers), whose books about Isadora have contributed much to our understanding of her life and art, succumbed in Santa Barbara, California, on September 20, 1977. Anna Duncan, blinded by a rare blood disease, died in Yonkers, New York, on March 7, 1980, while she was struggling to complete her book of reminiscences about Isadora. Of those remaining, Erica Lohman Duncan withdrew from the dance many years ago to practice painting, and Maria-Theresa Duncan (Mrs. Stephan Bourgeois) alone is still dancing. All have much they can teach us through their recollections and their knowledge of Isadora's dances, if their memoirs and records are preserved.

The growing interest today in Isadora is in marked contrast to the situation some twenty years ago, when I first tried to find out what Isadora's dances were like. I looked in the New York Telephone Directory but could find no mention of Duncan dancers, Duncan dance teachers, or the Duncan Dance Guild. I had heard that Isadora's dance was still being taught here and there, but where could I go to see it? I was at a loss until one day I noticed in the Sunday *New York Times* the picture of a dancer billed as Maria-Theresa. In the days when she danced as one of Isadora's girls, she was always listed on the program merely as Thérèse, but I saw at once from Maria-Theresa's stance and her Grecian draperies that she must be an authentic Duncan—one of the original six. I went to her recital, met various Duncan pupils there, and eventually wound up taking lessons in Duncan dancing. (I do not mean to give the impression that I am a dancer. Certainly no one who has ever seen me in action would be under that illusion.)

I studied first with Mrs. Augustin Duncan, then with Julia Levien. To both I am deeply grateful. During the same period I went to all of Maria-Theresa's recitals, and although she was at that time dancing her own compositions, not Isadora's, I learned much about Duncan movement from watching her, and from listening to her impromptu remarks. I had the good fortune one afternoon to see Irma Duncan teach a master class to Julia Levien and Hortense Kooluris. I also consulted Mignon Garland about some of Isadora's dances. Lastly, for two years Anna Duncan had the kindness to let me watch her master class, whose members included Julia, Hortense, Gemze de Lappe, and Ruth Perryman. These sessions with Anna were invaluable to me.

While interest in Isadora's dance has been reawakened, speculation about her life and character has never ceased, and that interest seems to be increasing. The critic Robert Kimball notes: "One striking reason for the Duncan revival is the almost insatiable yearning today for stars, . . . charismatic leaders who can serve as role models in the struggle for reassertion of the individual in an increasingly homogenized society. Isadora Duncan is correctly perceived as such an individual."[2]

Why does she appeal to us?

Fernand Divoire describes[3] a dance which she once improvised as an encore at the end of a concert at the Théâtre Lyrique de la Gaité. She said, "I am going to dance the philosophy of my life." To Divoire, she seemed to be standing before an invisible bronze door. Again and again she hurled herself against the door, and again and again the unyielding door felled her. Finally, bruised and shaken, with a tremendous effort of will, she gathered up all her strength and flung herself against the invisible door. And the heavy door, unhinged, at last fell open.

The tragedy of Isadora is that she was broken by the effort of opening the door—nevertheless she forced it open. Life broke her, but it never diminished her. Her conceptions, goals, and efforts always retained heroic stature.

The sense of heroic effort, regardless of consequences, is one reason why we are so moved by Isadora's dances. She is ourselves before life has taught us to be "reasonable" (unambitious) about what we hope to accomplish.

She is ourselves while we are still at one with nature, and she has an innocence and a youthful sense of wonder about all living things.

She has compassion, without shrinking at pain and ugliness, hatred and grief.

She has eagerness, and above all she has courage. She will batter down that door if it kills her.

And because we feel this, she gives us a tremendous sense of release, a sense of our own possibilities. She teaches us not to calculate the cost, but to see what must be done and to do it.

This is why her dancing came as a revelation, a religious experience to many people. They were changed by it. Max Eastman called her "beautiful, a militant and mighty woman, the symbol of those who put on their courage like armor and fought for the affirmation of life in America."

Gordon Craig, looking back in old age on the first time he had seen her dance, captures the enchantment and sense of release he felt on watching the young Isadora.

> . . . Into this dangerous world leapt Isadora, possessed of immense courage. . . . All she did was done with great ease or so it seemed—this it was which gave her an appearance of power. . . .
>
> How is it we know she is speaking her own language? We know it for we see her head, her hands, gently active, as are her feet, her whole person.
>
> And if she is speaking, what is she saying? No one would ever be able to report truly, yet no one present had a moment's doubt. Only this can we say—that she was telling the air the very things we longed to hear and till she came we never dreamed we should hear; and now we heard them and this sent us all into an unusual state of joy, and I—I sat still and speechless.[4]

Gordon Craig loved her, left her, and wrote about her. Most of the books about Isadora have been written by people who knew her. These books have the quality of intimacy, and they usually focus on that period of the dancer's life which they knew best, to the exclusion of other periods. As for her autobiography, though it bears the imprint of her personality—one might say the sound of her voice—it is full of omissions and inaccuracies and it ends before her trip to Russia.

The present book can make no claim to personal reminiscences of Isadora. It is an account of the dancer's whole life—an attempt to put her character and works in historical perspective. It introduces new material. It also inevitably contains much material familiar to readers of other books about Isadora, but it is hoped that the cumulative effect of such material will present a fuller and perhaps somewhat different picture of her than that which emerges when such information is widely scattered among many books. The narrative does not deal in any detail with Isadora's relations with her pupils because there is already one first-hand account of the subject, *Duncan Dancer,* by Irma Duncan, and two other first-hand accounts in the process of being finished, one by Maria-Theresa Duncan Bourgeois, the other by the late Anna Duncan, now being completed by a young friend. Nor does the present book attempt to incorporate the material from Russian sources which is made available to western readers, much of it for the first time, in *Isadora and Esenin,* by Gordon McVay, since his book covers that part of Isadora's life in detail. I have, however, used his account to fill in a few dates or facts, and, when I have found myself disagreeing with his sources' interpretation of events or people, I have so indicated.

Though Isadora's inspiration was Greek, she did not believe in the Just Mean. She was Dionysian, not Apollonian. "My motto: sans limites," she once wrote in a letter to Irma Duncan. Her commitment was total, her abandonment complete. To Rodin she was, quite simply, "the greatest woman the world has ever known."

If my book manages to increase the reader's understanding of the dancer's life and art, while evoking the living Isadora, I shall be satisfied.

Acknowledgments

 THANK the following institutions and individuals for permission to examine and/or quote from manuscripts and other materials in their possession or under their care:

The New York Public Library, the Library for the Performing Arts at Lincoln Center (The Dance Collection and The Craig-Duncan Collection)

The Library for the Performing Arts at Lincoln Center, the New York Public Library (The Irma Duncan Rogers Collection)

The Archives de la Préfecture de Police, Paris, France

The Archives de la Seine, Paris

The Bibliothèque de l'Arsenal, Paris

The Bibliothèque du Conservatoire de Musique de Paris: Isadora Duncan file

The Bibliothèque Nationale, Paris: Collection Gordon Craig

The Bibliothèque de l'Opéra, Paris: Archives Internationale de la Danse

The California State Library in Sacramento: Microfilm Collection

Acknowledgments

The Collection of Mme. Fernand Divoire, Paris

Letters from Fernand Divoire to Isadora Duncan in the Duncan Collection, the Library of the Performing Arts at Lincoln Center

Harry Ransom Humanities Research Center, the University of Texas at Austin, The Craig Archives; also the Albert Davis Collection (photographs)

The Maurice Magnus–Isadora Duncan–Gordon Craig Collection: Temporarily on loan to the Library of the Performing Arts at Lincoln Center

The Collection of Mme. Mario Meunier and Christine Dalliès: Photographs and drawings, including drawings by Grandjouan, Sartorio, Lucien Jacques, Bourdelle, and Dalliès, and fifty-one photographs

The Musée Bourdelle, Paris

The Musée Rodin, Paris

The Museum of the City of New York: The Arnold Genthe Collection in the Theatre Collection, and the Mary Fanton Roberts Collection in the Theatre Collection

The New York Public Library Newspaper Collection at Twenty-Third Street, and many other departments, including the Slavonic Collection, the Theatre Collection, and the Music Collection

The Louis Sue Collection of letters from Isadora Duncan

The Donald Oenslager–Edward Gordon Craig Collection in The Beinecke Library, Yale University Library

The University Research Library: Department of Special Collections, University of California at Los Angeles, Edward Gordon Craig Collection and the Mary Desti Papers

I should also like to thank the following individuals for their valuable help:

TRANSLATORS: Peter Golden, Katya Ford, Jane Harris, Geraldine Rinehart Lykins, and Edward Meywald.

RESEARCHERS: Nancy Hallinan, Jane Harris, Renee Gregoire Miller, and Mme. Olivier Ziegel, as well as Soviet dance scholar Elizabeth Souritz, who kindly found some information for Chap. 13.

My thanks and gratitude also to the following: Mlle. Lucienne Astruc; A.K. Baragwanath, senior curator of the Museum of the City of New York; my mentor and old friend, Jacques Barzun; Mme.

Acknowledgments

Aia Bertrand; Mrs. Hilda Bohem, The University Research Library, Department of Special Collections, UCLA; Mrs. William A. Bradley; Susan Braun; Witter Bynner; George H. Cabaniss, Jr.; Selma Jeanne Cohen; George Copeland; Edward Gordon Craig; Mme. Fernand Divoire; Anna Duncan; Mrs. Augustin Duncan; Irma Duncan (Mrs. Sherman Rogers); Maria-Theresa Duncan (Mrs. Stephan Bourgeois); Raymond Duncan; Ms. Ellen S. Dunlap, research librarian at the Humanities Research Center, the University of Texas at Austin; Hugh Eames; Marion Evans; Paul Fabri; Bernardine Szold Fritz; Mignon Garland; Els Grelinger; Paul Hertelendy; Jean and Lawrence Heyl; Martha M. Kaihatsu; Simon Karlinsky; Richard H. Koch, II; Julia Levien; Isaac Don Levine; Mme. Anne Lotsy; Jeanne and George Maloney; Joseph E. Marks III; Gordon McVay; Mme. Mario Meunier; Jeremiah Newton; Donald Oenslager; Genevieve Oswald; Alexander and Helen Pickering; Al Pischl; Harrison Salisbury; Ted Shawn; Francis Steegmuller; Louis Sue; Fredericka Venables; David Weiss; and Andrew Wentink.

I should also like to thank these members of my family—my parents, Frank Tuttle, and Fredericka Staats Tuttle Callaway, for their encouragement and support; my brother-in-law, Taras Votichenko, for making available letters and pictures formerly in the possession of his father, Sacha Votichenko; and my sister Helen Tuttle Votichenko—and my friend Nancy Hallinan for their criticism and help with this book. Above all, I should like to thank my husband Jerome Hastings for criticism, typing, encouragement, and help in so many ways that there is not room enough to list them here.

Isadora Duncan at the Portal of the Parthenon, Edward Steichen, 1921 (*Collection, The Museum of Modern Art, New York*).

Signs and Portents
1877

ISADORA Duncan, that spiritual daughter of classical
Greece, shared with the ancient world the convictions
that significant events are foreshadowed by portents
and that certain people are marked by fate for eminent
and terrible destinies.

"Like the family of the Atrides," she wrote in an early draft of
her memoirs, "there are strains of blood . . . [which seem to be]
continuously enveloped in tragedy."

". . . My first recollection—a clear sensual remembrance of being
thrown from a burning window to the arms of a policeman."[1] The
place where she lived was going up in flames, as shortly before, her
parents' marriage and the Duncan fortunes had gone up in smoke.
These memories—the blazing hotel,[2] her frantic mother, her absent
father, and comforting arms around her—assumed symbolic proportions for the little Isadora.

She begins her autobiography: "The character of a child is already
plain, even in its mother's womb. Before I was born my mother

was in great agony of spirit, and in a tragic situation. She could take no food except iced oysters and iced champagne. If people ask me when I began to dance, I reply, 'In my mother's womb, probably as a result of the oysters and champagne—the food of Aphrodite.' "

What was this tragic situation that Isadora never reveals? As in Greek legends, the story begins before the heroine's birth and is the consequence of the actions and ancestry of her parents.

Her mother, born Mary Isadora (Dora) Gray, was the daughter of Thomas Gray, a man of some prominence in San Francisco. A native of Ireland, Gray had first immigrated to Illinois where he fought in the Black Hawk War (and incidentally struck up an acquaintance with another volunteer, Abraham Lincoln). Between forays, Captain Gray scoured the country seeking recruits, and in St. Louis he met Mary Gorman, a slight young woman with a strong-featured "Spanish type of Irish beauty"[3] who succeeded in recruiting *him*. At the end of hostilities, he and his bride crossed the Great Plains in a covered wagon; according to family tradition, their first son was born during an Indian raid. The Grays settled in San Francisco where they multiplied and prospered. In 1850 Thomas Gray started the first ferry service between San Francisco and Oakland. He served in the Civil War, rising to the rank of colonel and suffering the loss of a son who had also enlisted. After the war, he returned to the west coast, where he was appointed Naval Officer of the Port of San Francisco. He was subsequently elected three times to the California legislature.

The Catholic Grays must have been dismayed when their daughter Dora, a properly raised and accomplished young woman, announced her intention of marrying Joseph Charles Duncan. Not only was Duncan an Episcopalian, he was also thirty years older than Dora, divorced and the father of four grown children. That he was, however, a man of energy and enterprise, the Grays could not deny. Born in 1819, he came of an esteemed Philadelphia family; among his forebears was General William Duncan, who had served in the American Revolution under General Washington and was later an associate of General Jackson.[4] General Duncan's restless grandson, after working on a newspaper in New Orleans and engaging in an unsuccessful business venture in Springfield, Illinois, came to California in 1849. There, after various unremunerative jobs, he started a profitable auction firm, the Chinese Salesrooms, which offered Oriental art to the gold-rush millionaires of San Francisco. After selling the firm to his partner, he next opened a picture gallery on Pine Street, offering paintings he himself had selected in Europe. His interest in painting was more than commercial and led to his founding, along with his brother and others, of the San Francisco Art Association, of which he later became president. Joseph Duncan also dabbled in literature, and some of his verse was published in an anthology called *Outcroppings,* edited by Bret Harte.

In the days when he was still financially inexperienced, Duncan had run a lottery in San Francisco, a fairly usual occupation in the "get rich quick" atmosphere of that boom town. Unfortunately, too few people bought tickets and he failed to the amount of $225,000. "But," said his former partner, James Tobin, in an interview in the *San Francisco Evening Bulletin,*[5] "Duncan was the ablest and most indefatigable worker I ever knew. He was as sober as he was industrious. . . . After the lottery failure he resumed the auction business and started the publication of the *Morning Globe,* the *Evening Globe,* and the *Mirror.* He conducted three papers and his auction business at the same time." His diligence was finally rewarded. "He . . . figured in a $90 homesteads enterprise in which he made money. With the proceeds of the Homestead speculation he started The Pioneer Bank."

Thus, when the 50-year-old Duncan sought the hand of the 20-year-old Miss Gray, he was renowned as a man of property, an amateur and patron of the arts, and a person of some standing in the community.[6] He had, moreover, great charm and persuasiveness, so much so that Thomas Gray found himself consenting to become president of the bank that his son-in-law was then in the process of forming.

The Pioneer Land and Loan Bank was organized during 1869 and 1870, with a capital variously reported as $1 million and $2 million. In 1874, Duncan founded the Safe Deposit Company, for which he erected a handsome building, and, three years later, he inaugurated the Fidelity Savings Bank. His plans for still another institution, the Union Bank, did not achieve fruition, however, for on October 8, 1877 headlines proclaimed the collapse of the Pioneer Bank.

The failure created little surprise in financial circles. The *San Francisco Evening Bulletin* noted:

The payment of 1 percent per month's interest by Duncan's bank while other banks were lending money at 7 and 8 percent per annum was regarded as a suspicious circumstance. For the past three months or more, checks on the Pioneer Bank have been discredited at many of the banks of the city. . . .

It is reported that considerable sums of money have been loaned by Mr. Duncan on San Francisco lots. Until recently bankers have regarded this class of security as second or third rate. . . .

James de Frémery, President of the San Francisco Savings Bank . . . said that the manner in which the Pioneer Bank had been conducted was against all the rules for carrying on a legitimate savings bank business. . . . Most of the so-called loans were really investments in real estate, some being made with money borrowed at high rates of interest.

Despite this, the first news stories were not unsympathetic to Duncan. The *Evening Bulletin*[7] also described him as a "man of sanguine temperament, great energy, full of push and pluck, qualities that are eminently good when . . . under control of a conservative mind."

But the tone changed the next day when it was discovered that Duncan and his son-in-law, Benjamin F. Le Warne, had fled, leaving the books of the bank in a state'of confusion. Listed among the assets were stocks of the affiliated Safe Deposit Company (managed by Le Warne), which proved to be in even worse financial condition than the Pioneer Land and Loan Bank. The remaining Pioneer Bank officers knew nothing about the bank's transactions. The institution, wrote the *Evening Bulletin,* ". . . seems to have been endowed with a dummy President and a figurehead directory . . . Thomas Gray confesses that he was only nominal president . . . having no voice in its management, and totally ignorant of its business; that he held the position and performed ornamental functions only. . . . It is extremely doubtful whether Mr. Gray held any of the bank stock." The strongboxes of the bank were discovered to be virtually empty, and the cashier said that at no time had the money on the premises amounted to more than $8000. The four business buildings that Duncan owned were found to be heavily mortgaged. Warrants were issued for the arrest of Duncan and Le Warne.

For Dora Gray Duncan the catastrophe was devastating. Married for eight years, she now had four young children, the youngest (Isadora) not five months old. The pride she had taken in her successful family had been dashed. Not only was her husband in hiding, but her father too was in disrepute for his dealings with his headstrong son-in-law. Also affected were Le Warne and William T. Duncan,[8] son-in-law and son, respectively, of Joseph Duncan by his first marriage. Both men had held posts in the bank besides being depositors; even if the family name could be cleared, they faced financial ruin.

Each day's headlines brought fresh revelations and rumors. "There seems [sic] to be no securities in the bank at all. Everything is cleared out. . . . Duncan stated that all real estate owned by him belonged to the bank, but thus far it has not been possible to learn what the real estate is, as there is no memorandum in the bank." Among the assertions printed in the paper, one paragraph must have struck the already distracted wife with particularly painful force: "A letter addressed to Duncan was received and opened by the [receivership] committee yesterday. It is signed with initials but it is evidently written by a lady who knew all about the affairs of the bank and was also cognizant of an intention to realize and flee on the part of Duncan. The lady is not Duncan's wife, but who she is cannot be surmised."

Perhaps in an effort to bring some kind of order into her shattered life, on October 13, 1877, Dora Gray Duncan brought her baby daughter to Old St. Mary's Church in San Francisco to be christened. The baptismal register reads (in Latin):

On the 13th day of October in the year of our Lord 1877 was baptised Angela I. Duncan, born on the 26th day of May, in the same year, of Joseph and Mary Duncan of this Parish, Godparents were William T. Duncan and Mary Morrison.

J. MacSweeney, Ass't. Pastor[9]

This birth date, May 26, 1877, is worthy of note, since it differs from the previously accepted date given by Isadora's older brother Augustin of May 27, 1878. The birth records of the four Duncan children, together with the vital statistics of other San Franciscans, were destroyed in the fire that followed the earthuake of 1906. Years later, on January 2, 1947, Augustin Duncan appeared before Superior Court Judge Edward Murphy to testify to the birth dates of the four Duncans as follows: Mary Elizabeth, November 8, 1871; Augustin, April 17, 1873; Raymond, November 1, 1874; and Isadora, May 27, 1878.[10] Contrary to the date given in the deposition, Raymond Duncan always insisted that Isadora was born in 1877, and the baptismal register shows him to have been correct.

It is curious that almost five months were allowed to pass between Isadora's birth and her baptism. The explanation may be that the ill health and low spirits that characterized her mother's pregnancy, according to Isadora, continued through the first months after her daughter's birth.[11] In any case, the baptism in October seems to have been Mrs. Duncan's last formal act as a Catholic. Her mind and emotions were in a state of turmoil. Her husband was not the model of perfection she had believed him to be, but duty and religious training bound her to him. Moreover, she had reason to believe that his feelings for her had changed. She later told her daughter-in-law that if her four children had not been so close together, the marriage might have succeeded. Perhaps if she had devoted more time to her husband, he might not have drifted away. Her Catholic upbringing, she felt, had not prepared her for the uncertainties of existence.

Joseph Duncan, meanwhile, had taken refuge in a hiding place found for him by friends, waiting for an opportunity to escape from the city.

Isadora later told the writer George Seldes a different story.[12] Her father, she said, had initially hidden himself at home, but a mob had burst into the house, shouting "Kill Duncan!" When they saw that his frightened wife was pregnant, they hesitated and then retreated. After they had gone, she released her husband from the closet in which he had secreted himself, then collapsed and was carried to bed, where she remained for several months. It was at this time that the doctors prescribed the diet of champagne and oysters for Mrs. Duncan, which Isadora later felt had such a decisive prenatal influence upon her own career. Duncan then went into hiding in the city, convinced by this incident that his house was no longer safe.

As we have seen, however, Isadora was five months old at the time of the failure of the Pioneer Land and Loan Bank, therefore her mother's diet of champagne and oysters can have had no prenatal effect upon her own life. The story of the mob breaking into the house seems to have been another flourish of Isadora's imagination. (However, there were indeed riots in San Francisco at that time. Unemployed workers demonstrated against Chinese immigrants, and the labor leader Denis Kearny, who headed the riots, later threatened to seize the Pioneer Bank buildings in the interests of the depositors.)[13]

During that autumn, Duncan's whereabouts remained undiscovered, and the depositors of the Pioneer Bank offered a $5000 reward for the capture of Duncan and Le Warne or "the recovery of their bodies." Gradually, however, stories about the fugitives disappeared from the papers and the public turned its attention elsewhere. Then, on December 22, the city was aroused by the disclosure that Duncan and Le Warne had been concealed for weeks in a cottage near Washerwoman's Bay in San Francisco. Their suspected whereabouts had been communicated to the mayor, who had waited until the next morning to advise the chief of police who, in turn, had waited another day before ordering the place searched. By the time the house was entered, the two wanted men had fled.

These curious delays did not pass unnoticed. A grand jury which investigated the escape disclosed the fact that the mayor was not only a director of the Safe Deposit Company but had also sold the company its safes. "One feature . . . in connection with the report of the Grand Jury which has caused considerable comment," dryly noted the *Evening Bulletin,* "is the absence of any indictment . . . of the persons who, as *particeps criminis,* harbored [the fugitives] and aided them during their flight."

Meanwhile the hunt for the absent bankers continued. In mid-February of 1878, Police Captain Lees, acting on a promising tip, boarded the barkentine *Ellen J. McKinnon.* There he found a quantity of articles marked "J.C.D." and trunks presumably belonging to the financier. The captain of the ship told the police officer that a go-between had paid the passage for "two Spanish gentlemen and a servant" who wanted to travel to Central America. The fugitives, of course, were not found on board, but this time the trail was fresh.

Then, on February 25, over four and a half months after he had disappeared from view, headlines proclaimed "Duncan Captured."

Discovered in a rooming house at 509 Kearny Street, the former banker had recently recovered from pneumonia and he appeared pale and worn. At the police station where he was booked, he told reporters that he had believed, up to the last moment, that he could avert the Pioneer's failure. "I have not intended to defraud anyone in the whole affair. I have transferred no property to anyone. I hoped to save the bank and I did everything that I could. My son put $140,000 into it and that was lost. . . . I am wrecked financially, physically and mentally." Some time after Duncan's arrest, Le Warne was seized in Oakland.

Joseph Charles Duncan was brought to trial four times. Perhaps because the official attitude toward the case was equivocal, the first three trials ended in split juries.[14] At the fourth trial, he was acquitted.[15] Having been divorced by Dora Gray Duncan, he remarried and moved to Los Angeles, with the intent of making a new career for himself. Isadora's mother was left with four children to bring up and provide for as best she could.

❧ 2 ❧

A Missing Father
1878 – circa 1894

OR several months after the crash, the Duncans lived on in their big house at Taylor and Geary Streets, San Francisco, where Isadora had been born. Then, some time between Isadora's baptism on October 13, 1877 and the following spring of 1878, Mrs. Duncan and her four children moved to Henry House (at present called the Portland Hotel) located on Ninth Street between Broadway and Washington Street in Oakland. Presumably their San Francisco home was sold to pay creditors.

From Henry House they moved to 764 Fourth Street where, according to city directories, they lived through 1881. From 1886 on they are successively listed as living at 1254 San Pablo Avenue, at 1156½ Seventh Street, and eventually at 1365 Eighth Street, where they remained for seven years, until 1894. The frequency of their moves in the early years bears witness to their difficult financial circumstances.

Mrs. Duncan supported herself and her children by giving piano lessons. She left early in the day and returned home late; often she rose at daybreak to knit caps and mittens which she sold to stores as a means of supplementing her slender earnings. Despite her best efforts, she never seemed able to keep abreast of the mounting bills; often it was doubtful if she would have the money to pay the grocer.

When Isadora was five years old, Mrs. Duncan entered her in the Cole Elementary School on Tenth Street between Union and Poplar Streets in Oakland. Isadora later remarked, "I think my mother prevaricated about my age. It was necessary to have some place to leave me." The child intensely disliked the chalk-smelling classroom with its hard benches where she was forced to sit for hours, her limbs aching with inactivity. Every sound and smell wafting through the half-opened window enticed her to revel in the buzzing, blossoming, swarming life outside. She took no satisfaction in memorizing subjects she did not understand, that seemed to have no bearing on anything she might conceivably do with her life. She was conscious, too, of being poorer than her classmates, and that made her shy and awkward. "I can never remember suffering from poverty at home, where we took it as a matter of course: it was only at school that I suffered."[1]

Two memories of her school days stood out with particular vividness. The first was a Christmas party. One consequence of her mother's revulsion against her Catholic upbringing was that she had become an atheist. Resolved to rear her children without pious sentimentality, she had revealed to them early the identity of Santa Claus. At the party in question, a teacher distributed cakes and candies, telling the class, "See what Santa Claus has brought you." Isadora, then six years old, stood up and said, "I don't believe you, there is no such thing as Santa Claus."

To this defiance the teacher replied, "Candies are only for little girls who believe in Santa Claus."

"Then I don't want your candy," retorted the child, who would not be silenced. "My mother told me she is too poor to be Santa Claus and give presents."

Sent home from school in disgrace, Isadora anxiously related the

Isadora in San Francisco, 1889, photograph by Kervel (*Archives for the Performing Arts, San Francisco*).

episode to her mother: "Wasn't I right? There is no Santa Claus, is there?"

Mrs. Duncan comforted her daughter with the austere words: "There is no Santa Claus and there is no God, only your own spirit to help you." Looking back on the incident, Isadora wrote, "I never got over the feeling of the injustice with which I had been treated, deprived of candy and punished for telling the truth."[2]

Isadora has told us the other memory in that first draft of her autobiography quoted earlier:

> . . . Once, when I was about eight years old, the teacher asked each child for a story of their short lives. The other children's consisted of accounts of gardens, of toys, of pet dogs, etc. Mine ran somewhat as follows:
>
> First we lived at 23rd Street in East Oakland. The man kept asking for the rent, until we moved to a small house on 17th Street. But again we were not allowed long to remain. In three months we moved to two small rooms on Sunpath Avenue. As Mama could not take the furniture, we had only one large bed for all. But again the unkind landlord became disagreeable, and we moved to . . . etc., etc. This continued through fifteen moves in two years.
>
> The teacher thought I was playing a bad joke on her and summoned my mother to appear before the board of directors. When my mother read the "life" she burst into tears and said that I had written only the truth. I remember her eyes were red for days afterwards, and I could not understand. The state in which we lived, continually hunted, had seemed to me the normal thing.[3]

She repeats elsewhere in the same manuscript, "I remember all through my childhood a distinct feeling of the general unpleasantness of life as being a normal condition."

This constant feeling of unease was certainly increased by anxiety over her missing father. "When other children at school spoke of their fathers, I was silent," she later wrote.[4] She knew that her parents were divorced (in itself a shameful fact that had to be concealed) and—ominous circumstance—that he had left the family shortly after her birth. But what was he like? "All my childhood seemed to be under the black shadow of this mysterious father of whom no one would speak."[5] She evidently felt that she must not raise the subject with her mother, for she addressed her question to an aunt. "Your father was a demon who ruined your mother's life," was the alarming reply, which could hardly have succeeded in quieting the little girl's fears.

She sensed, too, that there was some mysterious secret about her family. From her mother and grandparents she gained the impression that the Duncans were gifted and important people who had once been prominent and wealthy. Yet now they seemed to be under a cloud. Was it because they were poor? Did it have something to do with the divorce? If divorce was so disgraceful, perhaps it was unsafe for women to marry! The consciousness of not having a home like that of their classmates had the effect of drawing the four Duncan children and their mother close together—it was the "Clan Duncan" against the world.

The four were, in order of age, Elizabeth (Mary Elizabeth), Augustine (he was to drop the "e" later), Raymond, and Isadora.[6] There was a year and a half difference in age between each of the older children; Isadora was born two and a half years after Raymond. With Mrs. Duncan out at work during the day, they led unsupervised carefree lives, climbing walls and trees and risking their necks in many stimulating ways. When their mother came home at night (if she was not too tired), she would play the piano or recite poetry, losing her weariness in Schumann and Mendelssohn. There were no fixed bedtimes, and sometimes, buoyed up by the presence of her children and comforted by the harmonies which her daily life did not provide, she would forget the lateness of the hour. At other times she would read to her children from the works of Robert Ingersoll, the atheist philosopher whose follower she had become. Isadora regarded these evenings as her true education. School was simply something to be endured; it taught her nothing.

A passion for the arts was inherited by the young Duncans from both sides of their family. Their grandmother, the small lively woman with still more than a trace of her "Spanish type of Irish beauty," loved to declaim Shakespeare, and, as her older grandson recalled, she "had the voice for it, too."[7] Sometimes she would amuse her grandchildren by dancing a reel or a jig. Her daughter Augusta had a lovely singing voice and a talent for acting and took part in their private theatricals with great success. Although her parents applauded her gifts, there was no question of Augusta's using her talents on the stage; the Grays were too straight-laced for that.[8] Nevertheless, they considered the arts to be important and discussed the merits of painters, actors, musicians, and writers with an intensity which other people might devote to politics or business. To the young Duncans, excluded by their family's circumstances from the society to which they would normally have belonged, the arts must have offered a glimpse of a world that was noble, spacious, and coherent where they would not feel like exiles.

Drama appealed to all the Duncan children. Raymond, the younger boy, was enthralled by the story of Joan of Arc, and at age nine he made his first school speech about the patriot-saint. He managed to impart his fervor to Isadora, and, when she was given a new doll, he persuaded her to use it for playing St. Joan. Enthusiastic at first, Isadora wept copiously when the doll was about to be burned. However, she did not snatch it back from the fire; she felt, even then, that the arts demand sacrifices. Besides, she did not want to earn her brother's contempt.[9]

Away from the classroom, Isadora was happy much of the time. Visiting the ocean always made her feel liberated and strong. She would skip along the hard damp sand—her wet skirt whipping about her bare legs and her long hair flying—and consider how everything was in motion—the wind, the waves, and herself. And, in the spring, the meadows, gold with California poppies, seemed to her the color of joy: she would remember them years later when she was in Budapest and in love.[10] Swaying poppies, soaring birds, sweeping waves—all seemed to be dancing, and she danced with them.

Dancing, she had recently discovered, also had a practical use: if she performed for the girls next door they would let her ride their bicycle around the block. And when she took charge of the smaller neighborhood children to earn pocket money, she would keep both them and herself amused by teaching them to move in rhythm.[11]

Raymond Duncan told a reporter for the *Oakland Tribune* in 1948 that Isadora had given her first dance recital at the First Unitarian Church, which still stands at Fourteenth and Castro Streets in Oakland. The date was probably late in 1890, which would have made Isadora thirteen years old.

From an early age, the Duncan children helped in whatever ways they could to improve the family's material circumstances. To ease the strain on the budget, Elizabeth lived for a time with her grandparents. The boys took odd jobs, and, when they were old enough, Raymond worked in the railroad yards and Augustin "drove a mustang and cart"[12] for *The San Francisco Post,* picking up newspapers fresh from the press and delivering them to newsboys. Isadora sometimes peddled her mother's knitting from door to door, and, when it became necessary to persuade the butcher to extend their credit, it was she as the youngest and most appealing who was sent to wheedle him. (Used to coaxing and cozening tradespeople from childhood, she ultimately developed a protective blindness toward debts that was to be the despair of her friends and business managers.)

Later the Duncans began giving lessons in social dancing. They taught polkas, schottisches, and waltzes while Mrs. Duncan played the piano. At first only the three older children taught, but presently Isadora left school, which she considered useless, pinned up her hair, and joined them in giving classes. (Isadora said that she was ten at the time, but actually she was older; she was often mistaken about dates, and when she wrote her memoirs she had professional as well as the usual feminine reasons for wanting to take several years from her age.)[13]

Cut off now from formal education, she depended for learning on her musical mother and on her own lively curiosity. She was a voracious reader with a will to learn, and she had the advantage of living in a family where ideas were constantly discussed. All her life Isadora was drawn to thinkers: scientists, statesmen, philosophers, artists, musicians, and writers. She was as interested in hearing their ideas as in expressing her own, and thus she never stopped learning.

Her brothers and sister, too, contributed to the shaping of her mind and talents. Her sister, Elizabeth, said many years later that it was she who had taught Isadora to dance. This is doubtless true— in part. As is true of families where the members are lively and creative, the Duncans stimulated and criticized one another. The "esthetic" or "fancy" dancing that Elizabeth and Isadora presently began to teach may have owed something to the suggestions of their brothers as well as to the inspiration of both girls. (Isadora's *adult* compositions were of course her own work.)

A strong influence on Isadora's dancing in this early period appears to have been the teaching of François Delsarte or at least the theories of bodily movement that went by his name. The chief source of information today about Delsarte's theories of movement is a book by the pioneering American dancer, Ted Shawn. In *Every Little Movement,* Shawn describes Delsarte's theories as they appear in books by his students and as they were taught to him by Mrs. Richard Hovey, a pupil of Delsarte's son, Gustave Delsarte.

It has been suggested by Allan Ross Macdougall[14] that since Delsarte was mainly a teacher of voice and since his only American pupil, Steele Mackaye,[15] was an actor, "the bodily and facial expressions later mistermed Delsartism were really, it would appear, the creative addition of Steele Mackaye to his master's methods." But, whatever Mackaye may have added to the contributions of Delsarte, this word of caution fails to account for the facts that the aforesaid Mrs. Hovey also stressed bodily movement and what Shawn learned from her he understood to be the teaching of the older Delsarte. The degree to which François Delsarte's teaching was devoted to gesture and bodily expression cannot be determined exactly at this writing, since the collection of material on and by Delsarte is in the possession of Louisiana State University and is not open to consultation by anyone other than the graduate body. In refusing Shawn permission to study the collection, the curator, Dr. C. L. Shaver, explained that it would be valueless to a dancer since Delsarte's work dealt with the singing and speaking voice. There, for the time being, the matter rests.

There is no doubt, however, that Isadora studied what she believed to be Delsarte's theory of movement. Gordon Craig, in his auto-biography,[16] tells of finding a book on Delsarte in a trunk of Isadora's, and Isadora herself is quoted in a dance periodical as saying, "Delsarte, the master of all principles of flexibility and lightness of body, should receive universal thanks for the bonds he has removed from our constrained members. His teachings, faithfully given, combined with the usual instruction necessary to learning dance, will give a result exceptionally graceful and charming."[17]

Who was Delsarte and what were his theories (or the theories taught under his name) that evidently had some influence on the young Isadora?

François Alexandre Nicholas Delsarte (who was born in Solesme, France, on November 19, 1811 and died in Paris on July 20, 1871) was not a dancer. He was a student of music, a theorist of movement, and a voice coach. Originally a singer who had studied at the Paris Conservatory, his own voice had been ruined by poor training, and he thereupon resolved to discover the proper way to teach. In order to learn how the larynx was constructed, he practiced dissection at medical school. Anatomy awakened his interest in the effect of structure on movement, and that in turn led him to examine the relation between movement and emotion. He spent many years observing how people move under both stress and ordinary circumstances; he watched children at play and adults at work; he visited insane asylums and the scenes of accidents. "From his observations," Margaret Lloyd tells us in *The Borzoi Book of Modern Dance,* "he devised a system of dramatic expression, and some of his pupils were the great actors of the day." According to Ted Shawn, "While Delsarte himself was known during his lifetime largely as a professor of singing and declamation, and perhaps two-thirds of his lectures dealt with diction, tone, and other aspects of the singing and speaking voice, it was his laws of gesture, ignored and not even recognized by the dancers of his day, that so profoundly affected the American dance some thirty years after his death."[18]

In the September 1898 issue of the dance magazine *The Director,* Mrs. Richard Hovey, Gustave Delsarte's pupil, is quoted as saying, "Sit a little forward . . . it is less tiring and more artistic, and then it is the natural way. In truth, that which is best for hygiene is right for beauty always. . . . If one would have fine attitudes without thinking of them, it is necessary to put the feet in the right position, then relax and the force of gravity will make you graceful." And the "right position" is discovered "by giving a little thought to the mechanical laws which govern your body." These remarks touch on several of Delsarte's theories which particularly impressed Isadora. The natural is the most beautiful: and natural movement is that which is made in accord with both the structure of the body and the pull of gravity. The young dancer was struck by his observation that all natural movements are expressive of something such as a thought, a feeling, or a motive. According to Shawn, Delsarte noted, "There is nothing more horrible or deplorable than a gesture without a motive, without a meaning," and he pointed out that involuntary movements reveal much about a person's feelings. He divided the body into three main zones—the head (the mental), the upper torso (the emotional and spiritual), and the lower torso (the vital and physical)—and he stated that all movements take their meaning from the zone in which they originate.[19] It is worth noting that when Isadora later decided that the source of movement lay in the solar plexus (the upper torso) it was the emotional and spiritual impulses that she was most interested in exploring in the dance.

The Delsarte system which Isadora appears to have studied in her childhood in San Francisco was probably greatly modified from that taught by the French master. When the Duncans were growing up, Delsarte inspired a craze: young men declaimed poetry with what they hoped were the appropriate Delsartean gestures, and young girls in Greek robes,[20] with whitened skin and white wigs, held classical poses.[21] It was perhaps the memory of this flummery which caused Isadora in 1925 to say to a young friend, the journalist Walter Shaw, that she had "studied Delsarte" and had understood nothing about it.[22] This was not what she had felt when she was growing up in San Francisco, for she also told Walter Shaw that she had had "Professor of Delsarte" printed on her professional cards.[23]

The Duncans' dancing classes continued to grow, so it was fortunate they soon had a large enough place in which to teach. This was the Castle mansion in San Francisco on the northwest corner of Sutter and Van Ness Streets,[24] which Joseph Duncan, after recouping his fortunes in Los Angeles, saw fit to provide as a proper home for his second family. (Made cautious by his past reverses, he kept title to the property, however.)[25]

According to Isadora, Duncan had dropped out of his children's lives after the divorce, and she, a baby at the time, had no memory of him at all—except for an incident that happened later when she was about seven. As she recalled, a stranger in a top hat asked the child to direct him to Mrs. Duncan's apartment.

> "I am Mrs. Duncan's little girl," I replied. . . .
>
> And suddenly he took me in his arms and covered me with tears and kisses. I was very much astonished at this proceeding and asked him who he was. To which he replied with tears, "I am your father."
>
> I was delighted at this piece of news and rushed in to tell the family.
>
> "There is a man there who says he is my father."

Her mother was startled and distraught at first and refused to see him, but later she relented and allowed the children to get acquainted with him. Isadora discovered, to her relief, that her father was not only presentable but charming as well, and she became very fond of him.[26]

It was several years after this reunion—in 1893, when Isadora was sixteen—that Duncan presented the family with the Castle mansion. It was a handsome house with large dancing rooms and open fireplaces. To the Duncan children, who had grown up in a series of cramped dwellings, it must have seemed a palace. To add to its glamor, it possessed a secret passage—or at least a space between the walls that was wide enough for the young Duncans to hide in.[27] On the grounds were a tennis court, a windmill, and a barn. Augustin converted the barn into a theater, where he acted the part of Rip Van Winkle, wearing a beard that had recently been part of a fur rug.[28] Quick to follow on this triumph the Duncans put on a series of plays that were received locally with enough success to warrant the family troupe's making a tour up and down the coast. The Duncans were determined to become professionals and artists.

In 1894, while they were living in San Francisco, the youngest Duncan was listed for the first time in Langley's *San Francisco City Directory* by the name and title she was to make world-famous—"Miss Isadora Duncan, Teacher, dancing."

Shortly after this, Joseph Duncan suffered a new financial reverse, and the Castle mansion and its grounds had to be sold. But it had served to give the beleaguered family a short period of ease and respite from material worries, and they would always remember their two years there with gratitude.

3

Apprenticeship in the Theater
1895–1899

FTER the loss of their home, the Duncans decided to take energetic steps to repair their fortunes. Isadora went to the manager of a traveling company then playing in San Francisco and asked for an audition. The man watched critically while she danced on the bare stage to Mendelssohn's "Songs Without Words" and then said to the girl's mother: "This sort of thing is no good for a theater. It's more for a church." Though he was wrong in his appraisal of her commercial possibilities, he was right in recognizing the impulse that prompted Isadora's art. She was later to write, "Art which is not religious is mere merchandise . . . ," and again, "My dance is not a dance of the body but of the spirit. My body moves because my spirit moves it." Disappointed but undaunted, she decided that if there were no openings in San Francisco, she would try her luck elsewhere, and she convinced her surprised but accommodating mother that they must go to Chicago.

It is remarkable how often Dora Gray Duncan—a woman suf-

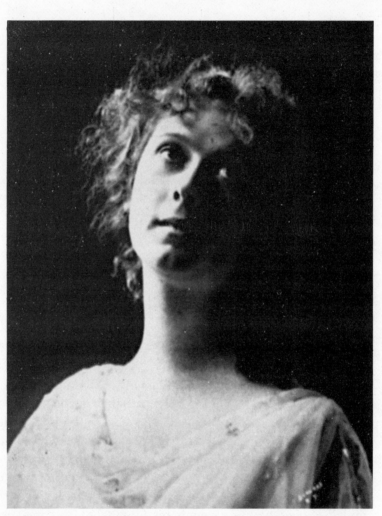

Isadora in New York, photograph by Jacob Schloss (*Hoblitzelle Theatre Arts Collection, Humanities Research Center, University of Texas at Austin*).

ficiently strong-willed to have rejected her religious upbringing and divorced her husband—fell in with her children's suggestions. Her relation to them in that regard seems to have been something like that of an older sister, always ready to join in their schemes and to take them into her confidence. Perhaps in her loneliness and inexperience in making a living, she had fallen into the habit of turning to them for advice; perhaps she had an adventurous nature. At any rate she never appears to have insisted that they abandon any project because of financial riskiness (they had so little to lose, after all). She was determined, moreover, that her children would have successful lives. What they willed would be her will and their triumphs would be her triumph.

Mrs. Duncan and her 18-year-old daughter arrived in Chicago in June 1895, having left the other young Duncans behind in San Francisco. Their assets were a small trunk, filled with their belongings, some old-fashioned jewelry, and $25 in cash. They had exhausted their meager funds before Isadora managed to find an engagement, and she wrote later "I can never see the streets of Chicago without a sickening feeling of hunger." Fortunately she carried a letter of introduction from the San Francisco Press Club to the Press Club of Chicago. Ike Fleming, a member of the latter club, introduced the two women to "Old Bohemia," a circle of writers, actors, musicians, and artists. At the Bohemian Club, Isadora made many friends, one of whom brought her to Charles Fair, the manager of the Masonic Roof Garden.[1] She danced for Fair and was hired to appear for three weeks at the roof garden for a weekly fee of $20. Billed as "The California Faun," she alternated (at the manager's suggestion) her solo to Mendelssohn's "Spring Song" with an "interesting turn—something peppery with kicks and frills."

Her entree into "Old Bohemia" did more for her than turn up a job; it also introduced her to someone who in the succeeding months was to become increasingly important to her. This was a reddish-haired, bearded, 45-year-old Pole named Ivan Miroski, a writer and painter who earned an inadequate living at some nondescript business in Chicago. Miroski admired the young dancer and sometimes took her and her mother out for dinner or went picnicking with them in the woods near Chicago. Isadora and Miroski confided in one another during their long walks in the country, and she soon grew to count on his presence. Miroski, for his part, had fallen in love with her, and one day when they were alone together he asked her to marry him. Moved by his passion and the feelings of tenderness which it awoke in her, and envisaging their life together as a romantic idyll, Isadora consented.

For the time being, however, marriage was out of the question; Miroski was as poor as she, and Isadora had her career to consider. An acquaintance by the name of Harry Bowers[2] had provided her with an introduction to the theatrical producer Augustin Daly, who was then in Chicago. Daly saw her dance and hired her for a small part in a pantomime called *Mme. Pygmalion* that he was staging in October in New York. Her mother was overjoyed. But how were they to raise the money for train tickets? After some debate, they telegraphed to a friend in San Francisco, asking for $100 so that Isadora could go to New York for a "triumphant engagement" on October 1. The money arrived, and with it came Elizabeth and Augustin Duncan, who had assumed from the telegram that the family's fortune was made. So Isadora said farewell to Miroski, consoling herself with the thought that as soon as she had earned some money she would be able to rejoin him.

But money did not come easily in New York. From the date of her arrival in New York until November 18, the opening date of the pantomime, Isadora rehearsed unpaid. This was standard theater practice of the period, but it imposed great hardship on the Duncans, who had used up most of their borrowed funds in traveling to New York. Isadora had no money for lunch, and when the noon recess was called, she would hide and sleep in one of the stage boxes; then, without having eaten, she would rehearse all afternoon. To add to her misery, the star, Jane May, was temperamental and easily angered, and the pantomime proved exasperating in its witlessness. Still, it offered a toehold in the theater world, and, in any case, Isadora could not afford to give up her job.

After three weeks in New York, the play went on the road. This meant the exhaustion of one-night stands, looking for affordable lodgings in each new town (she was determined to send half of her $15 weekly salary to her mother), and sometimes having to discourage the attentions of men who assumed that a young actress was fair game. She remembered one boarding house in which the men were drunk and where she did not feel safe until she had barricaded the door to her room with a heavy wardrobe.

The tour lasted two months,[3] after which the company returned to Manhattan and Isadora was given the part of a fairy in *A Midsummer Night's Dream,* starring Ada Rehan. A longer tour followed this time, which took her back briefly to San Francisco before returning to the east coast.[4] On the road, she found relief in pouring out her feelings in letters to Miroski and in receiving his loving replies. When the company at last arrived in Chicago, she was overjoyed to be reunited with him. Before she left, he promised to follow her to New York where they would be married. She communicated this happy news to her family, and, on her return to New York, they greeted her with the truth: one of her brothers had made inquiries and had discovered that Miroski already had a wife in London.[5] Heartsick, Isadora broke off the engagement and returned to the drudgery of the theater.

Her work had never seemed more meaningless: she had been given the part of a singer in *The Geisha,* and, since she could not carry a tune, she merely went through the motions, open-mouthed. After *The Geisha* closed on November 21, 1896, Isadora found a more congenial use for her talents. With three other women, she performed an incidental dance in *Much Ado About Nothing.* She also took the part of a spirit in *The Tempest* and performed a gypsy dance in *Meg Merrilies,* a dramatization of Sir Walter Scott's *Guy Mannering.*[6]

After *Meg Merrilies,* the Daly Company was sent to England, and although Isadora did not mention the trip in her autobiography, she went with them.[7]

In London, Isadora took ballet lessons with Ketti Lanner, the first dancer of the Empire Theatre. She also probably gave some dance recitals for private gatherings, although there is only indirect evidence of this.[8]

She sailed for home at the end of 1897 or the beginning of 1898.

Back in the United States, she broke her ties with Daly and con-
centrated on building an independent career. *The Director* reported
a series of five concerts in 1898: "The dance recitals of Miss Duncan
were first given in New York in February . . . shortly after her return
from London. They have created a deep enthusiasm among the
cultured people of that city, and the manner in which they are
heralded by the press as the arrival of a new creation in art has
aroused a general and widespread interest. . . ."⁹ Presumably these
recitals were given in private homes; among Isadora's patrons, the
magazine lists such socialites as Mrs. Whitlaw Reid, Mrs. Bolton
Hall, Mrs. Charles Oelrichs, and Mrs. Frederick W. Vanderbilt.

More importantly *The Director* gives her repertoire at the time
(late 1898). Among her dances were:

Ophelia and *Narcissus,* both to music by Ethelbert Nevin

The Spirit of Spring, to a waltz by Strauss

The Rubáiyát of Omar Khayyám: four quatrains to a waltz by Strauss,
and three quatrains to a song by Mendelssohn

A Dance of Mirth, to a pizzicato by Strauss

A Sonnet to the Beautiful, from the French of Joachim du Bellay, to a
song by Mendelssohn

L'Allegro (Milton), to "Une Promenade du Matin" by Gustave Lange

Il Penseroso (Milton), to "Il Penseroso" by Stephen Helm

A Dance of Wandering, to "Melodie" by Paderewski

These dances were pastoral and lyrical in mood and leaned heavily
on literary sources. Isadora appears to have felt that unless she
provided her audience with clues, they would be unable to understand the emotions she was expressing.

A reviewer in *The Director* gives us a glimpse of these naive early
works, which, nonetheless, were already characteristic of her style
and choice of subject.

In . . . *The Spirit of Spring* . . . the dancer bounds on stage with uplifted hands and face, the incarnation of joyous spring breaking the icy fetters of winter. . . . She springs hither and thither, scattering the seeds as she goes, plucking the budding flowers, breathing the life-giving air, exhaling a joyousness of nature which is wondrous in its grace and beauty. . . .

In . . . *Wandering* . . . the dancer conveys the impression of a spirit roaming through the forests, bewildered at the strangeness of her surroundings, trembling at every sound, the rustle of the leaves, the sighing of the winds.

. . . *Narcissus* is another charming bit of pantomime. The fabled youth is depicted staring at his own image in the water, first startled at its sudden appearance, then charmed, fascinated at his mirrored beauty. Becoming more and more enamored, the dancer leans forward, seemingly viewing herself from side to side, sending kisses to the liquid image, stepping across the shallow brook and still finding the figure reflected from its surface. The poetry of motion, the first start, the gradually growing conceit, the turning and bending, the ecstasy of delight at finding himself so beautiful are all most convincingly enacted by the pretty dancer. . . .

Three quatrains from the *Rubaiyat* were exquisitely rendered. . . . The slow oriental movement, the intensity of desire, the mournful abandonment of all hope, and the final turning down of the "empty glass" . . . were a wordless poem. . . .

. . . The dancer [then] turned to *A Dance of Mirth,* and as she bounded and whirled in ecstatic frenzy, holding her sides aching from over-much laughter, one could realize how versatile and plastic Miss Duncan is. . . .[10]

However *Town Topics* (Sept. 15, 1898) was less impressed.

Miss Duncan is undoubtedly graceful . . . but I must confess that to see her once is enough. . . . I cannot see how the dances interpret, as is claimed, the exquisite quatrains of the *Rubaiyat.* I make this criticism with no reflection on Miss Duncan who undoubtedly has grace and ability but who should either enlarge her present repertoire or arrange a new one.

Most of these early pieces were soon dropped from her programs, but she continued to dance the Ethelbert Nevin *Narcissus* as late as 1905, when she made her second trip to Russia.[11]

That she performed to Nevin's music at all was due to her powers of persuasion. Learning that Nevin disapproved of dancers using his compositions, Isadora called on him at his studio in Carnegie Hall, where the Duncans, too, had a studio. When she showed him her choreography he was so struck with what he saw ("Surely the same spirit must have descended on us both!" she quotes him as saying)[12] that he invited her to take part in a concert of his works which was to take place on March 24, 1898 at the Carnegie Lyceum.

The day after the concert, an account, here printed in its entirety, appeared in the society notes of *The New York Times:*

> Carnegie Lyceum was well filled with fashionable guests at Ethelbert Nevin's entertainment yesterday afternoon. Mr. Nevin played *Misericordia, Il Rasigmuolo, La Pastorella* and *Arlecchino,* and Miss Julia Wyman gave eight soprano solos. Miss Isadora Duncan danced three Water Scenes, the music composed by Mr. Nevin and Mlle Serverin acted in pantomime, to musical accompaniment, *Florianne's Dream,* by Vance Thompson.[13]

The young dancer must have been disappointed by the brevity of this notice—it can hardly be called a review. Both its cursoriness and its placement in the society pages indicate the position of the dance at the turn of the century. Whereas music received more extended criticism in *The Musical Courier* and *Musical America,* the dance was not taken seriously as an art form except by one or two short-lived dance magazines, such as *The Director* (which in any case devoted much of its space to society news). Dance was merely an entertainment, an adjunct to a fashionable evening. Indeed, Isadora's career seemed to have reached an impasse. The only openings for dancers were to be found in musical comedy or the music halls— neither a field for a serious dancer—or in the opera corps de ballet.[14] Had she wished, Isadora might have qualified for the corps. In addition to her studies with Ketti Lanner in London, she had studied in New York with Marie Bonfanti, the former star of *The Black Crook.*[15] But everything about ballet ran contrary to Isadora's instincts. As she was to write in *My Life:* "I am an enemy to ballet which I consider a false and preposterous art."[16] False, because it seemed to be unnatural in every way: it was full of "set numbers," the holding of poses, and meaningless starts and stops. "No movement, pose or rhythm is successive, or can be made to evolve succeeding action." Worse still, toe-dancing ran counter to the structure of the human body: "Under the tricots are dancing deformed muscles . . . under the muscles are deformed bones."

As for the preposterousness of ballet, even its warmest admirers today would have to admit that that was the only word for the art as it existed at the time of Isadora's first public appearances. V. Svetlow, in his admirable *Le Ballet Contemporain* (published in 1912 in St. Petersburg, under the pseudonym V. Y. Ivchenko), tells us that these works abounded in peasants in high heels and Tartars in toe shoes, and that it was common practice for ballerinas wishing to display their technique to interpolate *pas de deux* from other ballets without regard for either unity of choreography or of music. (This sort of practice dies hard—witness the baggy-trousered men doing Russian knee-bends and the girls playing castanets in Renaissance Verona in the filmed version of *Romeo and Juliet* by the Bolshoi Ballet.) The scenarios were not known for coherence, and they were enlivened by such touches as "the happy troupe of fishermen who are stimulated to dance by the fatigue of their work." One is reminded of Jean-Jacques Rousseau's comment on the opera ballets of his day: "The manner of bringing about such festivities is simple: either the prince is sad and they dance to cheer him up, or he is gay, and they dance to take part in his joy."

But if the ballet offered the only opening for a serious dancer, what was Isadora to do? Her attempts to reach a wider public met with incomprehension or levity on the part of the press. *The Broadway Magazine* (in an article illustrated with some charming photographs by Jacob Schloss showing her wearing a lace dress and ballet shoes) criticized Isadora for being too ladylike. "She spurns Broadway with a large, thick spurn. . . . She is very, very classic, and is horribly,

horribly afraid of becoming anything but absolutely and painfully refined. It can thus be seen that Miss Duncan occupies a rather unique position among American dancers. . . ."[17] Yet on March 14, 1899, when she gave a complete recital of dances illustrating *The Rubáiyát of Omar Khayyám,* while Justin McCarthy (the English playwright, author of *If I Were King*) read the stanzas, the degree of nudity of her costume—she danced with bare arms and legs— proved so shocking that several members of her society audience walked out. One of those who stayed to watch her later told a reporter:

> When she stood still, she was like a Greek statue in grace of classic outline. But she had neither the color nor the immobility of marble. Her arms were bare to the shoulders, and her legs to the knee had the same semblance. . . . Her pose and movements were often eloquent with the ideas which were being read and in delightful unison with the music which was being played . . . The selections from Omar at this time were expressive of his love of wine and women. Miss Duncan's suitable pantomime was chastely graphic. Nevertheless whenever . . . her feet stepped far apart, one of her legs came forward, right out of that sedate drapery, and was on transitory view full-length, and skin-colored.

A few days after the Omar recital, Isadora was in the news again. She and her mother and sister had taken two rooms on the main floor of the Windsor Hotel on Fifth Avenue and 47th Street. This was a fashionable address which the family needed, for Isadora's concerts did not constitute a steady source of income, and the Duncans earned their living by giving dancing lessons to the children of New York's "Four Hundred."

On St. Patrick's Day, Isadora and Elizabeth were giving a class to about thirty children, accompanied by their maids, while Mrs. Duncan played the piano. Outside, the St. Patrick's Day parade was in full swing, and the sound of the band and the marchers could be heard faintly over the piano music. Suddenly a strange noise attracted Mrs. Duncan's attention and she looked up from the keyboard in time to see a woman's body hurtle past the window.

She said, "At first I thought there was something wrong with my eyes."[18] The falling body was followed by another. Mrs. Duncan signalled to a maid and asked her to go to the door. The latter returned and whispered that the corridor was full of smoke. Mrs. Duncan hurriedly explained the situation to her daughters. "The Misses Duncan bade the children be calm, and after gathering up their wraps with the aid of the maids marshalled them in line and led them out of the building, the Southern portion of which was by that time a mass of flame. . . . The Duncans, who were without wraps, were invited to the home of Arthur Von Briesen, at One East 47th Street."[19]

The flames spread rapidly next door, traveling up the elevator shafts and enveloping the upper floors of the hotel. Firemen fighting the blaze were hampered by the holiday crowds and by a poor water supply. By 4 P.M. almost all of the central part of the building had collapsed.

Later that day the Duncans moved to the Hotel Buckingham, also on Fifth Avenue, where they were interviewed by the press. The reporter from the *New York Herald* wrote:

> Miss Isadora Duncan had not entirely recovered from the shock of her afternoon experience when I saw her last night. She said mournfully that she had saved only the dress she wore, a house gown of dark brown material with flaring Elizabethan collar.
>
> All of her costumes and those of her sister were lost as well as the bric-a-brac which they highly prized. . . .[20]

Also lost (alas for the Duncans and for their future biographers) were family photographs and other mementos.

Once again the Duncans were penniless. Without enough money to live modestly at home, Isadora characteristically decided that the moment had come for them to go to London. She applied for help to the wealthy matrons at whose homes she had danced—many of whom had reason to be grateful for the rescue of their children—and, by raising $50 here and $50 there, she finally accumulated $300 in all. This was still short of what was needed to buy steamship tickets for the four Duncans who intended to go abroad,[21] but they managed to book passage on a cattle boat. On April 18, 1899, shortly before they were to leave, Isadora gave a farewell concert, which was reported as follows in a New York paper.

Under the patronage of 67 society women . . . an impressive function was held yesterday.

Miss Isadora Duncan, assisted by her sister, Miss Elizabeth Bioren Duncan, her brother, Mr. Augustine [sic] Duncan, with a large mamma in a blue gown that was monstrous and unnatural, and a diaphanous younger brother distributing strophes from Ovid in the background, gave for the first time in New York, some idylls from Theocritis and Birn, done into dance under the name of "The Happier Age of Gold" . . . [at the Lyceum Theatre].

Miss Duncan has recently had the misfortune to lose her wardrobe by the Windsor Hotel fire, which probably accounts for and excuses the fact that her sole costume for yesterday's dance was a species of surgical bandage of gauze and satin of the hue of a raspberry ice, with streamers of various lengths which floated merrily or mournfully as the dancer illustrated the bridal of Helen or the burial of Adonis.

Miss Duncan's melancholy brother kindly read extracts from Theocritus and Ovid as an accompaniment to the writhings and painful leaps and hops of his sister, while a concealed orchestra discoursed doleful music and the audience of tortured souls gazed at one another and blushed or giggled according to their individual form of nervousness.

When the final dance was finished there was a sigh of relief that it was over and that Miss Duncan's bandages hadn't fallen off as they threatened to during the entire show. Then the entire audience of 67 solemnly filed upon the stage to kiss Miss Duncan, her mamma and sister and wish them success in introducing "The Happier Age of Gold" to London drawing rooms in May.

Miss Duncan has fully determined on this reckless course, which is sad, considering that we are at peace with England at present.[22]

So much for the way serious dance was reviewed.[23] Is it surprising that Isadora felt that if her art was ever to meet with understanding she must cross the Atlantic?

❧ 4 ❧

Beginning in London
1899–1900

N May, two weeks after sailing from New York, the cattle boat docked at Hull, and the four Duncans entrained for London.

Isadora's biographer Allen Ross Macdougall is surely right when he says that in her memoirs Isadora exaggerated the hardships of her first months in England.[1] As he points out, not only were the Justin McCarthys and several of her New York patrons in London, but Ketti Lanner, as ballerina of the Empire Theatre, was in a position to provide her former pupil with helpful introductions.[2] Yet, despite some useful contacts, the problems that Isadora faced in London were essentially the same as those she had confronted in New York.

These were, first of all, how to find an opening for her art, and second, how to find an audience that understood what she was doing. All the conventional avenues to recognition as a dancer were blocked. She was not a member of a ballet company and had no desire to become one. Nor was her dance suitable for the music hall. The theater had been able to use her only as a chorus girl or at best a soloist, and, though she had met with applause, dancing the part of the First Fairy was not part of the career she had in mind. Her performances at the parties of leading hostesses and at recitals with Ethelbert Nevin and Justin McCarthy had been attempts to bypass the standard roads to success in the theater, allowing her to reach a social and artistic elite—the only elite, she foresaw, that could understand her art. But even the most eminent hostesses, she now recognized, could never launch her; in their view, she would always be a graceful interlude in a fashionable evening. She must somehow make her own openings, find her own audience, and create her own critics. For this, she would need the backing of artists and intellectuals.

Fortunately, at one of the London drawing rooms to which she was admitted, she met Charles Hallé, son of Karl Hallé, the German pianist and conductor. Charles Hallé was an artist and, luckily for Isadora, he was also the director of the New Gallery. He suggested to the young American that she give a series of three recitals there. She managed to find for the series an impressive list of patrons headed by the Princess Christine of Schleswig-Holstein, a daughter of Queen Victoria, and including the artists Holman Hunt, Walter Crane, and Sir William Richmond, the novelist Henry James, the playwright J. Comyns Carr, the composer Sir Hubert Parry, the music critic J. Fuller-Maitland, and the classical scholar, historian, and poet, Andrew Lang.[3] The first recital was reviewed the next day (March 17, 1900) in the London *Times* in an unsigned review by Fuller-Maitland.

Miss Isadora Duncan is a young dancer of remarkable skill, whose art, though it might fail to satisfy the average ballet master, has a wonderful eloquence of its own. . . . Miss Duncan's exceptional beauty of face and figure fits her for her . . . task of illustrating in dance . . . passages . . . chosen from the Homeric *Hymn to Demeter* and the Idylls of Theocritus; these were read . . . by Miss Jane Harrison,[4] and a small orchestra, conducted by Mr. J. E. Barkworth played accompaniments to the dancing. . . . Both in the passage requiring the eloquence of gestures, and in the more lyrical measures of regular dances such as the mazurka in *The Triumph of Daphnis,* or the rhythmic steps danced to Mendelssohn's *Frühlingslied,* the dancer made a success of no ordinary kind. Her powers were exhibited in a most favorable light in *The Water Nymph,* danced to some pretty music by E. Nevin, and from beginning to end the occasion was one of complete artistic enjoyment.[5]

A magazine article gives us a glimpse of the young Isadora:

. . . She dances Mendelssohn's musical poem, a *Welcome to Spring,* with a . . . grace that makes one think of flowers and birds and lambs at play. Her costume for this is appropriately copied from Botticelli's *Primavera.* The robe consists of several gauze slips worn one over another. The upper one has angel's sleeves and is of a dim, pale green color, painted here and there with delicate flowers. . . . Very Botticelli-like is the long dark hair, crowned with roses, and falling in small curls to the waist. Ropes of roses wind about the body and the feet are shod with golden sandals. Not a single stock step is taken, and the whole dance seems like something that might have happened in ancient Greece. Miss Duncan is lucky in that her work has been praised by the painter Sargent. Through that she is to dance in a few days for a representative assembly of artists and literary men at Mrs. Holman Hunt's. She has already danced for Princess Christian and Princess Victoria, and expects to dance before the Prince of Wales on the 29th of May . . . at the Court Theatre. . . .

A Californian by birth . . . she had her first (dancing) lessons in San Francisco, then put in a year at a ballet school in New York, and afterwards came to Europe to study. . . . Most of that time she has spent in the British Museum, analysing and memorising the steps and attitudes of the classic nymphs of antique art. Her work is thus the result of the application of poetic intelligence to the art of dancing, and her aim is to study nature and the classics and abjure the conventional.

. . . In appearance Miss Isadora is tall, graceful and slender, with a small oval face, good features, and a mass of thick, dark hair. She is beautiful on the stage and has particularly graceful arms and hands.[6]

Fuller-Maitland persuaded Isadora that she should dance to more serious music and dispense with the poetry readings.[7] Accordingly, in her second program, she danced to Chopin's C Minor Prelude, the mazurka in A Minor, and the waltz in C Sharp Minor, as well as Mendelssohn's *Spring Song* and a minuet from *Orfeo* by Gluck. Andrew Lang and Sir Hubert Parry delivered the introductory speeches on the first two occasions. For her third program, Sir William Richmond spoke on "Botticelli and the *Primavera,*" and Isadora gave a program inspired by Renaissance paintings: *La Primavera, Angel With a Violin,* suggested by the painting of Ambrogio de Predis (to "Nobilita d'Amore" by Cesare Negri, 1604), and Titian's *Bacchus and Ariadne* (to music by Giovanni Picci, 1621).

Dancing for artists rather than for socialites gave impetus to Isadora's creativity. These dances could be less pantomimic: she could express the emotions in a Chopin composition without having to depict a recognizable situation, as she had in *Wandering,* or a story, as she had in *Narcissus.* Isadora needed the stimulus of the intelligentsia and throughout her life she would seek out the company of artists, philosophers, scholars, musicians. Often she used ideas from their realms as the impulse for her art, sometimes finding them in places that were laughably far afield: "I would sit far into the night . . . poring over . . . Kant's 'Critique of Pure Reason' from which heaven only knows how, I believed I was finding the inspiration for those moments of pure beauty which I sought."[8] Isadora, let it be said, was far from being the mindless, humorless creature of legend.

Before the New Gallery series of concerts, Isadora had danced in a number of private drawing rooms, sometimes for pay and sometimes for charity, and had taken her old part as the First Fairy in the R. F. Benson production of *A Midsummer Night's Dream.*

She had also made an impulsive visit to Mme. Ivan Miroski, the wife of her former fiancé. About a year after Isadora's engagement had been broken, while the Duncans were still living in New York, she heard from a Chicago friend that Miroski had enlisted to fight in the Spanish-American War and had died of typhoid in training camp. This news came as a terrible shock to Isadora, who had so little recovered from her love for him that she still slept with his picture under her pillow. Unable to believe in the story, she went to Cooper Union and looked through files of old newspapers until at length, with incredulous eyes and stopped heart, she found his name listed among the dead.[9]

The letter from her Chicago friend had also given Mme. Miroski's London address, and now that Isadora was in England, she made up her mind to meet Miroski's widow. One day, without telling any member of her family, she called at the boarding school where Mme. Miroski taught. The teacher received her visitor with a certain reserve, but went on to relate that she had often heard about the young girl from Miroski, that he had intended his wife to join him in America as soon as they could scrape together enough money for her fare, and that they had both worked toward this goal for years. "And now," she said in a tone that wrung Isadora's heart, "he is dead." Isadora burst into tears and both women wept together in shared sorrow.

Isadora wrote: "I contrasted the fate of this patient little old lady—for she seemed very old to me—with my own daring voyages, and I could not understand it. As she was Ivan Miroski's wife, why had she not gone to him, if she had wanted to? Even as a steerage passenger. For I was never able to understand, then or later on, why if one wanted to do a thing, one should not do it. For I have never waited to do as I wished. This had frequently brought me to disaster and calamity, but at least I have had the satisfaction of getting my own way. . . . I remember I cried all the way home at the fate of Ivan Miroski and his poor little wife, but at the same time I had a strange exultant sense of power and a contempt for people who were failures, or who spent their lives waiting for things."[10] When she got back to her room, she gathered together Miroski's letters and photographs and locked them away in her trunk. Thus, she put an end to the past that had ceased to belong to her.

In London, Charles Hallé and his sister Maria took Isadora to the theater. Henry Irving made a deep impression on her in *The Bells,* and it appears that she also saw Irving and Ellen Terry in *Cymbeline.*

She was enchanted by Ellen Terry but apparently took no particular notice of a young man who was also in the cast and who was to play a decisive role in her life. This was Ellen Terry's son, Gordon Craig, whom she would meet later in Berlin.

Isadora was devoted to Hallé and she reserved her Sunday evenings for him. She was very fond too of Douglas Ainslie, a young Oxford-educated poet. She divided her time between the two men, being indeed a little in love with both. They quite naturally disliked one another, each protesting that he could not understand what she saw in "that fellow." With the days passing happily between her friend-ships and her work, she would have been content to remain in London. Raymond, however, had gone on to Paris and kept sending his family glowing reports of life in that city. At length he persuaded them to join him. (By now, only Isadora and her mother remained in London. "The gentle and cheerful Elizabeth"[11] had gone back to her pupils in New York, and Augustin was still on tour in the United States.) So mother and daughter took the channel steamer to Cher-bourg, and from there a train to Paris where they were met by Raymond.

5

Paris
1900–1901

RAYMOND'S quarters were not big enough to accommodate his mother and sister, and so the family took a furnished studio in the rue de la Gaîté in Montparnasse. The phenomenally low rent of fifty francs a month was explained at nightfall, when a series of crashes shook the floor and the walls. The apartment was over a night printing press, but since the Duncans had already paid the first month's rent, there was nothing to do but stay and make the best of it.

And to be in the capital of France in the springtime was compensation for much. Raymond and Isadora "used to get up at 5 o'clock in the morning, such was our excitement at being in Paris, and begin the day by dancing in the gardens of the Luxembourg."[1] They spent much of their time in the Louvre in the Greek collection, Raymond making sketches of the vases and Isadora imitating the postures of the statues, to the alarm or amusement of the guard. As was their habit, they also visited churches and monuments, Isadora being particularly struck by the dancing figures by Carpeaux on the facade of the Opéra and by the reliefs by Rude on the Arc de Triomphe. One afternoon, they had the great emotional experience of standing in the top gallery at the Trocadéro to see the tragedian Mounet-Sully in *Oedipus Rex,* after which the pair walked home "tipsy with inspiration."[2]

Summer came and Charles Hallé arrived from London, happy to see Isadora and eager to show her the delights of the Universal Exposition of 1900. Isadora was not impressed by the fairgrounds atmosphere which seemed commonplace beside the wonder of simply being in Paris, but she returned to two of the attractions again and again. These two were the Rodin Pavilion and the recitals of the Japanese dramatic dancer Sada Yacco, who was appearing with a small troupe at the theater which had been built for the American dancer Loie Fuller.[3] To the young San Franciscan, the supple, undulant movements of the Japanese dancer must have seemed like independent confirmation of her own reaction against the "artificial starts and stops" of ballet. As for Rodin, she was instantly struck by the force of his sculpture. Here was an artistic ally, someone who, like her, had studied Greek art in order to arrive at a spontaneous natural treatment of the human body. As for his habit of omitting the head or arms, disconcerting to some spectators, it posed no difficulty to one whose eye had been trained by Michelangelo casts, the Nike of Samothrace, and the Venus de Milo.

Hallé returned to London in the autumn, but, before he left, he introduced the 22-year-old Isadora to his fashionable 25-year-old nephew, Charles Noufflard, who in turn introduced her to two of his friends, Jacques Beaugnies and André Beaunier. The three men were enchanted with Isadora and enjoyed showing her off to their friends. Having seen her interpret Chopin, Beaugnies decided to present her to his mother, Mme. de Saint-Marceau. The wife of a sculptor and herself a musician, Mme. de Saint-Marceau gathered at her salon the elite of the artistic and social worlds of Paris.[4] She invited Isadora to dance one Friday evening, and, to the gratification of her three cavaliers, Isadora's performance was a great success. The Californian found herself launched in Paris society.

After her appearance at Mme. de Saint-Marceau's salon, Isadora danced in the drawing rooms of the Comtesse Greffuhle (the great beauty admired by Proust), the Duchesse d'Uzès, and the American-born Princesse Edmond de Polignac, who became a particular admirer of her younger compatriot.[5] Now well known in Paris (she had even danced at the Elysée Palace for the French president), Isadora thought of giving a series of concerts in the family studio. Invitation lists for these events exist in her own handwriting in a blue notebook (preserved among her papers in the Dance Collection of The Library of the Performing Arts). They reveal that Gabriel Fauré[6] and Octave Mirbeau[7] were among those invited. She also drafted a charming announcement for a recital to be given on December 12, 1901: "Miss Duncan will dance to the sound of harp and flute in her studio next Thursday Evening and if you feel that seeing this small person dance against the waves of an overpowering destiny is of ten francs benefit to you—why come along!"

By this time her material circumstances had improved sufficiently for the Duncans to give up their apartment over the printing press and move to a studio at 45 Avenue de Villiers. Here Isadora gave dancing lessons to children of socially prominent families while her mother played accompaniment on the piano. Here too she composed her own dances and received her friends. Of the three young Frenchmen, it was the shy, stocky André Beaunier who became her favorite. She says of him: "He was pale and round-faced and wore glasses, but what a mind! I was always a *cérébrale,* and although people will not believe it, my love affairs of the head, of which I had many, were as interesting to me as those of the heart."[8]

Beaunier was a writer. He introduced Isadora to French literature, he discussed his own work with her, and he took her for walks in the country or brought her to see Notre Dame by moonlight. Charmed by his sensitivity and wit, Isadora fell in love with him. Beaunier, however, remained too shy to express his feelings for her by more than a look or a pressure of the hand. Finally, Isadora decided to take matters into her own hands, and one evening when she was sure that her mother and Raymond would be at the opera, she invited Beaunier to a champagne supper at the family studio. He was so disconcerted to find her alone, dressed in her flimsy dancing tunic, that he hurried away early.

Hurt and baffled, Isadora then plunged into an intense flirtation with another more impetuous member of the trio (she does not say which one, but her description of him suggests Charles Noufflard). He took her to a hotel room and was on the verge of seducing her when some act of hers evidently made her inexperience evident. Overcome with remorse, he bundled her home to her mother. Isadora later wrote plaintively about still another such experience, "I had often heard about the terrible dangers which young girls risked by going into theatrical life but as my readers can see from my career so far, it was just the opposite. I really suffered from too much awe and respect and admiration which I inspired in my admirers."[9]

During this year in Paris, Isadora had the good fortune to form friendships with two men whose art she revered. As usual, her luck was the result of her own daring to risk a rebuff. Greatly moved by Rodin's sculpture, she mustered the courage to call one day at his studio. Far from being annoyed at the intrusion, Rodin showed her his work, and afterwards she danced for him. He was charmed and became one of the young American's warmest admirers, later writing: "She makes her dance sensitive to line, and is as simple as the Antiquity that is synonymous with Beauty."

She also became the friend of the painter Eugène Carrière, whose goodness and lack of artifice made her feel as if she had come into the presence of a saint. "A great tenderness for all stemmed from him . . . the beauty, the force, the miracle of his pictures were simply the direct expression of his sublime soul."[10] She became very much attached to him and his family and often visited them in their modest flat in Montmartre.

Isadora first met another lifelong friend in 1901—Mary Desti, a young divorcée with a year-old son,[11] who had come from Chicago to Paris where she was halfheartedly "studying voice." Impulsive, scatterbrained, uncritical, and outgoing, she became devoted to Is-

Three poses drawn by Bourdelle, circa 1909 (*Mme. Mario Meunier—Christine Dalliès Collection*).

adora, and, in her company, Isadora became the carefree girl she had never been able to be during her childhood in America.

Before this time, Isadora had always danced spontaneously. Now she began to analyze movement and to reexamine everything she had learned about her art. She practiced long afternoons in front of her mirror, trying to discover the true gesture and the expressive phrase. She became convinced that the body's center of motion lay *not* at the base of the spine, as taught by her ballet teachers, but in the solar plexus. "She read omnivorously in the archives of the Paris Opéra, filling notebooks with her researches. What other great woman dancer (and here is no wish to dim the fame of Taglioni or Pavlova) had ever been so well informed? Which of them ever doubted their teacher so profoundly, on such excellent basis?" It should be remarked that this passage was not written by a professional Duncanite or drumbeater for the modern dance but by Lincoln Kirstein, who later became general director of the New York City Ballet. He continued: "Few people have ever thought or felt so profoundly as Duncan on the sources and uses of lyric movement. It is all the more remarkable that she should have been so methodically curious, young as she was, free from any academic standard, lacking in practical background. . . ."[12]

This very freedom from academic standards, due not to ignorance but to her lack of commitment to any ready-made system, made Isadora question classical theories of the dance. The more convinced she became of its inadequacy, the more determined she was to follow her own path.

What was this new path in dance? To understand, we must look at Isadora's method of work. It is frequently said that she had no technique, that she was an inspired amateur. Whether or not this is true depends on what one means by "technique." (What, for that matter, is "dance"? Some Balinese dancers, on viewing classical ballet for the first time on a visit to New York, said, "It's very interesting, but, of course, it's not dancing.")

Certainly Isadora did not believe in mechanical exercises divorced from feeling and understanding. She wrote of "those systems of dancing that are only arranged gymnastics, only too logically understood (Dalcroze, etc.)."[13] She would later caution her pupils, "Remember always to start your movements from within. The *desire* to make a certain gesture must be there first."[14] John Martin, a dance critic for *The New York Times,* writing in *Dance Index,* spoke of "her insistence that the exercises of her young pupils . . . never lapse into . . . mere muscular exertion. . . . The dancer's habit of moving must be made such that movement is never an end in itself but always the outward result of an inward awareness. It follows then that no series of set movements, whatever their virtues for muscle development can be established as a training technique."[15]

But if "set movements" cannot be used, then what exercises, Martin asked, could Isadora have given her pupils to develop in them the necessary strength, control, and grace? Her solution, according to him, was to use as exercises "movement processes common to everybody . . . walking, running, skipping and the like. . . . Because Isadora's dance was simple in its gymnastic demands, she was undoubtedly able to develop all the needed strength, elasticity and endurance under cover of these natural movements."

This is true to some degree, though I would qualify his phrase "simple in its gymnastic demands." Martin forgot to add (perhaps he did not know) that Isadora and her pupils also used exercises at the barre for the purpose of developing strength and suppleness. Sometimes, the feet were kicked over the head in front, sideways and backwards. The knees were turned out for sidekicks, the leg was held straight, and the toes were pointed. In other exercises at the barre the knees were bent outward until the dancer sat on her heels; she then raised herself on her toes and sank slowly, holding her spine straight. (Irma Duncan, in *The Technique of Isadora Duncan,* refers to such exercises as "gymnastics.") In dancing, natural positions were employed. Neither knees nor feet were turned out, and in kicks the leg was usually relaxed, not tensed, though Isadora would use straight extensions in her *Bacchanale** from *Iphigenia* (Gluck)

---

*Anna Duncan said that Isadora did not use straight leg extensions in the *Bacchanale.* There is a difference of opinion about this. Both opinions may be correct because Isadora sometimes revised her dances.

and in the *Symphonie Pathétique* (Tchaikovsky). Many of her exercises were designed to develop complete fluidity in such ordinary movements as walking, running, skipping, and leaping. Irma Duncan would later write[16] that the exercise of lying down and rising

> teaches you control over the body through the unfolding of the movements one by one. Connect your movements by moving very slowly like a slow motion picture, without any breaks. You must seem to melt into the ground, into the very roots of things. Then after a moment of complete immobility, you rise with the strong desire . . . to reach up to the . . . sun. . . . Unfold your movements again slowly one by one in a continuous flow.

Abrupt transitions between kneeling and sitting must be avoided. The torso, too, was trained to be lithe, and movements made by the legs were continued through the body, not cut off at the hips as is sometimes done in ballet, which can make the dancer look like an articulated marionette.

Isadora also used "Tanagra figures," a series of movements derived from Greek art, for training her pupils in the basic vocabulary of her dance. But most of their technique was acquired not in exercises but in the course of rehearsing her dance compositions.

Although her dancers performed "movement processes common to everybody," these movements were not by any means easy to perform. Had they not been performed with training, they would have offered no esthetic satisfaction. Isadora once held an audience spellbound by slowly walking—a walk that was part walk, part dance—across the field of the Lewisohn Stadium in New York. The pioneer modern dancer, Helen Tamiris, remembers another occasion when the audience was transfixed by Isadora's "simple" movements.

> She was dancing the *Pathétique*. She started on the ground, lying close to the floor and—it took a long time—the only physical action was the very slow movement which carried her from prone to erect with arms outstretched. At the finish everyone was crying and I was crying too.[17]

That Isadora was able to produce such an effect with movements "common to everybody" is surely an argument for the existence of technique. Nor could the Duncan technique be acquired rapidly. Maria-Theresa, one of Isadora's six original pupils, said in disgust of a student: "She wanted me to teach her how to walk in a *day*! A day!!! It's taken me *years* to learn how to walk properly."[18]

Even Duncan-trained dancers find Isadora's "simple" movements difficult to execute correctly—as one can see by attending any Duncan class. For dancers with different training, however advanced, her movements present additional obstacles. On one occasion, some Duncan dancers asked a ballet soloist of reputation and ability to join their group in demonstrating Isadora's dances. Despite the soloist's quickness in learning the steps, she found she could not break herself of the habit of holding her body straight, which made her look rigid next to the other performers. This is not surprising, when one considers that the ballet technique in which she had been well schooled is founded on a different and opposed set of principles. To quote Agnes de Mille:

> The [ballet] posture is based on a straight and quiet spine, a stiffened straight knee (and this is the only form of dancing in the world that uses the stiff knee), and level hip line. The hips may not lift, thrust out or rotate. The shoulders may not ripple. . . . The knee, except when flexed in a bend, is held absolutely taut and straight. It is never relaxed. . . .[19]

Isadora's technique, on the contrary, aimed at fluidity. In contrast to ballet, which is based on the principle that the body's weight is centered primarily at the base of the spine, Isadora believed that the body's center of gravity is the solar plexus. Her figure moved forward with the weight placed as in the Nike statue or the figurehead of a ship—the upper torso leaning forward and the limbs following. According to Isadora, the body moved first in walking, running, or leaping, then the arms followed, with the movement unfolding through upper arm, forearm, wrist, hand, and fingers. The movement developing through the body had a gracefulness as satisfying to observe as the spring and descent of the impala. The fact that Duncan movement travels more slowly through the arms and the back leg as the body descends from a leap adds to the impression of lightness, as if the limbs were draperies gently settling after the descent of the body. All dancers use these means to some extent to create an illusion of weightlessness, but they were particularly characteristic of Isadora, and they have been used far more frequently by choreographers since Isadora showed their wealth of possibilities.

Analyzing her method of composition, Martin wrote:

> She has described her search for certain key movements which should arise out of elemental emotional experiences such as fear or love. . . . The only possible means that lay within herself was memory. . . . A state resembling fear itself must be recreated to stimulate the impulses of suitable movement. This could only be done be recalling previous experiences of fear and allowing these memories freely to induce their own emotional and bodily states.[20]

The similarity between this process and Stanislavski's preparation for acting is obvious. (When Isadora later met him, the two artists immediately recognized the kinship between their methods.) Martin was far from denying that Isadora possessed technique; in the same article, he proposed that Isadora's scattered writings about the dance be collected. "Such a task adequately performed would probably result in the greatest textbook of the dance ever written."[21]

Once Isadora had discovered the key movements, she could begin the work of developing them, of transforming them into a dance. Her inspiration often came from music, and she would try to express its "meaning," that is, try to project whatever joy, despair, or other emotion lay in it, rather than impose on it some story of her own. Her way of composing—in which the movements are personal, not formal, and are based on emotional experience, not on convention (like the traditional "hand on the heart" as an expression of love)— is of course the approach to choreography of the modern dance, and Isadora was the first to use it in our times.[22]

But the discovery and projection of her own feelings in natural movement was not, so far as Isadora was concerned, the ultimate goal of the dance. That goal was the expression of universal feelings, flowing from the dancer's own sources of deepest emotion. To achieve this, the dancer must become unaware of the movements of the body, allowing them to act as the medium for transmitting the impulses of the unconscious. In Isadora's words:

> His body is simply the luminous manifestation of his soul. . . . This is the truly creative dancer, natural but not imitative, speaking in movement out of himself and out of something greater than all selves.[23]

What she did not add is that it is necessary to pass through the stages of psychological and physical self-awareness to reach this final stage of self-forgetfulness, of surrendering to the music and the promptings of one's innermost being. She did write elsewhere, however, "Natural dancing should only mean that the dancer never goes against nature, not that anything is left to chance."[24] Thus the self-forgetfulness that Isadora advocated is not the denial of technique, as some critics maintained; rather, it is the achievement of a state in which technique becomes unconscious and the dancer's body is free to express his spirit.

❧ 6 ❧

Berlin and Vienna
1901 – 1902

HORTLY before the close of 1901, Isadora met another American dancer who had already won fame in Paris. This was Loie Fuller, whose success in the French capital had been so great that she now owned her own theater. Isadora apparently had already seen her[1] and considered her to be a superb artist.[2] Mme. Emma Nevada, the American opera singer and an acquaintance of the Duncans, brought Miss Fuller to the Duncans' studio one evening where Isadora danced for them.

Loie Fuller was impressed. She was about to leave France with her troupe for an extended tour of central Europe, and she invited the young woman to join them. As Fuller already managed Sada Yacco, the Japanese dancer whom Isadora greatly admired, she accepted with alacrity and agreed to meet her new impresario in Berlin.

What happened next is described quite differently in the memoirs of Loie Fuller and of Isadora, but it seems possible that both accounts are correct. Fuller, by the way, never mentions her protégée by name, but since she characterizes her as a performer who "danced with remarkable grace, her body barely covered by the flimsiest of Greek costumes," her identity is unmistakable.

When Isadora arrived in Berlin at the beginning of 1902,[3] she was surprised at the oddly demonstrative atmosphere of Loie Fuller's entourage. "A dozen or so beautiful girls were grouped around her, alternately stroking her hands and kissing her."[4] Still more unexpected was the fact that, though the company had been quartered in a palatial suite, there was apparently not enough money to pay the hotel bill, and when it came time to leave, the trunks were held by the Hotel Bristol.

Isadora's misgivings vanished, however, when she saw her colleague on stage.[5] "No imitator of Loie Fuller has ever been able even to hint at her genius!" Fuller danced with scarves under changing lights. The compelling feature of her performance lay not in her footwork, which was simple, but in the play of light on her draperies. These she extended by means of sticks held in her hands, playing out the material with breathtaking grace to create the effect of wings or unfolding petals. There is a tendency today to dismiss Loie Fuller's art as "well-manipulated yardgoods," but two pioneers of the modern dance, Isadora and Ruth St. Denis, saw her innovations differently.[6] They learned much from her use of lights and were quick to see the expressive possibilities in her use of drapery to extend the gesture, a use which they incorporated in their dances and which has been further developed in the choreography of such moderns as Alwin Nikolais and Frank Holder. St. Denis, indeed, thought so highly of Loie Fuller that she included her as one of the three originators of the modern dance (the other two being Isadora and herself).[7] As for Isadora, she wrote of Fuller: "That wonderful creature—she became fluid; she became light; she became every color and flame, and finally she resolved into miraculous spirals of flames wafted toward the Infinite."[8]

From Berlin, the troupe travelled to Leipzig, Munich, and eventually (in February 1902)[9] to Vienna, where it was the intention of Loie Fuller to present Isadora to a select public. To secure suitable patrons for the event, Loie herself delivered invitations to the Princess Metternich and to the British and American ambassadors, though she was sorely tempted to leave the younger dancer in the carriage "because of her . . . appearance. She wore an Empire robe, grey and with a long train, and a man's hat, a soft felt hat with a flying veil." On the afternoon of the performance, ten minutes before the concert was to begin, Loie went backstage.

"I found her with her feet in warm water, in the act of dressing her hair in a very leisurely manner. Startled, I begged her to hurry, explaining that she ran the risk through her negligence of offending an audience that would definitely give her her start. My words were without effect. Very slowly she continued her preparations. . . ."

Seeing that there was nothing further to be done, Loie rejoined her guests.

All at once she made her entrance, calm and indifferent. . . . But it was not her air of indifference that surprised me most. She appeared to me nude or nearly so, to so slight an extent did the gauze which she wore cover her form.

She came to the front, and while the orchestra played a prelude from Chopin she stood motionless, her eyes lowered, her arms hanging by her side. Then she began to dance.

Oh, that dance, how I loved it! To me, it was the most beautiful thing in the world. I forgot the woman and all her faults, her absurd affectations, her costume and even her bare legs. I saw only the dancer and the artistic pleasure she was giving me. When she had finished no one spoke.[10]

Then the princess whispered, "Why does she dance with so little clothing on?"

The reason for the general silence now became clear to Loie who said quickly in an audible voice that Miss Duncan's luggage had not arrived, and, rather than disappoint the waiting public, she had consented to dance in her rehearsal costume. Disaster was averted.

Isadora's next two performances—for the press and for the artists of Vienna, two notably less straitlaced groups—were unqualified successes.

Fuller next took the Californian to Budapest where she again presented her before an influential audience. Among those present was a Hungarian impresario, Alexander Grosz, who was very much impressed by the young dancer. Isadora then left for Vienna with the leader of Loie Fuller's orchestra to fulfill an engagement which the latter had arranged for her. It was here that the break occurred between the two women.

Loie wrote that after the concert, the conductor returned to Budapest alone and reported that Isadora had no intention of re-joining the company. Loie then telegraphed the girl to find out whether she meant to return and received the reply: "Only in case you will deposit to my credit ten thousand francs in a Viennese bank before 9 o'clock tomorrow morning." Loie lamented that "This proceeding was all the more cruel as she knew that I had just lost more than one hundred thousand francs through a Viennese manager who had broken his contract with my Japanese Company. . . . After I left Budapest the dancer came there to fill the engagement I had secured for her."[11]

Isadora tells the story somewhat differently. According to her, in Vienna she had been assigned to a hotel room with another member of the troupe, a volatile young woman who had already disconcerted Isadora by her affectionate manner. This girl had taken a strong fancy to Isadora. For some reason—possibly the wish to combat her strong feelings for Isadora—the girl appeared one night at Isadora's bedside with the announced intention of strangling her. On the pretext of saying her last prayers, Isadora got out of bed and fled down the corridor in her nightgown screaming, "Lady gone mad!" Hotel attendants intercepted her pursuer, but Isadora, un-nerved, dispatched two telegrams, one severing her connection with Fuller, and the other begging her mother to join her. In need of work, she remembered the Hungarian manager, Alexander Grosz, and sent off a message to him. In reply, he offered her a contract to dance at the Urania Theatre in Budapest.

Isadora's account of the episode gains some credibility from Loie Fuller's own description of her entourage. If Isadora did indeed have the experience just described, her unceremonious break with her patron is not surprising.

Yet, despite the unpleasant prelude, her stay in Hungary was to be a happy one, for in Budapest she experienced her first great popular success, and here too she met the actor Oscar Beregi, the young man enshrined in her autobiography and in her memory as "Romeo."

Drawing by Sartorio, 1911 (*Christine Dalliès Collection*).

7

Budapest—and Romeo
1902

N her notebook, under the date of May 11, 1902, Isadora jotted down notes for a press conference. She meant to speak about the dance, but she was so happy that she found it difficult to concentrate on the subject. A clue to her feelings might be found in the brief glossary of Hungarian words inscribed by another hand on the previous page: "The sun, sunshine, my soul, I am, yours."

In preparing her talk for the press, Isadora wrote:

How beautiful is the Spring in Budapest!—In the Garden of the National Museum there are some lilac trees in blossom. One hardly sees a green leaf—they are one radiance of purple blinding to the eyes . . . exhaling a perfume so wonderful. . . . Could I dance the happiness of one little tree in this Garden—one little tree bursting with blossoms and gladness!

I have known many springs but never such a one. I must stay here longer—I feel something of the youth and strength of this country creeping into my spirit. This country has much to teach. I must not go until I learn all. . . .[1]

She was in love. To have a gifted, handsome, and ardent young man in love with her, to know that she was successful and worthy of his love, and to feel all her senses blossoming with delight—all this she had dreamed of so often in her twenty-four years that to experience it was scarcely believable.

Everything had gone astonishingly well since her arrival in Budapest. Instead of dancing for small, select groups, as she was accustomed to doing, Alexander Grosz wanted her to dance for the general public. Isadora was doubtful; she had not forgotten the articles in the New York papers, and she worried that her work might mystify her audience. Grosz laughed at her fears. If she wanted to reform the dance, he contended, she must stop treating her art like smuggled goods, reserved for an exclusive minority.[2] With some trepidation, Isadora began to prepare for her public debut at the Urania Theatre on April 19.

Interest in the young American ran high. The reporter for *Pesti Naplo* was able to tell his readers:

> Miss Duncan's greatest dream is to erect a temple in Athens where she would educate young girls to become priestesses . . . of the dance. This sounds somewhat Californian but we cannot fail to repeat that so much conviction and simple enthusiasm radiates from Miss Duncan's inner nature that we have no right whatever to be skeptical.[3]

And in *Uz Idök,* Mari Jazai, who had attended one of her practice sessions, wrote:

> This infinitely ambitious . . . young girl . . . considers her art as sacred. She would like to deal only with difficult problems, despising those whose solution seems easy. After one of her rehearsals, the musicians began to play the *Blue Danube* Waltz, and, carried away by the enticing music, she performed a charming dance of a type never seen before. The onlookers were so enthusiastic . . . that every-

one begged her to include this beautiful number in her program.

By heaven! You should have seen her wide eyes fill with tears of indignation. She was just as much offended as she had been earlier when a gentleman kissed her foot in helping her to put on her slippers. In tears she told us: "Why should I tread the pioneer's thorny path in order to perform a commonplace, profane dance before a cultured audience?—the kind of dance I've known since I was four? If that were my purpose, I'd go into vaudeville . . . and make a lot of money. . . ." It was quite useless to tell her that she should include this number in her program to . . . show her audience how she is able to create a noble work out of a common dance. Without uttering another word she walked away. . . . How miraculous is her dedication to this classical art!

Her [ordinary] clothing, a naive mixture of ancient and modern styles, is exotic to such a degree that if she appeared on the street she would block traffic in a few minutes. And she would not even notice it.

. . . she performed a dance showing how the musical angels of Angelico pay homage to the Lord, how they praise God with the music of their violins. And seeing this dance, I had the feeling that from now on every other dance would somehow strike me as slightly clumsy and forced.

. . . She is even more irresistible as gay Nausikaa tossing a ball, as an ecstatic bacchante or as a nymph chasing a fawn. These are truly herself. . . .[4]

The reviews after her debut were equally enthusiastic. They spoke of her freshness, her "angelic face" ("If Miss Duncan were quite candid she would admit that she chose [to dance] the *Primavera* because her features exactly correspond to Botticelli's idea of beauty. Not everyone can make that boast!"),[5] her joyousness, and her "touching modesty," which was apparent despite her revealing costumes and bare feet. The critic of the newspaper *Pesti Naplo* noted (on April 20, 1902) that, in spite of the spontaneous quality of her dancing,

This new type of art . . . is not merely a harmony of haphazard movements, it is already . . . a codified art. . . . She has discovered entirely new movements of the human body. . . . This is, in fact, the magnificently free dance of nymphs on a Greek chalice where the feet carry the slender body with breathtaking ease. . . .[6]

And yet there was something here more intangible than technical mastery. An article in the same issue of the paper* tried to analyze the curious effect she produced.

At the beginning you perceive something unusual, almost strange. Generally, the speech of the feet is thought to be full of sensual enchantment. Her feet, however, though they are beautifully shaped, do not speak that language. They try to impart something which we feel we have seen once in a dream. And immediately her hands, her face, the lines of her magnificent body tell us wonderful things— in a word, they become eloquent of the soul itself. . . . The audience gazed at her as if they would like to absorb through their eyes the sunshine and springlike flavor of her sweet soul.

This critic's observation is worth noting for it shows that Isadora's conception of the dancer "who . . . has attained such a degree of understanding that his body is simply the luminous manifestation of his soul"[7] is no empty figure of rhetoric; it corresponds to a state that can evidently be felt by an audience.

Her second performance at the Urania Theatre on April 20 was another triumph. When she had finished the last number, *Bacchus and Ariadne,* the audience did not want to leave the theater. Suddenly making up her mind, Isadora asked the orchestra to play *The Blue Danube,* and, as the familiar strains of the waltz sounded forth, she began to dance with "almost unbelievable impetuousness." If she had been applauded enthusiastically before, this time she received an ovation. Her rapturous abandonment to the impulse of the music and the apparently artless spontaneity of her dance made it the most popular of her compositions, and, from that time, someone in the audience whenever she appeared was sure to call out for *Die Schöne Blaue Donau.*

*The writer is not identified in the translation owned by The Dance Collection.

For these first two performances at the Urania, Grosz had engaged a leading young actor, Oscar Beregi, Artist of the National Theatre, to recite the classical idylls and odes that served as her accompaniment. The 24-year-old Isadora could hardly have failed to notice that this handsome young man, tall and well built, with thick black curly hair, watched her with admiration and intensity. They met again at a party where his expressive dark eyes and lively manner left no doubt in her mind that he was powerfully attracted to her. "When he smiled, between his red sensual lips gleamed strong white teeth. From our first look every power of attraction we possessed rushed from us in mad embrace. From that first gaze we were already in each other's arms and no power on earth could have prevented this."[8]

Sensing her response, he invited her and her mother to see him in *Romeo and Juliet* at the Royal National Theatre. His acting in the title role deepened the impression that his sensual good looks and impetuous manner had made upon her. After the performance he invited the Duncans to supper and henceforth became a frequent visitor at their apartment.

What "no power on earth could have prevented" took place one night, after Mrs. Duncan, supposing Isadora to be in bed, had gone to sleep. Beregi secretly called on Isadora. At first he was content to talk quietly, but gradually emotion made his words falter, then cease. His ardor and "a great pity for what he seemed to be suffering" overcame her fears, and they secretly became lovers. At last she was cherished and adored. Eager to share her happiness and proclaim her love to everyone, on the evening of her final appearance in Budapest she performed a series of dances to the Hungarian gypsy songs which he had taught her. The next day they ran away to the country for several days. "We knew for the first time the joy of sleeping all night in each other's arms, and I had the unsurpassed joy of waking at dawn . . . to feel his arms around me."[9]

Mrs. Duncan was greatly distressed by this escapade, which both shocked and worried her, and she must have been relieved when her daughter's concert schedule took her from Budapest. At the end of this tour, however, Isadora returned to the Hungarian capital where she met Beregi. He spoke of their marriage as if it had been already settled and took her to look at apartments where they might live. But his manner had undergone a change. He seemed preoccupied and had to spend much time away from her at the theater where he was rehearsing the part of Brutus in *Julius Caesar*. Finally, Isadora wrote, "he asked me if I did not think I should do better to continue my career and leave him to his . . . I still remember . . . the cold chill that struck my breast. . . . My last vision of him was the mad enthusiasm of the theatre audience, while I sat in a box swallowing my tears and feeling as if I had eaten bushels of broken glass."[10]

Her only remedy would be to get away from both him and the city that held so many reminders of her former joy. She immediately went to Grosz and signed a contract to appear in Vienna and the cities of Germany. The next day she took the train for Vienna, a journey she described as "one of the bitterest and saddest I ever experienced." In Vienna, she fell ill and had to be placed in a hospital. An alarmed Beregi came from Budapest to be at her side, but, despite his concern, Isadora could not deceive herself that his love for her had revived. After he had left and Isadora had sufficiently recovered to leave the hospital, she went for a rest first to Franzensbad and then to Abbazia. It was a long time before she recovered her full strength. She had loved wholeheartedly and given herself without reserve. The rejection of her love was a terrible shock, and the thought of her past happiness only served to increase her present misery. Gradually, however, the kindness of friends and of Grosz and his wife began to dull the edge of her grief. She experienced that sudden return of interest in her surroundings so characteristic of convalescence. She remarked about a palm tree outside the window of her villa: "I used to notice its leaves trembling in the early morning breeze, and from them I created in my dance that light fluttering of the arms, hands and fingers, which has been so much abused by my imitators; for they forget to go to the original source and contemplate the movements of the palm tree, to receive them inwardly before giving them outwardly."[11]

But Isadora could not rest long in the sun, watching the ruffling of palm fronds. Her illness had depleted her savings, making it necessary for her to return to the theater. Grosz booked appearances for her in the principal German cities. Once again, she prepared herself to appear in public; her dance enriched with what she had learned of joy and sorrow.

Isadora drawn by an unidentified artist, perhaps Gordon Craig (*Mme. Mario Meunier–Christine Dalliès Collection*).

❧ 8 ❧

Convalescence, Success, and a Manifesto

1902–1903

AFTER Isadora had recovered from her illness, she went to Munich where her manager was arranging appearances for her. He had decided not to spend much money on publicity at this stage of the campaign; the important thing, he felt, was to win the support of artists—the approval of the public would follow. The artistic center of the city was then the Künstler Haus, a rendezvous for such well-known figures of the day as the painters Lembach, Von Kaulbach, and Stuck; it followed that Isadora should make her debut there. Lembach and Von Kaulbach offered no objections, but Stuck opposed the plan; in his view, the dance was frivolous entertainment, not art, and it certainly was not worthy of being shown in such august surroundings.

Isadora resolved to convince him of his mistake. If her account is to be trusted, she went to his home and asked his permission to dance for him. He gave it. She danced, and then, hardly breathless, "talked to him . . . without stopping on the holiness of [her] mission, and the possibility of the dance as an Art."[1] He was the one left winded by this encounter. If her enthusiasm was touching, her self-assurance was patently godlike. Yet, when she danced, she seemed unconscious of either herself or him. It was as if she were alone and dancing for her own delight in some forest clearing. He was astonished and charmed, and he melted. Of course she might appear in the Künstler Haus!

Her recital was a great critical and popular success. From that night her reputation in Munich was established, and it continued to grow throughout her engagement. The newspapers were full of articles either attacking or defending her art, but, even in denouncing it, they tacitly recognized its importance. The discussion was not limited to intellectual and artistic circles. The public, eager to join in the controversy, flocked to see the 25-year-old performer. Under the heading "Isadora Duncan's Poetic Dances Have Divided Germany," a correspondent for an American newspaper noted with some surprise that tickets to her concerts sold out rapidly, though their price scale was scandalously high—50¢ to $2.50, as compared to the 18¢ to $1.50 top which prevailed elsewhere—this "without any sensational advertising, no pictures on billboards or in the store windows . . . merely here and there a modest poster giving date of performance and program."[2]

The same reporter provided a glimpse of Isadora as she appeared in one of her recitals in a dance inspired by Botticelli's masterpiece, the *Primavera*.

> Her dress is of some soft grey stuff with printed blossoms, a copy from the draperies of one of the figures in the painting. And now, with wreathing arms, and undulating body, and bare . . . feet she present[s] to us the . . . pulsing, ecstatic quickening of all life, the langorous . . . *dolce far niente* of this marvelous season.

After noting the wide emotional range of her dances—among them, a fiery bacchanal and *Orpheus Mourning the Death of Eurydice*—the writer concluded:

Her grace is indisputable. Never an abrupt movement. Never a sharp angle. And to those with whom modesty, intelligence and feeling in the human countenance count far more than the expressionless regularity of features, she is more pleasing than the much vaunted Mérode[3] whose immobile countenance affords about as much inspiration as would a wax mask.

The students of Munich also fell under her sway. Night after night, after the performance, they uncoupled the horses from her carriage and drew her home themselves. What made her all the more appealing to them was that she was young—their own age— and that she so plainly delighted in giving them pleasure. Long accustomed to coolness, now Isadora basked in the warmth of their enthusiasm. On one occasion the students took her to their café, where she was lifted dancing from table to table. Although the evening ended with her dress being torn to ribbons by her admirers, she described the party as "really . . . most innocent."[4]

Usually, however, when Isadora was away from the theater, she devoted her time to serious pursuits. The atmosphere of Munich stimulated her and she took up the study of German and philosophy. Everything seemed to provide inspiration for her work—the conversation of the people she met, the museum collections, the new pictures in the studios, and the theories of Schopenhauer on the relation of music to will.

Tempted by the nearness of Munich to the Italian border, she interrupted her performances to travel to Florence for a few weeks' vacation.[5] While she was there, she immersed herself in the painting and sculpture of the Italian Renaissance, finding much in their movement that she later incorporated into her art.

In her autobiography, Isadora wrote that this was her first trip to Florence, and that she composed her *Primavera* after seeing Botticelli's masterpiece in the Uffizi Palace. Here her memory played her false. In fact, she had created and danced the *Primavera* in London, where she had been influenced by the Italian Renaissance paintings in the National Gallery. She was also familiar with Botticelli's work from reproductions.

The date of her first trip to Italy is uncertain. She seems to have visited Florence before her appearance in Budapest, if her remarks to reporters in that city are to be trusted. But wherever her first acquaintance with Italian Renaissance art took place, she was a sensitive critic, as revealed by her remarks in *My Life*[6] on the *Primavera*.

From Florence she went to Berlin, where Grosz, her manager, had hired the Philharmonic Orchestra and the chief opera house, the Kroll, for her debut.[7] He was risking his entire capital to present her handsomely, but he no longer held doubts about her reception. His confidence was justified: Isadora repeated and improved upon her Munich success. From that time, she danced to packed houses. The newspapers, struck by her sense of mission and the ethereal quality of her dancing, began to call her "the holy, the divine Isadora."

It must not be supposed that there were no dissenting voices in this chorus of praise. The president of the Berlin Artists' Society, Herr von Werner, urged his colleagues to reject Isadora's offer to admit art students to her recitals at half price.[8] To encourage students to see her, he said, was to foster immorality.

The critic of the *Berlin Morgen Post* objected to her art on aesthetic grounds. In an article headed "Can Miss Duncan Dance?" he complained that the American had no technique; her style could not be considered an art form. The art of the ballerina of the Berlin Opera was vastly superior to her art. He invited the ballet masters of the world to watch Isadora Duncan and to judge whether what she did was dancing. Isadora did not allow such a challenge to go unanswered. Replying to the *Morgen Post,* she wrote:

Dear Sir:

I was very much embarrassed on reading your esteemed paper to find that you had asked of so many admirable masters of the dance to expend such deep thought and consideration on so insignificant a subject as my humble self. I feel that much excellent literature was somewhat wasted on so unworthy a subject. And I suggest that instead of asking them, "Can Miss Duncan Dance?" you should have called their attention to a far more celebrated dancer—one who has been dancing in Berlin for some years before Miss Duncan appeared. A natural dancer who also in her style (which Miss Duncan tries to follow) is in direct opposition to the school of the ballet today.

The dancer I allude to is the statue of the dancing Maenad in the Berlin Museum. Now will you kindly write again to the admirable masters and mistresses of the ballet and ask them "Can the Dancing Maenad Dance?"

For this dancer of whom I speak has never tried to walk on the end of her toes. Neither has she spent much time in the practice of leaping in the air to find out how many times she could clap together her heels before she came down again. She neither wears corsets nor tights and her bare feet rest freely in her sandals.

I believe a prize has been offered for the sculptor who can replace the broken arms in their original position. I suggest it might be even more useful for the art of today to offer a prize for whoever could reproduce in life the heavenly pose of her body and the secret beauty of her movement. I suggest that your excellent paper might offer such a prize and the excellent masters and mistresses of ballet compete for it.

Perhaps after a trial of some years they will have learnt something about human anatomy, something about the beauty, the purity, the intelligence of the movements of the human body. Breathlessly awaiting their learned reply, I remain, most sincerely—

Isadora Duncan[9]

From the letter, it is obvious that Isadora found the fight stimulating, and that at age twenty-six she knew how to defend herself.

As a result of this exchange, she was invited to lecture on the dance by the Berlin Presse Verein. Her speech was later republished in pamphlet form as *The Dance of the Future*,[10] and it is now one of the seminal works of modern dance theory.

Nature, Isadora said, is the source of the dance. Every creature moves according to its nature—that is, according to its feelings and its physical structure. "It is only when you put free animals under false restrictions that they lose the power of moving in harmony with nature and adopt a movement expressive of the restrictions placed about them." The movements of the savage are natural and beautiful, but those of civilized people, hampered by clothes and conventions, have become distorted.

Ballet dancing, with its artificial starts and stops and its holding of poses, is, according to Isadora, the antithesis of natural motion. The ballet's movements and rhythms do not flow naturally and successively from one another. Ballet tries to "create the delusion that the law of gravitation does not exist." Worse still, it permanently warps the body: "Under the tricots are dancing deformed muscles . . . underneath the muscles are deformed bones." (On this point, see a recent issue of *Dancemagazine:* "Doctors, therapists, even physicists are rattling as well as realigning the bones of the dance profession. And their first target is the grand plié. . . ." The dancer's continued bending of the knee in the fifth position eventually yields a knee injury.)[11]

Greek sculpture portrayed natural movement; the sculptors understood that each gesture must be in harmony with the body that makes it, and that a "ripe and muscular" man will dance differently from a child. If her own dance looked Greek, Isadora said, it was only because she used natural movements. "To return to the dances of the Greeks would be as impossible as it is unnecessary."

She added: "But the dance of the future will have to become again a high religious art as it was with the Greeks. For art which is not religious is not art, is mere merchandise."

It follows that the purpose of the dance is not mere entertainment, and that the issue between Isadora and the ballet is not simply an issue between two kinds of dancing.

It is not only a question of true art, it is a question of . . . the development of the female sex to beauty and health, of the return to the original strength and to natural movements of woman's body. It is a question of the development of perfect mothers and the birth of healthy and beautiful children. The dancing school of the future is to develop and show the ideal form of woman. . . .

In this school I shall not teach the children to imitate my move-

Drawing by Fritz von Kaulbach in Munich in 1902, on a 1904 cover of *Jugend* (*youth*) magazine (*Blair Collection*).

ments but to make their own. . . . The dances of no two people should be alike. . . .

The dancer of the future will be one whose body and soul have grown so harmoniously together that the natural language of that soul will have become the movement of the body . . . O, she is coming, the dancer of the future: the free spirit who will inhabit the body of new woman . . . the highest intelligence in the freest body![10]

Isadora insisted that the dance must be natural (suited to the structure of the human body), individual (expressive of the person's age, build, and, more important, emotions and character), and possessed of a serious purpose, even beyond the purpose of art, which is the physical and spiritual liberation of the dancer. All these ideas were novel, and we are still exploring their implications.

Her speech was well received and commented on at length in the newspapers the next day—she received almost as much publicity as a diplomat or scientist. She had established the premise that the free dance was an art, worthy of serious discussion. She would, in any case, have been assured of a respectful hearing through the eminence of some of her admirers, who now included, if we are to trust the press, two reigning monarchs.[12] Whatever the truth of this publicity story about the kings, by April a committee had been formed to raise the money for a theater in Berlin to bear her name, and the Countess von Bülow, wife of the German Imperial Chancellor, was among the project's sponsors.

In May, Isadora went to Paris to prepare for a series of ten performances at the Théâtre Sarah Bernhardt. The theater was a large one, and the dancer, afraid that it might not be filled on her opening night, took the precaution of distributing free seats to the students of the Ecole Nationale Supérieure des Beaux-Arts. Many of them became her ardent admirers, and one of them, the Spaniard, José Clara, later published a book of drawings of Isadora.

The Paris critics were coolly favorable; Isadora did not receive the kind of triumph she had become accustomed to in Germany. Nevertheless, as the engagement progressed, the audience apparently warmed to her, for by July the columnist Helen Ten Broeck wrote, "She has been a tremendous success . . . she is deservedly quite the rage."[13] But this success did not come soon enough to offset her earlier losses, and, in the *New York American* of July 1, 1903, it was reported that, while she was giving a dinner party, a bailiff arrived to collect a debt of $500 which she had incurred during her tenancy at the theater.

Shortly before this incident, on June 30, Isadora had been invited to a picnic given for Rodin in celebration of his being awarded the prize of the French Legion of Honor.[14] Among the other guests was a young Scottish pupil of Rodin, the sculptor Kathleen Bruce, who would later become the wife of the explorer Captain Robert Falcon Scott.

Kathleen Bruce (later Lady Kennet) wrote in her autobiography, *Self-Portrait of an Artist:*

> After lunch at the picnic, a fine old Norwegian painter, Fritz von Thaulow, tuned up his fiddle, and somebody said the lovely dancer must dance. Isadora had a long, white high-waisted Liberty frock on, and shoes. She said she could not dance because her frock was too long. Somebody said, "Take it off," and the cry rose, "Take it off." So she did, and her shoes too, and as the fiddler began to play, Isadora, in a little white petticoat and bare feet, began to move, to sway, to rush, to be as a falling leaf in a high gale, and finally to drop at Rodin's feet in an unforgettable pose of childish abandonment. I was blinded with joy. Rodin was enchanted. . . . Rodin took Isadora's and my hands in one of his and said, "My children, you two artists should understand one another."[15]

So began a long friendship between the two unusual young women. Later, Kathleen Bruce went on tour with Isadora to Brussels and The Hague.

> No friends had we at all in these foreign towns. If pressmen came, the dancer was self-conscious and austere, and since she talked nothing but American, the interviews were brief. We got up early, ran in any park that was near, and did a few gymnastics. Whatever

happened later, and terrible things did happen, at that time the dancer was a healthy, simple-living, hard-working artist, neither beautiful nor intelligent apart from her one great gift for expression. Moreover she was not musical in the usual sense of the word, though her rhythm could rouse the greatest and the least to delirious rapture.[16] She was open-handed, sweet-tempered, pliable and easy-going. "Oh, what's the difference?" she would say, if I, who hated to see her put upon, wanted to stand out against overcharges. "What's the difference?" But she ate carefully, and drank nothing at this time but water or milk. She was making enormous sums of money.[17]

Isadora then returned to Germany, where she spent the rest of the summer and the early fall in touring the various cities. She was now a well-known figure and she could command high prices. It seemed hardly the moment, in the opinion of her agent, to interrupt a promising career. Isadora took a different view. For the first time in her life, she could afford to do as she liked. Her brother Raymond had just returned from America and Augustin had rejoined them earlier; thus, after several years of dispersal, the whole family was once more reunited. It had always been the Duncans' dream to visit Greece; what better time to go than the present? Unable to dissuade them, Grosz was forced to let them go, and Isadora and her family set out for the country which she already knew so well in her imagination.[18]

❧ 9 ❧

Pilgrimage to Greece
1903

HE Duncans were pilgrims in search not only of a new country but also of the past; they, therefore, resolved to travel to Greece by primitive means, to duplicate the conditions of antiquity. Embarking at Venice, they sailed to Santa Maura in Ithaca and there hired a fishing smack to sail them across the Ionian Sea. Isadora has given us an unforgettable picture of Raymond's explaining to the fisherman in a mixture of ancient Greek and pantomime "that we wished our voyage as nearly as possible to resemble that of Ulysses." At Karvasaras on the other shore, they spent the night in the town's only inn. Isadora reports that they slept little, partly because "Raymond discoursed all night on . . . Platonic Love," and partly because of the fleas. The next morning at dawn they set out for Agrinion, with Mrs. Duncan and the baggage ensconced in a carriage and her hardy children escorting her on foot, bearing branches. Isadora tells us that so great was their joy in being in Greece that they sang and shouted, and, when they came to a mountain stream, Isadora and Raymond insisted on baptizing themselves in its rapid current and were nearly swept away.

"We had our lunch in a little wayside inn, where, for the first time, we tasted wine preserved with resin in classic pigskin. It tasted like furniture polish, but making wry faces, we insisted it was delicious."[1]

They passed the night at Agrinion, and the next day they took the stagecoach to Missolonghi to salute the memory of Byron. Afterwards, they took the steamer to Patras and from Patras they travelled by train to Athens.

Now at last they were in the heart of Greece: they had reached the goal of their pilgrimage. Their first act was to climb the Acropolis and stand silently in the Parthenon. They next visited the monuments and historic sites of the ancient city, keeping a lookout for a suitable spot on which "the Clan Duncan [could] . . . build a temple that should be characteristic of us."[2] This was to be Isadora's school of the dance. As all the Duncans were now wearing sandals and robes, their progress through the streets of modern Athens created a considerable stir.

One day, in their explorations of the countryside around the city, they climbed a hill and suddenly saw that they were on the level of the Acropolis. Because of the clear, dry air, the temple of Athena looked startlingly clear four kilometers away. They determined to acquire this land as a site for their temple, and, after some inquiry, discovered that the hill, named Kopanos, belonged to five peasant families who used it for grazing their sheep. The peasants had never considered the land to be valuable, but as soon as they learned that a group of presumably rich Americans (and from their costumes undoubtedly mad) wanted to buy the property, they set a stiff price. After some negotiating, the Duncans accepted the terms, and the bargain was sealed at a banquet of spitted lamb and raki.

It then became necessary to choose a design for the building. Following the typical Duncan style of doing nothing by halves, Raymond decided to use the plans of the palace of Agamemnon, and he set about hiring workers and masons. The laying of the cornerstone was accompanied with appropriate ceremony. Isadora

Photograph taken by her brother Raymond in an Athens amphitheater (*Blair Collection*).

and Raymond danced in a pattern which indicated the shape of the foundations. The presiding Greek Orthodox priest blessed all the stones of the house, its future inhabitants, and then, using the cornerstone as an altar, he slit the throat of a black cock. Although Raymond had persuaded his family to become vegetarians, the incongruity of this ceremony with their beliefs does not appear to have struck any of the Duncans. They were in fact enchanted by the merging of the ancient and new in Greece, so that the past seemed ever present. In a country where children were still baptized "Athena" and "Antigone" and where the Christian church was said to have preserved in its music hymns to Zeus, what could be more appropriate than for an Orthodox priest to sacrifice a cock?

Though it was autumn, the weather was still warm. Too elated to leave the sight of the walls that were slowly taking shape before their eyes, the group decided to camp out on the hillside. By this time, the party had been joined by Augustin's wife, Sarah, their little girl, Temple,[3] and Kathleen Bruce, who describes the excursion in her memoirs. They all "camped on the thyme-covered slopes of Mt. Hymettus . . . Very early one morning when it was just getting light, I heard a playing on a reed pipe. I sat up on the grassy ledge I had chosen for my bed to see whence came the lovely plaintive notes. It was a young goatherd at the head of a troupe of goats. I watched his beautiful movements, so light and sure-footed, his bare shoulder and arm bronzed and supple, his ragged clothes, and his tossed hair. I was delighting in the grace of him when suddenly he caught sight of me. With a wild, piercing note on the reed to his goats he turned and fled down the grass and rocks, his herd bounding behind him."

She also speaks of the "native riders [who] stripped would come down to water their horses in groups of eight or ten, looking for all the world like the Parthenon frieze, glorious in pose and a marvel of color, their red-bronze limbs against the blue sea."[4] How Isadora must have enjoyed such sights!

Years later, in 1938, Kathleen Bruce returned to "Kopanos, where in 1904 (I think) Isadora and the Duncans and I built a wonderful house. . . . There it was, quite untouched and half-roofed only. It all came back, how we used to go out separately with a rug and a stick and a petrol tin to sleep on the hillside. The tin was because we only had one revolver among us, and if we heard anything suspicious we banged on the tin and fired the revolver into the air."[5]

The first night on the mountainside brought to their attention something that had not occurred to them before: there was no water on Kopanos. Raymond hired more workers, but their digging produced nothing but additional expense. This was a serious drawback, but the Duncans were still so elated to be in Greece that nothing could dampen their enthusiasm. When they were not camping on Kopanos, they stayed at the Hôtel d'Angleterre, and there, on November 3, 1903, Isadora gave an interview to a reporter from *The World*.[6] Explaining her early interest in Greek art, she said, "I was brought up in San Francisco where my father's house was plentifully supplied with reproductions of classic art in sculpture and engraving. In this artistic atmosphere I breathed the first years of my childhood. There I became inspired with high artistic ideals, and, while a little girl, my inborn taste for dancing was developed. While playing in the garden of my father's house I tried by instinct to impart to my childish dance what I saw exhibited in the models of art." It is notable that Isadora does not say that her father was not in her "father's house." She was still ashamed of her parents' divorce and of the poverty of the greater part of her childhood. Her mother, too, must have found the divorce an embarrassing topic, for in Budapest she had told a reporter that her husband "had died so young that he could not have had the faintest idea that his tiny daughter had inherited his love of Greek art." Actually Joseph Duncan had drowned on October 14, 1898, with his third wife and their young child in the shipwreck of the *S.S. Mohegan,* off the coast of Falmouth, England.[7]

It is impossible not to feel a pang of sympathy when one reads Isadora's early statements on her privileged upbringing as the daughter of an art-loving banker: they show how sensitive she must have been to the irregularity of her childhood.

In his Sunday-supplement prose, the reporter of *The World* gives us a glimpse of Isadora:

> The feet were bare save only for the sandals. . . . It was a wondrous figure, slim but rounded. There was a finely shaped head with a coil of glorious hair setting against the back of the neck, two arms exquisitely molded—the very classic simplicity of the costume only made the wearer all the more beautiful, the more graceful. . . . In her sweet, soft voice there was just the faintest thrill of rhapsody that spoke of deepest feeling . . .

Isadora, in fact, was living in a state of exaltation. Since her arrival in Greece, everything she saw excited her interest and sometimes her tears. In each new city she visited, Isadora was an eager visitor to the museums. She steeped herself in Greek art and literature. Stirred by her reading about the Eleusinian mysteries, she and her brothers and sister danced the thirteen miles from Athens to Eleusis, pausing where the road overlooked the bay of Salamis to imagine the maneuvering of the Greek fleet against the forces of Xerxes.

Once, on returning from an exploration, they learned that the king of Greece and his entourage had paid a visit to their temple on Kopanos. She noted, "We remained unimpressed. For we were living under the reign of other Kings, Agamemnon, Menelaus and Priam."[8]

Isadora had come to know the archaeologist Philadelpheus and the poet Angelo Sikelanos,[9] whose sister, Penelope, would marry Raymond. With these and other intellectuals, she speculated on the nature of ancient Greek music. It was the belief of many scholars that the modal chants of the Orthodox liturgy had originated in classical Greece; once sung to celebrate the gods of Olympus, they had been appropriated by the Christian church. The Duncans were enthusiastic about the idea of presenting Greek tragedy in its pristine form, with the choruses sung to the ancient music.

One night when the little group of travelers was sitting in the ruined theater of Dionysus, the unearthly voice of a young shepherd soared out of the darkness, singing a plaintive song. They listened, enchanted. The next night he was joined by a companion, and on subsequent evenings (the Americans having distributed drachmas) the number of singers grew. A contest was held to choose the ten boys with the most beautiful voices, and these were placed under the charge of a seminarist and taught the choruses of *The Suppliants* by Aeschylus; Isadora was to accompany them in dance.[10]

During the stay in Greece, Isadora had given several public recitals. On November 29, she gave the final one, attended by the king and the royal family.[11] With her funds exhausted by the heavy cost of building the temple on Kopanos, she was forced once more to go on tour. So, saying goodbye to their Greek friends and accompanied by the ten singers and their teacher, the Duncans boarded the train for Vienna.

Isadora's mother (*New York Public Library*).

Isadora's father (*New York Public Library*).

As first fairy in *A Midsummer Night's Dream,* 1896 *(New York Public Library).*

Wearing her mother's lace curtains, 1898 (*New York Public Library*).

Dancing the *Primavera*, Paris, 1900 (*New York Public Library*).

Mrs. Dora Duncan (Isadora's mother), Walter Schott, and Isadora, 1903, in front of Schott's sculpture of Isadora (*New York Public Library*).

Isadora and Edward Gordon Craig on the day they met, Berlin, 1904 (*New York Public Library*).

Isadora Duncan, Temple Duncan, and Mary Desti at Bayreuth, Germany, 1904 (*New York Public Library*).

Isadora with Grünewald students in 1905 (*New York Public Library*).

Isadora in Belgium in 1905, photograph by Edward Gordon Craig *(New York Public Library)*.

Isadora, Deirdre, and Patrick at Versailles, 1913 *(Mme. Mario Meunier—Christine Dalliès Collection)*.

❧ 10 ❧

Germany—and Bayreuth
1903–1904

N their return from Greece, the Duncans went to Vienna where Isadora was to dance the choruses from *The Suppliants,* while the ten Greek singers whom the Duncans had found chanted the words. The Viennese public received this attempt to revive the classical drama with some bewilderment, though the critic for the *Neue Presse,* Herman Bahr, wrote a series of enthusiastic articles about the production. But it was the second half of the program, with its lighthearted dances, waltzes, and *The Blue Danube,* which ensured the success of the engagement. A pupil remarked:

Today, when one visualizes Isadora dancing, one is apt to think of her doing an interpretation demanding great dramatic power of expression. But in her youth she really excelled in the lighter offerings, the sort known as popular numbers. She was superbly fitted for such dances. Little dance poems—similar to the ones I most often like to recall—a Chopin mazurka, a Brahms waltz, and the ineffable "Dance of the Happy Spirits," executed to a flute solo from Gluck's *Orpheus*—represent what the true dance should be. They are lightfooted, graceful, expressing the soul of Terpsichorean art, which is really joy in action. . . .

These were Isadora Duncan's masterpieces, and they were performed with a brilliant technique of her own requiring perfect nimbleness of limbs and body and genuine elevation. This latter, the most important technical quality in a dancer, was always produced by Isadora and [later] her pupils under their own power and never artificially induced as in the ballet, where the ballerina is lifted off the ground by the strong arms of her partner. On that point alone, Isadora's technique stands far above that of the ballet. The remarkable quality of her elevation gave her dance creations in the gayer mood the incomparable effect of being executed off the ground rather than on it.[1]

Cheers and applause greeted every performance, and *The Blue Danube* was encored again and again.

In Munich, the Greek choruses created a great impression. The boys were praised for the purity of their voices and Isadora for her expressiveness and grace; nevertheless she felt the inadequacy of trying to portray by herself the "fifty daughters of Danaus," and often at the end of her performance she apologized for its inevitable shortcomings. Soon, she assured her audience, she would open a school, and, with her pupils, she would be able to dance the fifty maidens convincingly.[2]

From Munich, she traveled to Berlin where she had once again taken an apartment. The German capital responded to her program as had Vienna: the audiences politely applauded the antique choruses but reserved their real enthusiasm for *The Blue Danube*.[3]

It was perhaps lucky for Isadora that classical tragedy was not more popular, for the boys' voices were beginning to change. Isadora and her family saw what they must do. After bestowing farewell gifts of clothing on their protégés, the Duncans took the youthful singers and their tutor to the rail station and regretfully, but with finality, saw them off on the train for Athens.

Now that her time was once more her own, Isadora began giving weekly receptions that were well attended by literary and artistic Berlin. At one of these parties Isadora met a young writer named Karl Federn. It is Federn whom she credited with awakening her enthusiasm for Nietzsche's philosophy. So much in Nietzsche must have seemed to her like a prophetic confirmation of her own ideas— his image of the wise man as a "dancer" whose virtue it is to express the truth with "lightness"; his saying, "Count that day lost in which you have not danced"; and even his heralding of the superman— "the highest intelligence in the freest body." What else was Isadora's envisaged school but a plan for creating the superwoman? Isadora found herself looking forward to her frequent sessions with Federn, and he, too, enjoyed them, for he later wrote of his pupil:

> Her singular mixture of highest rapture for Greek culture and German philosophy, together with her sure, free and youthful Americanism, struck me as charming. . . . Her complete dedication to her idea compelled my friendship and help.
>
> Isadora was then very slender and pretty. She had read a great deal, was full of fun and high spirits; was carefully guarded . . . by her mother, much admired by her brothers and sisters [sic] and even a little feared, since she turned out to be not without feminine malice although at bottom kind-hearted and good.
>
> Her spiritual and physical resistance were astounding. She could practice all day and in the evening, give a two-hour-long performance, go from the theatre to the station, take a train for St. Petersburg, and while her companions went to bed and rested, continue on to the theatre on arrival for rehearsal and give another performance at night without feeling tired.[4]

Isadora soon became so immersed in her studies that she grew reluctant to interrupt them even to fulfill engagements in nearby Leipzig and Hamburg. She turned a deaf ear to her manager's entreaties that she undertake longer tours, even though, as he pointed out, her costumes and choreography were being imitated by other dancers and praised as original.[5] He must have wondered what kind of performer he was managing—one who would interrupt her career at its height to spend months poking among ruins, who enjoyed dancing on tables in a student café, and who took even greater pleasure in reading philosophy and writing letters to scientists. An example of the latter was her correspondence with Ernst Haeckel, the distinguished evolutionist whose neo-Darwinian work, *The Riddle of the Universe,* had made a deep impression on her. On the occasion of his seventieth birthday, Isadora had impulsively sent him a note of congratulation:

Dear Master . . .
Your genius has brought light into the darkness of many human souls. Your works have given me religion and understanding which counts for more than life with me. . . .

all my love
Isadora Duncan[6]

To her surprise, she received a reply to her letter. On the back of a printed card of acknowledgment, Haeckel wrote:

Bordighera, Park Hotel
2 March, 1904

Much admired artiste!
The receipt of your amiable letter together with the present of your beautiful pictures have given me much joy on my 70th birthday and I want to thank you heartily for them.
I have been for quite a while a sincere admirer of your classic art (being an old admirer of the Greeks) and I hope at last within this present year to have the pleasure of making your acquaintance. As author of the "Anthropogenie" I would be charmed to see in the harmonious movements of your graceful person the greatest creation of nature!
I shall remain for the rest of the month in Bordighera at the Park Hotel. Middle of April, I go back to Jena. As a return gift I shall then send you my picture. Please forward me your address for the month of May and let me know if you desire some of my pamphlets.

With thanks and best wishes for the growing success of your art-reform along the lines of evolving nature, I remain, your sincere admirer,

Ernst Haeckel

She hastened to answer:

Dear Master,

I consider it a great honor that you have written to me. I have read your dear letter many times and can hardly believe that you, dear Master, have written in this way to me. I have just returned from my performance at the Philharmonic and in the solitude of my room am thinking of you. Of your wonderful life-work, of your great human heart that has worked for all mankind. . . . How I would love to dance for you! I am going to be in Bayreuth this summer and perhaps I can come to Jena and dance for you, in the open air perhaps under the trees. But my dances will be only a poor way to express my love and gratitude for you. . . . Now I must go to sleep since I have to travel tomorrow to Mannheim, Hanover, Luebeck and Hamburg, etc.—and later to Paris. Goodnight dear Master, your

Isadora Duncan[7]

Her astonishment and gratitude at this letter from Haeckel whom she would later meet were genuine. Among people who were merely prominent or successful, Isadora was well aware of her worth, but before those whom she considered great, she felt profoundly humble. Rather than her own gifts, it was her *conception* of the dance, she believed, that entitled her to respect. She often doubted the adequacy of her talent compared to the magnitude of the task she saw ahead of her.[8] And yet here, in spite of her shortcomings, the brilliant and profound Haeckel had addressed *her* as "Much admired artiste" and had voiced a desire to meet her!

As she mentioned in her letter to Haeckel, Isadora intended to spend the summer in Bayreuth. Her decision to go had been prompted by a note the previous August from Cosima Wagner, inviting her to take part in the coming year's production of *Tannhäuser*.[9] This

mark of recognition must have been flattering to the dancer, for
Isadora greatly admired Wagner's widow. "I have never met a
woman," Isadora later wrote, "who impressed me with such high
intellectual fervour as Cosima Wagner, with her tall, stately carriage,
her beautiful eyes, a nose perhaps too prominent for femininity, and
a forehead which radiated intelligence. She was versed in all the
deepest philosophy, and knew every note and phrase of the Master
by heart."[10] Isadora presumably saw in Cosima a rebel like herself—
a rebel, moreover, whose personal standards had become law for
an influential part of society. A pioneer for women's rights in both
art and love—had she not left her husband for Wagner?—Cosima
had survived criticism to overawe her detractors. Isadora regarded
her with reverence as one whom she wished to emulate.

In her letter to Isadora, Cosima Wagner explained that the composer had always been dissatisfied with conventional ballets as being
inadequate to the demands of Music-Drama. She wished to know
if Isadora would dance the first Grace in the Bacchanal of *Tannhäuser*.
Isadora accepted eagerly, conscious that she had been accorded
unusual attention by this habitually reserved and unbending woman.
Resolving to merit the honor, she arranged to go to Bayreuth in
May.

Just before her departure, Isadora's close friend, Mary Desti,
arrived in Berlin, and Isadora persuaded her to accompany the
Duncans to Bayreuth. She also persuaded the impressionable Mary
to discard her ordinary clothing and don the tunic and sandals which
by now the dancer had adopted for street wear. When the august
Cosima, meeting her protégée, saw the pair in their Greek robes,
she exclaimed in surprise: "Why, Isadora, do all Americans dress
like you?" "Oh, no," Isadora replied airily. "Some wear feathers."[11]

It is hard for us to imagine how startling her clothing must have
been. This was a time when women compressed their feet into
pointed-toe, high-heeled shoes and their bodies into stays, when
even ballerinas danced tightly corseted, and when women consoled
themselves for their discomfort with the French motto "One must
suffer to be beautiful." Isadora's abandoning of corsets, shoes, and
conventional dress, not only on stage but in her daily life for reasons

of health and aesthetics, was nothing short of revolutionary. She struck at the basic principle of feminine fashion: the traditional belief that it was the duty of women to attract men at whatever cost to themselves. Isadora quite simply believed that it should be the goal of women to be natural, healthy, and intelligent, and that men were naturally attracted to healthy and intelligent women. Since many men found her attractive and intelligent, this gave force to her argument.

The designers Fortuny and Poiret would put the stamp of fashion on the classical Greek lines that Isadora had brought to the public's attention—Fortuny in 1906 with his Delphos gown and Poiret somewhat later—but it was Isadora who began the revolution in women's dress.

Isadora and Mary Desti wore their tunics even to formal dinner parties at the Villa Wahnfried. An invitation to the villa was like an invitation to court, a court presided over with queenly dignity by Frau Wagner, whose entourage included writers, artists, grand dukes, and princesses. The musicians Richter, Muck, Mottl, and Humperdinck were frequent guests, as was Cosima's son-in-law, the writer and teacher Heinrich Thode.[12] However proud Isadora may have felt at having earned a place in such a brilliant gathering, she remained ingenuous. With total candor, she attempted to explain to Cosima Wagner what was wrong with Music-Drama:

> One day during luncheon . . . I calmly announced, "Der Meister hat ein Fehler gemacht, eben so grosse wie seine Genie" ["The master has made a mistake, despite the greatness of his genius"].
>
> Frau Cosima fixed me with startled eyes. There was an icy silence.
>
> "Yes," I continued with the extraordinary assurance which belongs to extreme youth, "der Grosse Meister hat einen grossen fehler gemacht. Die Musik-Drama, das ist doch ein unsinn" ["The great master has made a great mistake. Music-Drama is nonsense"].
>
> The silence grew more and more troubled. I further explained that drama is the spoken word. The spoken word was born from the brain of man. Music is the lyric ecstasy. To expect a possible union between them is unthinkable.
>
> I had uttered such blasphemy that nothing further was possible.

I gazed innocently around me, to meet expressive visages of absolute consternation.

Thinking to dispel the frost by making herself completely clear, Isadora concluded:

The speaking is the brain, the thinking man. The singing is the emotion. The dancing is the Dionysian ecstasy which carries away all. It is impossible to mix in any way one with the other. Musik-Drama kann nie sein.[13] [Music-Drama cannot be.]

It speaks well for Cosima that her friendship for the younger woman survived this shattering piece of frankness.

Despite Isadora's, one might suppose, major reservation about Wagner, she steeped herself in his music with all the immense enthusiasm of which she was capable. To become conversant with Wagner's thought, she attended the rehearsals not only of *Tannhäuser*, but those of *The Ring* and *Parsifal* as well. She was apparently so successful in divining what the composer had had in mind, that once, after she and Cosima had disagreed on the dancer's conception of the Bacchanal, Cosima came across some notes in her husband's handwriting that bore out Isadora's interpretation of his meaning.[14] Cosima, generously conceding her mistake, vowed henceforth to give the Californian free rein.

Isadora had hired a cottage, Phillips Ruhe, for the season, where she and her friend Mary Desti lived alone. Late one night, when Isadora was getting ready for bed, Mary called her companion to the window. A man was standing in the garden below, his eyes fixed on the house. She felt herself becoming alarmed when Mary told her that he had been watching Isadora's room every night for a week. At that moment, the moon came out and shone down on the rapt face of Heinrich Thode.

Isadora threw her coat over her nightgown and ran out into the garden. Thode, startled and delighted, confessed that he had fallen in love with her. At the urgency in his voice, all the eager and painful longings which she had refused to admit—had not even

Portrait by E. Bieber in Berlin, circa 1904 (*Picture Collection, University of California at Los Angeles, Department of Special Collections*).

been aware of feeling since the unhappy end of her affair with Beregi two years before—began to revive in her. Faint with hope and apprehension, she led Thode back to the house.

He, however, was a married man, too aware of his situation to do more than kiss her, yet too much in love to force her from his mind. So he began the custom of calling on her every evening after she had returned from the theater. Even when he was speaking of art or reading the *Divine Comedy* to her, Isadora understood that he was telling her indirectly of his love. They had so much to say to one another that often dawn was breaking when he finally left the cottage. Yet never, Isadora wrote, "did Thode make one gesture of earthly force toward me . . . although he knew that every pulse [of my body] belonged only to him."[15]

Beregi came from Budapest to visit her and, though their affair had ended painfully, she was happy to see him. Perhaps because her love of Thode seemed to have no possible future, she was delighted to get away for a few days to Helgoland in the company of Beregi, her little niece Temple, Mary, and Mary's son, Preston Sturges. After a short stay on the North German island, Beregi returned to Hungary, and the others returned to Bayreuth.[16] Once there, her former schedule reestablished itself.

Each night Thode visited Isadora at Phillips Ruhe. Each day Isadora danced or rehearsed at the theater. She hardly slept at all, and she was so preoccupied by her thoughts that she hardly noticed her fatigue. Her performance and appearance were widely commented on. A correspondent wrote:[17]

> The peculiar feature of the Bayreuth festival this year is the bare-foot dancer, Isadora Duncan, who some time ago made the conquest of Berlin . . . even during this festival time at Bayreuth the serious beauty of this dancer is something quite conspicuous.
>
> She drives about the town in an elegant carriage . . . and is always accompanied . . . by a female companion [Mary] dressed like herself in Greek costume . . . sandals on their feet, and ribbons drawn through their hair which is dressed in Greek style . . .
>
> On the dancer's face, so I am told, is always an expression of

sadness, which does not wholly disappear even when she joins in the gay laughter of her companions.

Miss Duncan dances in *Tannhäuser,* and therefore this opera, next to *Parsifal,* and the *Nibelungen Ring,* excites the greatest interest.

The ballets, however, danced by the Vienna and Berlin ballet corps are far more Parisian than Wagnerian in type, and it strikes one as a pity that Bayreuth should have introduced anything of this style. The dance of grace is, without a doubt, danced by Isadora Duncan.[18]

The "expression of sadness" which this writer mentions was a reflection of Isadora's inner state. By this time, she was hopelessly in love with Heinrich Thode: ". . . the slightest touch of his arm sent such thrills through me that I turned faint . . . I completely lost my appetite for food. . . . Only the music of *Parsifal* brought me to the point where I dissolved into tears and wept, and that seemed to give me some relief from this exquisite and terrible state of loving which I had then entered."[19]

The summer was drawing to a close, and Isadora went on tour, but to be away from Thode, while she was still in the same country with him, brought no release from her longing. She lay in bed, wakeful. "Constantly I saw Heinrich's eyes and heard his voice. From such nights I often rose in agonized despair and took a train at two in the morning traveling over half Germany only to be near him for an hour. . . . The spiritual ecstasy with which he had inspired me in Bayreuth gradually gave place to an exasperated state of uncontrollable desire."[20] She says earlier, "Though I had spent so many nights with Heinrich, there had been no sexual relations between us."[21]

It may be wondered why Isadora did not put an end to a situation that caused her so much suffering. Probably she was too deeply in love with Thode to have the courage to refuse to see him. What remains surprising is that she apparently never threatened to stop seeing him as a means of winning him to her, nor did she make any attempt to seduce him beyond letting him know of her love. She did not, presumably, allow herself to think of marriage. Rather, she seems to have accepted the relationship on his terms, perhaps because she was afraid of the greater pain and involvement that a liaison would bring. Her love affair with Beregi had ended unhappily when he broke their engagement. Miroski had become betrothed to her with what seemed bigamous intent. These disappointments and, most of all, her father's abandonment of her family shortly after her birth must have suggested to her that men's love was not to be depended upon. Thus, if Thode could offer her neither marriage nor an affair, she must try to control the demands of her senses. She succeeded so well that she "finally could eat nothing at all and was attacked by a queer faintness."[22]

At the end of the summer, Thode left for a lecture tour. After going to Venice to see Mary off for America, Isadora toured Germany, but she continued to make Berlin her headquarters. Weary of wasting her energies on a hopeless passion, she began to devote herself to a project that had long been in her thoughts: this project was her school.

In the latter part of 1904,[23] she bought a house in the Grünewald district of Berlin. At the same time she announced to the newspapers that she was looking for young pupils willing to consecrate themselves to the dance. The children were to live at the school and Isadora would feed, house, clothe, train, and educate them at her own expense. Isadora was immediately swamped by applicants. She chose twenty[24] girls between the ages of four and eight. Isadora was later to write in her autobiography: "Certainly the sudden opening of this school without the proper premeditation or capital or organization was the most rash undertaking imaginable; one that drove my manager to distraction."[25] But, as she said in another context, "I was never able to understand ... why, if one wanted to do a thing, one should not do it. ... This has frequently brought me to disaster ... but at least I have had the satisfaction of getting my own way."[26] And if the school was to be a constant financial drain on her resources, it was also a source of artistic fulfillment and consolation in times of sorrow.

Twin Souls

1904

N December, at nearly the same time as the founding of her school, Isadora met a young man who was to play a decisive part in her life. Edward Gordon Craig was at that time a tall commanding man of thirty-two, with the straight nose and sensitive mouth of his mother, the actress Ellen Terry. He had the Terry magnetism, a quick elastic way of moving, and the beautiful voice of the trained actor: his original profession.

Like Isadora, Craig was a revolutionary: he aimed at nothing less than remaking the theater. His sense of mission had evolved slowly and not without wrenching his life out of established patterns. Married at twenty-one to May Gibson[1] and at the threshold of a successful career (his roles already included Macbeth, Romeo, and Hamlet),[2] he had abandoned the stage for which birth and talent seemed to have destined him. In the emotional turmoil of finding himself, he had embarked on an affair with the young actress Jess Dorynne,[3] by whom he had a daughter, Kitty. The affair had broken up his already failing marriage, and the resulting bitterness made it impossible for him to see at will his four children by his wife.[4] Meanwhile he was trying desperately to make a living. He started a magazine, *The Page;* he sold sketches and drawings to newspapers. At the end of 1899, he and his friend, the conductor Martin Shaw, decided to produce Purcell's *Dido and Aeneas.* After this production, Craig knew he had found his life's path. Purcell's *The Masque of Love,* Handel's and John Gay's *Acis and Galatea,* and Laurence Houseman's nativity play, *Bethlehem,* followed in distinguished succession, each adding to Gordon Craig's reputation as a maker of original and breathtakingly beautiful stage settings.

But while he was struggling to establish himself, he was drifting apart from Jess Dorynne. Groundlessly he began to suspect her of trying to maneuver him back into the theater as an actor and presently he left her.

In the same year, he met and fell in love with the young violinist Elena Meo. She too fell in love with him and was in despair to learn from his friend Martin Shaw that Craig was married, for though he assured her he was expecting a divorce, she was a Roman Catholic and a divorce would not change the situation. Eventually, after a severe inner struggle, she decided that Ted meant more to her than anything else and that she would devote her life to him. Three children would be born of their union: Nellie (1903–1904), Ellen Mary Gordon Craig (Nelly, 1904–   ), and Edward Anthony Craig (Teddy, 1905–   ).[5]

Yet, despite his love for Elena, Craig was apparently not ready for married life. Perhaps the memory of his ill-fated marriage and the loss of access to his four children was too strong. Very likely he felt that marriage was a trap. He may have felt also that it was essential to be independent until he had established himself professionally and financially. For, although his reputation continued to grow, his income remained precarious. William Rothenstein, Max Beerbohm, Arthur Symons, Yeats, and Graham Robertson[6] all had praised his settings, but Ellen Terry had lost money on the two productions, *The Vikings* and *Much Ado About Nothing,* that he had mounted for her. Such *succès d'estime* had the effect of convincing

Edward Gordon Craig in 1895 *(University of California at Los Angeles, Department of Special Collections).*

producers that he was too costly to use (this despite the fact that
he had had nothing to do with the business management of either
Terry play).[7] In short, he found himself simultaneously artistically
established and unemployed. Fortunately, the German Count Harry
Kessler had seen his work and persuaded Dr. Otto Brahm to invite
him to the Lessing Theatre in Berlin.[8] Thus Gordon Craig came to
Germany, and in the last month of 1904 he met Isadora.

Accounts of the meeting differ. Isadora, in *My Life,* says that Craig
attended one of her recitals and afterward came backstage in a "wild
state of excitement," half jokingly accusing her of "stealing his
ideas."[9] Craig, in his unfinished autobiography, *Index to the Story of
My Days,* wrote that their meeting occurred in a roomful of people
before he had ever seen her dance.[10] He adds that when he did see
her dance and later visited her in her dressing room, he kept silent,
being moved and too conscious of her fatigue to want to disturb
her with chatter.

He later gave details of their meeting in a letter.

> I was taken to see her at her flat in Hardenbergstrasse (was it *no.*
> 11—?) by Miss Elise de Broukere [sic]—when I got into the room
> where there was a big piano. I first came face to face with the little
> sister Elizabeth D. and took her to be I.D. (Ho! Ho!) Gus D. was
> there too, I believe and his loved Sarah, mother of their little girl—
> Temple Duncan. Then turning I saw Isadora and we talked—I
> suppose—what about I don't know. The concert to which I went
> was 1, 2—3 or more days later—I forget. So its [sic] not true that
> I met her for the first time AFTER the concert.[11]

Craig does not believe that the account in *My Life* was written
by Isadora. Since she died before her book was published, and since
the original typescript, perhaps with corrections in her hand, has
disappeared, it is impossible to tell whether she or an editor wrote
that passage. Though the episode in *My Life* sounds unlikely (Craig's
coming backstage and at once praising Isadora, as well as angrily
claiming that she had stolen his ideas), I am inclined to think that
she wrote it (which does not necessarily mean that it is accurate).
Isadora sometimes invented anecdotes to make a point, and here

her point seems to be the unexpected kinship between her ideas and those of Gordon Craig.

But Craig would see the point of the anecdote as being his supposed accusation that Isadora had stolen his ideas. Since he was very sensitive on the subject of people's stealing *his* own ideas, this recounting of such an incident in *My Life* would of course make him angry.

A more extensive account of this first meeting appeared in Gordon Craig's day books, which Edward Craig drew upon in his biography of his father.[12]

In Berlin in December Gordon Craig met by chance Elise de Brouckère, whose sister Jeanne he had known in London at the time of *The Masque of Love*. While he and Elise were lunching at her apartment, he talked about his ideas for a school of the theater, and the sort of movement he would teach there. Elise asked him whether he had ever seen Isadora Duncan; the kind of movement she made to music might be what he had in mind. When Craig replied that he had never seen her, Elise persuaded him to come with her to the Duncan apartment nearby at 11 Hardenbergstrasse.

According to Gordon Craig's account, the Duncan family was there: Mrs. Duncan, Augustin, his wife, Sarah, and Elizabeth. A Mrs. Maddison was playing Fauré on the piano, and Craig watched Isadora's face as he listened to the music; her expression reminded him first of one of his previous loves, then of another. To Isadora, the fact that he was the son of Ellen Terry—"my most perfect ideal of woman!"—seemed no less fateful.[13] They were seized with a sense of wonder, discovery, and recognition which made the other people in the room fade into unreality. "We became friends and lovers from the moment we stood there at the piano," Craig later wrote in his diary.[14]

The next day Isadora appeared at a showing of Craig's work at Friedemann and Weber's Gallery. Her enthusiasm fired him and he poured out explanations of his drawings and his ideas on the theater. She, for her part, invited him to see her dance. Later that day he wrote her a letter and left it at her apartment. "It was, I remember, a letter of love, if ever a letter held love in it."[15]

The concert he attended on Isadora's invitation was a Chopin Evening; Craig preserved the program, noting on it, "the first I saw." It reads in part:

"Mazurka A flat op 17, no 4"—after which he has commented, "faultless."

"Mazurka H flat op 33, no 4"—his note: "amazing—it is so beautiful."[16]

In his autobiography, he later wrote:

I shall never forget the first time I saw her come on to an empty platform to dance. Berlin—the year 1904, the month December. Not on a theatre stage was this performance given, but in a concert hall, and you may recall what the platforms were like in 1904.

She came through some little curtains which were not much taller than she was herself—she came through and walked down to where a musician, his back to us, was seated at a large piano—he had just finished playing a short prelude by Chopin when in she came, and in some five or six steps was standing by the piano, quite still—you might have counted five or eight, and then there sounded the voice of Chopin in a second prelude or etude—it was played through gently and came to an end—she had not moved at all. Then one step back or sideways, and the music began again as she went moving on before or after it. Only just moving—not pirouetting or doing any of those things which a Taglioni or a Fanny Elssler would have certainly done. She was speaking in her own language, not echoing any ballet master, and so she came to move as no one had ever seen anyone move before.

The dance ended, she again stood quite still. No bowing, no smiling—nothing at all. Then again the music is off, and she runs from it—it runs after her then—for she has gone ahead of it.

How is it that we know she is speaking her own language? We know it, for we see her head, her hands, gently active, as are her feet, her whole person.

And if she is speaking, what is she saying? No one would be able to report truly, yet no one present had a moment's doubt. Only this can we say—that she was telling the air the very things we longed to hear and till she came we had never dreamed we should hear;

and now we heard them, and this sent us all into an unusual state of joy—and I—I sat still and speechless.

I remember that when it was over I went rapidly round to her dressing-room to see her—and there too I sat still and speechless for a while. She understood my silence very well—all talk being unnecessary. No one else came to see her, so far as I remember, so far as she remembered—afar off we heard applause going on and on. She put on a cloak, shoes, and we went out into the streets of Berlin where the snow looked friendly and shops were still lighted up, the Xmas trees all spangled and lighted—and we walked and talked of the shops. The shops—the Xmas trees—the crowd—no one heeds us.[17]

After visiting her school and attending another of Isadora's recitals[18]—*Iphigenia* this time[19]—he again visited the Duncan apartment, where Mrs. Maddison was again playing the piano. When she left, Isadora and Craig impulsively accompanied her to the door in the hope of leaving secretly, but they were intercepted by Augustin. They found their opportunity a little later when Karl Federn and his sister were going home in a car large enough for two extra passengers. In high spirits, they decided to drive to Potsdam. On the way, Craig and Isadora told each other all they felt and thought and hoped and imagined. "We talked sort of three-ply, if you can guess what I mean."[20] At dawn they took coffee at a little hotel on the outskirts of the city, then drove back to Berlin. By this time, it was 8 A.M., so they decided to visit Elise de la Brouckère at her flat at Spinchernstrasse 7. "We had a cheerful champagne breakfast in the tower—four of us, Isadora, a lovely Belgian lady (the sister of Senator de la Brouckère), Gordon Craig and myself," wrote Karl Federn later.[21] "It was at that time that her friendship with Craig began, very differently from the way it is told in the Memoirs."

After breakfast, Isadora began to worry about her welcome at home. Elise therefore called on the Duncans and came back to report that their attitude was chilly. It seemed wiser for Isadora not to try to return for the time being, so she decided to spend the night with Elise. While Craig was still with them, Elise took four photographs of Isadora, two with her and Craig seated together reading from a book. On the back of one picture, Craig noted, "1904. In Berlin about Christmas time when we had taken shelter with Elise de Brouckère . . ." and then, in apparent reference to the disapproval of the Duncans, "Two villains, Dec 16, 1904." Another snapshot shows Isadora praying in an attitude of mock penitence. The inscription reads, "1904. Dec 16, I.D. Topsy." (Topsy was Craig's pet name for Isadora. She called him Ted.)

The following day at tea time Isadora rejoined Craig at his studio at Siegmundshoff 11. It was a vast cold room with a balcony, and there were artificial rose petals strewn on the black waxed floor. Unfortunately there was no stove or heat—the gas had been turned off. Nor was there any couch. Craig lived in a little room down the block at Siegmundshoff 6. They made up a bed as best they could on the balcony with several rugs, Isadora's fur coat beneath them, and a sheet and two more rugs over them. She already knew that he was her love, the other half of herself, her "twin soul."[22] If this seems a sudden conviction, they had plenty of time to get to know each other, for as Craig later explained, "In Prussia in 1904 an hour had 700 minutes if it was a good hour."[23]

That night they talked a great deal, some of it high-spirited nonsense, some of it serious conversation. Craig told her that he was going to be married to Elena in about four months. Isadora replied that she did not believe in marriage.[24] If she did not take his marital plans seriously, she can hardly be blamed; his letter to her, his ardent looks, and his lovemaking seemed to proclaim that he had no thought for anyone else. It seems likely that Craig did not even intend to convince her that he was committed to another; he was not forthright in his dealings with women, often because he did not know what he himself wanted. (Elena Meo had fallen in love with him before she learned, not from Craig but from his friend Martin Shaw, that Craig was already married. He then told her that he was expecting a divorce, but since she was a Catholic, this did not eliminate the difficulty for her. Only after a severe struggle did she resolve to devote the rest of her life to him.)[25]

The following afternoon, December 18, Isadora was supposed to appear at a reception at her own house. Craig evidently urged her not to go, for she sent him a note afterward. "Dear you are quite right it was a sort of Blasphemy to go among a lot of people only dear Frau Begas gave the party in my honor." However, she took the precaution of waiting until the reception was underway before arriving, to avoid maternal lectures. After the party, she slipped away again to Craig's studio.[26]

Isadora and Craig fell in love with what may seem unusual rapidity, but it must be remembered that they were both sensitive, impulsive, and impractical people. Craig as a young man was "Excessively attracted sexually by women. . . . When the amorous feeling in me came surging up, I did not know what on earth to do—there was no man about in our house to show me a way out of my dilemma. [His parents had separated when he was three years old.] If I saw a nymph and felt attracted to her, I might go right up to her and attempt to kiss her. . . . It distressed me—these sudden attacks bewildered me—and only much later on I saw some relation between sex and creative ability in my work."[27]

His son Edward Craig later wrote about the stimulus that sex provided to his father's creative impulse:

> If one or another person exhilarated him to the extent that it helped him with an idea, he would consume that person, then discard their shattered and disillusioned remains—in the same way that other creative artists consume spirits and toss the empty bottle into the dustbin. And in this respect he was particularly ruthless with women.
>
> Inwardly he lacked self-assurance, and like his father was always looking for some boost to his ego—hence his tremendous outpouring of letters and the almost feverish concern with which he awaited the replies. He particularly liked writing amorous letters to women; they generally succumbed easily to his charm so he was certain of the kind of reply that would provide the boost he required.
>
> He had no time for people who were not outspoken and fearless, and he liked those who treated him as their equal *provided that they respected his only love—the theatre.* . . .

When he was working on some idea anything irrelevant to that idea would not be tolerated: "Get rid of, that chattering fool; she's getting in the way of my thoughts. . . ."

Under the self-assured facade that most people encountered was a man that few knew: the real, tragic, despairing, self-doubting artist, struggling with perspective and sciagraphy, trying to teach himself to write and to draw.[28]

This being so, Isadora's creative gifts must have heightened for him her already considerable charm. So temperamentally akin were they that they often spoke of one another as twins. Craig's large-scale way of looking at things was a trait belonging to Isadora, as was his engaging humor. They both had the capacity for seriousness and for intensity without solemnity. They were eager and light-hearted. In artistic creation, everything came easily to them. (In art, as it has been remarked, everything is either easy or impossible.) Both were reformers whose purpose it was to strip their respective art to its essentials. Yet this pruning of dead wood was not due to a paucity of ideas; the artists were confident that they had something to put in its place. To Isadora, Gordon Craig would have stood out immediately as a kindred spirit. And as unrequited love for Rosaline had prepared Romeo for his passion for Juliet, so unsatisfied longing for Thode had prepared Isadora for Craig.

The two had something else in common, as they must have discovered with surprise and sympathy. Both had been reared by energetic and devoted mothers in the absence of their fathers. Both recognized that the mystery surrounding their missing fathers—a shameful difference to be concealed from other children—had clouded their childhood.

Craig's parents had not married. At the time that Ellen Terry had eloped with the architect Edward William Godwin, she was still married to her first husband, the pre-Raphaelite painter G. F. Watts, although they had been legally separated for three years. Ellen Terry was sixteen when she married Watts, then a man of forty-seven. As might be expected in view of their disparate ages, their marriage was fraught with difficulties. Watts' purpose in marrying her had been, in part, patronizing: "To remove an impulsive young girl from the dangers and temptations of the stage."[29] Before his wedding, Watts had lived at Little Holland House, the home of Mr. and Mrs. Thoby Princep and of Mrs. Princep's two sisters, Lady Somers and Mrs. Cameron. Once married, Watts saw no reason to let his new status change his domestic arrangements. After the ceremony, Mrs. Princep continued to act as Watts' hostess, while the inexperienced Ellen remained in the background, ignored by the triumvirate of ladies. Not unnaturally, the marriage failed, and Ellen was sent home to her parents. She went back to work on the stage, and sometime later she renewed her friendship with Edward Godwin, an old acquaintance of her family. Presently they fell in love, and she eloped with him. She was then twenty-one years old. The couple subsequently had two children, Edith and Edward, but the alliance came to an end when the boy was three. Like Isadora, Edward felt anxiety about his missing father. ("Every other boy I knew had his mother *and* father. Not having mine—not hearing of mine—this grave sensation of something being wrong grew and grew into a fixed sort of small terror with me.")[30] The similarity of his circumstances to Isadora's must have increased his feeling that he had found his twin. In his copy of her autobiography he wrote, "Exactly" next to her statement, "All my childhood seemed to be under the shadow of this mysterious father of whom no one would speak, and the terrible word divorce was printed on the sensitive plate of my mind."[31] Earlier, where Isadora quoted her aunt's remark, "Your father was a demon who ruined your mother's life," he noted on the page, "As my sister said to me of my father."[32]

An entry in Craig's autobiography reads: "Isadora and I saw each other daily. We could see little else. We were indeed full of admiration for each other. Astonished too—but I would say to her, 'It is not of course *real.*' "[33] The fact that his parents had separated and that his own marriage had ended in divorce, as well as his awareness of his sexual susceptibility, made him cautious about admitting to himself that he loved her. In the same book occurs the revealing passage:

. . . To please women became my deepest real delight . . . yet often I felt it was all acting—not real—for real was Father and Mother, and see where that reality led me to. . . . Only once in my life a real woman and I came face to face. She won. . . . Such courage I did not possess: I can understand it, seeing it, but I have no such courage. All courage, face to face with love, is what that other one had when we cried and laughed and said it was not real—she came to mistrust that saying of ours—she came to tell herself it *was* real—that led her into immense sufferings.[34]

(Here the "real woman" is Elena; "that other one" is Isadora.) If from the beginning Craig told himself his feelings were not real, it was because he could not reconcile them with his feelings for Elena Meo. On March 3, he wrote in his notebooks:

I am in love with one woman only, and though others attract me how could it ever obliterate what exists of her in my heart and soul, or how could it alter my heart and love to her—but I am keenly attracted to another woman, who may be a witch or a pretty child (and it doesn't really matter which) and I find it hard to be away from her. She not only attracts me, she revolts me also. . . .

When she talks about herself incessantly for a quarter of an hour— when she drinks more wine than she needs or wants—when she cuddles up to other people, men or women, relations or not relations—it is not that she does so repulsively but I see they are equally attracted as myself—and I object to be equally anything in such matters.

And my confession is that I have a contempt for her and do not like to feel I have a contempt—because I find her so dear and delightful.

Still I cannot trust her, and even friendship, much more love demands absolute trust.

Not that I love her—it is not possible to "Love" twice.

And that is where perhaps a clever idiot would get mixed, for though I do not love her, I tell myself and her that I do—still I also tell her that I am unable to tell what love is.[35]

At the same time, he wrote to his friend, the musician Martin Shaw, about Isadora:

Artist or not—this is a marvelous being—beauty—nature and *brain*.

I don't like brainy women but brains and intelligence is a rare and lovely thing.

If you could see *one* dance you would understand how wonderful it is. Beauty and Poetry is art when it is created, no matter how, but a living being—

I have seldom been so moved by anything—It is a great, a rare, rare gift, brought to perfection by 18 years of persistent labour—and we may all agree to worship such things.

. . . Inspiration is given out by the thousand volt per second from Miss D. And I am alive again (as artist through her—you know how life giving or taking one artist can be to another.—We gave each other some darned stunning inspiration once—.)[36]

From the very beginning, indeed, Isadora seemed untroubled by doubts about the reality of their love or its outcome. She wrote to Craig, shortly after the beginning of their affair:

Thank you, thank you for making me whole, happy, complete. I love you, love you, love you, and I hope we'll have a dear sweet lovely Baby and I'm happy forever.

Your
Isadora[37]

However, it was necessary for her to turn her attention elsewhere for she had an engagement to tour in Russia. In the midst of preparations for her departure, she took time out to write to him:

I'm packing my trunk.

Everyone is calling on me to hurry.

Darling until we meet again. Until I return to the heart in which I was born. . . . I love you as the essence of all that is good and sweet in Creation. And I am above everything else Grateful-Grateful-Grateful to you. . . . I am your love if you will have me. If not—but I am your Isadora.[38]

Traveling away from him in the night, the train crossing an inky river which flowed between moonlit banks of snow, she felt like a soul crossing the river Styx of the underworld "to the land of Shadows." The click-clack of the train wheels seemed to intone, "*How* I love you—*How* I love you—*How* I love you." She felt torn with longing for him. The very severity of her pain reassured her, serving as it did as a measure of her joy. "Last night I cried *real* tears . . . I'm rather glad to know it's possible to feel so bad. Things inside me hurt in a most incredible way—I was rather glad."[39]

In Berlin, Craig returned to his empty studio at 11 Siegmundshoff[40] and found the place oddly deserted. He noted on a scrap of paper:

Home here at 5 o'clock and find myself saying, "if only she were here." She is not here. She is rushing through space away from me—Oh, you *dear* one.[41]

Then (presumably reminding himself once again that what he felt could not be *real*), he erased the last phrase, but the words remained faintly legible, permanently engraved on the page by the force of his stroke.

Isadora, meanwhile, at every train stop, took the opportunity to mail him postcards and notes. The enforced delay at the Russian customs station gave her a chance to write him a long letter. Between waves of homesickness for Craig, the thought of appearing in St. Petersburg before the most dance-conscious audiences in Europe made her blood race in anticipation. She was in Russia! In Germany, the ballet had been her foe; now she was taking her campaign into enemy territory. On the platform of a rural depot, she noted, "I walked up and down looking out over the waste and I felt just like Napoleon."[42]

❧ 12 ❧

Introduction to Russia
1904–1905

SADORA arrived in St. Petersburg on the morning of December 25 (December 12—Russian calendar),[1] and, after checking in at the Grand Hôtel d'Europe and refusing the proffered bridal suite (much too mournful alone!), she dispatched a telegram to Craig in Berlin: "Happy Christmas Hearts Love."

She was to make her Russian debut on December 26, 1904, but, initially, she was more preoccupied with the absent Craig than with her surroundings. She wrote to Ted: "I think the best thing to do with St. Petersburg is to forget it and pretend I'm not here. I'll not see it—I swear I won't. . . . If I could only sleep till the 30" (when she hoped to be home).[2]

Isadora was to appear at the Hall of Nobles at a benefit performance for the Society for the Prevention of Cruelty to Children. Since Her Imperial Highness and sister of the czar, the Grand Duchess Olga, was a patron of the society, Isadora was thus assured of imperial patronage. That fact, as well as widespread curiosity about the unconventional American dancer, meant that tickets to her concert sold out rapidly, and a second concert was scheduled for December 29 (December 16—Russian calendar).

The audience that attended her two concerts included the Grand Duke Vladimir Alexandrovitch with the Grand Duchess Maria Pavlovna, the Grand Duke Boris Vladimirovitch, and leaders of St. Petersburg's social, intellectual, and artistic worlds, among them Fokine and Diaghilev.

Critics and public alike reacted strongly to her initial performance, an all-Chopin program. The December 1904 issue (number 51) of *Teatr i Iskusstvo (Theatre and Art)* declared:

> Isadora Duncan . . . performed on the 13th of December for the first time before the St. Petersburg public which completely filled the hall of the Dvorjanskoe Sobranie [Assembly of Nobles]. . . .
>
> However for Duncan, the usual established meaning of the word "Dance" does not apply. . . .
>
> A semi-naked young girl makes her appearance in a light, semi-transparent Greek tunic, giving full freedom to her movements and not concealing the form of her body. Her feet are bare; no tights are visible. A well-proportioned figure. Her countenance is not outstanding for its beauty, but she has a very attractive, modest face.
>
> Nevertheless, the first impression is shocking because of its unusual quality.
>
> But as the chords of a Chopin Mazurka (C-sharp, Opus 7) rang forth, and as Mme. Duncan became alive and began to dance, the first impression faded away. Before us was not a woman creating a sensation. Before us was an artist.
>
> The rhythms of this and the other six randomly chosen mazurkas, the alternations from profound perpetual sorrow to unrestrained joy—this entire complex range of human feelings so finely expressed by Chopin,—was reflected in the plastic movements, in the dance, in the gestures and mime of Mme. Duncan. . . .
>
> The Nocturne (C-flat, Opus 48) was performed under blue illumination. Her body appeared like marble. There was so much pleasure, such passionate melancholy, such expectation and rapture. What expressive hands!
>
> Her interpretation of the Polonaise (A-sharp, Opus 53) was ex-

traordinary. The artist . . . in a short bright red tunic . . . danced in a kind of Bacchic ecstacy. . . . In the midst of a dance she would suddenly fall, and this always corresponded to the musical measure.

In a word, it is necessary to have a great, original talent to create such an impression in this field which so many consider mere nonsense. . . . And Mme. Duncan showed to what degree of expression one can lead the arts.[3]

N. Georgievich, in the December 14 *Petersburgskaya Gazeta* (December 27—western calendar), wrote of her

. . . marvelous plastic sensibility. Her body is as though bewitched by the music. It is as though you yourself were bathing in the music. Then, the expressive hands. Have you ever heard of mimicry by hands? . . . And yet Duncan's hands are expressive as her face. And the legs? For after all it was the legs, the bare feet that were supposed to be the sensation of the evening. . . . This is not a *nudité* that arouses sinful thoughts but rather a kind of incorporeal nudity. . . .

Duncan has thin pale feet. . . . but they are expressive like all else about her and sometimes they are even eloquent. Being bare, they touched the ground lightly, soundlessly.

Duncan has no ballet technique; she does not aim at *fouettés* and *cabrioles*. But there is so much sculpture in her, so much color and simplicity, that she fully deserves the capacity audience which she is already assured for next Thursday.[4]

Not all the critics were equally enthusiastic. Commenting on this same performance a little later, the double issue (numbers 51–52, 1904) of *Russkaya Muzykal'naya Gazeta (Russian Musical Gazette)* remarked:

. . . Certain poses and gestures actually reproduced figures from Pompeian frescoes, but these gestures and poses have long since been stylized by ballet choreography. Attentive copying still cannot substitute for creativity and talent, but the latter is not observable in the monotonous dances of Mme. Duncan. . . .

Organized applause in one or two sections of the hall did not gain strength at the conclusion of the performance.[5]

But, despite his comments about the applause, this critic appears to have been in the negative minority.

The performance of Thursday, December 29, *Dance Idylls,* was cheered by the public and warmly received by the critics. So much interest was expressed in her work that further performances were scheduled for St. Petersburg and Moscow early in February. But at the moment Isadora was interested in nothing but getting home. She wrote to Ted: "I think that as an inspiration for a dancer *you* are not a success. . . . You give me only one inspiration and that is to run away from all publics and the like and rush to you."[6]

The return journey from Russia to Berlin seemed interminable to her.

> Darling, this darned old train is 3 hours 3 centuries 3 eternities late late late—we will arrive about ten and the secretary and the maid will *yank* me up to Hardenburgstr but I will slip away as soon as I can and come to no 11—I *won't* come to No 6 because I haven't the outside key. Darling I've come Back Back from the land of snow and ice—I feel I discovered the North Pole—will you wait for me at No 11— oh sweet—I am almost crazy and half dead—you Darling—.[7]

The separation had been too painful for them both, and shortly after her return, when Isadora was scheduled to appear in Dresden on January 15 and in Hamburg from January 24 to January 31, Craig went with her. In Hamburg, he watched while Isadora held auditions for her school. (One of the applicants whom she accepted, on Craig's advice, was the nearly 8-year-old Irma Erich-Grimme, who would later become known as Irma Duncan.) On the train to Dresden, they amused themselves by passing back and forth a piece of paper on which they carried on a written conversation. Their dialogue, joking at first, soon became serious, and Isadora, thinking of the child she had longed for ever since she had met Craig, wrote:

> Dearest Baby if you come perhaps you would like to know that you were *Wanted.*[8]

To this Craig added:

And you, Babe, will know with me what all that word means. She your mother is wanted. She my darling is wanted. . . . You will want *her* right to the *end.*

He had abandoned his cautious habit of reminding her that their love was not real. *Not real?* He longed to be near her wherever she went. Thus, though it meant interrupting his work, when she returned to St. Petersburg for her performance of February 3, Craig accompanied her.[9] He has noted in *Index:* "Feb 6, to Moscow with Isadora,"[10] and among his papers[11] there is a drawing made that day from their Moscow window. Apparently, no letters written by Isadora about their trip have been preserved. Since Craig was with her, she had no need to record her impressions for him. This is unfortunate, for between her first and second Russian tours, an event took place that would have a profound effect both on Russia and on the direction of Isadora's future. Was she then aware of the influence it would have on her? Or did she think of it as a tragic act totally unconnected with her? There is no evidence in her letters to provide an answer.

❧ 13 ❧

Russia:
Signs of Two Revolutions
1905

HE new year in St. Petersburg had opened with an outbreak of violence which would ultimately depose the Romanov dynasty and destroy the Russian empire. On Sunday, January 22 (January 9, 1905, by the old-style Russian calendar), a crowd of workers, led by the peasant priest Father Gapon, assembled in front of the Winter Palace to petition the czar for redress of their grievances. The czar's troops fired into the unarmed crowd, killing 500 men, women, and children and leaving hundreds more lying wounded on the bloodstained snow. A wave of alarm swept over the city. These events were still fresh in all minds when Isadora returned to Russia.

In *My Life,* she tells us that her train, delayed by snowdrifts, arrived at 4 A.M., and thus she chanced to witness the funeral procession of the murdered workers, whose rites were being performed under cover of darkness to avoid popular demonstrations. But if the events in Gordon Craig's diary are correct—that Isadora was in Dresden at the Hotel Bellevue on January 15 and in Hamburg from January 24 to January 31—it seems unlikely that she could have witnessed the cortege for the victims of the massacre which had taken place on January 22.[1] A government so anxious to forestall outbreaks of unrest that it required funerals to take place in the middle of the night would hardly have permitted them to be performed as late as February 1 or February 2, when she would presumably have been arriving for her first concert, which was to take place on February 3.[2] Moreover, Gordon Craig evidently had doubts about Isadora's account, for, in his copy of *My Life,* he noted, "Each day she wrote to me—I have the letters—I must compare those pages." Finally, there is among the Duncan-Craig letters in the New York Public Library an advertisement for a performance of *The Magic Flute* on January 22, 1905, with a notation in Craig's hand: "Dresden, we at Hotel." Of course, Isadora and Craig might already have left before this performance took place, but, if they did not go to it or expect to be in Dresden on January 22, there seems to be no reason why Craig would have kept this announcement. Therefore, the inference can be made that Isadora was in Germany with Craig at the time of the massacre. It is, however, possible, as Francis Steegmuller suggests,[3] that some of the wounded who died later might have been buried during the early days of February. Since all victims were buried at night by official order, Isadora might have seen their funeral cortège. But whether or not she was an eyewitness to these somber events, there can be little question of the impression they left on her spirit or of the fruit they were to bear in her future life.

The riots had apparently not diminished the brilliance and liveliness of St. Petersburg's social season, however, for, on the morning of her February 3 return engagement, the newspaper *Novoye Vremya* announced that the house was entirely sold out and that honorary tickets would not be valid for her performance.[4]

From news items on January 20[5] in *Novoye Vremya* which announce the upcoming February concert, we learn that Isadora was to give an all-Beethoven program, consisting of the presto from the *Sonata Opus 10,* a minuet (arranged by Hans von Bülow), and the adagio from the *Sonata Pathétique, The Moonlight Sonata,* and the *Seventh Symphony.* The music would be played by the Symphony Orchestra

of the New Opera Company of Count A. A. Tservetely and conducted by Leopold Auer. The piano soloist was to be Isadora's Berlin
accompanist, Professor Hermann Lafont.

Isadora's first two Russian performances had been enthusiastically
received by critics and public alike, but in the interim since her last
appearance a reaction had set in. Musicians who had been offended
by her dancing to compositions not specifically intended for dance,[6]
and who had already criticized her for dancing to Chopin, were
outraged at the thought of her all-Beethoven program, and their
disapproval seems to have communicated itself to the performers.
Lafont was criticized for playing poorly during the first part of the
program. Leopold Auer, attacked by his fellow conductor, Ziloti,
for his participation in the concert, later made excuses,[7] explaining
that he had never seen Isadora dance before that evening, and that
he was so horrified by what he was witnessing that he refused to
look at the stage. Not surprisingly, his conducting was lackluster,
and Isadora herself was affected by the lack of musical support. In
the eyes of many of the onlookers, her dancing never caught fire.
Trying to explain what had happened, the critic N. S. Shebuyev
wrote: "The dancer was not in the mood. Perhaps because of the
conductor's hostility, perhaps because of trouble with the admin-
istration, perhaps something else, but she was not in the mood—
inspiration failed her, and her dancing lost its brilliance, faded,
wilted."[8]

Nonetheless, the influential critic L. Vilkina, writing about this
and Isadora's previous concerts in *The Scales, A Monthly of Art and
Literature,* praised her warmly, stating, "Isadora Duncan was the first
in our day to resurrect the creative side of the dance."[9] In the *Seventh
Symphony* she compared Isadora's movements to those of a flutist
on an Etruscan vase, to "Botticelli's Venus . . . born anew," to a
Maenad, to an Amazon "whose smooth flowing movements are
transformed into impetuous leaps," to a Bacchante who "abandons
herself to love, [whose] wild dance intoxicates," and to a seeker for
something unknown which lures and frightens her. "One is unable
to catch a single moment because the next comes into being too
rapidly. . . . The music fades away and ceases. The symphony is

finished. Exit Duncan. To the enthusiastic curtain calls there is no end. What do they mean? Did the spectators understand . . . or did the nudity of the eccentric American rouse their blunted senses? Who can tell?"[10]

Another witness who, like Vilkina, had been moved by the Beethoven evening was the poet Andrei Bely,[11] who had attended it and the earlier Chopin concert with Alexander and Lubov Blok.[12] Bely wrote:

> I remember in those revolutionary days in Petersburg Isadora Duncan performed the 7th Symphony of Beethoven and a series of numbers of Chopin and I remember how we (principally L.B. [Lubov Blok, wife of the poet] and myself) . . . were together at the concert: I will never forget the appearance of Duncan in the allegretto (the second part of the Symphony) and will never forget the 12th Prelude of Chopin. The sounds of the 12th Prelude and the motions of Duncan were for us the symbol of the new, young revolutionary Russia.[13]

Immediately after the St. Petersburg performance, Isadora and Ted traveled to Moscow,[14] where three performances had been scheduled. Public interest made it necessary to add a fourth. Constantin Stanislavski was in the audience, and his initial reaction to her costumes is instructive: "Unaccustomed to see an almost naked body on the stage, I could hardly notice and understand the art of the dancer." Yet, by the intermission, he had become "a newly baptised disciple of the great artist."[15]

Despite the unlucky all-Beethoven concert, the two Russian trips in December 1904 and February 1905 and Isadora's subsequent appearances in Russia were to have a profound effect on the history of the dance. As Allan Ross Macdougall writes in *Isadora: A Revolutionary in Art and Love:*

> The date should be kept in mind, for since the dancer's death it has appeared in innumerable articles and books on the dance as 1907 or 1908. Even in certain issues of the usually fact-sure *Encyclopaedia*

Britannica, there is a lack of exactitude. . . . The English ballet critic Cyril Beaumont in his book on Fokine also flatly pontificates: "It has been stated that Fokine's reforms were inspired by Isadora Duncan. But the dancer did not visit St. Petersburg until 1907!" But the date 1905 must be reemphasized for it is an important one in the annals of the dance and particularly in the history of the Imperial Russian Ballet and its colorful offspring the Diaghilev Company.[16]

Macdougall is right in stressing that Isadora came to Russia earlier than frequently supposed, but he apparently did not know of her two performances in St. Petersburg at the end of December 1904.

Though many conservative balletomanes and dancers were shocked by Isadora's innovations, the reaction of the ballet was by no means totally hostile. The young Tamara Karsavina, ballerina at the Maryinsky Theatre, later wrote:

> Isadora . . . rapidly conquered the Petersburg theatrical world. There were of course the reactionary balletomanes to whom the idea of a barefoot dancer seemed to deny the first principles of what they held to be sacred in art. This, however, was far from being the general opinion, and the feeling of a desire for novelty was in the air. . . .
>
> I remember that the first time I saw her dance I fell completely under her sway. It never occurred to me that there was the slightest hostility between her art and ours. There seemed room for both, and each had much that it could learn to advantage from the other.[17]

Another dancer who apparently felt the same way was the 25-year-old choreographer Michel Fokine, who attended her first concerts with his friend Diaghilev. To Fokine, who had long raged at the absurdities then enshrined in ballet, and who had in fact, in 1904, sent a letter to the director of the Imperial Theatre with specific suggestions for its reform, it must have come as a heartening experience to see in Isadora's work the embodiment of so many related principles. In his letter to the Imperial Theatre, he had written:

The dance need not be a mere divertissement introduced into the pantomime. In the ballet the whole meaning of the story can be expressed by the dance. Above all, dancing should be interpretive. It should not degenerate into mere gymnastics. It should, in fact, be the plastic word. The dance should explain the spirit of the actors in the spectacle. More than that, it should express the whole epoch to which the subject of the ballet belongs.

One no longer demands the eternal short skirts, pink tights and satin ballet shoes. One can give way to the freedom of artistic fantasy.

The ballet must no longer be made up of "numbers," "entries," and so forth. It must show artistic unity of conception. The action of the ballet must never be interrupted to allow the danseuse to respond to the applause of the public. . . .

Through the rhythms of the body the ballet can find expression for ideas, sentiments, emotions. The dance bears the same relation to gesture that poetry bears to prose. Dancing is the poetry of motion.

Just as life differs in different epochs, and gestures differ among human beings, so the dance which expresses life must vary. The Egyptian of the time of the Pharaohs was different from the Marquis of the 18th century. The ardent Spaniard and the phlegmatic dweller in the north not only speak different languages but use different gestures. These are not invented. They are created by life itself.[18]

It should be noted that Fokine was a reformer and Isadora a revolutionary: that is, Fokine wished to change certain things within the framework of the ballet, while Isadora wished to abandon the ballet altogether, feeling that its system of movement was unnatural and that its aim—entertainment—was insufficient. Fokine felt that the ballet was capable of greatness if it was pruned of irrelevancies and triviality. To what extent Fokine's dissatisfaction with conventional ballet had been crystallized by what he had read about Isadora's ideas prior to seeing her cannot, of course, be determined. But Allan Ross Macdougall is surely correct in pointing out that Isadora's theories must have received much publicity in a country where dance was enshrined as an art.

From her first public appearance as a solo performer in Budapest in 1902, the young American iconoclast was a subject made for publicity. . . . As early as 1903, Isadora Duncan gave a public lecture on *The Dance of the Future.* This appearance before a large audience . . . did not exactly go unnoticed either in the German press or elsewhere. It can be assumed that the strictures on the ballet may well have seeped into the ballet-conscious periodicals of the Russian capital. . . . That [her] reputation as a particularly articulate apostle of a new style of dancing had preceded her to St. Petersburg cannot be doubted.[19]

It is thus highly likely that Fokine was familiar with Isadora's ideas when he wrote his famous letter. Even if this were not the case, his work would have borne a certain resemblance to hers, nonetheless, for he was, like Isadora, a student of Greek and Renaissance art whose studies had intensified his dissatisfaction with ballet. It is not astonishing, therefore, that he admired Isadora's dance. It is certain that Isadora's example made it easier for the artistic authorities and the public to accept his innovations. In 1904, the directors of the Imperial Theatre had not even bothered to acknowledge his letter.[20] In 1907, in contrast, after Isadora's Russian tours, he was able to produce the Greek ballet *Eunice,* even though his dancers were not permitted to perform barefoot.

Sergei Diaghilev, at any rate, did not doubt the effect that Isadora had had on Fokine. In a letter from Monte Carlo dated February 17, 1926, he wrote to W. A. Popert: "I knew Isadora very well in St. Petersburg and I was present with Fokine at her first performances. Fokine was mad about her, and the influence of Duncan on him was the foundation of all his creation."[21]

The eminent Russian critic V. Svetlov,[22] too, felt that Isadora's outlook had colored all of Fokine's work. In his admirable book *Le Ballet Contemporain* (published in 1912 in St. Petersburg), he remarks: "Fokine was the first independent propagator of these [Isadora's] principles on a wider scene. Fokine's *Eunice* not only does not move away from Duncanism, but indeed bears manifest traces of it."[23] He cites the ballet *Carnival* as an example of dance which it would not have been possible to choreograph before Isadora's tour, for it had "no 'literary subject' . . . no ballerina who predominates over everyone and everything."[24]

And Karsavina adds:

> Fokine . . . made *Eunice* (1907) as a direct tribute to [Isadora]. . . . In truth *Eunice* was a compromise between our tradition and the Hellenic revival embodied by Isadora. The leading part, taken by Kshessinskaya on the first night, displayed in its texture an almost complete vocabulary of classical ballet. Pavlova . . . and the whole corps de ballet had bare feet or make-belief [sic] ones. Tights were not to be discarded; ten toes pencilled in had to suffice the illusion . . . a perspective of years between this first creative effort of Fokine's and his later mastery shows how timid was the initial manifestation of his rebellious spirit.[25]

On this first visit to Russia, Isadora was cheered not only by the public but was also warmly received by the ballet. Mathilde Kshessinskaya, the prima ballerina assoluta of the Maryinsky Theatre, came in person to the American's hotel to invite her to a performance. A box was placed at her disposal and, although Isadora disapproved of ballet, she could not refrain from applauding Kshessinskaya's consummate grace and the artistry of another ballerina, Anna Pavlova. In fact, she and Pavlova became mutually admiring friends, with such high regard for one another's gifts that Isadora henceforth would urge her pupils to attend Pavlova's concerts,[26] and Pavlova would tell inquirers that she had learned the fluidity of her arm movements in *The Dying Swan* from Isadora.[27]

On February 6, as we have seen, Isadora and Craig left for Moscow,[28] where she gave a fourth performance by popular demand. A review in the February 27[29] issue of *The Scales,* signed "S.S.," said in part:

> Bodily movements are as spiritual as sound. One can have no doubt of that upon seeing Isadora Duncan.
> Isadora Duncan gave us a presentment of that state of the flesh which I call "spiritual corporeality." In her dance, form definitely

overcomes the inertia of matter and every movement of her body is an incarnation of a spiritual act. [Isadora's phrase "The dancer who, after long study, prayer, and inspiration, has attained such a degree of understanding that his body is simply the luminous manifestation of his soul" is thus no mere figure of speech but the description of an actual state which can be felt and communicated.] Exhilarated and joyful, with every step she shook off the path of chaos, and her body appeared extraordinary, sinless and pure. This was such a victory of light over darkness that I felt ineffably glad, but I also felt sad—sad because she was pure, while all around there were the impure, and because she was wise, while all around there were fools.

After praising her dances, which apparently included the *Primavera,* the *Angel with the Violin, Narcissus,* and the *Lament* and *Bacchanale* from *Orpheus,* the writer concludes, "Isadora Duncan's dance is a serious portent of the future."

After a brief appearance in Kiev, Isadora ended her Russian tour and returned to Germany, leaving the Russians to ponder her art and to reappraise their current works in its light. The critic Svetlov later wrote: "The dance, formerly the highest of the arts, was deprived of its spiritual and religious bearing . . . Duncan came to simplify the dance, to purify it of these excesses and these conventions. . . . The ballet of today must become penetrated with [Duncanism]. And once having become so, it will throw overboard all that is conventional and false, and raise itself to a height hitherto unknown." He adds, "The influence of Duncanism on the choreography of the 20th Century is much wider, much deeper than one would believe at first sight."[30]

❖ 14 ❖

The Birth of Deirdre
1905 – 1906

ER tour of Russia completed, Isadora and Craig returned to Berlin. Isadora resumed teaching at her school and made brief concert appearances at nearby towns.

Craig, too, was working hard. "This year and 1906 saw me designing a number of scenes for plays and a few of these came to be reproduced in *Towards a New Theatre* [Craig's book]. To the friendship and inspiration of Isadora I owe some of the best designs of these two years."[1] He was becoming known throughout the country. Exhibitions of his drawings were held in Dusseldorf, Berlin, and Cologne.

Craig appeared to have forgotten that his feelings for Isadora were not "real." Certainly there was nothing in his behavior to her which would have made her doubt his love. He accompanied her to Hamburg, Dresden, Cologne, Breslau, and Frankfurt, "she dancing and I doing little," as he wrote in *Book Topsy,* "resting and being happy with her."

In a letter to his friend Martin Shaw, Craig confided:

Personality is a wonderful force. It is that which so many of us lack—and I. has it. The electric personality which sweeps out in a torrent takes everything prisoner.[2]

And again to Martin:

She's a genius—and more. A *Sun* Genius, horribly like me—only I'm not a genius and the sun knows me only sometimes. . . . I am drinking in American 'push'—Walt [Whitman] in a book is alive— but Walt walking, dancing is LIFE.[3]

In March, Isadora wrote a bitterly self-accusing letter to Craig about something—we don't know what—that had taken place between them. It indicates that Isadora at last understood the extent of Craig's commitment to Elena Meo. For, though he had written after the night of his first lovemaking with Isadora, "I tell her that I am going to marry in about 4 months time—She does not believe in marriage," it seems probable that he had withheld the information that he already had two daughters by Elena (the first of whom had died) and that she was expecting a third child by him early in January. (It must be remembered that Craig had hesitated to tell Elena of his marriage to May. Elena was already in love with him when she learned the truth from Martin Shaw. So it would not have been surprising if he had shown a similar reluctance to tell Isadora of the strength and number of his ties to Elena.) On January 3, 1905, his son by Elena, Edward Craig, was born. Possibly the discovery of this birth, and of her lover's continuing feelings for Elena, prompted Isadora's letter, written in Berlin around March 10, 1905. In later years, Craig professed to be baffled by it, for he wrote on the top of the note, "I wonder what this was? letter opening? jealousy?"

Dear—I feel awfully ashamed—ashamed is not the word.
I feel dust and ashes—it was an awful kind of rage that took possession of me—
Let my pain atone for it—I'm afraid you will never be able to think of me in the same way again.

And I didn't mean to tell you.
That is the worst of it—
You are so dear and kind
but I know what you must *think* of it.
    I would give I can't write about it—I hate myself—I am in
despair over it—
forgive me—
but you can't make it *undone* can you—.

At the bottom, Craig wrote: "It is—for I forget what it was. (1944). Ted."[4]

In her next letter, Isadora wrote: "Save me from the Green Demon Jealousy! And the Red Devil Desire for complete Possessorship." She was ashamed of her jealousy. She had learned at an early age that love is not necessarily permanent—witness her parents' divorce and her father's remarriage. How could she refuse to acknowledge the existence—or, indeed, the just claims—of a rival? To love childishly, possessively, was not Isadora's true nature. Much later, in 1907, when Elena [Nelly] was ill, she would write:

> I will be anxious to hear of N's health—bring her down in the *sun* and she will get well—or what can we do? Heaven knows that there are no complications which Love cannot make simple—for me I am ready to be simple—simple as the primitive earth and sky—I feel full of Love and nothing else. Suffering is caused by a misunderstanding of love—.[5]

Isadora's evident remorse and Craig's fervor soon swept away the pain between them, and their passion continued even more ardently than before.

Meanwhile, Craig was conscious of an unacknowledged tug of war between himself and Mrs. Duncan. He noted: "Isadora had a strong sense of Duty to her family. She loved the family very much. Released . . . and off we went whenever we could. . . . It is this which all great public performers have to be assured of and even given— their freedom after work hours."[6] During the week of March 25 to March 30, he made the entry: "Topsy [his pet name for Isadora] and I at Villers-la-Ville, Belgium. Here we went from Brussels, to get away from the crowd. Jealousy was on the increase in that crowd."[7] Mrs. Duncan, of course, disapproved of Craig and was alarmed by her daughter's involvement in the affair. Isadora adds that her mother was "furiously jealous" of Ted. "Now that we [she and her brothers and sister] found interests so absorbing that they continually took us away from her, she realized that she had actually wasted the best years of her life on us, leaving nothing for herself. . . . [The] uncertain humors on her part increased . . . and she continually expressed the desire to return to her native town."[8]

Besides her mother's disapproval, Isadora presently had the censure of the sponsors of her school to contend with. "When they learned of Craig, they sent me a long letter, couched in majestic terms of reproach, and said that they . . . could no longer be patronesses of a school where the leader had such loose ideas of morals."[9] The dancer reports that she was made so indignant by what she believed to be her critics' hypocrisy, that she hired the Philharmonic Saal and delivered a lecture on the topics of the dance as an art of liberation and the right of women to bear children with or without marriage—a discussion "which was considerably in advance of the Women's Movement of the present day."[10]

If this incident took place, it seems likely that it was in March, for there were signs that the young Californian's usually easygoing temper was wearing thin. On March 25, 1905, the [N.Y.?] *World* reported that she had been fined $30 for insulting a government bailiff.[11] "The official called to hand some documents to Miss Duncan, who, hearing he was a bailiff, kept him waiting a long time, then called him an insolent person and ordered him to leave the house instantly." In court, she explained her action by saying that she was "nervous and hysterical from overwork." Perhaps it would have been true to add that the arrival of the bailiff had probably prompted disagreeable memories of the evictions of her childhood.

On April 17, Haeckel came to Berlin, and Isadora had the happiness of taking Craig to hear the lecture of her friend and mentor.

On April 22, Craig began work on his first book, a short but revolutionary essay called *The Art of the Theatre*. He was so immersed in his subject that he finished the book in seven days. This speed was typical of his absorption in his art, in which he so resembled Isadora.

This resemblance did not automatically foster compatibility, however. As Isadora once wrote, "My life has known but two motives—Love and Art—often Love destroyed Art, and often the imperious call of Art put a tragic end to Love. For these two have no accord but only constant battle."[12] Love and art are more time- and emotion-consuming than most other activities, and Craig and Isadora were both dedicated artists. Isadora, moreover, needed the income from tour appearances to support her school and her mother, and, on occasion, her sister and brothers. She had for so long been the chief breadwinner of the "Clan Duncan" that it would never have occurred to her to refuse them assistance.

Now she was also supporting Gordon Craig. They had incorporated themselves as a firm called Direktion Vereinigter Künste (United Arts Management) and hired an engaging but dubious German-American called Maurice Magnus as their manager.[13] Then Craig and Duncan had opened a joint account at the National Bank für Deutschland. So far Isadora was the only depositor. Craig had written his friend Martin Shaw, "I'm not making a penny but living like a Duke." And later, from Moscow, he had written to Shaw, "As you may guess, I'm not paying my own hotel bills and I haven't a sou in the world—but I'm damned if I'll starve or sit on a stool and wait for things." Meanwhile his drawings were being shown in a number of German cities.[14] Isadora, for her part, was touring Germany.

Her frequent absences were a strain on the relationship. They both agreed that he was moody: ". . . he was always either in the throes of the highest delight, or the other extreme . . . when the whole sky seemed to turn black."[15] Or, as he described himself, "The face smiling and patient—but the hands . . . hinting at a fearful impatience somewhere in the hinterland."[16]

Yet they had an immense appreciation of one another's work and, when Craig finished writing *The Art of the Theatre,* he immediately read it to Isadora. She was delighted with it and made a few suggestions,[17] and later wrote an article about him for a German magazine, *Die Schau Bühne* (July 1906).

The Art of the Theatre was to prove as revolutionary for the stage as *The Dance of the Future* was for choreography and, like the latter, his little book was as much a manifesto as an essay.

Craig pleaded for a unity of style and mood in costumes, scenery, acting, and lighting. (For one thing, he felt that footlights should be abolished—they are useless.) The stage director is the most important of the theater personnel: his is the task of fusing the various elements. "He . . . reads the play, and during the first reading the entire colour, tone, movement and rhythm that the work must assume come clearly before him." The words of the play are only one of the many elements in a theater piece, and they are not more important than the others. The piece ". . . is incomplete when printed in a book or recited . . . incomplete anywhere except on the boards of a theatre." In this sense, Shakespeare's plays are not theater pieces, ". . . they can but lose heavily when presented to us after having undergone stage treatment . . ." *Hamlet* was finished—was complete—when Shakespeare wrote the last word of his blank verse, and for us to add to it by gesture, scene, costume, or dance is to hint that it is incomplete and needs these additions.

The purpose of these reforms is to make the theater "a place in which the entire beauty of life can be unfolded, and not only the external beauty of the world, but the inner beauty and meaning of life. It should not only be a place to show facts in a material way, but *the* place to show the whole world of fancy and in a spiritual way. . . . The Theatre of the Future shall be the Temple of Life— the Temple of Beauty; and it shall be for the people."

He adds, "The art of the theatre has sprung from action— movement—dance . . . the father of the dramatist was the dancer."

Isadora must have been struck with the similarity of some of these ideas to her own—particularly with his emphasis on the spiritual purpose of the theater, for had she not written, "All art which is not religious is not art, is mere merchandise"[18]?

Although the theater today largely ignores Craig's definition of the real "theatre piece" (which is "incomplete except on the boards of the theatre"), it has adopted his other ideas about costumes, settings, and lighting. There is probably not a stage director or a lighting expert in the world today—excluding those in Asia and Africa—whose work has not been heavily influenced by Gordon Craig.[19]

On July 20, at Kroll's Opera House in Berlin, Isadora gave her first recital with the children of her school.[20] Craig was present and afterward he wrote:

> I saw this first showing at a matinee . . . where after dancing her own dances she called her little pupils to come with her and please the public with their little leapings and runnings. As they did and with her leading them the whole troupe became irresistibly lovely . . . we all wept and laughed for joy.
>
> And to see her shepherding her little flock, keeping them together and specially looking after one very small one of four years old, Erica was her name, I believe, was a sight no one there had ever seen before or would ever see again.[21]

The spontaneous quality of these childish dances was remarked upon by a later observer who noted:

> For the most part, all the evolutions [of the dance] were carried out with marvelous accuracy . . . but often the severity of the figures relaxed and the little ones skipped about at their own sweet will. This had a special charm and even a special interest of its own for it showed clearly how well they had been taught to move. Indeed it must be admitted that there was a generous absence of anything like stiltedness or affectation. The whole thing was like some voluntary game played by gay and frolicsome children, but directed by someone who could enter lovingly into a child's idiosyncracies and capacity for expression.[22]

In December 1905, Craig noted in his diary: "In Holland. Topsy's thoughts were all of baby clothes."[23] Isadora had just learned that she was pregnant. "There could not be the slightest doubt about it."[24] The child whom she had longed for since the beginning of their affair was to come at last. If she was apprehensive at the thought of bearing a child out of wedlock, it seems probable that she did not voice her fears. Craig wrote: "we two,—Topsy and I—did not use the *usual* arguments to each other—those of self-interest, used by all the world."[25]

It is certain that much of the time she was intensely happy. She looked forward to the birth of their baby with delight and was indignant when her doctor "offered to adopt it. I'm really getting scared. . . . The future king of Ireland must be protected from these conspiracies."[26] Outwardly, Isadora's life went on much as before. "I continued to dance before the public, to teach my school, to love my Endymion."[27]

This surface calm was marred by an incident that was reported with some confusion by the American press. Isadora was banned from dancing in Berlin, supposedly because her bare feet were shocking. The American papers expressed bewilderment. Isadora had been appearing barefoot almost since the beginning of her career, moreover "in a country where women, even of the upper classes, sometimes swim in public in costumes which would cause their arrest in Atlantic City or Narragansett Pier, it is inconceivable that this circumstance caused the official order."[28]

It was not Isadora's costume, however, but that of her little pupils that had been found objectionable, as a news story in the January 9, 1906, *Kölnischer Zeitung* makes clear. The children, who had been appearing at the Theatre des Westens, were found to be "so scantily clad that the sense of modesty of the girls, who are still minors, was not protected." They were forthwith prohibited from giving further performances by the Berlin and Charlottenburg police. Isadora, backed by a phalanx of notables, among them Thode, Humperdinck, Baron Harrach, and Cosima Wagner, immediately protested the order; and though the episode ended with the lifting of the ban and a victory for her, it must have been an uneasy reminder to the pregnant dancer of the force of prudery. Flouting convention was not going to be easy.

In the spring, Isadora left Berlin to tour Scandinavia. While she was in Stockholm,[29] she visited the Gymnastic Institution, but was not greatly impressed: ". . . it takes no account of the imagination, and thinks of the body as an object, instead of vital, kinetic energy." In short, her objection to Swedish gymnastics was the same as her objection to ballet technique. "The whole tendency of this training seems to be to separate the gymnastic movements of the body completely from the mind. . . . This is just the opposite from all the theories on which I have founded my school, by which the body . . . is medium for the mind and spirit."[30]

While returning from Sweden by ship, she became quite ill, and she decided not to undertake any more tours for the time being. Her pregnancy was advancing, and she wished to be away from prying eyes.

In June, Isadora rented the Villa Maria in the village of Noordwijk on the North Sea: "It's splendid to go out without meeting a soul."[31] Her little niece, Temple, the daughter of Augustin, stayed with her for three weeks. Craig visited intermittently, torn between his work, exhibitions in various cities, Isadora's desire to have him with her, and his instinctive avoidance of painful situations.[32] They wrote to each other almost daily, expressing their love and exchanging books and ideas. Isadora commented on the drawings that Craig sent her or amused him with accounts of her domestic life. Her notes to him are full of contentment.

> A letter from you is a touch from your hand filled with vitality— and gives me new life. . . . I am what you make me—very happy.
>
> Your Topsy[33]

Sometimes she voiced her longing for him. "Wish I could trip up to Amsterdam [where Craig was staying]. Couldn't I some *dark* night, and return the next *dark* night"—"dark" because, despite her happiness, she was conscious of having to avoid scandal.[34]

In another letter, she wrote:

> I wish you would know that in all the hundreds of times you have kissed me there hasn't been *one* that everything in me hasn't

Deirdre at Versailles, 1911 (*Mme. Mario Meunier—Christine Dalliès Collection*).

cried out—make me fruitful—give me a child—not once—I have always had that constant longing impossible to control—and I think that if it hadn't come I would have gone crazy from the struggle— as it is I can't help feeling happy about it—I *can't* help it—I have the most exquisitely happy feelings at times—but that's no good to you.[35]

Why it was no good to him her letter does not explain. Most of her notes to him are cheerful, indeed gay, although there is evidence that sometimes this gaiety was forced. In August, Kathleen Bruce, who was living in Paris, received a letter from Isadora. Kathleen later wrote in her memoirs:

> It was a queer cry, childish and pathetic. Would not, could not, I come to her? Her need was very great . . . I went at once. I found her pitiful, helpless and for the first time, endearing. "Poor darling, what is the matter?" "Can't you see?" cried the dancer spreading high her lovely arms. Slowly, and with many a lie the story came out at last . . . her baby was due in a month or two. She had dared tell nobody, not her mother or her sister. . . . She was lonely and miserable. In after years, when the war had given different value to these things, she said and probably believed that she had done this deliberately, and was proud of her courage and independence; but at the time she was still nothing more than a frightened girl, fright- ened and pitiful. . . . For the health of the future son the mother must be cheered and cared for. I would not let Isadora see that I was shocked. . . .
>
> We two girls settled down to a queer anxious life in a little seaside villa on a lonely foreign beach. The days were long. Isadora stitched some little clothes like any sweet mother and was sometimes peaceful and even radiant. But there were other terrible days and nights when a fierce cloud of doubt, fear and loneliness would descend upon her.[36]

On one horrid occasion, ". . . a press reporter had tracked the poor girl down and had come to interview her. Of course she refused, but the reporter hung about the house." Kathleen dressed herself in the dancer's robes and ran up and down the beach to mislead the intruder in case he should have heard any rumors about Isadora. To the relief of the two women, the man finally left.

That night I woke in the small hours, aware that not all was well . . . I got up and peered very quietly into Isadora's room. The bed was empty. . . . The front door was open. . . . Some instinct sent me rushing directly to the sea's edge, and there, straight ahead in deep water . . . I could surely see dimly a head and two hands and wrists extended. The sea was calm. I rushed in. The figure ahead did not move. As I neared it, calling, she turned around with a gentle, rather dazed look, and stretched out her arms to me with a faint childlike smile saying, "The tide was so low, I couldn't do it, and I'm so cold."[37]

Kathleen led her ashore, got her out of her wet clothes, put her into bed with hot-water bottles and gave her hot drinks as she murmured words of comfort.

What a change when, not long after, Isadora's lover arrived without heralding, to stay we knew not for how long! Isadora was radiant and masterful. He was to be treated as the Messiah; everything was to fall before his slightest wish. Our simple fare must be supplemented; wine must replace the customary milk; everything must be turned to festival. . . . He was gay, amusing and argumentative; only once or twice did wild outbursts of uncontrolled temper pass with a wave of terror through the little villa . . . Isadora herself remained externally beautiful and serene. Endowed always with an abundance of generosity towards those about her, she seemed ready to forgive, to condone, to accept, to give herself up to ministering to [Craig] . . .[38]

Her happiness in his presence would have given him no clue to her previous despair, and Kathleen says nothing about his being told of the suicide attempt. Isadora's account of the reporter episode (if, indeed, it is the *same* episode) in a letter to Craig sounds so unconcerned that Craig imagined her smiling as she wrote it.

For the last week a mysterious individual has seated himself opposite our house and stared for hours at the windows—causing us much uneasiness. . . . Today he called in high dungeon [sic] said the police were following him on the Beach [sic] . . . he explained he was a *reporter* and wanted an interview. . . . The old one [the cook] is in a fearful tantrum and we can't tell why. She abused me like a pickpocket. . . . It isn't so easy to have a peaceful existence. [Craig: "her smile"] I have developed a positive talent—I am too modest—genius for crochet! You'll be s'prised.[39]

It is possible that Craig never guessed the extent of her fears. This conjecture is strengthened by a poem he wrote about Isadora at the time, which appeared in his portfolio of six drawings of the dancer, published by Insel Verlag, in August 1906.

> I see Calmness and Beauty, both the strong and
> the sweet advancing now with perfect ease . . .
>
> Not yet has she depicted a Gloom or Sorrow
> unbearable . . .
>
>> This is the great power.
>> She comes of the lovely family.
>>
>>> The Great Companions . . .
>>> The Courageous Giants
>>> The Preservers of Beauty
>>> The Answerers of all Riddles.[40]

Calmness, beauty, and ease do not suggest desperation. That she was able to conceal the anxiety beneath the surface of her courage seems all the more likely from a letter Craig wrote her years later on a different occasion:

My darling, I know how you can suffer and never show more than
   a smile—. . .
Never was there one so weak or strong as you— . . .
My heart has often broken to see your weakness—large chips (you
   shouldn't have noticed them, for I, as you, will never show those)
My heart has often shaken with *terror* to see your strength. . . .[41]

It also seems possible that Isadora, being without him and unsure of the extent of his love, would have concealed her anguish lest she drive him away. We know from her letters that shortly after Kathleen arrived, Isadora unaccountably did not receive any mail from Craig (who had gone to London for ten days), and his silence made her very anxious. "I thought you were run over by a London cab. I thought you were *ill*. I thought the boat had gone down in a storm Saturday night." Then, guessing that Craig might have been visiting Elena Meo, Isadora added: "I am . . . glad you see your dear Mother or see any that you love and I can only repeat—'if there is anyone you care for very much who feels unhappy and wants to come with you she can have half my little house with *all my heart*. It will give me *joy* and love is enough for all——.' "[42]

Isadora's experiences with Miroski and Beregi must have convinced her that being in love was an impermanent condition. So thoroughly had she learned this lesson that when she was in love with Thode she had not dared to make any demands at all.

Craig was in England between July 18 and July 21. He had indeed visited Elena. He had seen her only once briefly since the birth of their son Teddy, and now, feeling trapped because Isadora's baby was due, he rushed to Elena's side. Afraid to tell her the whole truth about Isadora, he "merely said that some woman who was infatuated with him was giving him trouble, the breach between him and Isadora was gradually widening, and he probably made himself believe, at the time, that it was a one-sided affair."[43] Touched by Elena's devotion, he resolved to make some money as soon as possible so that he could send for her and the children.

Now he was back with Isadora and Kathleen. Isadora was outwardly serene; only once did she betray her uneasiness. On that night, the house had become stifling and first Craig and then Kathleen decided to sleep on the beach, leaving Isadora a prey to unfounded jealousy.[44] Most of the time, however, when Ted was with her, Isadora appeared cheerful and happy, and Craig apparently chose to accept her gaiety at its face value.

When his stay at Noordwijk ended, "Isadora sank back, exhausted,

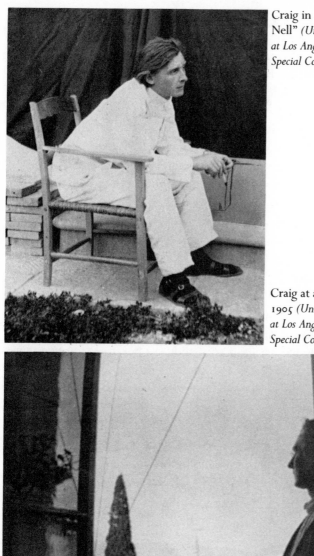

Craig in 1907, inscribed "to Nell" *(University of California at Los Angeles, Department of Special Collections).*

Craig at a window in Berlin, 1905 *(University of California at Los Angeles, Department of Special Collections).*

into the monotony of a long wait."[45] In August, she engaged Marie Kist, who would become her fast friend, as a nurse. The time of delivery came at last and the local doctor was summoned. Craig, in Rotterdam, hurried back to Noordwijk.[46]

Isadora's labor was long and difficult; the baby may have been awkwardly placed, or perhaps tension, caused by the thought of the world's—and worse, her mother's—disapproval,[47] added to the rigors of her travail. Kathleen Bruce wrote: "I knew little of anesthetics and Isadora less, but in our respective agonies we implored the foreign doctor, as best we could, to administer them. He seemed to reply only that there wasn't time, he could not leave, to get it ready. So the frenzied agony went on and on. A terrible bungle! But at long, long last, just before final exhaustion set in, the birth came."[48]

Thus, on September 24, 1906,[49] after two days and nights of labor, Isadora's daughter Deirdre was born. This experience left the 29-year-old Isadora convinced that "it is simply absurd that with our modern science painless childbirth does not exist *as a matter of course*. It is as unpardonable as if doctors should operate for appendicitis without an anesthetic!"[50] Yet the thought of her sufferings receded somewhat when the baby was placed in her arms. "Oh, women what is the good of us learning to become lawyers, painters or sculptors when this miracle exists? . . . What did I care for Art! I felt I was God, superior to any artist."[51] And years later, she would write of her achievements in ascending order of importance: "I had created an Art, a School, a Baby."[52]

❧ 15 ❧
Duse,
Rosmersholm,
Illness
1906–1907

HORTLY after the baby's birth, Craig left for Berlin and Amsterdam, while Isadora, the baby, and the baby's nurse stayed behind in Noordwijk. Isadora's letters to Craig at this time, in which she reports on the baby's progress, are full of serenity.

Autumn turned cold and stormy, however, and Isadora decided that they would be more comfortable inland. Late in October, she and Fräulein Kist packed up Craig's and her belongings at the Villa Maria and moved to the Hôtel du Vieux Dolen at The Hague. Ted was staying nearby in Amsterdam, preparing for an exhibition of his work that would take place in November at the Kunst Kring in Rotterdam.[1] Presently, they all moved back to Berlin where Isadora delightedly showed her baby to the pupils of her school.

But Isadora and Craig were not to stay long in Berlin. Juliette Mendelssohn, a patron of the school and wife of the banker who managed the business affairs of Eleonora Duse, introduced the couple to the great Italian actress. A friendship developed between the three, and presently Duse proposed that Craig design the set for Ibsen's *Rosmersholm* which she was to produce in Florence that December. Craig consented "chiefly," he wrote, "for the sake of Isadora." Why he should have hesitated, in view of Duse's position as "queen of the Italian stage" and of his admiration for her acting, remains unclear; perhaps it was because Duse's production of *Electra,* for which he had done the designs the previous year, had not materialized. He had been disappointed also that summer by E. Verkade, a wealthy member of the Dutch biscuit family, who had offered to establish a theater for him in Holland. The plan fell through, and Craig noted: "How could I tell that he was later on to establish a theatre with some of my ideas in it, but under his own name?" This experience increased his suspicion of projects over which he was not in charge. "For the sake of Isadora" appears to have been in part a face-saving phrase, in the light of what happened later. But Craig also wished to please Isadora, and he was eager to have the chance to show his work in the theater where it belonged. So he accepted Duse's commission.

On November 17, he wrote to his Dutch friends, the Van Looys, to say that he was just leaving for Italy. Then he, Isadora, the baby, and the nurse, Marie Kist, all boarded the Nord-Sud Exprès.

In Florence, Craig's settings for *Rosmersholm* progressed but not without difficulty. Various reasons have been given for the complications he encountered. In *Index to the Story of My Days,* Craig has noted: "I find the following written in my day books of 1906. Today I would write it differently—excusing poor Duse—but at that time, counting on her strength, I wrote:

> With Isadora to Italy, there to prepare the scene for *Rosmersholm* for Eleonora Duse. . . . Wasted time, owing to the helplessness of Duse to be of assistance to me—and she in Italy, and an Italian, and queen of the Italian stage!
>
> How utterly trivial all these "great" women are, and how they play into the hands of rascally fellows . . . who . . . trick them into doing ill unto the most sacred of things, their stage.[2]

Part of the trouble was that the workers Duse found for Craig could neither understand English nor grasp the effects he wanted. Craig finally had to find his own assistants, but, because of the language barrier, he was compelled to do most of the work himself. Furthermore, he and Duse had completely different conceptions of what the scenery should look like, and Isadora, who was acting as interpreter for the two artists, found it diplomatic to keep Duse out of Craig's way.[3]

When Duse finally saw Craig's setting it came as a shock to her, although she had enough artistic appreciation to recognize its genius. So moved was she, indeed, that she wept and threw her arms around Craig,[4] and later, after the performance on December 5, 1906, she sent him a warm note of thanks, expressing the hope that he would work with her again.[5]

Unfortunately, Duse was playing in repertory and there were to be no further performances of *Rosmersholm* in Florence. Still more unfortunate, the expenses of Isadora's school were depleting her bank account, and she was forced once again to go on tour. Leaving her baby with the nurse, she said good-bye to Craig and Duse and set out for Poland.

Evidently rumors about Isadora's baby had reached Warsaw, for on December 3, 1906 the director of the Warsaw Philharmonic wrote to Craig who was acting as Isadora's manager:

> We beg to acknowledge receipt of your favor of the 1st, inst.; and in order to be able to arrange the Réclame [publicity] in time, we would ask you to give us an early reply to the following:
> 1) Name of Miss Duncan's husband.
> 2) Newest portraits of Miss Duncan for exhibiting in windows. . . .
>
> signed: A. Rajchman

On the bottom of this letter, Craig noted tersely:

> 1) Not the affair of the public.
> 2) No pictures. . . .[6]

On December 17, Isadora arrived in Warsaw. She was scheduled to dance the next night and did so despite a toothache that necessitated an immediate trip to the dentist and six[7] subsequent trips before the pain could be relieved. Nonetheless, she gave an inspired opening performance. On December 18, she wrote to Craig, who had remained in Florence:

> Dearest—I slipped into my old dresses and my old dances like a Charm. After rehearsing orchestra all day—and great agony of spirit—suddenly felt myself dancing like a miracle. *Art* or *whatever* you choose to call it—every little finger movement came in its old place. I was hardly conscious of my body at all—I feel I have cause to triumph a bit. . . .
>
> The House was entirely *sold out* . . . I wish someone were here to make the [box office] count (I feel a little nervous about it) but *not you.* I can't tell you what I felt when I witnessed your wonderful work in Florence. Probably you have no idea how truly great and beautiful it was. It was like something supernatural that a man with a thousand million geni [sic] at his disposal might create. I felt conscience-stricken too that I had perhaps been the cause of your wasting some of your time on me. It would be a *sin.* . . .[8]

But shortly afterwards she found herself having to write to Craig:

> Dearest: This Business is *Maddening.* The House was *sold out* last night—*crowds standing.* They brought me a muddled account this morn.—1700 roubles (a rouble is 2 francs) in *House.* Then a long list of so-called *expenses* and *taxes,* ending in wanting to hand me 440 roubles. This is obviously absurd. So I telegraphed you to come if you could come or send a Business Man to unravel the mystery. . . . You might send Mr. G. if you don't want to come. . . . This *Contracting* and *accounting* is *Death* to any *Nobility* of life or thought.[9]

And indeed, managing Isadora's affairs was a drain on Craig's time and creative energy. Little more than a year later, he was to write to his friend De Vos, a Dutch actor: "I cannot act as impresario to Isadora *forever*—that would kill me."[10] And in the draft of a letter to Isadora some time afterwards, he spoke of trying "for a time to obliterate myself [in your work] and only succeeding in pretending to the obliteration."[11] As often happens in the artistic world, Craig was in danger of neglecting his own work while trying to further the career of another artist. Thus, in 1907, he listened as patiently as he could to Isadora's appeals to find her a musical director. Rajchman had substituted another orchestra for the one that had played at her rehearsals, and she felt that she must refuse on artistic grounds to dance to it.

She had by this time returned to creating her own dances, and she wrote to Craig:

> Something is on the way but comes slowly. It's this music question. I must settle once for all—antique? Early Italian? Gluck? Modern? or None? You know it's a subject worth thinking about. You have a superior think box in your head than mine—What do you think?
>
> . . . it's very interesting because when they compose a Ballet the Ballet Master composes the dances. . . . Then he brings this to the poor musical composer & says "Make me so many bars of 2/4 time, so many of 3/4, and then so many of 4/4." The musical director . . . who composes ballets says that it's quite impossible to compose any music worth anything in that way. The whole question ought to be worked out by a head stronger than mine. I screwed up my nose & thought for a few hours yesterday & evolved the following—or I'll enclose it. [The enclosure is missing.] Tell me if it's any good—I feel my poor head is very faible. But I've found one new movement which I think will stonish you. . . .[12]

This letter is worthy of comment for two reasons. It shows Isadora preoccupied by a subject to which she would return many times— the relation of dance to music. Should music or dance be composed first? Or should a dance be created independent of music? Equally interesting, it shows her writing to her lover in a way that belittles her own intelligence. At least two later readers of her letters, the perceptive critics Anna Kisselgoff (in *The New York Times*, January 11, 1975) and Emily Leider (in the *San Francisco Review of Books*, April 1977), found Isadora's propensity for using childish words ("think box" and "stonish you") and even "inane baby talk" (as Emily Leider puts it) disconcerting and distasteful.

Indeed, Kisselgoff finds Isadora's choice of words so jarring that in a review of Steegmuller's *Your Isadora,* entitled "Behind the Legend, Baby Talk," she dwells on this unexpected, self-deprecatory aspect of Isadora, that "symbol of liberated woman." (It must be said, in fairness to these critics, that it takes a lover's indulgence to enjoy "When you coming to see yo' po' old rabbit?") But aside from the fact that such words were certainly not intended for public view, to be surprised at or critical of their use is to miss two points: first, that the letters were written specifically to a deeply insecure lover who felt threatened by a competing artist, particularly since that artist was a woman; and, second, that Isadora had arrived at her own radical convictions slowly over time. Her irregular childhood, her experience of bearing an illegitimate child, and the difficulty she had in dealing with someone as vulnerable, as prone to anger and depression, as Gordon Craig were all contributing factors. Loving Craig and admiring him as an artist, she wanted to protect his pride and encourage his work. It was only later that she began to assess the costs to herself and her own work.

However, she did not think of Craig as an opponent. It was the place of women in society—the laws governing property, marriage, divorce, and the custody of children, as well as the customary double standard—that Isadora wished to reform, but, in her eyes, men were not the enemy. "It seems to me that if the marriage ceremony is needed as a protection to ensure the enforced support of children, then you are marrying a man who you already suspect of being a villain and it is a pretty low down proposition. But I have not so poor an opinion of men that I believe the greater percentage of them to be such low specimens of humanity."[13]

Isadora gave her final concert in Warsaw on January 10, and the next day she returned to Berlin, where Craig, back from Florence, was waiting for her.[14]

She could not stay with him for long because she had a contract to tour again in Holland. Since they had many bills to settle (including four or five months' salary owed to Fräulein Kist, the baby's nurse),

she dared not postpone her departure. Craig's old friend and collaborator, the musician Martin Shaw, was to meet her in Holland,
having been engaged as her conductor.

On January 16, Ted's birthday, she sent him a telegram and the
following letter from Amsterdam:

> I long for [the baby]. I long for you—and I miss the Wonder and
> the Inspiration that you add to all the moments. Even the suffering
> which you sometimes cause is joy compared to being without you.
> Oh do you think the day will come when I can stay with you and
> be some help to your work and so further my own better than by
> bumping about the country like this. . . . You are the Wine and Poetry
> of Life—Without you how flat & cold. . . . If you were going to
> Italia I might come with??? Yes—[15]

When Isadora had left Florence in December to tour Poland, she
had sent the baby and nurse to San Remo, on the Italian Riviera.
She wrote Ted from Holland, in January.

> O how I would long to see our Baby, but Dr. told me to change
> her milk and bring her to a cold climate *now* might be fatal so I
> don't dare. Frl. writes me she is leaving—she promised to stay till
> March. I will find a nurse here that I can give full instructions to
> & send her down—I must *see* the nurse myself who is to care for
> Baby.
>
> Stumpff [her manager in Holland] wants more dates here—O
> Darling I am so sad & distracted, but will try & be brave—Ray
> [Raymond Duncan] telegraphs for money—[16]

Her first concert in Amsterdam was played to a packed house.
She told Craig:

> The sweet strong words of your telegram gave me strength to
> dance last night as nothing else could. I put them up on mirror &
> between each dance they *shone* for me—
>
> This morn. I found I was *"ill"* so have been lying flat all day as
> it is necessary—[17]

The following day she was still too "ill" to go out. She wrote:

Dear—My star seems to have been a yearning star, & it is decreed
I spend my life in longing longing longing. Sometimes when I dance
or when I am with you it is stilled—yes you can still it—but no
one else & nothing else, only sometimes my dance. . . .

No letter from you today!—

Kathleen [who had been visiting her in Amsterdam] left this morn.
for London—She was very sweet and cheerful. I have been lying
down all day as am rather too "ill." Tomorrow I must go to Harlem
for a rehearsal of Chopin music—

Darling, I am going to bed now with a book of Blake's Job!

What a funny life!!

I want the Baby—I want *more*—you. I am filled with yearning
and unrest. . . .

Do you say "be sensible Topsy, go to bed & get well"—I dance
here 25 & 28 then Berlin?

I have to pay the Beastly Bills here as they come in—or they
would make trouble.

Hotel Doelen—Hague	500 guldens
Prof. Trul.	150 "
Dr. Van Ness	300 "
Frl.	225 "
Hotel here 9 days	225 "
	1430 !!!
	awful!

Frl. telegraphed for 450 frs. I had to send it as thought perhaps
they were in some difficulty.

Almost the receipts for 2 evenings—dreful [sic]—as soon as they
stop coming in I will send you all accounts, receipts, dividends, etc.
Elizabeth writes she must have 1000 gulden back she lent, to pay
House Taxes with. . . .[18]

Craig, in Berlin, was working on the scenery that Duse had
commissioned.

I have done 4 of the designs for *The Lady From the Sea* & only like
one—& the scene painters are a bit expensive—taking every sou

& nine of what D [Duse] pays me. It's queer this idea of an artist working for positively *nil.* . . . A good steady wage like Otto gets [Otto was the concierge at 11 Siegsmundshoff] would be preferable. . . . The school (my project for a school for Theatre) . . . must wait. All good things wait & if 30 years is worth a fairly good thing a *good* thing is worth 100 years.

I shall then appear "for the first time on any stage" as Yorick.

But before this ultimate debut, there was Duse to satisfy. The great actress seemed to be wavering in her choice of plays, and Craig, immersed in his work for her, found her reversals trying.

> By the way, Duse will not do "Tintagiles"—She has a new play— It is pitiful—yet she had evidently forgotten Mr. Rosmer and M. Magi and Co. when she spoke of "Tintagiles". Yet even with all this forgetting and changing she is the best of her land.[19]

Isadora's "illness," meanwhile, had not improved with rest. We find her writing to Ted:

Dearest—
This is the third day I must lie in bed. Horrid, when I was working so well—
Patience—
Can't even read as my head swims—will be all right tomorrow I hope for evening. [This would presumably be January 25, when she was scheduled to give her second Amsterdam Concert.]
Silly me to get so ill—
Can't understand it—[20]

It was probably after this performance that Isadora "fell prone upon the stage and had to be carried back to her hotel." She was extremely ill. In *My Life,*[21] she refers to her malady as "milk fever," but Francis Steegmuller remarks that it was presumably menstrual in origin. If he is correct, as seems likely from the way she writes "ill" in quotation marks, and, if it is remembered, as Kathleen's Noordwijk diary had noted, that Isadora had suffered tearing of tissue in giving birth to Deirdre, it is not surprising that she now felt acute pain during her period, especially considering the heavy concert schedule she had undertaken. But whatever the initial cause of her illness, Steegmuller is surely right when he suggests that worry over debts, her enforced absences from Ted and her baby, and most of all an awareness of Craig's restlessness had increased her discomfort. Craig, burning to get at his own work, had become impatient with her claims on his time. Isadora sensed this, and her uneasiness alternated with exhaustion. Nonetheless, he came briefly to Amsterdam to visit her sickbed. On January 23, after his return to Berlin, he received a telegram from Duse, apparently forwarded by Isadora. "I have a new play that is very beautiful but I must discuss it with you. Can you come to Nice? I shall be putting on Rosmer February Ninth."[22]

On seeing this telegram,[23] Isadora felt a premonition that all would not go well between the two, without herself to act as a go-between. Her fears proved all too well founded.

According to Isadora, Craig arrived in Nice "to find that, without the knowledge of Eleonora, they had cut his scenery in two." He "flew into one of those terrible rages of which he was at times the victim" and denounced Duse for allowing his scenery to be ruined. As he continued his furious tirade, the actress became angry and told him that she wished never to see him again. "That was the end of her intention to devote her entire career to the genius of Gordon Craig," wrote Isadora.[24]

Craig, writing later in *Life and Letters,*[25] stated that this account of the affair was nonsense, that he attributed Duse's saying that she wanted him to design her other plays to kindness, and that he could understand her behavior, although he "certainly felt most unhappy" when none of the other plays materialized. As for reports of a terrible quarrel between them, "Fancy anyone treating the mighty Duse badly, being cross, banging a table, *I* of all people, too—I who in her presence always dwindled to the age of eighteen or nineteen, thought her a kind of divinity, barely uttered two words in her presence—and never would have dared to say Bo [sic] to her shadow."

Yet Edward Craig, in writing his life of his father, confirmed Isadora's account:

> He left for Nice on February 7 and on the following day went round to the old Casino Theatre to see if all was going well. To his horror he discovered that the stage manager, on finding the proscenium opening at Nice so much lower than the one at Florence, had calmly cut two or three feet off the bottom of the whole set . . . [Craig's] fury knew no bounds, and after telling everyone in the theatre what he thought of them in English, with the introduction of various French and German words such as "crétins," "imbeciles," and "dummkopf," he rushed off to find Duse. She could not understand any of his words, but she disliked his outburst and lack of self-control. All was over between them. They would never work together again.[26]

It must be added that Craig seldom knew what his rages were like; he tended to think of himself as mild and put-upon.

Several days after Craig's stormy encounter with Duse in Nice, he went to nearby Monaco[27] to regain his equanimity. Isadora, far from well and evidently believing Craig to be still in Nice, made the taxing trip from Amsterdam to the Riviera. She apparently arrived to find him back from Monaco but ready to depart for Italy. Shortly after he left she sent a letter,[28] postmarked 21 February, 1907, to Craig at the Luchenbach Hotel Metropole in Florence.

Hotel des Princes
Nice

Dear—

I hope you're all right—Four good men & true carried me down in a chair & brought me over in a wheeled chair. Excruciating pain, but glad to be here—so *quiet* & I can look right out on the sea. I am in a good deal of pain—must lie flat.

I feel a bit of a Fool, but it's no use fretting over spilled milk— so patience Topsy—The latest torture invented for me is Mustard Plasters—I thought they were out of date!

Love to you, dear dear soul. I feel a very foolish & inadequate
Topsy—
Poor thing
I envy you to see all the Beauty of Florence again—"our Don-
atellos."

Craig's abrupt departure is not difficult to understand. He had
already interrupted his work to visit the sick Isadora in Amsterdam.
Now he was threatened with further interruptions, for Fräulein Kist
and little Deirdre were about to join Isadora in Nice—and as Isadora
later wrote to him, "Why, the very *Goo* of a baby makes you look
for a time-table book."[29] Mrs. Duncan, too, with whom his relations
were strained, was also expected to join them. But, furthermore,
his attention to Isadora's business—securing bookings and arguing
with managers about accounts, orchestras, and publicity—had been
taking time which he felt he needed for his own art. He had not
turned his back on England and acting to end as Isadora's secretary.
He had felt imprisoned, until the blow of Duse's dismissal sprung
the trap and released him. He had written to Martin Shaw:

The Rosmer scene was CUT down—pity me a little—yet I care
so little, for I want to fly far beyond that haphazard work . . .
My whole being is sick by the delay of the birth of that which is
burning in me . . .[30]

He no longer intended to work for others or to be subject to their
whims and changes of plan. (The volatile Duse had first asked him
to design sets for *The Lady From the Sea* and *John Gabriel Borkman,*
then Maeterlinck's *Tintagiles,* then an unnamed new play—all within
the space of a month and a half!) It was time for him to invent a
new kind of theater where the movement of light, sound, and masses
alone would provide the emotion, and where the use of figures,
whether for scale, emphasis, or contrast, would be under his direction.

This idea was not, as so many thought, to exclude any other form
of theatre, for he loved the theatre in all its forms . . . but he wanted
to create a new kind of theatre that was an art and on its own.[31]

Florence seemed to promise him asylum. He had friends there:
Martin Shaw, who was searching for fifteenth-century music for
Isadora, and the American art collector Charles Loeser, who during
Craig's previous visit had offered him the loan of a villa. Ever since
the success of *Rosmersholm* in Florence, he had loved that art-nur-
turing city whose atmosphere, both stimulating and sober, promised
accomplishment. Also, good workers cost less than in Germany. So
Craig escaped to Florence, which he resolved to make his headquarters.

Despite the shock, humiliation, and alarm she must have felt at
Craig's sudden flight, Isadora did not voice her bitter disappointment.
She was aware of her own shortcomings and of her provisional hold
on him. Moreover, she hoped that his move portended nothing even
more serious. So she made no reproaches; even when she wrote of
her illness, she carefully lightened her account with jokes.

I had two awful days yesterday and before, pains like 170,000
devils—but am *much* better today. Mustard plasters all over—talk
about Dante's inferno he forgot to put in a shop labelled "Mustard
Plasters."[32]

Still feeling his freedom threatened, Craig found Isadora's un-
willingness to complain exasperating. In a letter to his mother, he
explained that Isadora was "in Nice with her Mama . . . & with
nurses to look after her as she is really rather ill—and so I have
come here to go on with work because *business* has laid its . . . little
claw on me for so long . . .[33] It is dreadful to see people ill who
have almost superhuman *patience*—only the impatient ones relieve
themselves."

Isadora's trip to Nice had been exhausting, and she suffered from dizzy spells whenever she got out of bed. She wrote on February 23:

> It kills me to say it, but I'm afraid March 10 is impossible—O Lord! I am still lying very flat & *pains* all over . . . I will be in bed a week more the Dr. says, & then it will be at least 2 weeks before I am strong enough to walk—practice—dance— . . .[34]

By this time Craig had moved into Loeser's empty villa at 4 Viuzzo della Gattaia, on a hill above the Arno and the city of Florence. It had orange and lemon trees growing in earthenware jars on a vine-covered terrace. Here he was to begin work on *The Mask,* the magazine which was to be his mouthpiece for his ideas in the theater. Later a young Englishwoman, Dorothy Nevile Lees, who had written two successful books on Tuscany, would give up her own work to help Craig produce *The Mask.*[35]

Isadora wrote:

> So you have a villa—Bedad! It sounds very imposing—
> I sat up an hour today . . .
> Fraulein has found a quiet hotel up on the hill over-looking the sea—12 frs a day—an improvement over this. If the Dr. allows I will move . . . I still take these powders which make my head continually spin . . .
> I look at the Baby & look out over the sea & think of you—& if my poor body is racked with silly pains my heart is filled with love & love—& so it's all right.[36]

The doctor had variously diagnosed her illness as neuralgia and nervous prostration. Isadora was indifferent to the name of her illness, but she noticed that her pains lessened when she had a letter from Ted.

The date of her recovery kept receding.

> The Dr. . . . has just been here. He says no performance possible till the first of April! . . . I am taking extra strong powders & can't read— your letters & the dear Baby keep me from despair. [sic]
> The Baby is beautiful & so intensely alive . . .[37]

Afraid that her letters might have alarmed him, she sent him a word of reassurance:

> Dear you need not worry about me. It is true I am somewhat ill & [in] a good deal of pain but your power of giving me joy is so great that the dear lines you wrote make up for all else. It is perhaps just from having to lie so still and being so much in pain—it sounds a bit Irish but it is really so—life dulls things a good deal & this being in a way half out of life—Love shines more clear. So don't worry about me—*I'm not unhappy.*[38]

But slowly her health began to return. On March 9 she wrote Craig to tell him that her strength was coming back, and a few days later she told him:

> Today I walked in the Garden, certain I love life. This is like being released from prison. All the smells of Earth were so good to breathe— I wanted to kiss all the plants & dance—too weak yet but *soon*— Yes, life is delicious . . .[39]

A walk to town, or in the hills with the nurse, were events marking the stages in her recovery. She wrote Craig that she was almost well and would be able to practice in a few days. But his last note to her had prompted some uncomfortable thoughts.

> I couldn't help thinking your letter sounded rather hard on Nord-wijk where *doors did slam* and Topsy *did* chatter and make a noise. My heart felt a bit sore & I wondered does he want me ever—even in *another* cottage? . . . the Bird likes to live with his mate in the nest—even the lion stalks about with his lady at his side—but you—O—you say "Go away disturber of the Peace" . . . Good night dear—I love you—Your Isadora.[40]

On the bottom of this letter, Craig wrote: "I don't say 'go away'— but I do say 'stay by me—and give me that pin' And you and your talking about giving me the Earth & fail to—then why not try a pin that I ask you for—"

Presumably he did not communicate this complaint to Isadora. Like her, he had been hurt and was therefore subsequently more careful to hide his feelings. The "pin" he spoke of was the money Isadora had promised to send him to help pay the workers who were building his scenery. This she had offered in good faith, but her illness had forced her to cancel her engagements, and her letters show that she was hard-pressed for money. But other people's financial difficulties never had any reality for Craig.

Nonetheless, he was working well without her distracting presence, as Isadora could not help noticing when he sent her some etchings that he had just finished. After commenting on their beauty, she wrote:

> I can't live without you that's true—I think my Body & soul contains [sic] parts of you—& I long for you but I'd rather you be a million miles away from me & know you happy or at least happy you know what I mean than close to me & unhappy . . . Good night my love—My own heart & soul more than Brother Helper Friend. All, *your* Isadora.[41]

Touched, Craig has written beneath her words: "My wonderful Topsy—Yes! Yes! but don't you protest too much?"
At last Isadora was strong enough to work again.

> I practice a little each day. The beginning is like breaking stones. One loves to work when once begun but it is so difficult to reach the right state to begin . . . A feeling of battering for ages against an impassible barrier & then suddenly & sharply a glow a light a connection with the idea like entering into a God . . . That's what I feel when I try to work only many times I get only as far as the suffering & battering & then a blank fall to despair.[42]

But, despite the difficulty of working and a recurrence of neuralgia, Isadora knew that she must resume touring soon. In the latter part of March she wrote to Craig:

> My *Munee* is going out—perhaps it is better I should start for Holland before I am quite bankrupt? What do you think? If you think so I

will start next Wednesday or so. Also the Dr. says it would be better to stop over a night on the way.

Well. I'd rather go to Florence.

Forgive me for worrying you but that's what I was put on Earth for.

All my love.

your
Isadora.[43]

On March 24, Isadora was finally well enough to leave Nice.

Dear—I am just starting for the station . . . Goodbye Blue Sky, Sunshine & Baby—O—I didn't like it. I wish I was going toward you instead. How joyous I would be then—How I would *fly* . . . Couldn't you find me a . . . cottage in Florence . . . I promise not to bother you at all. Goodnight darling . . . Love your Isadora a little if you can.[44]

Undated drawing by Christine Dalliès
(*Christine Dalliès Collection*).

❧ 16 ❧

On T'Other Side
of a River
1907

SADORA arrived in Amsterdam on Easter night, March 31, 1907. Weary from her trip, she wrote a brief note to Craig, then fell into bed.

Next morning she awoke to find letters from Craig waiting for her. They had been brought from Stumpff's office to her room at Brock's Doelen Hotel. Reassured by this sign of Ted's love, she wrote him a happy letter.

Dear, you ask what you give me—but you *know* what you have given me— . . . Life— . . . What the Sun gives the Earth . . . My soul is but the reflection of the rays of your love . . . I feel my body & soul becoming divine—through you. I would give myself to you a thousand thousand times until all passed into flame— . . .

I thank you that you wrote to me about N. [Nelly,¹ Elena Meo]. I have often wanted to speak with you about her. I *know* it is a good heart and filled with love for you—and I have often thought of her and I thank you because it shows when you write to me so that you have forgiven my stupid jealousy of which I have been many times ashamed——but I swear to you there is not a vestige of it left. Perhaps it was the pain of the Baby which cleared it all out—only love is left—& I am so grateful if you write me all your pains—& so proud that you *can* write to me. Couldn't you find a pretty place for her in Italy or South of France that she might rest in the sunshine & get *well*—Tell me what you think & let me help any plan—There is so much unnecessary pain that should not be— . . .

Tell me what I can do to help you about N. What I wrote you to London[2] I meant & mean with all my heart—. . . . It's just Love Love Love—the God of Love—& the Kingdom of Love—We will enter it & all who love you with us.

> your
> Isadora[3]

Though she wrote that she no longer felt jealous of Elena, was it really possible for Isadora to overcome her original intense feelings of hurt and anger? Why should she have felt any need to apologize for "my stupid jealousy of which I have been many times ashamed"? Why was she not more outraged at Craig's having several families?

To Isadora, it was natural for men to love more than once and to have children by the women they loved. Her own father had had several families, and, whenever he had had enough money, he had tried to be responsible for all his children. Isadora took it as the desired norm for a divorced husband to remain on speaking terms with his former wife. The relief of meeting her father, the unknown "demon" of whom no one would speak, and of finding him affectionate had been so enormous that she could not bear—she refused to contemplate—the possibility that two who had once loved should become enemies or, yet more chilling, strangers.[4]

As for herself and Elena, she saw that their situations were alike, and this realization helped her to deal with her jealousy. (Even in the last lonely months since Deirdre's birth Isadora had seen more of Craig than had Elena, a fact that would have made her feel less threatened.)

She dreaded Craig's rages *not* because she was afraid of fighting, but because the thought of losing his love was unbearable to her. Despite their mother's devotion, the young Duncans had grown up in a state of social ambiguity and economic precariousness due to their father's disappearance. The only respite was their time in the Castle mansion, which they lost in the receding tide of another of Joseph Duncan's fortunes.

But, for the boy Teddy and his sister Edith, their father's absence, though in its own way even more damaging, had not resulted in the loss of economic security. On the contrary, Godwin was a poor provider and the family fortunes improved after mounting bills impelled Ellen Terry to return to the stage.[5] Nor did it lessen their mother's protective love. Though illegitimacy had made the children's social status uncertain in the world at large, in the theater, Ellen Terry's world, her great gifts and the force of her radiant personality had made her children not only accepted but also welcome. So, for Craig, unshakeably sure of his mother's love and protective power, it was not the loss of women's love that he feared, but rather being overwhelmed by its excess. Women, he felt, treated him as a child, belittling his masculinity and threatening his work. He particularly feared professional competition from women. He needed the love of women, yet he periodically revolted from emotional entanglements and family ties and fled to his studio where, in a less encumbered setting, he could dedicate himself afresh to his work. So, from the safe distance of Florence, he waited for news from Holland.

Isadora gave the first concert of her resumed tour at Amsterdam on April 3, and the next morning she wrote to Craig from The Hague where she was staying.

Everything went well last night. My legs were a bit *weak* & *wobbly* but I took great joy in dancing & thought of you & danced to a harmony of Love. . . . Your telegram came to me just before I went on the stage and I rose to your message . . . you teach my spirit to climb . . . I am *made* of your Love and your thought and nothing else. Without you I would never have gone further than the door. You opened the door for me—I feel so rich from you, but what can I give you in return—Can the created being return something to the Creator—Body & Soul you have ploughed deep & sown & they blossoming and bearing fruit only from your sowing—What can I ever be to you in return? . . . Once I had to come in contact with horrid people and talk about contracts & dates but you have taken that off my shoulders & now I float in and dance—only—feeling your protection all round me like a big wall. . . . I would I were some God who could do for you what you do for me.[6]

She gave concerts in The Hague on April 4, in Utrecht on April 6, in The Hague again on April 8, in Leyden on April 10, and in Harlem on April 12,[7] which should have left her with a tidy sum of money. But Stumpff, her booking agent for Holland, informed her that the contract which said she was to *engage* the orchestra did not mean that he was to *pay* for it: the payment must come out of her share of the proceeds.[8] She wrote Craig:

Let Stumpff revel in his old guldens. I will go up to Berlin as this Hotel simple robbery. I will send you by bank tomorrow what is left of the fray—And I will send you a list of my expenses etc.— Indeed I have made no bills but there were the old ones—the hotel, Dr., nurses, etc., etc.[9]

Back in Berlin, Isadora was happily reunited with her baby. Craig was to join her soon and be with her at the Grand Hotel in Stockholm for a series of recitals she was to give between May 4 and May 15. After their brief reunion in Sweden, they returned via Heidelberg, where they separated, with Craig traveling to Florence and Isadora heading for Berlin. It would be many months before they were together again. Isadora began making plans for concerts in Germany, but it took time to get bookings. She had recitals scheduled for June 4 and June 7 in Baden-Baden. On June 5, from Baden, she wrote to Craig:

. . . not a large House—only 2019 & over a half . . . for expenses— & Hotel-bill almost 700! . . . have come to a more reasonable hotel here & hope to do better all round . . . We now have Baden June

7, Lucerne June 13, Zurich (?) June 15 & Berlin for June 28. Also started for the open air performance at Mannheim for July & waiting to hear from Weisbaden & some other places—it is not at all going as *quick* as I desire & I go crazy with Impatience.[10]

Adding to her irritation was the fact that the police department was giving the children of her school "the usual old trouble about permission to appear"[11] in the Berlin recital of June 28. "Police director ordered a special rehearsal this morn. We put all the little girls in long dresses & he looked in vain for a single leg. . . . He created an awful atmosphere. . . . As if that wasn't enough they've called up that *eternal* Gerichtsvollzieher's [marshal's] case again for 9 o'clock tomorrow morning & threaten to send the Police if I don't come. How can I dance in the evening with *that* in the morning?"[12] Meanwhile, Craig's Berlin studio had been opened and his possessions attached, presumably for back rent. Isadora called a lawyer to deal with the matter.

> Berlin is simply impossible with these things. Your studio looked as if snow had fallen, with sticky papers [put on Craig's possessions by the bailiff]. But don't worry, we will get them off all right. How Elizabeth goes along in this sort of an Inferno I don't know—She keeps up against it with really wonderful courage. They are even attacking me again on the taxes question— . . . Darling, forgive me all this stupid letter. One gets in a Stimmung [mood] here that is impossible for man or beast—a sort of fever of bumping one's head against a stone wall. I do not send you the details of all the places that have disappointed us. The sale for tomorrow is already 1600 so that looks well.[13]

Fortunately, permission was granted for the children to dance, and, on June 29, Isadora wrote Craig:

> Darling, a wonderful House last night. They shouted from the first number & made ovations all evening. We will *repeat* the evening next Friday. . . . There was over 4000 in the house last night. We made *net* about 1500. That would be all right if it was done 3 times

a week—but only *once* isn't enough. The papers say . . . "Her Art has ripened . . ."

There are no dates between Berlin & Mannheim although Gus has almost worked himself into a Brain-fever trying to book some—but it really seems impossible at this time of the year. . . . Dearest will you come to Mannheim on the 12th because I really don't think I can exist much longer without seeing you.

Gus keeps his books in perfect order & as he hasn't made dates enough refuses to take any salary whatever, but Hélas the enormous expenses eat up everything. He is now making a mighty effort to book *August solid,* 3 dates a week.[14]

Some time after Isadora's performance in Mannheim on July 12, Craig wrote in response to one of her notes:

Sweetheart mine—a wee lecture bowered in kisses all the time. My letter (Kiss) you say is not marvellous sympathetic (Kisses) & no one can appreciate difficulties (Kiss) except those wading in them. (Kisses) *Sympathy never pulled all those guns over the Alps in 1792!* Sympathy sits down at these moments and lets her Disciplined sister step forward. (Kiss) And so far as I can see sympathy has caused you to waste a few thousand marks instead of saving at least a few thousand. (Kiss). It is not discipline to *begin* & then say "I'm afraid financial things won't turn to much until the season begins" when you've had receipts amounting to

Heidelberg	2000 ?
Baden	1500 ?
Kiel	1000 ?
Berlin	3600
Mannheim	4000 etc.[15]

In another letter to Isadora, probably written before the one of July 12, Craig sent Isadora suggestions as to how savings could be made.

1st you must call your cashier to you & say to him *this:*
"The object of this tournée is to make a regular *profit* at each

town *not* to cover expenses or lose: If your xpenses—grand total per week—exceed your takings *you are to reduce the expenses*. I expect you to hand me *never* less than 500 marks profit after all expenses are paid." And you are to say to him: "If you wish to know how to reduce the expenses—take a list of each item and reduce each by 5%. Do *not* reduce these following:

> *Printers Bill*
>
> *Carriages for Lady*

but reduce all the rest: Hotels—eating—expenses in theatre or hall, salaries—& stop the leaks . . ." Unless you keep this RULE you'll reach October with only 3000 marks in hand. . . .

My darling—As I told you my regiment are a picked lot & are working in good order.

I hope I shall not have to disband them all a month from now—for I could only with *greater* difficulties begin again after another reverse . . .

Never before in my experience . . . has the work been going forward so *steadily* & *productively* . . . I shall only break the rythmn [sic] if I have to stutter out "Haven't any more oil for the machine" . . . Till then for the 1st salaries and material we rely on your lieutenant relieving the fort with an occasional 2000 marks . . .[16]

From the Rotters Park Hotel, Hamburg, around July 20, Isadora wrote:

> Dearest, After all the Enormous Effort—Hurrah & Huréh—after paying all expenses, childrens' [sic], Capelmeister's & everything, I have only a little over 2000 marks left!! I send you 1000 and keep 1000 for running expenses. I dance here on the 24th. . . . I have been quite desperate over the possibility of making any money this summer. The only thing to do now is to rest and make next season *good* from Oct. on.[17]

Isadora's finances did not improve as the summer continued. She gave a recital in Zurich in August (where she stayed at the expensive Hotel Baur au Lac), danced in Munich on August 20 and 22 and was to dance in Baden-Baden on August 24. She wrote to Craig:

I hate to send you disappointing letters and I can't send any other. . . . My money is at an end. I will have to fly to Berlin where I can at least get my board until then. . . . Frl. Kist has gone home & I had to send money for new nurse. Gus flew off to America sending me word of his going only from the boat. . . . I should have known that summer is always a rum time. . . . I wish I could get in the train & come to you but that would only be making things worse as I would not then have enough money to get back to Baden on Aug. 24.

This is a very rummy way to spend the summer, & I feel tired to tatters.[18]

By now, Craig was feeling desperate for lack of money. In a frantic letter, he asked Isadora to get the necessary funds from Dr. Zehme or from some other friend.

Please answer my letter Isadora about the 6000 marks. Or is the ship to go down once more—If so I go down with [it] & then goodbye to all such rush work. Do you always do what Elizabeth tells you? Or any other stray influence? What has made all these tours utterly unproductive? & why in Walt's name was I fool enough to start? . . . So why should I talk & try to show you. You don't seem to realize how serious this thing is. How can you write to me about *everything* except the one thing we all thought was what you were working for.

In a few days I shall have to pay out 2000 marks or close up & end the whole affair. That would mean 3 or 4 processes [lawsuits] as I have contracts with my workers. I am laid up with a foot red hot & I read at night instead of sleeping—Ice in bags makes foot pleasant at times. It's about 14 days I've been laid up & I could take it easily except for the weight of the money affair hanging like a hell in the air—flames downward. . . .

And then I expected to see you the day after Mannheim—but I suppose you have lost the map—or your head—or some other trifle— . . .

[Work at] this end is going ahead with fearful & divine energy & success—fearful to me & to see, because I see by side of it the words "useless—for Isadora has forgotten."[19]

The unfairness of this letter speaks for itself. From Berlin, Isadora wrote:

> You and I are not very practical people but this summer our impracticality is the limit. You will have to tell your people that they must wait till winter [to be paid]. There is no other way. . . . My banker here wouldn't lend me anything if I was dying! . . . Every now and then everything at your studio is attached—I asked Mr. Magnus [Maurice Magnus, Isadora's and Craig's business manager] to help me pack your pictures & take them out of danger of further attachments. . . . I must pay 100 marks to raise the attachment today or everything will be sold.
>
> Gus left for America because he rec. a letter from Frohman offering him a better part. Frl. Kist lent him the money for his ticket.
>
> I feel so dreadfully anxious about you. I will try and send at least 2000 marks or so tomorrow if I can get them. . . . I have to go through a treatment, otherwise the Dr. says I will not be able to dance next winter. Can't you insist on Mr. Loeser doing Something?[20] The Dr. won't let me practice so I can't continue on my new programme. . . . I wish I could write something to comfort you. . . . I committed a grave error in judgment thinking I could be able to make money in summer—something I never yet have been able to do in my life. . . .
>
> Dearest Dreamer this is a pretty silly world & I'm afraid you needed someone a bit stronger than your poor Topsy to help you. [Craig has written here: "All this is Elizabeth's influence."]
>
> All my hearts love to you—it can't do you much good though can it?
>
> your Isadora[21]

Isadora's letter, calling them *both* impractical and telling Craig that he would have to postpone paying his assistants until winter, must have been wounding to receive. However, Craig failed to notice that Isadora had repeatedly paid the bailiffs to prevent his possessions from being attached, besides sending him whatever money she could manage. If she did not send more money, it was because she did not have any to send.

On September 1 and 3, Isadora danced in Munich. On September 2, she wrote to him: "I am much in need of a rest and if possible from a financial standpoint I will come to Venice and bathe for a week. Will you meet me there?" Despite her announced concern about finances, Craig could not have helped noticing that she was staying at the far from inexpensive Grand Hotel Continental. Though he had urged her to cut costs, still he never complained to her about her choice of expensive hotels, perhaps realizing that a performer has to maintain a certain scale of living for publicity purposes.

Isadora did indeed need a rest. Beset with business worries since her collapse in Holland, she had been driving herself to find bookings, interviewing reluctant managers, arguing about receipts, travelling, performing, and dealing with bailiffs. And there was nothing she could do to reduce her regular running expenses, which included support for her family (her mother, Elizabeth, her baby, the nurse, and sometimes her brothers), all the expenses of the school, and payments to her doctors.

She travelled to Venice on September 8 and wrote Craig the next morning from the Hotel Royal Danieli (another de luxe hotel):

> Dear Love—I am so tired if I don't rest I will be ill— . . . If only you were here—well if you don't come I'll come & see you. . . . Address me Cook's Bureau . . . as I won't stay in this Hotel.[22]

Nevertheless, she was presumably still at the Danieli on September 15, as a note on its stationery from her to Craig indicates:

> If at the end of the week you don't come, I will come & see you—if you want me—do you—your Topsy—O the Sunset and the Moonlight—all a bit maddening.[23]

In still another note she repeats her invitation: "O wonderful city—do come here if only for three days?"[24] On the margin, Craig wrote bitterly: "How had I 1000 Lira to pay for 3 days to & from Venice?"

And so, as he was unable to come to her, Isadora went to him at Il Santuccio—San Leonardo, outside Florence. As Craig described it,

> It was a house with a lot of olive trees at the back and an open piazza in little, a square one, led on to those trees which were on a gently sloping bit of hill. In this piazza the peasants worked & made their stacks of hay or piles of beans or barrels of olives—each season a new work was begun with clocklike regularity. I had a small garden of my own.[25]

The young Englishwoman, Dorothy Nevile Lees, who had given up her own writing to help Craig with *The Mask,* lived opposite Il Santuccio in a small villa where she typed Craig's manuscripts. (Devoting herself to Craig, she would bear him a son, David Lees, in 1915.)[26] Other helpers included Michael Carr and his wife, and Gino Ducci, a postman and amateur printer. Later in October they would be joined by another Ducci family member who would act as cook and carpenter's assistant in return for board and lodging and occasional pocket money.

To this place Isadora came eagerly to be with her beloved, and here she was confronted by an implacable Craig.

Writing about what had happened, years later, after Isadora's death, Craig explained that before his departure for Florence Isadora had promised to supply him with funds for his material and his workers.

> This was not a very immense undertaking—her receipts might be anything between 3000 and 8000 marks per performance & she would send me 100 marks per show to let the work go on.
>
> I went off to Florence—waited—not a word—not a mark arrived. I waited & began to work—I got two men to commence—One a young artist from the Bordeghera gave up his house there on the strength of my assurance and damme if Madam Duncan didn't let *me* down & *him* down—& what's worse, sent no word of excuse. From that day on I have never forgiven this: I don't mind what anyone does or says to me—but if they in any way show disrespect for my work once I am at work (when warm at it) then click goes

the apparatus & it's all over between me & whoever has played me the trick. . . .

About a month later she suddenly arrived in Florence: Expected to find me willing to go on working with her—but she seemed to me like a sort of stranger & in spite of all her dear old attractions nothing could make me look on her as anything more than a wonderful dear thing, *across there on t'other side of a river.* There I put her, since there she seemed to be, & I never crossed over to her side again.[27]

So Isadora stayed in Florence for a day and left in despair. From Cologne she wrote to him:

Dearest:

A very long journey with rain outside and tears inside. Köln looks the personification of gloom. Thank the Gods that you have something Beautiful to look at about you. . . .

Mr. Magnus arrived here all right & Stumpff will keep the contract in spite of his threats. It begins Oct. 7 in Hague—I will send you the other dates tomorrow.

Dear Ted you have a funny effect on your Topsy! You fill me with a Longing & Pain that are Terrible. I felt I would rather die than leave Florence & each jog of the train was like Torture. It is probably better that I am not there. I have no strength when I am near you—I only want to fly into you and die. It is the music of Tristan that you don't approve of at all—and it is the most horrible suffering. I am *two* people really—& each would be fairly decent if the other wasn't there but the combination is frightful. [Craig has underlined this sentence.]

Your house in Florence is Beautiful. There is nothing in it but it is filled with Beauty. I can't tell you all I think about it.

I am very tired from the long journey & will tumble into bed now.

All my hearts love to you—& what I can't express.

your Isadora[28]

Remember me to Mr. & Mrs. Carr [two of his helpers]. They are splendid.

Craig has written at the top of her letter: "1907—She came and I couldn't say 'how late you come'—but we had been parted at Heidelberg by Elizabeth and 'ambition' and I was alone. This she must have seen & felt." (Craig believed that Elizabeth was hostile to him, and he suspected that she had advised Isadora that family and school expenses must take priority over anything she could send to him.)

At the bottom he has made a later entry: "1944—My darling— I know—I had shown you that our kissing had come to an end because I felt mortally hurt. . . . FORGIVE ME, I PRAY YOU—I too had a heart." However, if in 1944 he understood her feelings and her anguish, in 1907 he could feel nothing but pain and a sense of betrayal by being "let down by Madam Duncan." On October 27, he wrote to her:

> Write no more to me—think about me no more. I no longer exist for you *since that for which I live is less than nothing to you.*
>
> I am ashamed—*Red hot with shame* that I ever thought you part of that.
>
> all my letters to you lie here unsent. I shall write more I believe— I fear. I believe too I shall not send them. It is all my fault—
>
> now for *this* instant I am beyond all misery miserable—disgusted & bruised to death—
>
> & Now—I forget—[29]

The worst of it was that he continued to miss her. In one of the unsent letters dated October 24 ("recd a loveless letter from her, so why send them"), he wrote:

> I sigh and say, "well, there *is* a girl for Gordon Craig but only one—all the others are for Teddy & I am no longer him. And if that girl doesn't love you, you would be a fool to try & fill her place: leave it empty: it's easier. . . .
>
> And Gordon Craig sends his greeting to that girl Isadora Duncan and wants to know more. He wants to know a lot more about Isadora Duncan—He has heard a lot—& knows just a little but

would like to know much more—though he dare not hope—ALL. Only the Journalist wants to know *all.* . . .

Isadora Duncan I love you—and I ought not to say it—for it is almost ALL . . .[30]

If he had been able to send this letter, it might have spared Isadora much further pain, but he preferred to believe that Isadora's actions proved she did not love him, which absolved him from the responsibility of breaking with her.

What had caused the break? Though Craig had convinced himself that Isadora had let him down by failing to send the money he needed "without one word of excuse," he must have known that her long illness and her few engagements that disastrous summer had left her without money to send. From the beginning of their lovemaking, when he had told her "but of course it is not real," there had been signs that there were reservations in his love for Isadora. He felt guilty about Elena. Although he found Isadora's art stimulating, at the same time he felt threatened by Isadora's talk of artistic collaboration:

> She now and then touched on the possibility of dancing on a stage which I should arrange for her. I did not want to do this and I managed to evade the suggestion every time it came up. . . . "I will slip in—do my dance—& skip out & your performance will go on—then I will step in later again & do my other dance and again step out." This I thought was the very way not to collaborate to any worth, but I saw a practical something about her notion. But I didn't like it.[31]

He was afraid of being exploited by Isadora and wrote in the same memorandum:

> Artists she was fond of—really fond of them and their art, but nothing could prevent her American nature from pretty soon attempting to use their art (& even themselves) to somehow serve as Réclame for her career.[32]

Craig always found it extremely difficult to work with other people. Fearful of having his ideas stolen, he tended "to impose impossible conditions" on anybody wishing to employ him in the theater, "thus deliberately abort[ing] most of the productions he was invited to design," as Francis Steegmuller wrote.[33]

> He obsessively insisted on his "independence"—but much of what he called "independence" was a fear of the world. . . . Edward A. Craig links his father's fear and his defensive arrogance to the pall of illegitimate birth. The fears that prevented Craig from working with others were reproduced in his private associations.*

All sons need to break away from their fathers in order to establish themselves professionally on their own merits. But, in Craig's case, it was his mother from which he needed to establish his independence since he had little memory of his father. He never forgot that, during his staging of *The Vikings* for his mother, Ellen Terry, when the actors and business manager had wanted to overrule his decisions, they had appealed over his head to her. So, if he was suspicious of fellow workers in the theater, he was particularly suspicious of women. He wrote to Isadora:

> Woman as a rule being the most material packet of goods on this earth, makes a good effort to kill the desire for an Ideal . . . and is trying to break the man of his worship of King-monarch—Stars and Gods—that he may have no other gods than Her. And she will succeed until she reaches the artist, and then she will utter a shriek and like the sphinx will throw herself off the cliff . . .[34]

*These fears often reached exaggerated proportions. His son Edward Craig has related that, hoping to help his father with the mechanical movements of the model of *Scene,* he had consulted a friend who was studying hydraulics at the University of Genoa. His father exploded with a terrifying display of rage: " 'How dare you! You fool! You fool!' . . . As usual, when he worked on something that was particularly dear to him, he had become apprehensive of the imagined 'enemy' ready to steal and prostitute his ideas. In his nervous state, he imagined that I had betrayed him. . . . Later we discovered that his nervous condition was critical." (GC, p. 317.) As Craig grew older, he had two nervous breakdowns, during which he suffered attacks of suspicion and depression. (His father, the architect William Godwin, had been similarly afflicted.)

(It seems hardly an accident that the sphinx destroyer was Oedipus!)*

At the same time, Craig expected women to be endlessly indulgent
and generous to him, as his mother had been. (She was still supporting his children by his wife, May, and by Elena Meo.)[35] Isadora
was, like his mother, fascinating, a public figure, a star—in short,
a rival as well as someone he loved. And though she had sacrificed
much for him, he was not the only part of Isadora's life. She also
had her art, her school, her baby, and her family. ("What you don't
need Elizabeth will (by right) demand—& what Elizabeth don't get
Raymond has a right to—& then here is your poor love old ma &
Gussie likes a leg up of f20 now and then—& I—like all or nothing.")[36]
Elena, in contrast, lived for Craig and their children. Craig often
felt entrapped by domesticity. If it had any attraction for him, it
was in the company of the selfless Elena and not with Isadora, whose
business affairs made demands on his time and thought and whose
position as a star overshadowed his.

Isadora, in writing about the break years later in *My Life,* would
give quite another explanation for the end of their affair:

> I adored Craig . . . but I realized that our separation was inevita-
> ble. . . . To live with him was to renounce my art, my personality,
> nay perhaps my life, my reason. To live without him was to be in
> a continual state of depression, and tortured by jealousy, for which,
> alas! it now seemed I had good cause.[37] Visions of Craig in all his
> beauty in the arms of other women haunted me at night, until I
> could no longer sleep. Visions of Craig explaining his art to
> women . . . saying to himself, "This woman pleases me. After all,
> Isadora is impossible." All this drove me to fits of alternate fury and
> despair. I could not work, I could not dance. . . . I realized that this
> state of things must cease. Either Craig's Art or mine—to give up
> my Art I knew to be impossible. . . . I must find a remedy.[38]

According to Isadora, the remedy presented itself in the form of an
ornamental young man called Pim whom she persuaded to accom-

---

*Craig thought of himself also as Hamlet and his mother as Gertrude. "I too had lost a
father. I too saw my mother married to another. . . . I was always haunted by this father who
was, yet no longer was there—." (ITTSOMD, p. 162.)

pany her to Russia on her next tour. But Isadora did not go to Russia until December 1907, so Pim—if indeed he existed and is not an invention[39]—was certainly not the cause of their break. It was too painful for Isadora to say that her affair with Craig had been broken off over an issue of money; it was too humiliating to depict herself as suffering passively from jealousy. Better to write that she had retaliated by taking off with a rival.

Much later, writing in *The Real Isadora,* Victor Seroff, Isadora's last lover, attributed the break between her and Gordon Craig to Isadora's jealousy: "In the case of Craig, she exhausted herself with her own manufactured doubts about him. . . ." About her consequent trip to Russia with Pim, he wrote, "This irrational episode put an end to her two-year-old passionate affair with Gordon Craig."[40] Evidently, Seroff did not have the opportunity to consult the Duncan-Craig correspondence. He apparently relied on the account in *My Life* and on what he knew of Isadora's character in her later years when desertions and heartbreak had made her lonely and possessive.

On October 14, Isadora wrote to Ted from The Hague. The tone of her note is affectionate and calm; evidently she still clung to the hope that a reconciliation was possible. She urged him to "Go & see Duse & be *nice* to her. Don't expect such wonders of people . . ."

After her tour of the Netherlands, she stopped off in Berlin for a brief visit with her baby before traveling to Warsaw. From Warsaw, she wrote again to Craig. By this time she had admitted to herself the seriousness of the situation.

> You haven't written to me for an age & your last letter was rather enigmatic.
> I have been en fete perpetuel here champagne & dancing it was the only alternative to suicide. The only way possible to stand Varsovie was to be continually drunk![41]
> . . . Mama insisted on taking the steamer to America & is now on her way there . . .
> You do not write me so I do not know what you are doing . . .[42]

She went back to Berlin for a week of rest and then gave a concert in Munich on November 20. From Munich on November 23, she sent Craig a postcard from a restaurant:

Oh, Ted, forgive me—I am sowing the wild oats I forgot to sow in my youth—Topsy[43]

The card perhaps was intended to make Craig jealous, but they must have been fairly tame wild oats, for Elizabeth and the baby were with her, as well as a fourth person identified only by his initials—"SNTG."

On Saturday, November 30, 1907, Craig wrote Isadora a long letter. This draft was among Craig's papers; whether he ever sent the letter itself remains unknown:

You send me a postcard my dear girl to say that I don't write you any news of myself. But I never have from you a list of future addresses . . .

To the beautiful Mme Duse I sent my good Ambassadoress Mrs. Carr—who speaks clear and quiet French. I sent her with a letter—2 letters & 6 of my best etchings—Duse made a tragedy out of the whole parcel & made me most proud (of myself) by refusing to look at—or even open the parcel of etchings. This is quite the Dumas *Junior* style—Not the older & greater man. On getting my parcel returned to me unopened I sat & wondered why she was so tragic about it for she told Mrs. Carr she thought I was a godsent genius & necessary for the stage . . . & cried & said she wished she could make it easy for my work to be done under even fairly comfortable circumstances—*wished* she had 100,000 francs—*wished* she could help me, etc. etc.—*and yet would not look at my etchings in which lies* [sic] *my soul* and I—I feel twice as strong as ever . . . She Duse is unwise to feel I should be grateful for 100,000 francs. I should be grateful for her hand: a friend's hand.

. . . I am far from well for I have had so little to eat lately but *feel* splendid on it really. . . . I go out to dinner whenever I can in my old clothes & good Lord much in tatters sandals & everyone as kind as *English* can be at times. And I have issued a portfolio of Etchings only 30 copies ever to go out—16 or 400 francs per portfolio & with that Carr & his girl shall be paid & fresh wood brought & lunch.

The little pricking difficulties of finding a new house in a month from now & paying my poor & faithful old Ducci . . . these sink into insignificance under the deeper heart crumblings which are going on in my own house. . . .

And now you have my news. I want no help from the pocket. I want all the *hands* of friends. I can take care of the pocket business right enough for it is the easiest part of the problem.

I am no longer afraid of anything—except that the love of my loves in which I trust—except that:

This very love may turn to hate:

Unconscious love to unconscious hate:

Unconscious kindness to unconscious acts of unkindness—

Well then let us think neither of ourselves nor of one another, but each only of his Ideal. . . .[44]

❦ 17 ❦

Stanislavski and a London Interlude
1907–1908

T the end of December 1907, Isadora went to St. Petersburg, where she gave several concerts. On January 10 she left for Moscow, planning to stay there until January 20. In Moscow, she met Constantin Stanislavski, director of the Moscow Art Theatre.[1] They were both at once struck by the common quality of their ideas. As Stanislavski was later to write: "We understood each other almost before we had said a single word." After the debacle with Craig, the meeting with Stanislavski was both reassuring and enormously stimulating to her. They discussed their theories of dance and how to act, of how to make movements express thought and emotion, of how to find the true and revealing emotion behind the movement, and of how to keep this emotional truth alive through many performances.

Each drew inspiration from the other. Aware of Stanislavski's admiration for her, Isadora could not resist trying to turn it into something warmer. She describes the well-known incident in *My*

Life. Once, when Stanislavski was leaving, she kissed him on the mouth and, though he returned the kiss,

> . . . he wore a look of extreme astonishment . . . then when I attempted to draw him further . . . looking at me with consternation [he] exclaimed, "But what should we do with the child?" "What child?" I asked. "Why, our child, of course. What should we do with it?" "You see," he continued in a ponderous manner, "I would never approve of any child of mine being raised outside my jurisdiction, and that would be difficult in my present household." . . . I burst into laughter, at which he stared in distress [and] left me. . . . I was still laughing at intervals all night. But, none the less [sic], in spite of my laughter, I was exasperated and angry, too. . . . I think I then thoroughly understood why some quite refined men might slam on their hats after certain meetings with the highly intellectual, and betake themselves to places of doubtful reputation. Well, being a woman, I couldn't do this.[2]

Yet, Isadora's frustration and Stanislavski's embarrassment did not damage their friendship; if anything, the incident may have increased their regard for one another. And it is likely that Stanislavski was more seriously attracted to Isadora than his actions betrayed, if the following exchange of letters between the two of them is any indication. Isadora wrote to Stanislavski from St. Petersburg on February 4, 1908:

> Dear Friend:
> I have just come back from Madame Duse. [Duse was then on tour in Russia] . . .
> I danced last night. I thought of you and danced well. I received your cards and today received your telegram. Thank you. How good and thoughtful of you! And how I love you!
> I feel a surge of new, extraordinary energy. Today, I worked all morning and put many new ideas into my work. Rhythms again.
> It is you who have given me these ideas. I am so glad I feel like flying to the stars and dancing round the moon. This will be a new dance, which I will dedicate to you.

I have written to Gordon Craig. I told him about your theatre and about your own great art. But couldn't you write to him yourself? If he could work with you it would be *ideal* for him. I hope with all my heart that this can be arranged. I will soon write you again. Thank you once more. I love you. I still work with joy.

Isadora[3]

P.S. My tender love to your wife and children.

Stanislavski answered:

Dear Friend:

I am so happy! I am so proud. I have helped a great artist to find the atmosphere that she so badly needed . . . In the greatest rapturous feeling and artistic admiration I have felt up until now, I feel the birth of a deep and true friendship.

Do you know what you did to me? I haven't yet told you about it.

In spite of the great success of our theatre and the great number of admirers who surround it, I have always been lonely. (My wife alone supported me in moments of doubt and disappointment.) You are the first who has told me in a few simple and convincing words the chief and fundamental thing about the art I wanted to create. That gave me strength at a moment when I was about to give up my artistic career.

Thank you sincerely, thank you with all my heart.

Oh, I was waiting impatiently for your letter and danced with joy when I had read it. I was afraid you would put a wrong interpretation on my restraint, and mistake my pure feeling for indifference. I was afraid that your feeling of happiness, strength, and energy, with which you had left to create a new dance, would desert you before you reached Petersburg.

Now you are dancing the Moon Dance, while I am dancing my own dance, which has as yet no name. I am satisfied. I have been rewarded . . .[4]

In another letter, Stanislavski wrote:

... Do you know that I admire you much more than the beautiful Duse? Your dances have said more to me than her beautiful performance I saw tonight . . .

After your departure I kept looking in my art for the thing you had created in yours. It is beauty, as simple as nature . . .

I implore you, work for art and, believe me, your work will bring you joy, the best joy of your life. I love you, I admire you, and I respect you (forgive me!)—great artist. . . .

I kiss your classical hands a thousand times and

au revoir
Your devoted friend K.S.[5]

It is noteworthy that in this ardent exchange of letters Isadora did not neglect to remind Stanislavski of Gordon Craig's art. She had spoken to Stanislavski at length about Craig's theories, and she welcomed the opportunity to proclaim her belief in Craig's genius. Perhaps also in the back of her mind was the hope that Craig might forgive her for her dereliction if she could enlist Stanislavski's interest in his work. She showed Stanislavski *The Art of the Theatre* and he was impressed. Their conversations resulted in Stanislavski's inviting Craig to stage and direct a play of his choice for the Moscow Art Theatre. (This play was to be the historic production of *Hamlet,* given by the Moscow Art Theatre in 1912.)

Meanwhile Stanislavski also tried to interest Vladimir Telyakovsky, the director of the Imperial Theatres, in backing a school of Duncan dance. However, this project failed to materialize—not, according to Victor Seroff,[6] because of lack of appreciation of her work by Telyakovsky, but because Rimsky-Korsakov and other influential Russian composers disliked Isadora's use of serious music, music not composed for the dance, as her accompaniment.

Isadora was scheduled to dance in Odessa, and she toyed with the notion of going from there to Alexandria and Cairo, hoping that she could tempt Craig to join her in seeing the pyramids. Nothing could have been further from his thoughts. He wrote on the margin

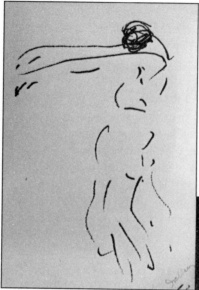

Drawing by Sartorio, 1911 (*Christine Dalliès Collection*).

Dancing to *Orpheus* by Gluck, drawing by Grandjouan (*Mme. Mario Meunier—Christine Dalliès Collection*).

of her letter: "She is expecting me to drop my work & follow her to Egypt!!! Great Gods what is her head made of?"[7]

To his friend, the Dutch actor De Vos, Craig sent a letter dated "February 13 or 14, 1908":

> Have I broken (gebrochen) with Isadora, you ask. Dear De Vos, you better than all else know that man does not break with love because he *can not*. That whether it is light or dark or good or wicked—cold or hot—a heavy or a happy love it is love—and when that is said or done—all is said & done & is unalterable.
>
> I love Isadora & I love this burden [his work] that I am carrying & though it will kill me . . . I shall love it forever. At one time I *dreamed* that Isadora was by nature (or perhaps even by love) bound up in this labour of mine—this fight for the freedom of our theatre—& had she liked she could I believe have taught me to do better what I am only doing to the best of my own ability.
>
> But little Isadora is very little & very sweet & weak & she has to do whatever her impulse tells her to do at the moment. . . . And then besides she has her sister and her school which absorbs all her time & attention—& then too she has to keep moving—first to Berlin—then to Moscow—then to Munich & then to Stockholm. So how can she have time to think quietly about anything or to work with me. . . .
>
> I have not a franc in the world at the moment I write—because I cannot act as impresario to Isadora *forever*—that would kill me—
>
> And so I make enough to pay for food & 3 workmen . . . so that this *damned, blessed* work may proceed. . . .
>
> Isadora came here to see me—she wanted me to give up my work & go rushing around the world with her—
>
> God, how lovely—but she does not understand that I cannot . . .[8]

At the beginning of April, Isadora, back in Berlin, wrote to Craig from the Hotel Adlon:

> Dearest—I arrived here from the North Pole today & am seeing the baby for the first time since three months. She is so splendid—rosey & strong—walking about & dancing on her toes—& talking. . . .

I wish you were here to see her—you would be so delighted with her & she is the image of *you*. . . . Forgive me for not writing for so long. Life is so queer—& difficult sometimes to write—I was ill a week in Varsovie in bed with fever & neuralgia. I found your letter here and if it was not that I have a contract to dance in Kief [sic] on Monday next I would take the train tomorrow night & bring the Baby to see you. . . .

I leave next Thursday night to dance Monday in Kief—after that, Odessa, then Carkoff [sic] & Rostov—& if it is a success, further . . .

I love you although you may think that my way of showing it is a bit strange. There are times when I can't write—if you ever ask me, I'll tell you why some day—if you like the Truth—but what is the truth—it's all an illusion—

But the Baby isn't an illusion. She's *lovely*.

I kiss your dear hands.

your Isadora.[9]

Isadora's letter prompted Craig to write a poem which he added to his pile of unsent messages to Isadora. It said, in part:

> No, you see that the Baby is no illusion
> because she heals & cheers.
>
> That which pains & robs
> Or trembles isn't truth . . .
>
> Do you give me pain—oh no—no—no
> For to give it you must first have it—
> & to have it must be that I caused it—
>
> > Therefore it is I who
> > gives myself pain
> > You give me nothing but
> > —yourself—carved
> > with the wounds I have given you . . .[10]

But most of the time he was more conscious of the hurt she had inflicted on him. On July 1, having received a letter from her, he wrote another unsent message:

Why, having forgotten me for so long should you wish to remember me now?...

Why, idiot, she can make some use of you now...[11]

Isadora, of course, had not forgotten him, but his mailed notes
to her were so cool and self-contained that she found it difficult to
write in answer. In London, however, encouraged by the affectionate
reception given her by his mother, Ellen Terry, she wrote on
August 3:

Meeting your Mother has been a very Great Thing. She is so
Marvellous—so Beautiful—so Kind. She was like a great lovely
Goddess Angel to me—& the two nights she came to the theatre
I danced as in a dream—I was so excited at her being there...[12]

Ellen Terry had been excited, too. Once, in fact, seated in the
audience and watching Isadora, she had been so moved that she
sprang to her feet and exclaimed: "Do you realize what you are
looking at? Do you understand that this is the most incomparably
beautiful dancing in the world?"[13]

Isadora's letter to Craig continued:

The whole visit has been most satisfying & my dear it is a shadow
of what will happen to *you* when London wakes up to you. *The Mask*
[his magazine] is fine and astonishes me every month anew....

I leave tomorrow for Ostend to get a breath of Sea Air. Will be
Aug. 6 in Paris & on the 8th I sail with Mr. Frohman to America—
it seems a funny time of year to open in New York but he says I
must get there before these dozens of copies who are all sailing on
Sept. 1. Your Mama says you are coming to Berlin in Sept. Couldn't
you come that we meet before I leave. I mean to find you some
Millionaire in America...I can't write I want to talk to you...

With all my love
Your Topsy Isadora...[14]

Craig answered bitterly in another unsent letter: "Great success to you, and keep all the millionaires you find for yourself... You need them."[15]

Isadora had reason to be pleased with the reception which she and the children of her school had received in London. The critics were enthusiastic. *The Academy* wrote:

> We have never seen an art so joyous, so purely beautiful as that of Isadora Duncan . . . Though, save in three dances danced by her delightful pupils she filled the whole program for three hours, yet nothing has ever been less monotonous. . . . We have never seen such joy of life as we saw in these children. . . . Miss Duncan, by her noble art, teaches us how this joy may be perpetuated and communicated to all.[16]

The program was Gluck's *Iphigenia in Aulis* and the little girls danced the choruses.

A member of the audience at the York Theatre on whom Isadora's performance made a profound impression was her compatriot Ruth St. Denis, who was then in Europe on tour.[17] Like Isadora, St. Denis had had to overcome the indifference and incomprehension of her fellow Americans to all forms of serious dance that were not the ballet. But whereas Isadora, having given up the unequal struggle on home ground, was dancing to public acclaim in Budapest in 1902, it took St. Denis, who had remained in America,[18] longer to win recognition. It was, in fact, not until March 6, 1906,[19] after giving a series of vaudeville performances to raise money, that she was able to present her first serious concert in New York, with the selections *Radha, The Cobras,* and *The Incense.* Later the same year,[20] she went abroad, where she met Isadora for the first time. By chance, a third American dancer, Maud Allan, an imitator of Isadora, was then appearing at the Palace Theatre Vaudeville and her presence was drawing away the crowds at the Duke of York Theatre. St. Denis later wrote:

> It is difficult to find words with which to pay tribute to the indescribable genius of Isadora. I can only say briefly that she evoked

in that pitifully small audience[21] visions of the morning of the world. She was not only the spirit of true Greece in her effortless, exquisitely modulated rhythms but she was the whole human race moving in that joy and simplicity and childlike harmony that we associate with Fra Angelico's angels dancing "the dance of the redeemed." Mary Fanton Roberts said years afterwards that "Isadora was Dionysiac and Ruth St. Denis Apollon," meaning that Isadora possessed the ecstatic liberation of the soul, which I translated into form, and it was some of this ecstatic quality of her soul that I received on this occasion, never to lose as long as I live. In one arm's movement was all the grace of the world, in one backward flying of the head was all nobility.[22]

The warm response of the public to her dancing was particularly gratifying to Isadora, since she vividly remembered "almost starving to death" in London eight years earlier. Her hopes of finding official patronage for her school soared when Queen Alexandra came to two of her concerts. The dancer was further encouraged when the Duchess of Manchester, eager for the school to settle in London, invited the American and her pupils to perform for King Edward and Queen Alexandra at the Duchess's country estate. The group received much praise, but nothing more tangible. Meanwhile, the school's expenses continued to mount, so Isadora, who had been appearing in London under the joint auspices of Charles and Joseph Schuman, decided to accept Frohman's offer of a contract to appear in the United States.

Regrettably, the influential Gerry Society would not permit the children of her school to perform in New York, so it was necessary to leave them behind, under Elizabeth's care, in Europe. A Mrs. W. E. Corey had generously lent her château (formerly the home of Emilie de Beauharnais, a niece of Josephine Bonaparte) to house the school.[23] The château was at La Verrière, forty minutes outside of Paris, and Isadora thought that the change in atmosphere would be beneficial for her pupils after "the somewhat confining influences of German life." She and Elizabeth were both tired of bureaucratic interference. "My sister was unwilling to be hampered any longer by the rules that are prescribed for all [German] schools," she told reporters. "Sometimes the red tape becomes very wearisome." At La Verrière, the girls had plenty of open space on which to dance on the grounds of the château and were still near enough to Paris to visit the Louvre and enjoy the city's other cultural advantages.

That the sojourn at La Verrière did not turn out as planned was not the fault of Isadora, though she was guilty of accepting too readily her sister's assurances that all was running smoothly. Elizabeth was then living in Paris with Deirdre in her charge. After leaving the little girls at the château under the supervision of their governess and a woman to cook their meals, Elizabeth, who was recovering from a personal loss, made no further visits to La Verrière.

Nor was Mrs. Corey in residence there. It was her mother, Mrs. Gilman, who decided that the girls would be better off living in a sparsely furnished building near the stables that had neither electricity nor plumbing. The children were not allowed inside the château—Mrs. Gilman feared for her parquet floors—and so they spent a lonely and depressing winter in Spartan surroundings. Eventually the disgusted governess left, and it was not until her replacement got in touch with Isadora that the girls were moved elsewhere. Their ultimate removal does not acquit Isadora—or Elizabeth—of the responsibility for the welfare of the children under their auspices.[24]

But these events were to take place much later, upon Isadora's return from America. She must now embark for New York, leaving behind her school, her little daughter, and Craig. She could be certain of a future reunion with her daughter and her pupils, but it must have been difficult for her to put an ocean between herself and Craig. Perhaps if she did find a millionaire to underwrite his work he would be able to forgive her. Perhaps too she could find a patron for her school. At any rate, she who had left for Europe on a cattle boat, an obscure dancer traveling on borrowed money, was returning to New York as an established artist with a European reputation. This time she would make New York take notice of her. The future of her school, and perhaps her reconciliation with Craig, depended upon her reception in America.

❧ 18 ❧

New York:
"Pure" Music and
the Dancer
1908

ISADORA arrived in New York in August and opened at the Criterion Theatre. In a city already satiated with Greek and classical dancers, it was an unfortunate time of year to hold what amounted to a New York debut. The audiences sweltered, but the critics remained tepid. *Variety,* already antagonized by the titles of her dances, some of which were given in French, spoke of the evening's "lofty pretensions to art." Isadora's performance was an "exposition—one could no more call it an entertainment than a public school lecture on Egyptology."[1] The more respectful *New York Evening Sun* noted: "Quite apart from the exquisite grace and beauty of her work, Miss Duncan displays powers of endurance that are quite phenomenal. . . . Unfortunately, the audience grows tired before she does."[2]

Mary Fanton Roberts, a writer and the editor of the magazines *The Craftsman* and *The Touchstone,* tells of going backstage after a performance of *Orpheus* and finding the dancer in tears, convinced by apathetic audiences and uncomprehending critics that she would never be a success in the United States.[3] Her unexpected praise heartened Isadora, and the two became lifelong friends.

Isadora also won the admiration and friendship of the sculptor George Grey Barnard, who introduced her to theater producer David Belasco, painters George Bellows and Robert Henri, and writer Max Eastman. The poets Edwin Arlington Robinson, Ridgeley Torrance, and William Vaughn Moody and the poet-playwright Percy MacKaye were others who gravitated to her circle. The public might be indifferent, but the artists quickly recognized her quality.

She had need of their encouragement, for she was becoming increasingly dissatisfied with Frohman's management. She felt that he had made a great mistake in presenting her as a Broadway attraction in midsummer[4] in the half-empty city—and with an inadequate orchestra. She became restive when, to recoup their losses, he sent her on a tour of the smaller cities with results even less rewarding at the box office.[5] She was reluctant to return to Europe with so little to show for her labors, and, with her friends urging her to stay in the United States, she decided to buy her way out of her contract with Frohman.[6]

She then took a studio in the Beaux Arts Building on West 40th Street overlooking Bryant Park. A reporter who came to interview her noted, "All unnecessary furniture had been removed, leaving only a tea table, a tabouret covered with photographs, and divans which are rolled about as desired."[7] In the post-Victorian world of knickknacks and heavy furniture, she had improvised a style of decoration that was simple, airy, and almost Japanese in its absence of clutter. Isadora hated clutter; she needed room in which to move. She herself was described as wearing "her short dark hair . . . parted simply, Madonna-like about her face . . . and coiled in a loose knot at the nape of her neck. She is five feet six and weighs one hundred and twenty-nine pounds." The reporter expressed surprise that she was not taller, for she looked "statuesque" on stage.

A reference to her young pupils showed why she felt the continuation of her school to be essential: "My children! . . . How could I hope to revive the lost art of dancing without their help? If I should die, if I should be disabled, who else would there be to carry on all the work on which I have spent all my years, all my resources?"

Soon she had cause to be glad that she had not returned to Europe. The conductor Walter Damrosch, whom she greatly admired, invited her to appear with him and the New York Symphony Orchestra. Isadora opened at the Metropolitan Opera House on November 6, 1908, [8] dancing Beethoven's *Seventh Symphony* to a full orchestra conducted by Damrosch. The house was completely sold out and this time, appearing in the fall season and accompanied by a first-rate musical organization, she was received with enthusiasm. Many critics, however, reacted to her choice of music with misgivings. The November *Musical Review* noted:

> Miss Duncan aims to "interpret Beethoven." To this end she has selected the 7th Symphony, "the apotheosis of the dance," as Wagner called it. And by doing that she invites serious people to a serious consideration of the question. She lays herself open to serious criticism, too. For she mutilates the symphony in that she does not employ it entire, taking only three movements,[9] and she uses the first movement of this monumental work as merely an introduction, dancing the other two movements. It is interesting, no doubt, but it scarcely brings Beethoven any nearer to the auditor. . . . Merely to see a single figure trip and pose through the length of two movements of the work is scarcely "interpreting" Beethoven.

In contrast, the critic of the November 11 *Musical Courier* declared, "Miss Duncan's share in this novel and beautiful program was delightful." And composer Reginald de Koven, writing in the *New York World,* stated, "I cannot better praise Miss Duncan's art than by saying that what she did was no infraction on the dignity and beauty of Beethoven's immortal work."

Isadora's dancing to the *Seventh Symphony* raises two issues—her musical understanding, and the propriety in general of dancing to music not specifically created for the dance. But first, perhaps, we must ask: Why should Isadora or anyone else *want* to dance the *Seventh Symphony?* What purpose could possibly be served by dancing it, or the *Pathétique,* or any other serious work?

The answer is found in examining Isadora's concept of the dance.

Dancing (*Théâtre de la Monnaie, Brussels*).

She felt that the dance must express *all* the great emotions, heroic as well as lyrical, not simply gaiety, flirtatiousness, yearning, love, but suffering, hatred, despair, resignation, courage, religious ecstasy. She could either dance such feelings without accompaniment or she must use music expressive of these emotions—in short, music by the great composers. She used the first alternative in her early composition, *Death and the Maiden,* but it was not a completely satisfactory solution, particularly for audiences accustomed to thinking of the dance simply as an entertainment. They needed the emotional clues provided by music. The possibility of commissioning music for her works seems not to have occurred to her. She had been familiar with the classical and romantic composers since childhood; furthermore, she was stimulated to creation by great music. Thus, it seemed natural to her to use it for her dances, even though she was aware that this solution was not wholly satisfactory.[10]

But let us return to the question of the propriety of dancing to music not specifically composed for the dance. First, it should be remarked that much concert music is written in dance form. Minuets, waltzes, sarabandes, mazurkas, gavottes, and the like legitimately fall into the dancer's province. Also music that has been designed for presentation on stage, as part of an opera, can be accepted as suitable for dancing since the composer expected it to be accompanied by some kind of visual action. Similarly, it is felt that where the composer has provided the work with a program (The Fantastic Symphony, Pictures at an Exhibition), his hints may justifiably be elaborated upon by a choreographer. The objections rise when "pure" music is used by the dancer. What are some of these objections?

First, that the composer did not intend the music to be danced, and this ignoring of his intentions is nothing short of sacrilege.

Second, that dancing can only distract the listener, preventing him from giving his undivided attention to the music.

Third, that dancing to the music implies that the composition is not complete in itself, that the composer's "meaning" is not fully set forth in the music but requires "interpretation." In providing interpretation, the choreographer superimposes his meaning on the meaning of the composer.

To take up the first of these objections, it may be true that the composer did not intend the music for dancing. At times composers have been known to grant permission for such use after seeing the work of a dancer (as Nevin did to Isadora), yet one can hardly hope for such dispensations from the dead. To many this must remain an unanswerable objection. Anyone who feels that it is sacrilege to dance to a particular composition had best stay away from the performance.

At the same time, it should be noted that music sometimes is used in ways not intended by the composer, without raising in us a feeling of sacrilege. Religious music is performed in the recital hall, ballet music is played without ballet, and operas are presented in concert form without benefit of costume, scenery, or acting. Why do these departures from the composer's intentions shock us so little? For one thing, we are accustomed to them. But there is a more important reason for our acceptance of these practices. Though elements of the complete work are missing, at least no new elements have been added which risk distorting the composer's meaning.

Distortion of the meaning, then, is the major crime we fear— having a work passed off as Beethoven's *Seventh,* when it is merely the capering about of Miss X, with Beethoven's music as background accompaniment. This being so, a test of the choreographer's success is the eloquence with which he or she has succeeded in conveying the composer's meaning.

I say "conveying" rather than "interpreting" because the word "interpreting" in this context is open to misunderstanding. It seems to imply that the dancer believes that the composer has not made his meaning clear and that it is up to the choreographer to help out. In short, it implies a patronizing attitude on the part of the choreographer, and it is against this imagined slight that music lovers react so strongly.

This was certainly not Isadora's attitude in dancing to music. "I am not a dancer," she once said, "I am there to make you *listen* to the music." She did not try to impose some program of her own on the composition; rather, she attempted to express its meaning, that is, to project in movement whatever joy, despair, or other emotion *lay in the music.* (There is notable exception to this—her choreography to Tchaikovsky's *Marche Slave,* in which she dances against the music.) If, as the American composer Roger Sessions said, "music is the gesture of the spirit," Isadora made the gesture visible.

Her understanding of the composer's intentions was far from superficial. As the critic of the *Post* wrote:

> People are apt to imagine Chopin all hues of melancholy. But Miss Duncan is an interpreter, and the gentle gaiety of her demeanor accorded with the familiar strains with a harmony that proved to demonstrate how wrong the cant acceptation of the composer is. People asked themselves, when they saw the long selection of Chopin numbers: "What can she do with them? Of what illustration are they susceptible?" Miss Duncan answered those questions with the completeness of a creative artist. There was nothing arbitrary about the evolutions which she associated with the music—nothing accidental. Miss Duncan was not merely filling out the music with a Terpsichorean accompaniment; she was realising the music through the medium of a sister art. . . . When the musician was sad, her movements—infinitely various, scrupulously simple—took their form from her mood. In one of the waltzes—probably it was the one in C sharp minor—she seemed the embodiment of one of the classic suppliants. She might have besought Creon for fated Antigone. She might have interceded for the Trojan captives. When she dances to the Valse in D Flat the mood was that of anticipation: She was the beloved of the Golden Age waiting for her lover. . . . She danced to some of the stately waltzes of Schubert and a Spanish dance of Moszkowski's as well as to Chopin, and so genuine, so documentary were her movements, that every musician present must have regretted that he did not bring the score with him and mark it with Miss Duncan's interpretations. She was Bacchic, but in the high inspirational Greek sense: the dance seemed in her to have come into its own again. We forget in these dull days of ours, that when Israel was in its prime, King David danced before the Ark of God.[11]

We should remember, too, that in Isadora's day dance recitals usually were reviewed by the music critic. Not a few found that her performances enlarged their understanding of compositions; eminent musicians reported the same experience.[12] Her feeling for the composer's form found expression in the structure of her dances. The *New York Tribune* noted: "Her appeal was as much to the mind as to the eye. She develops a theme as consistently as the composer she chooses to interpret. As the themes of Beethoven's *Allegretto* came and went they were caught into a new synthesis by the recurring movements and paces of the dancer. . . . The relations between the counterpoint and the figures of the dance were most lucid. Not only did they interpret. They translated."[13]

But, it may be asked, when composer and dancer are both saying the same things, is not the effect merely redundant? On the contrary, when the choreography is successful, there is a dialogue between music and dance, an interaction, an electricity which they generate that is not simply the result of adding one art to the other, but is also the stimulation of seeing how both compete, concur, and make the same statement in their separate ways. (This interaction accounts for much of the excitement of Balanchine's *Concerto Barocco,* set to Bach's *Double Violin Concerto.*) In such compositions, the relation of movement to sound manages to seem both inevitable and unexpected.

It should be said at once that a dance to a Beethoven symphony is not the original work, any more than a Shakespeare poem or play set to music and sung is the original poem or play. It is a separate work, and it must be judged separately. To many people, the idea of a classic recast in a new form is repellent. But the artist cannot stay away from the practice, for the arts are always cross-fertilizing one another. A great theme of literature may be exactly what a composer needs to express in his or her medium, and the fact that the theme is already known will make it possible to arrive at the heart of the statement more directly, wasting less time on the preliminaries, than if he or she were composing on an unknown theme. And it will make it easier for the public to grasp the composer's meaning. Thus, Craig, for all his feeling that *Hamlet* and *The*

St. Matthew Passion were complete in themselves, made designs for both, because the themes stirred him.[14] So it was not perversity that moved Isadora to compose dances to Beethoven's *Seventh Symphony* and Chopin's *Marche Funèbre*.

It must be added that Isadora had some technical grasp of music. Both Anna Duncan and the distinguished pianist George Copeland have assured me that the Californian could read an orchestral score. Victor Seroff, however, while not questioning Isadora's musical awareness, doubted that she could read music.[15]

One final remark about Isadora's musicality is necessary. As Allan Ross Macdougall so justly observed: "Though many of Isadora's detractors insisted that she had no musical culture, it is doubtful that without it musicians of the stature of Auer, Colonne, Damrosch, Ysaye, Thibaud, Messager, Gabrilovich and a host of others would have wasted a moment of their time even conversing with her, let alone placing their talents at her command."[16]

Her second program at the Metropolitan was *Iphigenia in Aulis,* a work that Gluck had designed for presentation on the stage. This time her performance aroused little controversy; indeed, her art met with widespread praise.[17]

In Boston, where she later danced *Iphigenia,* H.T.P., the critic of the *Boston Transcript,* wrote on November 28, 1908:

> The captivating quality of [her] motion is its innocence. No doubt behind Miss Duncan's dancing is some sort of technical system. . . . There is, however, no visible technique. . . . Rather it seems to spring spontaneously into being, to be the instinctive translation of the rhythm and . . . the mood of the music . . . in wholly natural movement. From the shore the Greek maidens see the approaching fleet; the joy of the sight wells in them and quickens their spirit. . . . Miss Duncan is . . . one of them. Her joy speaks in every motion of her body, in the play of her arms, in the carriage of her head, in the responsive flow and swirl of her draperies. The joy and the dance are as innocent, as free from self-consciousness as though there were no one to see. The buoyancy of her movement seems spontaneous and from within. . . .
>
> At the end of the evening she turned Bacchante to Strauss's waltz

of *The Blue Danube* and never was there more innocently sensuous Bacchante imparting the joy, the zest and the warmth of life that the music stirs within her. Her means were her body and its motions, and yet the impression was of disembodied and idealized sensuousness. So again with the sterner physical zest, the suggestion of the young barbarian in her *Scythian Dance* out of Gluck's opera. Each motion idealized the impulse that it would impart.

. . . She moves often in long and lovely sensuous lines across the whole breadth or down the whole depth of the stage. Or she circles it in curves of no less jointless beauty. As she moves, her body is steadily and delicately undulating. One motion flows or ripples or sweeps into another. . . . No deliberate crescendo and climax order her movements, rather they come and go in endless flow as if each were creating the next. . . . This pervading beauty springs most of all, perhaps, from the pervading lightness of Miss Duncan's movements. . . . [she] treads the stage as though it were the air. . . . Her dancing is as intangible, as unmaterial, as fluid as are sound and light. . . .

It is the custom to speak of absolute music—of music . . . that imparts nothing but itself, and that makes its own beauty and its own emotion . . . Miss Duncan's dancing is absolute dancing in a still fuller sense. It is peculiar to itself, it knows no rule and it has no customs except for those that she imposes. . . . It accomplishes its ends in seeming spontaneity and innocence. . . . It really achieves them—it is easy to suspect—by calculated, practical and reflective artistry.

What were some of the actual movements, still taught by Duncan teachers, which Isadora used in the dances to which the *Transcript* critic had reacted so strongly? Let us look at *Iphigenia: The Maidens Dance for Joy at the Sight of the Greek Fleet*—As the dance begins, the dancer holds her arms forward, raised above the shoulders, the palm of the lower hand held upward with fingers curved and the fingers of the upper hand poised lightly on them, while the front leg skips lightly, knee upraised. Then the body rocks back gently as the dancer skips on the back foot, before bringing it forward to skip in front. So, swaying forward and backward lightly, the dancer moves forward. Her arms meanwhile are upraised as she plays an imaginary

flute or trumpet. The arms are flung wide and hands brought together sharply to strike invisible cymbals. She skips upward, head
and arms raised, all her movements expressing joy. Next her lowering
arms swing wide as she strews unseen flowers from her skirt, then
she raises one arm as she rapidly circles her head with an invisible
wreath. None of this is mimicry; the gestures merely suggest.

The music has become a march, and the dancer, transformed into
a priestess, moves with measured steps, arms bent forward and
hands uplifted, bearing an offering. We see her climb the invisible
steps of the temple and raise her arms to make her sacrifice.

The joyful music returns and once again she skips forward, playing
the flute, striking the cymbals, strewing petals, and crowning her
head, as she rejoices at the sight of the Greek ships.

In the *Scythian Dance,* the dancer skips and, with arm upraised,
she makes a forceful downward stroke with her invisible spear.
Skipping on the other foot, with her other arm she makes the same
downward stroke. Then the arms come forward strongly holding
the spear upright.

At one point she leans forward, her weight on her bent knee and
her other leg stretched back, while, with the arm nearest the enemy,
she holds her shield to her body. The farther arm, upraised, with
hand clenched, is poised to hurl the spear down at her opponent.
Then her body recoils, and she sinks to her knee on her back leg
as she draws away from her enemy, while her forward leg is extended. Her forward arm raises her shield in front of her face and
her other hand, nearly on the ground, clutches her spear. Then,
with a sudden movement, she rises and flings her spear at her
opponent, who in turn falls back and sinks to the ground on her
back knee. Unlike the undulating movements in the welcome to
the Greek fleet, the movements here are strong, forceful, abrupt,
though graceful, and are suitable to her subject.*

(The descriptions above should provide a taste of Isadora's work;
Nadia Chilkovsky has recorded the exact movements of Isadora's

---

*Isadora danced the *Scythian Dance* as a solo. Later, her six pupils would dance it all together
in pairs. They also danced the welcome to the Greek fleet as a group.

compositions in *The Dances of Isadora Duncan,* published by the Dance Notation Bureau. Isadora's choreography can also be seen in the classes of those Duncan teachers who studied with her original pupils.)

At last in her own country, at the age of thirty-one, Isadora had the satisfaction of being a critical and popular success. She had finally begun to make a great deal of money. "At her fourth matinee," said the *New York Evening Sun* on January 1, 1909, ". . . the receipts exceeded $4800," and the takings in Boston were equally large. In Washington, no less a person than President Theodore Roosevelt came to her concert and afterwards expressed his delight in her art.

Although recognition was sweet, Isadora was not wholly satisfied with the results of her American visit. She had failed to find a backer for her school, which she estimated cost her a yearly $10,000 to run, and her recent profits were offset by her losses in August, when she was making so little that she had had to send to Europe for money with which to live. When she sailed for France on the thirtieth of December, 1908, to dance with the Lamoureux Orchestra at the Trocadéro in Paris, she had the satisfaction of having signed a contract to tour the United States with Damrosch and the New York Symphony Orchestra for five months of the coming year. Nonetheless, she had decided that as soon as she was back in Paris she would have to disband her school. She could not keep up deficit financing indefinitely. If only some millionaire would step forward . . .

❧ 19 ❧

Singer,
Stanislavski, and Craig
1909

N Paris, Isadora was met by Elizabeth, her pupils, and her daughter, now slightly over two years old. She had not been able to refrain from mentioning Deirdre to American reporters, though the child was always discreetly identified as "our youngest pupil, a daughter of Gordon Craig."

Craig seems to have dropped out of her life at this period. Before sailing from Europe in August, she had begged him to telegraph her about seeing her off, but she had neglected to enclose her address, apparently in despair of hearing from him. When she returned to Paris, he was still living in Florence and working on his magazine, *The Mask*.

Isadora's new manager, Lugné-Poë, who was also the manager of Duse and a friend of both women, had arranged for Isadora and her students to give a series of concerts with the Colonne Orchestra at the Théâtre Lyrique de la Gaité. These performances were immensely successful. "She is nature itself," commented the *Guide*

Musicale. "Hers is an extremely studied art, but an art which has arrived at such a degree that [artifice] has disappeared completely in spontaneity and naturalness . . . [She moves] in a continual and charming harmony, with a lightness that is incomparably supple and graceful. . . . Her little pupils are of a litheness and sweetness altogether rare."[1]

One afternoon at the theater, as Isadora was sitting in her dressing room, her maid presented her with a calling card on which the dancer read the name "Paris Eugene Singer." She remembered, "Suddenly there sang in my brain, 'Here is my millionaire!' "

An imposing man entered, six feet six inches tall, with curling blond hair and beard. Isadora thought to herself, "Lohengrin." He spoke to her graciously, but Isadora was troubled by the feeling of having met him before. Then she remembered that he had been at the funeral of the Prince de Polignac, one of her early patrons in Paris, in whose salon she had often danced. The Princesse de Polignac was one of Singer's sisters, as was the Duchesse Decazes, another early patron of Isadora. Following this meeting, Singer, an heir to the sewing-machine fortune, offered to underwrite the expenses of the school, so that Isadora would be free to teach and to compose new dances. With his characteristic generosity, he proposed to send the school to Beaulieu, near Nice, where the dancer and her young charges could rest and work in the sunshine of the French Riviera.

Paris Singer was then a commanding man of forty-one, with charm and aristocratic manners and bearing. His father, Isaac Merritt Singer, one of the inventors of the sewing machine,[2] had died when his son was still a child, and the boy had been reared as a ward of the British court. His upbringing and fortune allowed him to move in the upper ranks of English society—he was, indeed, a friend of Queen Alexandra[3] and his sisters' marriages had connected him with the French aristocracy. He had married in England, where he had been educated, and he was the father of five children. At first glance, his background could not have seemed more different from the Bohemian, often hand-to-mouth, upbringing of the young Duncans. But, in fact, their childhoods had one important point of similarity. Both the Duncans and the Singers had a sense of skeletons in the

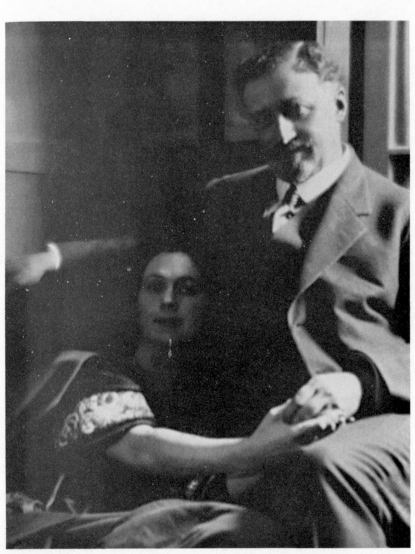

Isadora with Paris Singer, photograph by Arnold Genthe (*Museum of the City of New York*).

closet, old scandals that had rocked their families. If the Duncans had the bank failure of their father and their parents' divorce to contend with, the boyhood of Singer had been marked by a lawsuit of sensational nature.

Isaac Merritt Singer had died when his son, Paris, was eight, leaving "an estate valued at between 13 and 15 million dollars."[4] The boy's mother, Isabella, who was Isaac's second wife, was the only woman to benefit under the will. The first wife, Catherine Haley Singer, and one of his mistresses, Mary Ann Sponsler, the mother of ten of his children, brought suit to contest the will. The litigation was protracted, and, although it ended in a victory for the second Mrs. Singer, it revealed much about Isaac Singer's character and domestic arrangements which must have been painful for all branches of the family. "In an age of prudery, his uninhibited private life startled two continents. He married twice, maintained three mistresses and begot, in and out of wedlock, twenty-four children."[5]

The inventor had lived lavishly on a grand scale. His carriages were custom-built. "One of them, an enormous barouche, contained a lady's dressing room. Another could accommodate thirty-one passengers and had a bandstand near the rear. It took six to nine horses to pull it."[6] When he was in his fifties, he had married the 21-year-old Isabella Eugenie Boyer Summerville, an attractive divorcée of French and English parentage,[7] who was as different as possible from her flamboyant husband. One writer has characterized Singer as "vain and contentious. He quarreled with practically everybody who opposed his [wishes], frequently threatening bodily damage."[8] The repercussions of the lawsuits and their attendant publicity on his young widow and children can well be imagined.

This, then, was the background of the man who had come to Isadora's assistance. Paris Singer liked to "keep up" with the arts as befitted a man of his social position, and he was not without artistic aspirations himself, as the plaque reading "P. E. Singer, Architect" on the rear door of his Cadogan Square house[9] bore witness. Furthermore, he was an impulsive and generous person who shared Isadora's enjoyment of doing things on a large scale.

He swiftly transported Isadora's entire school and its delighted founder to Beaulieu. He himself was staying nearby at Nice, but he was a constant visitor at the school's villa, seeing to it that the young pupils had everything they needed for their comfort. His kindness and generosity won Isadora's gratitude and friendship. This consideration for the children sparked a glow of warm feeling in Isadora; indeed, she felt herself strongly attracted to him.

Not long after the move to Beaulieu Singer proposed that Isadora and her child take a vacation with him. But what was she to do meanwhile with the pupils of her school? To Isadora it seemed an appropriate moment to let the little girls, who had not been home for more than four years,[10] take a holiday with their families. Afterwards, Elizabeth and the governess of the school could be counted on to take charge of the children until Isadora had completed the organization of her school in Paris. Thus it was that Isadora casually transferred her young dancers to the care of her sister and of the new and, in some ways, rival institution that Elizabeth was setting up in Darmstadt; it did not occur to Isadora that Elizabeth and her musical director, Max Merz, would balk at returning her star pupils.[11]

So the little girls left for a joyful reunion with their families, while Isadora, Deirdre, and Singer boarded his yacht and sailed for the Italian coast.

Isadora wrote that during this voyage she and Singer had their first quarrel. Isadora was reading him her favorite poem, Whitman's *Song of the Open Road.*

Carried away by my enthusiasm, I did not notice what effect this was having, and when I looked up I was astonished to find his [Singer's] handsome face congested with rage.

"What rot!" he exclaimed. "That man could never have earned his living!"

"Can't you see," I cried, "he had the vision of a free America?"

"Vision be damned!"

And suddenly I realized that his vision of America was that of the dozens of factories which made his fortune for him.[12]

Whether or not this is a fair interpretation of Singer's thought, it is evident that his upbringing as a member of the privileged classes and its effect on his views were a source of friction between him and Isadora. Far from trying to gloss over their differences, it seemed that Isadora sometimes felt an unconscious need to goad him, as if to demonstrate that she could not be bought by gifts. Perhaps what bothered her was his attitude that money must always be earned as a reward for achievement. Yet *he* had never had to earn it. He had been born rich, while *she* had had to struggle to make her way. But if she could not be bought, she could be swayed by love, so their quarrels ended in reconciliations.

Isadora and Singer had to interrupt their vacation so that she could fulfill her contract to reappear at the Théâtre Lyrique de la Gaîté early that summer, before setting out for a brief tour of Russia. Singer accompanied her to Paris, but, fearing passport difficulties,[13] he remained behind while she went on tour.

In Russia, her path crossed that of Craig, who was there because of forces that she herself had set in motion. On a previous visit, she had spoken enthusiastically of Craig's work to her friend Stanislavski with the result that Craig had been invited to stage *Hamlet* for the Moscow Art Theatre. This production, not unveiled until 1912, was to prove epoch-making in the history of the modern theater. Isadora, who had never ceased to love Craig, was for a short moment "on the verge of believing that nothing mattered— neither the school, nor Lohengrin, nor anything but the joy of seeing [Craig] again."[14] But, as she was now committed to Singer, she tried not to allow the sway of other feelings to interfere with their relationship.

Their reunion in Russia ended in typically stormy fashion. Isadora tells us that "On the last evening, when we were just leaving for Kieff [sic], I gave a little dinner [in her suite] to Stanislavski, Craig and the secretary. In the middle of dinner, Craig asked me if I meant to remain with him or not. As I could not answer, he flew into one of his old-time rages, lifted the secretary from the chair, carried her into the other room, and locked the door."

Craig told it differently. In his account, Craig says Isadora ". . . tried to make me jealous by flirting in the most Café de Paris manner with poor horrified Stanislavski . . ."[15] And in his copy of Isadora's autobiography, *My Life,* Craig has noted: "She was all this time . . . kissing poor Stanislavski. I was of a mind to suffer but of two minds & decided *not* to suffer. So catching up the only other lady present I rushed her off and I closed the door. There we found the other room dark so no one can say, least of all I, what happened. I'm hanged if I'll say we sat stiff & dumb and looked at a picture book."

What did happen Craig told more completely in *Book Topsy.*[16] After he and the secretary disappeared into the bedroom of Isadora's suite, they listened behind the locked door while their hostess tried the handle, then they crept out by another door, went for a sleigh ride, and came back and registered at Isadora's hotel where they spent the night together. Late the following morning, the secretary, fearful of losing her job or of being left behind in St. Petersburg, dressed hurriedly and went to find the dancer. Craig lunched alone, and remembering that both women were due to catch their train, met them in the hall as they emerged to seat themselves in the waiting sledge. "As I helped to arrange the rugs I could not help saying [to Isadora] with polite smiles that I hoped she had passed a pleasant evening anyhow. [!] To this she said neither a yea or a nay, but, as was her custom when utterly bouleversé [sic], she uttered a brief sermon—said she, 'Try to emulate the virtues of the good *good* man with whom we supped last night,' and signing to the coachman to jolly well drive on she drove away. . . . Anyhow, off she went by train to join Paris Singer, her millionaire in whose millions she so thoroughly believed & whose millions she came to curse."

It seems probable that it was the thought of the waiting Singer and his money, even more than Isadora's obvious flirting with Stanislavski, that enraged Craig and provoked his retaliation. That Isadora had been looking forward to seeing Ted for the first time since their break a year and a half before, and that she must have anticipated a happy reunion—since, after all, it was she who had urged Stanislavski's invitation to Craig—apparently never occurred to him.

He did notice, fleetingly, that Isadora was utterly overwhelmed *(bouleversée)*, but the cause of her pain or of her flirting with Stanislavski was never consciously admitted by Craig.

Thus, at the end of her engagement in Kiev, Isadora returned, not to Craig in Moscow, but to the French capital. Here, she stayed with Singer at his apartment on the Place des Vosges, until the time came for her to leave for the United States and her second tour with Walter Damrosch.

This American tour reinforced the favorable impression that Isadora had made the year before. "When one says 'dances' one means not a dance of the feet only . . . but of the whole body," wrote *The Philadelphia North American*. "Miss Duncan dances as much with her gracile hands as do the Japanese, and she dances above all *with her brain*." [Italics mine.] And the critics who had formerly questioned the propriety of her costumes now found themselves siding with her against the philistines. *Musical America* voiced indignation because "a protesting bevy of Pittsburgh Sunday school teachers" had visited the Art Society, under whose auspices Isadora would be appearing in Pittsburgh, to ask "if Miss Duncan danced in bare feet" (bare feet presumably being a euphemism for scanty and immoral attire): "A vast Puritocracy—to coin the word—is the greatest obstacle to artistic growth in America."[17] The pioneering example of Isadora (and of another young dancer, Ruth St. Denis) was at last beginning to make an impact on accepted notions of decency in art and the dance.

In September, Isadora became aware that she was pregnant again; nevertheless, she decided to continue with her scheduled tour. It cannot be determined whether Singer accompanied her. The frequently inaccurate *My Life* says that he did and that he was "wild with excitement" at the prospect of visiting the United States, which he had never seen. Macdougall, in his biography of the dancer, says that Singer remained in France,[18] but the writer does not give any documentation for his statement. Since the passenger lists of the *George Washington*, on which Isadora sailed,[19] and the guest lists of her hotel, the Plaza in New York,[20] no longer exist, there is no way to settle the matter.

At any rate, we know that Isadora began her tour in Cleveland on October 10 and that she swung through the Middle West. In St. Louis, where she appeared at a charity benefit, she encountered problems. The "Rev. Dr. Fayette L. Thompson, pastor of Lidell Avenue Methodist Episcopal Church . . . delivered a scathing denunciation of Isadora Duncan. . . . Dr. Thompson without mincing words put her on a level with a midway dancer, said her show was beneath the character of a burlesque theatre, and called for police interference. After the sermon, Dr. Thompson told a reporter he did not attend the performance."[21] The minister's stand immediately came under fire from St. Louis society women, one of whom, Mrs. E. R. Hoyt commented, "Only an obscene mind could see anything vulgar in Isadora Duncan's dance." This was reported with glee by The Kansas City Post,[22] which was delighted to find such evidence of provincialism and dissension in a rival city.

If the Rev. Dr. Thompson later troubled to read the reviews of Isadora's subsequent appearances, he must have noted with surprise that the music in Iphigenia was found to be "particularly fitted" in its "nobility and lack of sensuousness to accompany the moods and poses which Miss Duncan portrays in her dances."[23] This appearance was in New York where Isadora gave a performance of Iphigenia in Aulis at the Metropolitan Opera House on the evening of November 9. Another reporter who attended the same concert observed, "In seeing Miss Duncan after a space of time, and especially seeing her in the same dances one realizes . . . how certain effects which one observed at first were not chances of the moment but the result of conscious artistic development which knew what it was about."[24] In short, for all the apparent spontaneity of her dances, they were carefully composed and performed with consummate technique. If this seems stating the obvious, still it must be said, for the notion persists that Isadora was an inspired amateur and that her dancing was merely "self-expression with a length of chiffon." If the latter were true, how can one account for the fact that only those of her imitators who had received dance training had any degree of success—and their successes were short-lived compared to hers—yet the means she used, chiffon included, were presumably available to everyone? As for her professional status, if teaching and founding a school, appearing before audiences since childhood, and supporting herself by public appearances are marks of the amateur, then it is the term for Isadora.

During her second concert at the Metropolitan, Isadora danced Beethoven's *Seventh Symphony,* a performance attended with mixed feelings by Carl Van Vechten, then music critic for *The New York Times.*

> It is quite within the province of the recorder of musical affairs to protest against this perverted use of *the 7th Symphony.* . . . However if one takes it for granted that Miss Duncan has a right to perform her dances to whatever music she chooses there is no doubt of the high effect she achieves. Seldom has she been more poetical, more vivid in her expression of joy, more plastic in her poses, more rhythmical in her effects than she was yesterday. . . . As usual she was most effective in dances which require decisive movement. One of the wildest of her dances she closed with arms outstretched and head thrown back almost out of sight until she resembled the headless Nike of Samothrace.[25]

Isadora had apparently intended to continue touring until the beginning of 1910. One day, however, a woman from the audience chided her on the obviousness of her approaching motherhood. The lady "came into my loge exclaimed: 'But, my dear Miss Duncan, it's plainly visible from the front row. You can't continue like this.'

"And I replied, 'Oh, but my dear Mrs. X., that's just what I mean my dancing to express—Love—Woman—Formation—Spring-time. Botticelli's picture, you know. The fruitful earth—the three dancing Graces *enceinte*—the Madonna—the Zephyrs *enceinte* also. Everything rustling, promising New Life. That is what my Dance means.'

"At this, Mrs. X. looked quizzical."[26]

Shortly thereafter, Isadora decided that her pregnancy was too far advanced for her to continue dancing, so, on December 2, she gave her farewell performance at Carnegie Hall before a very large audience.[27]

A few days later, on December 8, she sailed for Europe. She was accompanied by Augustin (who had just separated from his wife),[28] and his daughter Temple, a pupil at Isadora's school. She was feeling discouraged: not only had Loie Fuller given a well-received program which drew too heavily, Isadora thought, on the Duncan style, but the Metropolitan Opera Company, ignoring the fact that Gluck's music had long been in her repertory, had hired a Russian imitator of hers to arrange the dances for their next season's presentation of *Orfeo*. Speaking to reporters who came to see her off, she sounded doubtful about returning to America the next year, if ever.[29]

But this was only a temporary depression. Isadora's American tour had been successful. She was in love. And she was on her way back to France to see her cherished Deirdre. She and Singer planned to take the little girl with them on a sail up the Nile to pass the remaining months before the baby was born. Augustin and Temple would be in the party too. Her ship had at last moved into sheltered waters, and bright unruffled days lay smoothly before her.

Isadora on Paris Singer's yacht *(New York Public Library)*.

Paris Singer at the wheel of his yacht
(New York Public Library).

Deirdre on Paris Singer's
yacht on the Nile, 1910
(New York Public Library).

Isadora riding a donkey
in Egypt *(New York Public
Library)*.

Portrait by Otto, Paris, 1912 (*New York Public Library*).

Isadora and Hener Skene, 1913
*(Mme. Mario Meunier–Christine Dalliès
Collection)*.

Isadora and a French officer during the Great War (*Mme. Mario
Meunier–Christine Dalliès Collection*).

Isadora at the door of Bellevue
(*Mme. Mario Meunier—Christine Dalliès Collection*).

Isadora and a French officer, 1914, thanking her for lending Bellevue as a hospital to the French government (*Mme. Mario Meunier—Christine Dalliès Collection*).

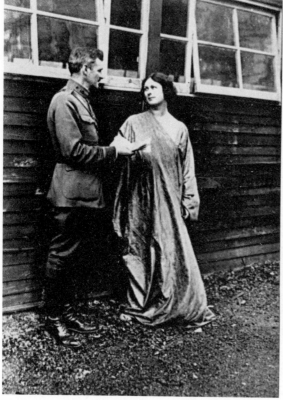

Anna Duncan, one of the Isadorables, photograph by Arnold Genthe in New York in 1915
(*Museum of the City of New York*).

The six original pupils of Isadora Duncan, photograph by Arnold Genthe
in New York in 1915. From left to right, Thérèse (Maria Theresa), Irma,
Lisa, Anna, Erica, and Margot (Gretel) (*Museum of the City of New York*).

Portrait by Arnold Genthe, May 31, 1916 (*Museum of the City of New York*).

Isadora and Walter Rummel in Bellevue, 1918 (*Mme. Mario Meunier—Christine Dalliès Collection*).

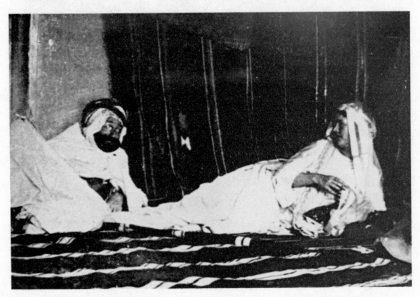

Isadora in Algeria (*Mme. Mario Meunier—Christine Dalliès Collection*).

❧ 20 ❧

Life with Lohengrin
1910–1912

N early 1910, Isadora, cruising up the Nile, sent two letters to her friend Mary Fanton Roberts in New York:[1]

Jan. 25, 1910
Luxor Winter Palace

Dearest Mary:

It is all so Heavenly and Wonderful I can't in any way get reconciled to the idea of your not being here—It is beyond any thing that I have ever dreampt [sic] or read or imagined—We have sailed up the Nile as far as Aswan seeing all the wonders and Glories on the way and now we return to Cairo—but we will not leave Egypt until the end of March. If you could only come over—if only for the Month of March! I received your dear letter it was forwarded to Luxor. Thank you—that in the midst of all your busy life you still find time to write to me. In comparison, I feel so lazy but in this boat the days and the banks of the Nile glide by like a dream—

and the great Temples and Monuments also seem like the conjuring of some Geni [sic] and not at all real. Do try if by some Miracle you can manage to come for the month of March. We are going to start up the Nile again from Cairo and you could easily join us then. Do try—and if not you will come with us another year—for this experience is too lovely to end, this year—we will surely come again.[2]

Our address till end of March will be c/o Cooks Cairo. Write me a line.

With all my Heart's Love to you and Love to Billy—your friend

Isadora

Dahabeah "Horus"—Cook's Dahabeahs on the Nile

Dearest Mary:

No word from you. Write me a line to say you are well—and did you recieve [sic] the letter & photos? We are sailing from Egypt March 8. So address me c/o Cooks Nice—where I will be during April and probably some part of May.

Will you tell me what impression is Miss [Maud] Allan making in America—the Boston and Chicago critics that Mr. Coburn[3] sent us proclaim her work as far superior to mine. If that is true I can cheerfully retire from the stage. Mary Sturges was to be in New York again for a short time at the Plaza did you meet her? Perhaps she is there still—but I think more likely on her way back—We are all in Good Health and happy but I guess Gus will give you all the news quicker than this letter—he sails back on the 22nd. I have never ceased to regret your not being with us. Well perhaps another time—Did Pavlova dance at the Met. If so I hope you have seen her. She is Wonderful.[4]

Give my love to Billy and remember me to all friends. With all my love to you.

Isadora

In March, they returned to the French Riviera to await the birth of the baby. Singer amused himself buying up land on Cap Ferrat, where he intended to build a great Italian castle. . . . I remained calmly in the garden by the blue sea, pondering on the strange difference which divides life from Art, and often wondering if a woman can really be an artist, since Art is a hard task-master who demands everything. Whereas a woman who loves gives up everything to life. At any rate . . . I was for the second time, completely separated and immobilized from my Art.[5]

At the Villa Augusta in Beaulieu, Isadora's son was born on May 1, 1910. This time the birth was an easy one. The child was registered at the town hall of Beaulieu as Patrick Augustus Duncan.[6] His parents were delighted with him, and Isadora wrote to her "dear and Great master," the philosopher, Ernst Haeckel: "My baby . . . is strong and sweet. I am just about to give him the breast. He takes up every minute of my free time but when he looks at me with his blue eyes I feel royally repaid."[7]

Shortly thereafter, they moved for the summer to the Trianon Palace Hotel in Versailles. Here Isadora and Singer gave a party for approximately fifty friends. One of them, Georges Maurevert, later wrote an account of the evening:

> The Colonne Orchestra [had been] specially engaged for the occasion. Thus, reclining in comfortable chairs . . . under the tall trees . . . we heard, as a sort of apéritif, Gluck's *Iphigenia* and Wagner's *Forest Murmurs*. . . . It was a wonderful beginning . . .
>
> Dinner did not lack charm, served under a vast tent, furiously battered by rain which luckily did not succeed in penetrating the thick canvas. At the little table where I seated myself I had . . . for neighbors Mlle Marie LeConte of the Comédie Française; Mr. Nijinsky, the young Russian dancer who is at present giving beautiful evenings at the Opéra; Mr. Henry Russell, the director of the Metropolitan [Opera House] of New York, who took advantage of the opportunity to make an engagement with Mr. Diaghilev, Nijinsky's manager. . . . At the other tables I noticed MM. Paul Marguerite, d'Humières, Lugné-Poë, Pierre Mille, René Blum, the deputy Paul-Boncour, d'Estournelles de Constant, . . . etc. . . . . . A noisy and joyful dinner, completely devoid of cant or arrogance.

When cigars were served, the cloth of the tent was rolled back and the garden appeared to us magically illuminated, with globes of all shades glimmering through the trees, and the lawns bordered with goblets of light...

And what joy... to see, circling about, to the sound of gypsy music, on the paths and the lawns, Miss Isadora herself, sometimes leaping under her white veils and fleeing toward distant groves, sometimes triumphant as the Victory of Samothrace, or grave as an antique suppliant incarnating the most troubling phrases of Schumann or Godard, Grieg or Beethoven...

The paths were damp and the lawns wet... the feet of Miss Isadora, protected only by sandals with gold straps, were otherwise bare...[8]

After Isadora's recital, the guests waltzed to the strains of a dance orchestra until the small hours of the morning.

Paris Singer was not present at this fête. He had gone to London for a few days, and there, a few hours before he was supposed to leave, he had been felled by a stroke. From the Hotel Capitol in St. James Square, where she hurried to join him, Isadora sent a note to Mary Fanton Roberts.

Thursday, July 7, [1910]

Dear Mary:

I am over in London for a few days with Paris he came over here and fell ill so I came to fetch him and then fell ill too—now we are both better and returning to France on Sunday We left Deirdre and the Baby at Hotel Trianon at Versailles. Paris is very anxious to know if you are coming to stay with us at Panginton [Paignton, Devonshire] in September? Afterwards we might run down to Venice [unclear] in October. Do come. We will have a glorious time. Gus and the Coburns are coming over. You could come on the same boat—you and Billy—Write me as soon as you recieve [sic] this and tell me what *date* you can come.

You will adore the Baby. He is perfectly Beautiful and seems to have the sweetest character. I am unhappy at being away from him even these few days. He looks like Paris—only his nose is turned up like mine—I gave a fete last week at Versailles. Had the Colonne Orchestra playing in the garden and dinner at little tables in a tent— it was a great success only I was desperate because Paris had fallen ill here in London & couldn't come.

Write me soon and tell me what date you sail.

Love to Billy and all my love to you.

Isadora.[9]

Paignton, in Devonshire, was the location of Singer's country estate, and here the lovers came at the end of the summer with a party of friends. This country sojourn was to be in the nature of an experiment. Isadora tells us that Singer was eager to marry her but that she felt marriage would not be practical; surely he would not be content to follow her around if she had to go on tour. But, he protested, she would not be under the financial necessity of touring if they married. Hoping to convince her, he asked her to Paignton to give her a taste of the life she would have as his wife.

It rained constantly. The house was full of guests, and the daily program was leisurely, but formal. According to Isadora's description of life among the English, they rise early and eat a hearty breakfast, after which "they don mackintoshes and go forth into the humid country until lunch, when they eat many courses . . . From lunch to five o'clock they are supposed to be busy with their correspondence though I believe they really go to sleep."[10] Then tea, and, after tea, some desultory bridge "until it is time to proceed to the really important business of the day—dressing for dinner, at which they appear in full evening dress . . . to demolish a twenty course dinner. When this is over, they engage in some light political conversation or touch upon philosophy until the time comes to retire. You can imagine whether this life pleased me or not. In the course of a couple of weeks I was positively desperate."[11]

Isadora's restlessness was increased by the fact that Singer, who had been seriously ill, still had a doctor and nurse staying with him. Isadora wrote: "They were both very emphatic as to my line of conduct. I was placed in a far-away room at the other end of the house, and told that on no account was I to disturb [him]."[12]

According to her account in *My Life,* Isadora was resolved to work, and so she wired Colonne, head of the Colonne Orchestra with which she had often danced in Paris, asking him to send an accompanist. To her dismay, the pianist who arrived was a man whom she knew to be in love with her and for whom she felt a strong physical aversion. She greeted him with the words, "How is it possible that Colonne has sent you? He knows that I hate and detest you." For several days, she practiced dancing while the accompanist played for her behind a screen, because she could not bear to look at him. When a friend reproved her for treating him so badly, Isadora relented and asked the friend and the musician to go with her for a drive. As they were returning, the car hit a rut, and Isadora was thrown into the accompanist's arms. "I . . . looked at him and suddenly felt my whole being going up in flames like a pile of lighted straw. . . . How had I not seen it before? His face was perfectly beautiful . . ."[13] When the pair returned to the house, the pianist drew her behind the convenient screen in the ballroom.

Victor Seroff, who knew Isadora very well in the latter part of her life, says that Isadora told him the anecdote in a different form, to illustrate her belief that music can transform an ugly performer into a beautiful person. To her, the musician, André Capelet,[14] was a striking illustration of this phenomenon. The screen and the automobile ride were not part of this story as told to Seroff, however, and he doubted that Isadora would have greeted Capelet with the words set down in *My Life.* "Whatever else could have been criticized in her character, charming and gracious behavior as a hostess was her special quality."[15]

From that moment, the two constantly sought to be alone together. But, as Isadora remarked, "These violent passions have violent ends." Eventually, word of the changed state of affairs reached their host, and the musician had to leave. We are left to guess Singer's view of the matter, but Isadora commented with irony: "This episode proved to me I certainly was not suited to domestic life."

She returned to the French capital, and here, at the beginning of

1911, she appeared at the Châtelet Theatre in the dances she had been working on in England to music by Gluck and Wagner.

These dances formed the chief part of her two programs at Carnegie Hall in February of 1911, when she opened her American season in New York. Her first recital, on February 15, 1911, included the Air and two gavottes for Bach's *Suite in D* and four works to music by Wagner—*The Flower Maidens* from *Parsifal* ("ideal and fitting music for such ideal dancing"),[16] *The Bacchanale* from *Tannhäuser* (performed, "though scarcely with sufficient wildness . . ."),[17] *The Dance of the Apprentices* from *Meistersinger* ("One of the most charming of Miss Duncan's achievements"),[18] and finally, the *Liebestod* from *Tristan und Isolde,* placed at the end of the program, so that those who did not wish to see the work (since it was not intended by the composer for dance) could leave beforehand. However, few took advantage of the opportunity to walk out.

The second program, on the afternoon of February 20 (which, like the first, was presented with Walter Damrosch as the conductor of the New York Symphony Orchestra), was notable because it included Isadora's first performance in the United States of the two *Dances of the Furies,* as part of her nearly complete version[19] of Gluck's *Orfeo.* These two dances, first given at the Châtelet Theatre on January 18, 1911,[20] show the development of an element in Isadora's choreography which was to have a profound effect on the modern dance—that is, the use of ugliness and weightiness for the sake of expression. She had already used ugliness for dramatic effect in the early *Death and the Maiden* (spasmodic movement and rigidity of the limbs as Death overtakes the dancer), but there it served as a contrast to the predominantly graceful gestures of the girl. In *The Dances of the Furies,* it dictated the character of the whole dance. The Furies (and Isadora embodied the infernal multitudes in her single person) were at once the damned and their tormentors—lost souls painfully striving to lift great rocks onto their shoulders, and their guardians jealously patrolling the entrance to the underworld. Their undirected prowling suggests suspicion and uneasiness. They know not where Orpheus will appear nor how he threatens them, but, stirred to dim memories of pity by his music, they are all the more determined to destroy him. Their movements are powerful and ungainly—with elbows out, fingers like claws, faces contorted with rage, mouths open in a silent scream. Sometimes, their hands are bound behind their backs, and, at other times, their freed arms writhe snakelike at the intruder. Their knees are strong and pliant. All their movements express tremendous force under constraint, conveying a sense of greater inner than outer speed. When Orpheus has passed between them, they renew their assaults with redoubled anger, but now there is a feeling of desperation—almost pathos—about their rage. They know they are defeated, for they seem to sense that love has brought Orpheus to the gates of Hades. It is their very inability to love which makes them Furies. Vanquished but unappeased, in a gesture of impotent ire they bend their heads as if to beat them against the floor, sweeping the ground with their hair. It is a work which, performed even today, has the power to purge the spectator with pity and terror.

We understand why it moves us when we compare Isadora's Furies to the evil spirits in Balanchine's *Firebird*. Despite superficial similarities, such as pouncing leaps and clawlike hands, Balanchine's Furies and evil spirits produce a completely different effect, understandably, since the choreographer's purposes are completely different. Balanchine's evil spirits are menaces appropriate to a fairy-tale ballet: they are inhuman and grotesque.* Isadora's Furies are something more than monsters. They are tragic, damned souls, who once were capable of salvation, and now are anguished as well as vengeful. It is our sense of their dual nature that involves us with them emotionally, as we cannot be by fairy-tale demons.

In this composition, then, Isadora's choreography stressed weightiness, resistance, and strength. In her essay, *The Dance of the Future,* she complained that the ballet strove for an impression of weightlessness, as if gravity did not exist. Her Furies, on the contrary, fling

---

*Balanchine's spirits for his *Orpheus* to Stravinski's music are shades, sleepwalkers, devoid of strength or emotion. Tormented furies would be out of place with this music. It would be instructive to see the choreography Balanchine devised to Gluck's *Orpheus*. Unfortunately, this work was performed for only one season in New York.

themselves to the ground and rise with difficulty, they bend under the effort of lifting huge burdens, and they beat with clenched fists against invisible walls. All is heaviness and weight, just as all is lightness and ease in the dance that follows in *Orfeo, The Dance of the Happy Spirits*. For Isadora, the determining factor in a choice of movements was not ugliness or beauty, nor even naturalness or unnaturalness (for the movements of the Furies are deliberately contorted as befits their deformed natures): it is, rather, *expressiveness*. The characteristic style of the modern dance, with a stress on tension and the overcoming of resistance, made its first full-fledged appearance in *The Dance of the Furies*. Quite apart from its seminal influence, *The Furies*—indeed, the entire choreography for *Orfeo*—is a great work.

After this concert, Isadora made appearances in Boston, Washington, St. Louis, and other cities before giving a farewell performance in New York on the last night of March.[21]

During this American tour, Isadora formed a warm friendship with the singer David Bispham. "He came to all my representations and I went to all his recitals, and afterwards at my suite at the Plaza we would have supper and he would sing to me . . . and we laughed and embraced and were delighted with each other."[22]

But Isadora could not be completely happy with Bispham and her other friends in America, however. She longed to be back in Paris with her children. Deirdre had written to her (in French):

Dear Mama

We are well. When are you coming home? Patrick is playing music. I had a good time at the circus. I know how to read and write now.

I kiss you.

Deirdre

At the bottom of the page, someone had helped Patrick to print in straggly letters "Mama, I kiss you."[23]

When she returned to France in April, she was joyously surprised

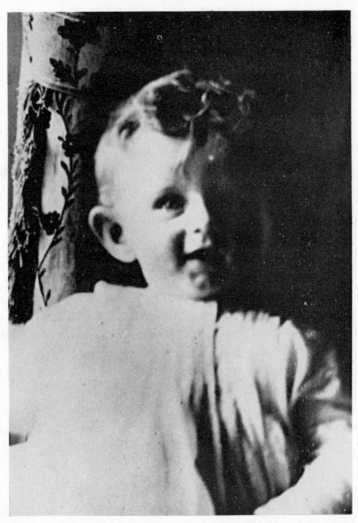

Patrick at Versailles, 1913 (*Mme. Mario Meunier–Christine Dalliès Collection*).

to see her Patrick run to the door to meet her—he had learned to walk in her absence.[24]

In 1909, Isadora had bought the house and huge studio of the muralist Henri Gervex in Neuilly.[25] It was admirably suited to her needs; the house where the children and their governess lived was separated from the studio by a large garden, and thus the dancer could practice in the late hours without fear of disturbing the others. The property was situated at 68, rue Chauveau, a wealthy residential section of Paris and a fair indication of the distance Isadora had traveled since the days of her studio above the printing press in the Latin Quarter. Paul Poiret decorated the Neuilly house for her. She dressed in Greek tunics designed for her by Poiret and Fortuny. Her surroundings and her clothes, at once fashionable and unique, bore evidence that she was at last "established." Artistic and commercial success, as well as Singer, had changed her mode of life.

He, too, had returned to Paris. The rupture between him and Isadora had not been complete; she had discarded the musician, Capelet, for him. It was not long before she and her "Lohengrin" had resumed their old intimate, affectionate, irritable, and intense relationship. They saw each other constantly, and he enjoyed entertaining the artistic and social worlds of Paris at magnificent parties in her garden. He was also full of benevolent schemes for a theater that he intended to build for Isadora. He had already bought the building site on the Rue de Berri, off the Champs Elysées, and had called on the architect Louis Sue[26] to draw up plans. It was Isadora's intention to make the theater both the headquarters of the school and a "meeting place and haven for all the great artists of the world,"[27] where actors such as Mounet-Sully and Duse could appear in Greek tragedy and other dramatic masterpieces in settings worthy of their genius. Gordon Craig would provide the settings and lighting. Augustin would play leads. There would be theater apprentices who would train for a year.

Unluckily, friction developed among the three chief collaborators—Singer, Sue, and Craig. Each wanted no interference from any of the others involved. Singer seems to have irritated Sue by suggesting where to put the exits and lavatories in the theater plans.

Craig and Sue were so determined to avoid each other that Singer proposed dividing the project into separate sections. There was much correspondence but few results.[28] Craig had initially written his acceptance to Singer on July 30, 1912, but, after reading various newspaper stories about Miss Duncan's projected theater, the stage designer sent an undated letter (from Morley's Hotel, Trafalger Square, London) to Singer, withdrawing from the project.

> . . . Thinking over your proposal to me I am afraid that there being no contradiction made by you in the Paris and American Press that the theatre you intend building is for Miss Duncan I am led to believe that the paragraphs are correct—
>
> Now although anyone might be honoured to build a theatre for Miss Duncan I have made it one of my rules lately to work for no performer however highly gifted or eminent, & I cannot break it.
>
> This therefore will make it impossible for me to go on with the idea.
>
> I am very sorry—& I had hoped things would have been different. With Good Wishes,
>
> > yours sincerely,
> > Gordon Craig.[29]

As Steegmuller noted, it was yet another of Craig's refusals to work in concert with others.

Singer must have been stimulated by the magnitude of Isadora's ideas. He was himself an amateur architect with a liking for large projects. Indeed, his life appears to have been a search for some cause into which he could throw himself wholeheartedly, as he did later in rebuilding Palm Beach as patron of the architect Addison Mizener.[30] Like his father, he seemed driven by ambition, but he lacked that sense of economic necessity that had proved such a spur to the older man. The younger Singer took no active part in the management of the Singer Sewing Machine Company, and, although he engaged in various business ventures, moneymaking was not a burning purpose in life to this man who was many times a millionaire.

This may explain why his moods varied between fits of energy and depression.[31] Isadora, who could always think of dozens of necessary and important things to do with money, had a tonic effect on him; she showed him how to direct his funds, taste, and energies into creative channels.

But all her qualities were not equally congenial to him. Her manners were informal and lively—too lively, he sometimes felt. Though she was in love with him, she apparently would have considered it hypocritical and a surrender of her painfully achieved freedom if she did not disagree with him when she felt so inclined, or if she stopped flirting with other men. Though she could devote herself to the man she loved, possessive behavior on his part immediately aroused in her a need to demonstrate her independence. The commanding Singer was not a man to react calmly to such provocations, as seen by the episode with the musician André Capelet.

One evening, when Singer and Isadora were giving an Asian costume ball at her studio, his sense of ill treatment suddenly became acute. He walked into an otherwise deserted room and found the playwright Henri Bataille and Isadora behaving in a way which suggested that the two were more than old friends.[32] Singer lost his temper and publicly broke with Isadora. He strode out of the house, but not before announcing his intention to cancel his plans for Isadora's theater.[33] Seeing her guests upset by the scene, Isadora, mindful of her duties as a hostess, tried to treat the catastrophe as a joke by dancing the *Death of Isolde*. But, inwardly, she was heartsick. Bataille, distressed at the quarrel, wrote Singer a letter of explanation, to no avail. The meeting that Isadora arranged to effect a reconciliation was not successful. Two days later, Singer left France for Egypt.[34]

❖ 21 ❖

Heartbreak
1913–1914

S always with Isadora, when love proved unhappy, she threw herself with renewed dedication into her work. In January 1913, she and her friend and accompanist, the pianist Hener Skene, left France to give a series of concerts in Russia. It was on this tour that she had the first of a series of hallucinations which seemed to foreshadow some terrible event. As they drove to her hotel, she began to see the heaped-up snow on either side of the road suddenly assuming the likeness of two rows of children's coffins, so real to her that she pointed them out in agitation to Skene. Another ill omen occurred one night on the train: "[I] heard Chopin's *Funeral March* all through the night and I had a sort of vision that impressed me so much that I danced it the following evening, *just as I had seen it,* without a rehearsal"[1]— though it was not her practice to dance improvisations in public.[2] (This visionary work, performed to Chopin's music and entitled *Marche Funèbre,* she later danced many times.) She felt a strong sense of death's approach: ". . . one evening before the performance I wrote a letter 'To be opened in case of death' containing my last will . . .'"[3]

While she was in Russia, she wrote an undated letter from the Hotel Astoria, St. Petersburg, to the architect Louis Sue. She and Sue had become friends during the drawing up of the plans for her theater. He had witnessed the disastrous confrontation between Singer, Bataille, and Isadora, and, even though this encounter had resulted in cancellation of the theater he would have designed, he and Isadora remained close friends. She wrote:

Dear Friend,

Thank you for your kind letter. I am here disconsolate—desolate in a temperature of 10 degrees above zero.

Lots of "success" but that doesn't mean happiness! I've worked very hard and am very tired. I leave after the last performance tomorrow—for Berlin, where I dance March 10–12–14—then I hope to return to Paris! What joy to see my Patrick and Deirdre again, I'm homesick.

Here I'm living like a monk and except for the moments of exaltation and extasy [sic] it's very depressing. Paris in Egypt *doesn't answer* my letters.

I'm trying to arrange to dance three farewell concerts at the Trocadéro before I leave for North America—because it's very cold here—not the slightest warmth, nor perfume, nor Love—I am desolate—When will spring come again? My soul is drying up.

Au revoir—Brute
Isadora

Say hello to our friends if you see them, also greet Paul Poiret for me.[4]

Her uneasiness vanished when she was met by her children who had travelled to Berlin with their Scottish nurse to rejoin her. Happily reunited, they journeyed back together to Isadora's house at Neuilly.

Deirdre at that time was six and a half years old and Patrick not quite three. The bond between Isadora and her children was a bond of art as well as of blood. From an early age, they had shown an unusual responsiveness to music and dancing, and Isadora watched them grow with an artist's critical satisfaction as well as a mother's partisan pride in their beauty, intelligence, and lovable natures.

Yet, even in the happy surroundings of her home, the disquieting visions recurred. "Each night, on entering my studio I saw three black birds flying about. I was so troubled by these apparitions that I called in Dr. R. B. He told me it was my nerves and gave me a tonic."[5] A dinner guest, a recent Catholic convert, was disturbed by her account of these recurrent hallucinations and privately went into the children's room and baptized them. The guest was Lord Alfred Douglas, Oscar Wilde's friend "Bozey."[6]

Advised by her doctor to rest in the country, Isadora took the children and their nurse to Versailles. The change had the hoped-for restorative effect. After a night in the quiet little town, she awoke feeling refreshed and happy. Her spirits rose even higher the next day when Singer, who had returned to Paris, telephoned and asked her and the children to lunch with him in the city. The luncheon went very well, with Singer overjoyed at seeing his little boy and Deirdre. All past animosities were forgotten, and the former lovers plunged delightedly into making plans for the future. After they had eaten, the party separated—she to go to a rehearsal, he to visit le Salon des Humoristes, and Deirdre, Patrick, and their governess to drive back to Versailles. On the trip home, the automobile stalled, and the chauffeur, Paul Morverand,[7] got out to crank the motor. He heard it start, and then suddenly the heavy vehicle backed away from him and rolled toward the Seine. He sprang at the door but could not pull it open—the handle wrenched out of his grasp. The car gave a lurch and careened with its three occupants into the river.

A small crowd attracted by the chauffeur's cries gathered to point at the spot where the vehicle had sunk. Two men tried to force open the doors of the car but the pressure of the surging water was too great. A M. Sire tried to dive into the Seine to free the trapped passengers, but he was restrained by the police. When the car was finally raised from the river, the two children and their nurse, Annie Sim, were dead.

Singer had the terrible duty of breaking the news to Isadora.[8] She did not weep. Those who were with her said that she sought only to lighten their grief, and to comfort Singer, her sister and brothers, the doctor who had been unable to revive the children, and the friends who had come to solace her. They came from all walks of life, friends begging to be of service. Gaston Calmette, the editor of *Le Figaro,* used his influence so that she was able to obtain the prompt release of the children's bodies from the morgue. The students of L'Ecole Nationale Supérieure des Beaux-Arts silently expressed their affection and sorrow by covering the bushes and trees of her garden with white blossoms. The sculptor Paul Bourdelle, with streaming eyes, threw himself on his knees before Isadora and put his head in her lap: "She looked at him as the Mother of God might have looked. All through that day with the different people coming to her, she seemed to be trying to console them. . . . She was in the most exalted state, as though some great spirit of pity had taken possession of her and she was sorry for the whole world. Truly, to have seen Isadora in such moments was to have known what a great being she was."[9]

In the midst of her grief, she did not forget to intercede with the public prosecutor for the unlucky chauffeur who was being held by the police. "He is a father, and I need to know that he has been released to his family, before I can regain some measure of calm."[10]

Her state of exaltation sustained her through the ordeal of the funeral (through some mischance she was admitted to the basement of the crematory, and the burning of the three coffins took place before her eyes) and through her visit to Singer at the hospital afterwards. "Lohengrin had been taken ill immediately after the tragedy and was in Doctor Doyen's Hospital . . . Isadora, standing over his bed, tried in her gentle way to console him."[11]

After the funeral, Count Harry Kessler, who had been Gordon Craig's patron in Germany and was now in Paris, wrote to Craig:

There was a most beautiful moving ceremony in [Isadora's] studio, the most moving ceremony I have ever been to. Nothing but exquisite music, Grieg's "Death of Aase." Then a piece of Mozart that seemed to embody the tripping of light children's feet on soft grass and flowers, and a wailing, infinitely moving melody of Bach. I thought my heart would break. Poor Isadora behaved splendidly. She knelt hidden by her sister and two brothers on the balcony. Then the coffins were carried out through the garden all strewn with white daisies and jessamine to the white hearses drawn by white horses. Everything most admirable in taste and restraint—but her brother tells me that she bears up wonderfully, and others who have seen her tell me that she is really *heroic,* encouraging the others, saying, *"there is no death."* Everybody in Paris is moved to the depths of their hearts.[12.]

Her family, at first reassured by her courage, presently grew alarmed, feeling that if she did not give way to her grief she might lose her reason. Augustin, knowing that the meeting might be more than his sister could bear, but convinced he must shatter her mortal calm, in desperation sent for her young pupils who were about to return to Darmstadt. At the sight of these other children, Isadora finally wept. She kissed the young girls and took them in her arms.[13]

In her absence, messages of condolences had been pouring into the studio. Most of them she could not bear to read but among them were two letters from Gordon Craig which she cherished and kept all her life. One reads:

Isadora dear—

I shall never be able to say anything to you. It's a mysterious thing but when I begin to think of you or speak to you I feel as though it was as unnecessary as if I should speak to myself. This feeling grows. And as I seem to be a man mad about something outside myself—I no longer seem to count.

A glimpse of myself—if I dared to lift a viel [sic] might kill me.

I have left myself (so it seems to me who dare not *look*) & what is me is a bag of sawdust with a head on one end & two leaden feet T'other end—& so on—

I seem to be outside myself—supporting myself by one arm or

by the hair—like a bunch of furies, & with some strength too, for I have serious things to attend to, get done, and then go.

My life as yours has been *strange*—you are *strange*—*but not to me*

And my darling I know how you can suffer & not show more than a smile—know your weakness which is that of a little, dear little fool

—for I, a big fool have looked at you. I know your strength too—

—for I who can taste strength

have seen all yours

Never was there one so weak or so strong as you—and all for Hecuba

My heart has often been broken to see your weakness—large chips (you couldn't have noticed them, for I, as you, will never show those)—my heart has often shaken with *terror* to see your strength. For my heart and your heart are one heart and an utterly incomprehensible thing it is.

I *want to be with you*—& it was only to say that that I write so much.—

And as I am with you, being you

what more is there to be said.

Let us not be sorry for anything or where should we begin.

You and I are lonely—only that.

And no matter how many came—or shall come—you & I must be lonely.

Our secret. I kiss your heart.[14]

Inside the letter was a small envelope and enclosed within it a sprig of pressed flowers and a message:

> Isadora
> there is much
> to do.
>
> 1913   T

Elena Meo also wrote Isadora. The mother of Craig's children Nelly and Teddy, Elena had been reunited with Ted since September

1908,[15] although at the moment she was in London. Any jealousy she may have felt in the past concerning Isadora had been swept away by the magnitude of the disaster that had struck the dancer. Isadora received two letters written in Elena's halting English, the second of which, dated June 19, 1913, read in part:

> I have so much and so great a sympathy for you and am very very sad at your troubles—a trouble so great that words become almost foolish. Poor little Deirdre—do not for one moment think I am so narrow or so small I could not love her—& little Patrick too—dear babes—I could have loved them both—if you were here in London—I would come and see you & perhaps help you bear your sorrow—I have suffered too and can feel for you very very much—& would help you if you would let me—should we ever meet. In one of your letters to Ted you asked for a photograph of us—here is a little one taken in the country.
>
> I have some work I am doing for Ted here—& will be here a month longer before joining him. If you came to London—will you come and see me—your sorrow is the saddest thing I know—but try & bear up—& keep strong.
>
> Elena Craig[16]

To express her thanks to the people who had written to her, Isadora sent a short note to the newspapers:

> My friends have helped me to realize what alone could comfort me. That all men are my brothers, all women are my sisters and all little children on earth are my children.[17]

With these duties accomplished, Isadora's strength deserted her and she fell prey to anguish. To distract her from her grief, Raymond Duncan urged her to join him and his Greek wife, Penelope, who were leaving to work in Albania among the refugees made homeless in the recently ended Turkish-Balkan War. Isadora agreed and set out to meet them, accompanied by Augustin and Elizabeth Duncan.

She broke off her trip in Corfu, where she replied to Elena's letter:

Dear

How sweet and good of you to write to me—Your first letter and your second letter came to me at the same time—the first had been mislaid by those who had opened the letters—Yes I have always thought of you as "Nelly" and I have thought so much of you. Some day if we meet I will tell you—I can't *write* it.

I have been with my brother walking over the mountains in Epirus—walking fifty miles a day and sleeping out under the stars— just to tire myself out and then it is better to weep with the stars looking down on you than in a room. We visited some of the villages burned by the Turks—poor people with their houses and crops destroyed if someone doesn't help them they will all die of misery. I am trying to organize some shelters for the children there—we return there next week—the poor little children so sad eyed and forlorn—and the poor women with nothing to give them—

I loved the pictures you sent me—something in the turn of the little boy's head like Deirdre—How she would have loved to play with them—she was so filled with joy and romping—Patrick only a baby but he toddled after her everywhere—Some mornings she would come to me dressed in a little white boy's sailor suit and say "Mama I'm not Deirdre today I'm *Jack*" She was so strong and gay like a boy—only when she danced she was like a little fairy—yes you would have loved them as I love *yours*—what dearer joy is there in all the world than to love them—ours or others—even those poor little dirty starved children in Epirus have some divinity in their eyes like Deirdre like Patrick it is the same divinity—As for me—I feel as if I had died with them what is here left seems such a poor shadow—what shall I do with it—all my life gone—and my work too—for how shall I ever dance *again*—how stretch out my arms except in desolation—if I had only been with them but the nurse had my place—It is so dear of you to say you will comfort me and if anything could be a comfort it would be to feel that love comes to me from you and Ted and your little ones. Yes I [take ?] the hand you hold out to me so sweetly and kiss it tenderly and love you and bless you. Yes I will come to see you if I can—and even if not I will feel often that I am with you—Isadora[18]

From the Villa San Stefano in Corfu, on June 23, Isadora answered Craig's inquiry:

Dear Ted—

Yes Nelly wrote to me but her first letter was misslaid [sic] amongst hundreds of others and I only received it two days ago with her second—very sweet and beautiful of her and I answered—

I don't know about the purpose of the war but to help those poor starving mites over there does something to keep me from dying in my desolation and despair—and then I think of Patrick and Deirdre would like to see those little ones eating and singing—and who knows perhaps among them we are saving some great spirit for future times—anyway what else can I do—my own work gives me such dreadful pain—even to think of it, and all my life seems like a fine ship on the rocks and no hope of ever going on to other voyages.[19] Also my poor head won't work right any more even to write to you—dear Beautiful wonderful spirit—you are creating the only world that is worth living in—*The Imagination*—this so called real world is the refinement of Torture—and if it wasn't for the escape the Imagination offers it would be Hell indeed—you go on opening the door—releasing poor souls from the Inferno of *reality* and *matter*—lift them up out of "life" into the *only life* up where the spirit can fly—freed from this abominable bad dream of matter— this only a bad dream—mirage—you find the only truth—freed from these infernal appearances that are *shams*. I know that all these so called happenings are *illusions*—Water can not drown people— neither can going without food starve them—neither are they born or do they die—*All is*—and the Eternal Truth is only seen in precious moments by such spirits as Phidias, Michelangelo—Rembrandt— Bach—Beethoven—others—and yourself—and it is only [unclear] with such glimpses that is of Importance—all the rest is semblances, illusions—veils—, I know that, but what will you—at present my poor Body cries out and my mind is clouded—I can only see Deirdre & Patrick—skipping and dancing about—and then lying there all white & still and cold—and shriek within myself *"What does this mean?"* All illusions I know they were but the appearance of Beautiful Spirit—Beautiful spirit existing everywhere needing no Earthly man- ifestation—Beautiful Spirit for us to find to portray in Eternal Im-

ages—to light others—but I am all torn to pieces and bleeding—
I wish I could see you a few moments. Bless you.

Isadora

did your Mother dearest receive a letter I sent to her[20]

In Corfu Isadora fell ill, and for days sat or lay motionless, exhausted by despair. Yet, even in her anguish, her artist's eye was making observations on her state: "When real sorrow is encountered there is for the stricken, no gesture, no expression."[21] She would remember that later when she sought through her art to convey grief.

Still repeating in her mind the events of that fatal day, she wrote to her friend, Georges Maurevert:

I am here alone with my brother and Elizabeth. We are living in a very isolated villa in the midst of olive trees by the sea. I know that my real self died with my children. I do not recognize what remains. I have always known that my children were the best part of my life—all the joy, the strength and the inspiration of my art. And now I feel that my life and my art died with them.

If I continue to exist it will be as another creature, kinder perhaps. But I'll never danse [sic] again.

Each morning, very early Deirdre and Patrick came to my room singing and dancing . . . Only on that last morning I heard Patrick weep. I went to their room. The child was sad and did not want to take his breakfast. I took him in my arms and consoled him. Then he consented to eat. He had just learned to speak: he said, *"Bread and butter, mama, bread and butter."* And then we laughed and played together. And I suggested we take an automobile ride. . . . We went to Versailles and then came to Paris. And then after lunch I put them in the car to send them back with their nurse. I kissed them, and they waved their little hands to say good-bye. . . . And then for a joke I kissed Deirdre's lips through the glass. The glass was cold against my lips and suddenly I had a strange apprehension—but the automobile went off. . . . And a few minutes later they were all dead. . . . It was the first time I had seen Death. . . . When they brought them back to me, when I kissed them, I recalled how cold the glass had been against my lips. It was like the kiss of Death . . .

And now I struggle with all my strength but I still see them in the car. . . . I must live for those who love me but it is really a torture too terrible. What shall I do? . . .[22]

In Paris, the need to console her comforters had given her strength to transcend her own suffering. But, away from people, it did not matter how she bore her grief. Nothing she did mattered. She was faced with the terrible knowledge that however well she bore her sorrow, nothing she did could make any difference to her children. No act of hers could affect them any longer. And there was no term set to her suffering. She could not say to herself that if she could only endure her pain for a while it would finally come to an end. It would come to an end only when her life ended. She was thirty-six, and there was nothing for which she wanted to live. To one of her temperament, accustomed to dealing with dangers by confronting them, with obstacles by overcoming them, the finality of her loss was surely devastating. If she had had a husband with whom to share her grief, she could have summoned up her energies to console him. But, though Singer and Craig sorrowed for her, they had other claims on their affections. Singer was a family man; Craig, who had rejoined Elena in 1908, had a little boy and girl by her, as well as five other children. Isadora had borne her children alone; now she must bear the grief of their death alone.

She wrote to Louis Sue from the Villa San Stefano on Corfu on May 14:

Dear Friend:

We are here in a villa overlooking the sea—completely isolated—one can walk miles among the olive trees wihout meeting *anybody*.

I've read Maeterlinck's last letter on death—I try to wear myself out with long walks—but night comes always when I cannot read any more or think and I fall a prey to tortures—What is surprising is that the body still lives—in spite of the fact that I drink nothing but milk—it agrees with me perfectly and I'm merely getting stronger; if only I could get ill it might be a great relief.

I would like to go to Epirus—to help the poor, but Paris who

at first was very enthusiastic about the idea, doesn't want me to—
He's in London.

My little brother Raymond with Penelope—have gone to Epirus—on foot with nothing. They're going toward Janina, what courage! They told me they would be back in a week and tell me the
exact state of the country and people—then if possible we'll raise
a subscription to help them. What do you think? They say there are
a thousand families dying of hunger. I thought I might go there and
do something for the children. If Paris would come it would be
simpler—but even alone I can perhaps do something. They say it's
a new country—magnificent—I even dreamed of founding a big
school there—an artist's colony. . . .

I am awaiting Raymond's return—I will write you—I would like
it so much if instead of sending you these stupid words in my bad
French, I could send you the view from my window—on the wide
space of the sea—I can see right to the mountains on the opposite
side which seem to float in the azure between earth and heaven—
like a vision of a promised land . . . Sometimes looking out on it I
think that maybe I'm dead with my children and have entered
Paradise—and I feel them close to me—and then comes again the
cruel physical suffering—my eyes will never see them, my hands
never touch them again, and I see once more the poor little things
waving their little hands—in the automobile driving off—and I
want to scream—but in fact it is life which suffers. [It is the living
self which suffers?] It is not the soul which stands apart and watches
all this suffering with astonishment.

Write me a line which will do me good—I think of you so much.
All that I know of you is strong and good.

May your work may everything in you be blessed.

Isadora[23]

In England, Singer, still recuperating from the shock of the children's death, had a premonition that Isadora was dying. He hurried
from London to be with her in Corfu, an act that awoke tender
feelings in her. "I had the hope," she later wrote, "that by a
spontaneous love gesture the unhappiness of the past might be
redeemed to feel again stirring in my bosom; that my children might

return to comfort me on earth."[24] According to Louis Sue,[25] Isadora asked Paris to give her a child, but the request jarred Singer, who took it as frivolous and inappropriate—or perhaps he found it less painful to interpret it as frivolity than as a heartbreaking attempt to remake her life. As Isadora related, "my intense yearning—my sorrow—were too strong" for him to bear, and one day he suddenly left.

Isadora saw then that if she was to survive she must work ("Isadora: There is much to do . . ."), and, summoning all her will, she returned to Raymond's refugee settlement in Albania.

At Santa Quaranta in the province of Epirus, a scene of endless wretchedness met her eyes. Families whose houses and crops had burned lived in makeshift huts and cooked their meager meals in the open. But Raymond was beginning to bring some order into the confusion. He had his sister's courage and drive and, in addition, a gift for organization. He managed to get under way, without funds or any experience in the field of relief, a project so vast that no government had been willing to undertake it. He decided that the best way to help the dispossessed was not simply to dole out food, but to issue tools and other implements so that the refugees could make the things they needed. To a reporter who visited the settlement on July 9, Isadora explained:

> Raymond bought raw wool in sacks at Corfu and took it to Santa Quaranta [where] he gave [it] to the hundreds of women who came just as soon as they knew what his object was. Hand spindles were supplied even to the children, and it was not long before the entire countryside was spinning coarse thread.
>
> My brother then paid the women a fair wage for this thread, which he at once sent to London and sold at a profit, all of which went back again into the purchase of raw wool. Once a day a great dinner was given to these starving women. So many children came with the women it soon suggested itself to us that a school was the natural sequence of the situation. Carpenters were sent for, and a master tent-maker. The carpenters made benches and desks and the tent-makers taught the women to make tents . . .
>
> Soon there was a . . . tent-city on the hillside. As an object lesson,

our effort ought to have a great and lasting value in that wonderful but uncivilized country, where there are no schools, and where the fleeing Turks burned all the villages and crops in their path. My brother and I visited at least forty of these villages, where at the present moment the women and children are almost without food or the necessaries of life. . . . On the other hand we found universal joy over the fact that Turkish rule was at last at an end.[26]

In *An Appeal for the Children of Epirus,* Isadora describes

a country whose strange and wild beauty, by the grandiose lines and astonishing profiles of its mountains, and the mysterious atmosphere of those arid valleys which always seem to be waiting for something, gives the traveller the impression that far from our world he is visiting some unknown planet . . .

And nonetheless, over there on the mountain slopes, brave men have dared engage in battle with this implacable nature; they have erected dwellings the color of the mountain rocks high up to escape fevers which rise from the valleys and barbarian invasions . . .

The Duncans lived in a tent on the rocky Albanian coast, and each morning, before beginning the day's work, they went swimming. Sometimes, as Isadora went about distributing supplies, she was soaked to the skin by thunderstorms, and she would remember that in ancient times this wild country had been the site of an altar to Zeus the Thunderer. The fierceness of nature briefly exhilarated and comforted her. Her hair, which had turned white, she cut off and threw into the sea.[27]

After several weeks of this strenuous existence, her health revived and with it her restlessness. In mid-August, she returned to Paris to raise funds for the refugee camp, intending to return to Epirus in September. While she was in France, she had a number of brochures printed, appealing for donations and offering for sale handloomed blankets and rugs made by the refugees. She also wrote to her New York manager, Fitzhugh W. Haensel (of Haensel and Jones), begging him to deny reports that she intended shortly to tour South America. In a letter from 68, rue Chauveau, Neuilly, on August 18, 1913, she said:

> I . . . will feel very much obliged to you if you will kindly contradict such rumors which seem to me infinitely shocking. It seems to me that if I could think of dancing at this moment it would be a crime against life itself and against the great lesson of death which I am trying to learn in silence. It will be a long time before I can even dream of my work again, and I hate to think that my friends who love me and whom I love in America should be led by the newspapers to think of me as dancing in South America.[28]

Back in Albania once more, Isadora took part in the work of the camp but found that there was little she herself could do to help rebuild the ravaged villages. Besides, she felt a growing need to see something besides misery, and so, persuading her sister-in-law, Penelope, to take a short holiday with her, she travelled to Constantinople—where she was not too absorbed by her own unhappiness to save the life of a suicidal young man by reuniting him with his beloved.[29] But a telegram from Raymond forced the two women to cut short their stay, and, hurrying back to Santa Quaranta, they found Raymond and his son Menalkas sick with fever. Raymond refused to abandon his work, and Penelope could not leave him, so Isadora, anxious and lonely, resumed her journey alone.[30]

Thus began months of wandering: to Switzerland with Augustin, back to the empty house in Neuilly which proved uninhabitable without the children, and to Italy where she briefly saw Craig. In *My Life*[31] she says that she passed through Florence, but did not get in touch with Ted because he had recently married and she did not want to cause discord. (Craig had, of course, not married; perhaps Isadora did not want to see him with Elena.) That she had refrained from seeing him earlier, on her way back to Santa Quaranta, is borne out by her letter of November 17, 1913. Later that autumn, in Florence, Craig and Isadora apparently did meet—two notes by Isadora (CD 234 and 235) refer to the occasion. Craig confirms it, noting in his copy of *My Life:* "Yes, we met—But you wanted to be weak instead of strong. Yes—I remember & you were still thinking all about *yourself* and not of an idea" (which seems a harsh judgment in view of Isadora's work at Santa Quaranta). It was around this time that Craig in a note (probably unsent) dated September 2, 1913, wrote, "Now again I want to help you and you won't be helped. It's not arms—not lips—not eyes—not anything touchable that will suffice for what you hunger for—only 1 thing will and that you won't have. Perhaps later—?" What was it that Isadora would not have? Work? Friendship? Had she wanted another child from Craig? That might explain the violence of his reaction when he read in her memoirs of the birth of her short-lived third baby: "I whispered, 'Who are you, Deirdre or Patrick? You have returned to me.'" Craig commented on the margin of his copy, "The crass idiocy of addressing a new life with an insult from the first!"

Her friend Eleonora Duse learned of Isadora's whereabouts and begged her to visit at Viareggio. Here, Eleonora tried to infuse her companion with her own compassionate strength, but Isadora was still subject to attacks of self-destroying anguish. One day, as she was walking on the beach, she saw the figures of Deirdre and Patrick skipping before her. She ran toward them but they disappeared in the spray, and Isadora, gripped by the fear of approaching madness, fell to the ground and cried aloud.

She felt a hand on her head, and looked up to see a young man bending over her. "Is there nothing I can do for you—to help you?"

In her despair, Isadora replied, "Yes. Save me—save more than my life—my reason. Give me a child."

Their union was to be a short one, for the young Italian was already engaged to be married. When he broke off the affair to go back to his fiancée, Isadora was not angry with him. Rather, she was grateful to have had his love, for once again she was pregnant, and she believed that this new baby would be Deirdre or Patrick returning to her arms.[32]

She broke the news of her pregnancy to Eleonora, who for once found herself baffled. Full of apprehension for Isadora, Duse poured out her concern—and her admiration—in a letter to their common friend Lugné-Poë.

She tells me that her little boy and little girl . . . were brought back to the house . . . The two little hands were clasped together, and the smile of the child unacquainted with Death, was there, smiling to the mother . . .

She, this mother, spoke of it for hours on end, and her grief was calm, gentle . . . and composed.

To have been with these two children *beyond* life—to have seen them hand in hand, smiling and dead! and still be able to see them living again! . . . What courage, what strength, what folly, what nobility, what distress, what error, what magnificent sweetness of heart! . . .

Nothing of that which is irreparable is understood by this magnificent and dangerous creature! Her generosity is quite as great as her error of imagination.

The "irreparable" which nevertheless exalts the tone of life— no—she does not even see it and she wishes to throw herself back into life, bleeding life . . . and see again . . . What?—the smile of the dead child *in another* smile of another child that will be hers!

Be sorry, my friend, for my littleness, for I understand nothing of *that will,* of that folly, of that supreme wisdom.

Isadora Duncan has on her side the Supreme Strength—greater than life itself . . .[33]

In Viareggio one day, Isadora felt moved to dance the adagio of the *Sonata Pathétique* of Beethoven for Duse. It was the first time Isadora had danced since the catastrophe, and in gratitude the older woman took the dancer in her arms. "Isadora, what are you doing here? You must return to your art. It is your only salvation."

When Eleonora left Viareggio for the winter, Isadora moved to the Italian capital. "I spent Christmas in Rome. It was sad enough but I said to myself: Nevertheless I am not in the tomb or the madhouse—I am here."[34]

Her accompanist, the devoted Hener Skene, had come to Rome with her, and another friend, the poet Gabriele D'Annunzio, called on her often or left little notes at her hotel to assuage her feeling of solitude.

Rome is a wonderful city for a sorrowful soul . . . Especially I liked to wander in the Appian Way at early morning when, between the long rows of tombs the wine carts came in from Frascati with their sleeping drivers like tired fauns reclining on the wine barrels. Then it seemed to me that time ceased to exist. I was as a ghost who had wandered on the Appian Way for a thousand years, with the great spaces of the Campagna and the great arch of Raphael's sky above.[35]

She was summoned from Italy and her sadness by a telegram from Singer begging her to return to Paris and her art. He had taken a suite of rooms for her at the Crillon. There she told him everything that had happened since he had left her—her sojourn among the refugees, her travels, and her despair. She spoke of the Viareggio episode and of the child she was carrying. After a silence, Singer told her that he had bought the hotel at Bellevue with gardens and terrace overlooking Paris. It was hers: he was giving it to her for a school. Would she be willing to put aside all personal feelings and for the time being exist only for her work? She consented.[36]

Soon the building had been remodeled, the fifty most talented applicants had been chosen, and six older girls, students from Isadora's first school, had arrived to help her with the instruction. It was generous of Elizabeth to let these girls go, since they were now the star pupils of *her* school, but the older sister had the magnanimity to say, "They've learned all they can, here. If they wish to become artists, they must go to Isadora."[37] Isadora now threw herself eagerly into the task of teaching, and, within a short time, her pupils had made such progress that the school became a meeting place for painters and sculptors who came there to draw inspiration from the liveliness and grace of the young dancers.[38] Other visitors to Bellevue were her friends Mounet-Sully, Cécile Sorel, D'Annunzio, Duse, and Ellen Terry.

Isadora's garden at Bellevue was next to that of the aging Rodin. "Here often at twilight these two rare and just spirits would walk together quietly without other guests."[39] Rodin had long admired Isadora, but now his admiration for her fortitude amounted to reverence. He later told Mary Fanton Roberts: "Isadora Duncan is the greatest woman I have ever known, and her art has influenced my work more than any other inspiration that has come to me.

Sometimes I think she is the greatest woman the world has ever known."[40]

It was the summer of 1914 and the air was full of rumors, but Isadora tried to shut them out of her consciousness with plans for her school and hopes for her coming child. In this period of anxious waiting, the assassination of the editor Gaston Calmette,[41] who had proved such a valuable friend at the time of the children's death, seemed a portent of some further disaster. Her pupils had left for a summer vacation at Singer's estate in Devonshire and the vast rooms of Bellevue were empty and depressing. Fortunately, Augustin and Mary Desti had remained with her.

On August 1, her pains began. Outside, under her open windows, criers were shouting news of the war mobilization, and, as the roll of the recruitment drum accompanied her groans, she gave birth to a son. The baby was small and frail and lived only a few hours. With its death, the flood of grief that she had been holding back engulfed her. She bowed to the needs of warfare and suffering. Even before she was able to rise from her bed, she had loaned Bellevue to Les Dames de France for use as an army hospital. "Shortly after this, I heard the first heavy steps of the stretcher-bearers, bringing in the wounded."[42]

❧ 22 ❧

Exodus
1914

HEN Isadora was well enough to move, she and Mary
Desti, who had been with her at the birth of the baby,
drove through the war zone to Deauville. Here they
took rooms at the Hôtel Normandie,[1] and, while Isadora slowly regained her strength, Mary worked as a nurse at the
former casino which had hurriedly been converted into a military
hospital. When the dancer was stronger, she helped out at the
hospital, too, running errands, reading to the soldiers, or writing
their letters home.[2]

Singer, meanwhile, fearing that there might be some awkwardness
in wartime England for the pupils of the school, a number of whom
were German, arranged to send them to the United States under
the care of Augustin and his beautiful new wife, the actress Margherita Sargent. Complications awaited the group on arrival. Because
the Duncans had no guardianship papers, the children were held at
Ellis Island. "Finally, through the kind offices of Frederic C. Howe,
then a very new Commissioner of Immigration, they were released

on a $500 per capita bond,"³ and they then proceeded to their new quarters in the Simeon Ford mansion at Rye, New York.

Elizabeth and her school had also emigrated to America and were installed in an estate in Tarrytown, New York. In response to the urging of her brother and sister, Isadora decided to join them and she sailed for New York from Liverpool on the *Franconia*. She was seen off by a doctor from the army hospital in Deauville,⁴ with whom she had formed a close friendship and who had accompanied her to England.

She arrived in New York on November 24⁵ and was met by Augustin and Elizabeth. Shortly after her arrival, she took a studio at 311 Fourth Avenue on the northeast corner of 23rd Street and Fourth Avenue, furnished it with her blue curtains and low divans, and reassembled her pupils. This studio she christened *The Dionysion.*⁶

Early in 1915, a group of Isadora's friends—among them the poet Percy MacKaye, the photographer Arnold Genthe, and the writers John Collier, Walter Lippmann, and Mabel Dodge Luhan—knowing that Isadora wanted backing for her school, arranged to invite the young reform mayor of New York, John Purroy Mitchell, to the Dionysion. The idea was that Isadora would charm the mayor, her young pupils would dance for him, and he would give his official endorsement to her work and perhaps make an armory available for her to practice in. But as so often happened when Isadora needed a patron, she was determined not to be patronized. She greeted Mitchell's fashionable party graciously, but during a sudden lull in the conversation she was heard to say: "Who are these people? What do they know about art, or what can they understand of my work? Who are these women? Wives with feathers!"⁷

Her friends quickly intervened and turned the talk into safer channels. But not for long. Isadora next chose to plead for Mrs. Ida Sniffen, who had killed her two illegitimate children and was now locked in the Tombs prison. Isadora said: "How do you suppose she feels, shut up there? How can *anyone* be certain that she did it? How can anyone believe that a mother would or could kill her children . . . that poor creature. I have wanted to go to her and sit beside her. . . ."[8] John Collier explained to Isadora that it was not within the province of the mayor to grant pardons.

Isadora then harangued the mayor on the sort of education her pupils received, contrasting it to the harshness of American life.

Mitchell, hopeful of restoring the amicability to his social visit, asked to see Isadora's work, and she replied coolly, "I do not think the children feel like dancing this afternoon."

Rebuffed, Mitchell and his party withdrew. After this fiasco, Walter Lippmann wrote to Mabel Luhan:

> Dear Mabel:
> I'm utterly disgusted. If this is Greece and Joy and the Aegean Isles and the Influence of Music, I don't want anything to do with it. It's an absurd mess and she is obviously the last person who ought to be running a school. I want you to let me off the committee! You can tell the others I'm too busy . . .
> I should have known better than to be dazzled into a shortcut to perfection—there are none and Isadora is not the person to show the way. . . .[9]

If Isadora had unconsciously used the subject of Mrs. Sniffen to get rid of the mayor, still her sympathy with the unhappy woman was genuine. Surely to lose one's children was punishment enough for any crime without also knowing that one was responsible for their loss. Who better than Isadora could gauge the pressure that society exerts on the unwed mother, pressure that perhaps had driven Ida Sniffen to her terrible act? The dancer had already written two letters about the case to the *New York Evening Sun*:

> Ida Sniffen is not to be considered as "wicked" but the present-day laws, conventions and prejudices as ignorant. They are not based on an understanding of the beauty of nature's forces. Ida Sniffen is a victim of that ignorance. Why are not the laws of the State founded on an understanding of Nature? . . .

And more fully:

Many persons have misunderstood my previous letter. It is difficult to explain an entire life's philosophy in one short letter, but it seems to me I said only very simple human things. Many accuse me of attacking the sacredness of marriage. Surely, let people live together if they love each other. I only said people could not be bound together by contracts if they did not love one another. I have not attacked "the sacredness of family life"—only suggested a remedy for family discords. . . . Why should the laws be like a great machine—once made and put in motion grinding out everything the same. Why not flexible laws? . . .[10]

One cannot help wondering whether Isadora's need to defy convention and those whom she regarded as conventional would have been so pronounced had fate allowed her to marry Gordon Craig. Before their meeting, she had apparently not been opposed to marriage: she had become engaged to Miroski and had later intended to wed Beregi. She certainly had been married, in an emotional sense, to Craig: while they were lovers, she had not sought other liaisons, she had wanted to bear his children, and she had expected to spend the rest of her life with him. As long as she was sure of his love, she had been able to minimize the pain caused by her mother's disapproval and anxiety and the censure of her school's sponsors. Kathleen Bruce informs us that in his presence Isadora was happy and serene. She could dispense with marriage while she had his love. Thus, their break had come to her with all the shock and none of the formality of a divorce, leaving her with an illegitimate daughter and a need to justify her position.

The latter was not a new experience for her. As an artist who was an innovator, she was accustomed to being embattled. Her dance had been attacked on moral as well as aesthetic grounds. All her accomplishments were made in the face of indifference, opposition, or ridicule, and, by now, she accepted opposition as the necessary precondition to accomplishment. Indeed, she found it a stimulus. However, society exacts heavy psychological penalties of nonconformists. In the effort to ward off increasing criticism, they may find themselves constantly assuming a stance of defiance and wasting their energies on issues that have nothing to do with their work.

The circumstances of her childhood had, in any case, predisposed Isadora to look at society with an outsider's eyes. The scandal of her father's bank failure and her parents' subsequent divorce had forfeited her a place in that sheltered and orderly world to which their position would have entitled her. Perhaps, as a theater person, she might simply have ignored the criticisms and conventions of society. But her proper though strong-minded mother had been reared as a member of the middle class, and, loving her mother, Isadora felt compelled to explain and uphold her actions. If she bore a child out of wedlock, she made it clear that she did so on principle. The artist whom Kathleen Bruce had described as "sweet tempered and easy-going"[11] felt an increasing need to attack the habits, standards, and institutions of society. She attacked those in power—bailiffs, officials, the respectable, and the rich—all those on whose goodwill the success of her work depended. Eventually, she would attack governments.

❧ 23 ❧

The Dionysion in New York
1914–1915

ON December 3, 1914, Isadora's six oldest pupils who were to become known as "The Isadorables," Anna, Irma, Lisa, Theresa, Erica, and Gretel (also called Margot), gave a program of dances at Carnegie Hall. It was the American debut of the girls.[1] *The New York Times* gave a brief review of the performance the following day. Under the title "Symphony Aids Dancers: Isadora Duncan's Pupils Appear with New York Orchestra," the critic wrote:

Six young disciples of the art of the dance as Isadora Duncan had conceived and expounded it, were presented yesterday afternoon at Carnegie Hall with the assistance of the New York Symphony Orchestra under the direction of Victor Kolas. . . .

The young dancers proved themselves well trained . . . though perhaps they did not succeed in making [their dance] so expressive and plastic as that of their instructress. The numbers which were played by the orchestra were the Allegro Moderato of Schubert's *Unfinished*

Symphony, Schubert's *Ave Maria* and the King Stephen overture of Beethoven. The dance program comprised Schubert's *Marche Héroique*, German Dances and *Marche Militaire*, [and] Florent Schmitt's waltzes: *Ballets d'Allemagne*.

Mme Namara-Toye, soprano, also took part in the entertainment. Edward Falck was her accompanist.

The *New York Herald* later announced[2] that Isadora had sent some of the proceeds of this recital to French children whose fathers had been artists called to war.

Isadora's own programs early in 1915 were serious in theme and liturgical in manner. It seems likely that she intended her return to the stage to be in the nature of a declaration of faith and a rededication of herself to her art, for her dances were interspersed with readings from the Psalms and the Beatitudes. Her selections[3] are indicative of her state of mind at the time: after *The Unfinished Symphony,* Augustin read, "Unto thee will I cry, O God, be not silent to me"; after the *Marche Funèbre,* "Blessed are they that mourn: for they shall be comforted. They that sow in tears shall reap in joy"; and, after the *Ave Maria,* "Praise ye the Lord. Praise him, all his angels . . . let everything that hath breath praise the Lord." It was as if, from the depths of sorrow, she had summoned up all her will to deliver a message of joy, a message which at that moment she did not feel capable of speaking unaided ("In the prison of his days/ Teach the free man how to praise").[4]

But, if she had personal reasons for this theme for her dances, they remained obscure to the critics. the *Boston Transcript,* which had dispatched a reviewer to New York, complained on February 4, 1915:

> Her performances are sicklied over now with the pale cast of some very immature and hasty thought. . . . It is a most disheartening and amateurish mixture of music and recited literature, from the Bible and other sources equally unsuited to any such purpose. . . .[5]

A reviewer from a Chicago paper,[6] however, rebuked New Yorkers for their coolness to Isadora: "Her . . . dances are beautifully classical. . . . Miss Duncan is an artist . . . I hate to say that she is casting pearls before swine. . . ." (Presumably, Chicagoans would know better how to appreciate her art.) The facts that emerge from both these reviews are, first, that Isadora's season had gotten off to an unsuccessful start, and, second, Isadora's concerts, successful or not, were now regarded as sufficiently important to warrant coverage by out-of-state newspapers.

Evidently stung by the barbs of unfriendly critics and disheartened by the box-office receipts, Isadora gave the first of two American farewell performances at the Metropolitan Opera House on the afternoon of February 25, 1915. At the end of the program, she made an impromptu speech in which she criticized Americans, particularly wealthy box holders, for their lack of support of the arts—a lack which was compelling her to return to Europe. If her admirers wished her to remain, they should build her a theater on the Lower East Side where the people needed and appreciated her dance.

Curiously enough, this scolding was the signal for her greatest ovation that year. "None of her points missed fire and almost every sentence evoked applause." After her last dance, she received twenty-seven curtain calls.[7]

Several times that season, she made this plea for funds, coupled with a denunciation of the rich. Her constant appeals for funds during this American engagement, and her bitterness against the rich suggest that Singer had again withdrawn his help. Possibly he felt rebuffed and hurt by her loan of Bellevue, his gift to her, to the French government. One would suppose that this was hardly the way to attract backers. Nevertheless, a millionaire, Otto Kahn, was moved to place the Century Theater, of which he was a "patron and subsidizer,"[8] at her disposal. Thus, on March 2 Isadora was able to announce to the newspapers that, thanks to Kahn's generosity, she was postponing her departure from the United States. Instead she was going to give a series of performances at the Century. "There are to be exhibitions of classic dancing, with Greek drama and orchestral music every evening for a month, the prices of admission ranging from ten cents to half a dollar."[9]

As if to compensate for their previous coolness, the public and critics alike reacted enthusiastically to her second opening.

> All the artists in town, half the local clergy, and the faculties of Columbia and N. Y. U. seem to consider the Century the correct rendezvous for their set these evenings, and even Pavlowa's evenings were less crowded than Miss Duncan's premiere.[10]

An important factor in the public's favorable reaction was the new setting which greatly enhanced the works shown.

> With gray hangings as a background, and hiding the boxes at the side and with the galleries in darkness, light falling only on the dancing figures, it is easy to imagine oneself back in ancient Greece itself. . . . [11] The program . . . was the same combination of Schubert, Beethoven and Brahms that had been given before, yet enlivened with so many fresh details . . . that the entire performance had the effect of complete novelty. Isadora Duncan's art is as potent as ever. . . .[12]

Less delighted, however, was Isadora's patron, who had not been consulted about the new decor. The photographer Arnold Genthe later wrote:

> I was standing at the back of the theatre as Mr. Kahn came in. I shall never forget the horror on his face when he saw that Isadora had covered the elaborate gold of the founder's lodge with unbleached muslin, and had had the first ten rows of seats taken out so that the orchestra would not be too close to the stage. Under the soothing influence of Isadora's art—she put on a beautiful program—he appeared to relent, but not for very long. . . .[13]

Her programs at the Century consisted in part of repetitions of the short dances given earlier that year: *Orpheus*, the *Iphigenias*, and *Oedipus Rex*. In *Oedipus*, Augustin appeared as the king, Margaret Wycherly as Jocasta, Irma Duncan and Margherita Sargent (Augustin's wife) as priestesses of Apollo, and Isadora as leader of the chorus. (Sarah

Whiteford, Augustin's first wife, was another priestess; evidently, she and the Duncans had remained on friendly terms.) On April 16, 1915, there was the first performance of the second movement of Tchaikovsky's *Pathétique* symphony, one of Isadora's important works. There were dances to poems by MacKaye, William Blake, and Poe, several Easter programs of music and dance, using extracts from Berlioz's *L'Enfance du Christ,* Bach's *St. Matthew Passion,* and Schubert's *Requiem March* and *Ave Maria.*

The *Ave Maria* is one of Isadora's great dances. She had composed it in two versions—as a solo, which she performed, and as a group dance, in which her pupils took the part of adoring angels. In the group version, each girl moves ahead, her chest forward. The arms are flung wide and then closed above the head, the wrists crossing, like the beating of great angelic wings. The action is so simple and subdued that when, in the third verse of the song, each dancer suddenly brings her knee up in a skip,* it comes like a sudden release or uprushing of the spirit. The body and arms make gestures of adoration and humility toward the Virgin and Child, but the movements are so strong that the humility seems only tender, not self-abasing.

At the end, the feet move very rapidly and smoothly (like the feet of Sylphides), though the angels move on half-toe, not en pointe, while the arms rise slowly upwards. There is nothing indecisive or sentimental about these gestures—they are Michelangelesque and immense.

The Virgin Mary shrinks back, as if from the Angel of Annunciation, then makes imploring gestures with her hands and arms. Then, though her head is bending low over the Child, her arms, wrists, and hands move backwards in a gesture of surprise. The angels' arm movements in the dance encompass the earth, reach to the sky, and come from the heart in yearning, as the dancers offer themselves to the Virgin and Child.

What makes the *Ave Maria* so tender is that the movements are very strong, but controlled, as if it is necessary to be gentle, not

*Anna Duncan taught an earlier version of this dance, without the skip.

frightening, to the Child. There is a sense of tremendous passion held in check through tenderness. There is also on the part of Mary a sense of humility and wonder: how could this great blessing have happened to me? Isadora and her girls would dance both versions of the *Ave Maria* many times in the coming years.

The consensus regarding these recitals was that the programs that relied least on words succeeded best. But, even if the theater had been sold-out for every performance, the low ticket prices and the missing ten rows of seats would have made it impossible for Isadora to make a profit.

Isadora also encountered trouble of another sort. On the night of April 23, the fire commissioner discovered that the twenty girls of her school were sleeping in a dormitory that had been set up in the former library of the Century in clear violation of the fire laws. The children were evicted and sent to a hotel, and, in protest, Isadora skipped her performances that afternoon and the evening of April 24. Explaining that the children had been housed backstage to save time, she declared that she was being persecuted by the authorities.[14]

According to Genthe, she had received Otto Kahn's permission to lodge the girls at the theater, but friction had developed between Isadora and her sponsor, and as a result the children were expelled.[15]

Meanwhile, Isadora's debts were mounting. Besides the cost of remodeling the Century, there had been the expense of those extra Isadorian touches, such as the hundreds of fresh lilies with which she had decorated the stage for her Easter program.

The pianist George Copeland reported a characteristic incident.[16] Isadora had asked for altars with roses on them to be placed at either side of the stage. At the dress rehearsal, she inspected the altars and expressed her dissatisfaction to her manager, Frederick Toye.

"Do you call that 'masses of roses'?"

Toye answered: "We can't afford 'masses.' Since you had most of the orchestra seats removed, even with capacity business we have a deficit of $3000 a week. Do you want to add to our deficit?"

Isadora was silent for a moment and then said gently, without irony, "How wonderful! You always know what everything costs! I just know what I want."

She got the roses.

Copeland first met Isadora in 1915. She had attended one of his concerts and had sent word that she would like to have him play for her recitals. At that time, Copeland had never seen Isadora[17] and considered her merely a silly woman who danced in scanty attire. He had, therefore, no desire to play for her. He was persuaded to meet her, however, and Isadora gave him an appointment one day at the Dionysion for 11:30 P.M. The unusual hour did little to mitigate Copeland's sense of foreboding. When Augustin Duncan met him at the door and silently beckoned him in, Copeland thought, "He's being Greek on Fourth Avenue," and he prepared himself for a pretentious evening.

He found himself in an immense studio. Isadora was not there, but the six girls were, dressed in their light dancing tunics. Presently, Isadora came in and asked him to be seated. The girls began to dance. After watching them for two hours, during which Isadora did not broach the subject of his playing for her, he surmised that this was an audition and that he would eventually be asked to perform for her. Being an established concert artist who never auditioned for people, he rose to go. Isadora detained him. In her view, the matter was already settled. She had asked the girls to dance so that he would have an opportunity to see *her* work.

Copeland made an appointment to come back and discuss matters. When he arrived, Isadora had just finished rehearsing and was lying on the floor between a plate of sandwiches and a pitcher of beer. Since there was no furniture in the rehearsal room, he joined her on the floor. She began to talk in her gentle voice. (In all the years he knew her—and some of the occasions on which he saw her were full of stress—he never knew Isadora to raise her voice. At the theater, she was always gracious to the stagehands, and she never left without saying "good night" to the electricians, dressers, and musicians.) They discussed the music she wanted him to play for her, and he agreed to give six Chopin recitals with her at the Dionysion.

After this, he saw her many times, and they talked about various aspects of the recital but not once did she rehearse with him. This fact did not occur to him, however, so entertaining and wide-ranging was her conversation, until the evening of the first performance.[18] Then Copeland went clammy with panic and called for Toye, her manager, to say he did not think he could go on. Toye sent for Isadora, who smiled gently and said: "You don't understand. It's the *music* which is important. Play as if I were not there, as if you were simply playing a recital alone, and it will be all right. You see, I can't dance without *the music*."

Since there was no alternative, Copeland did as she said. He played with such desperate concentration that it was a moment before he could identify the thunder that followed the first dance as applause. Startled, then reassured, he continued, and, by the end of the second concert, he could actually enjoy his part in the series.

Copeland remembered that Isadora was often half an hour late, or later, for her performances. On one such occasion when Toye, backstage, told her that the audience was waiting, she said serenely: "We must teach the American public the art of repose."[19]

With this attitude, she was certainly not going to indulge her audiences with light offerings if she thought they needed Greek tragedy.

Attendance at her performances had not been so heavy as she had anticipated. Lack of interest in her more ambitious projects (particularly *Oedipus*) and repercussions of the war in Europe, which was then having a depressing effect on all business enterprises,[20] combined to make her financial situation increasingly unstable. At the beginning of May 1915, she was obliged to make a public appeal for some wealthy person to guarantee the $12,000 she owed so that the trunks would not be attached before she and her pupils sailed for Europe. She said that she had spent $62,000 on her programs at the Century and had lost $12,000. She offered to put up her "Château in France" (presumably Bellevue), valued at $20,000, as collateral.[21]

The banker Frank Vanderlip,[22] the newspaper publisher Ogden Reid,[23] and other admirers (among them a young woman named

Ruth Mitchell,[24] who had never met Isadora but withdrew a large part of her savings to help the stranded performer) raised enough money to pay off the dancer's most pressing debts and to buy steamship tickets. Thus, on May 6, Isadora and her pupils sailed on the *Dante Alighieri* for Naples.[25] Her friend Mary Desti, who had come to see them off, impulsively remained on board, sailing without baggage.[26]

During this trip, an incident occurred which was to affect Isadora's relations with her young pupils. Isadora had asked her manager, Frederick Toye, to arrange a contract for her to dance in South America. Toye, however, decided to secure a contract for the four oldest girls, and without their knowledge—or Isadora's—sent a radiogram to Buenos Aires on their behalf. Isadora learned of his act and dismissed him at once, but his action left her with suspicions about her pupils' ambitions which never disappeared altogether.[27]

Isadora had intended the school's ultimate destination to be in Greece, but she feared traveling in wartime with her pupils, a number of whom carried German passports. She decided, therefore, to put the children temporarily in a boarding school in Switzerland, while she went to Athens to investigate the possibility of transferring her little group there. But, before she left her students, she gave a recital with them at the Grand Opera House in Zurich, and another on the lawn of their hotel. The receipts of the latter performance were divided between the French and German Red Cross—a most unusual act for those partisan times, indeed an unusual act for a partisan (Isadora was pro-Allied) during *any* war.

24

A Call to Arms: The Marseillaise

1915 – 1916

HEN Isadora landed in Greece, she found the country in a state of conflict. The government was undecided whether or not to cast its lot with the Central Powers (the king and court were pro-German—the queen was Princess Sophia of Hohenzollern). There was also a strong ground swell of pro-Allied sentiment among the followers of Eleuthérios Venizélos. It was a poor time to arouse official interest in backing a school of dance. But, if the Greeks were divided on the war, Isadora's allegiance was clear. Forgetting the purpose of her trip, she threw herself into the struggle. *The Pall Mall Gazette,* an English paper, reported:

> Isadora Duncan happened to arrive in Athens on the fateful day when despite M. Venizélos' parliamentary triumph, King Constantine refused to follow him down the path of destiny.
> More Greek than the Greeks, Isadora Duncan declared that someone must be up and doing for the national honor . . . and accompanied

by her brother, she snatched up a portrait of the popular statesman, and striking a characteristic pose in Constitution Square, endeavored to dance the Athenians into a sense of their responsibilities.

She only paused from time to time to harangue the people on their duties to their State and Country. "Let those who dare," she cried, "follow me! Forward to the house of Venizélos!" and with nimble feet and bewitching poise, she danced from square to square and from street to street in the hope of drawing all the town to the residence of the statesman.

Amused at first, and then not a little moved, the crowd poured breathlessly along with her; little by little, though, the people dropped off by twos and threes, until by the time the end of the journey was reached, her following was reduced to very small proportions.

Disappointed but not daunted, Isadora Duncan gave a final exhibition before the great man's residence, sang the *Marseillaise,* and sent in a handsome bouquet to the object of her admiration.

M. Venizélos sent out a word of thanks but did not show himself.[1]

Although Isadora's stay in the Greek capital was pleasant and she saw many old friends, eventually it became clear to her that at the moment Athens was not the place for her school. So, making a brief side trip to French Switzerland, where her school was now located, she traveled back to Paris.

Here she settled at the Hotel Meurice, and, on December 5, recovering from a bout of what may have been typhoid—the doctors were not sure—she wrote to Mary Fanton Roberts:

> . . . the school, after numerous tragedies is finally settled in Geneva and I hope will not be running away again.
>
> Paris is pretty sad but it suits my mood better than N.Y.
>
> . . . Yes, I went to Athens but things are in a deplorable state there. Oh where are the Heroes of Greece? I hope to be up again in a week or two and will write to you again . . . I received Wytter [sic] Bynner's *Iphigenia* and think it beautiful. Will you tell him as soon as I am better I will write and thank him. . . .[2]

Later she took a house at 23 Avenue de Méssine (on the corner of the rue de Méssine) and installed her belongings. Here she entertained her friends and many of the soldiers and officers who had been sent home as invalids or were in Paris on leave from the front. To one of these parties came Maurice Dumesnil, a young concert pianist and, until recently, a noncommissioned officer, who had been detached from the service following an attack of pneumonia. He was brought to Isadora's soiree by a colleague, the Chopin interpreter Victor Gille. "I immediately felt at home. . . . She had that special art of conveying warmth of feeling at the first contact."[3]

These parties were a heavy drain on her funds, for she provided food and drink with her customary lavishness and she never knew how many guests to expect. She had given orders that no one was to be turned away, a rule she adhered to even when a group of unkempt and rowdy Bohemians turned up at one of her distinguished gatherings. ("Oh, the poor things, they are artists and they are so hungry! . . . Perhaps among them is a future Carrière or a Rodin.")[4] Furthermore she no longer had anyone to help her underwrite her costs. "She had confided to her intimate friends that she couldn't count on Lohengrin anymore. Despite his . . . devotion the time had evidently come when he was tired of artistic temperament and he seemed to have faded out of the picture. . . ."[5]

To many of her guests, the salon where she danced seemed like the last sanctuary of light in a time of beleaguered darkness. Jacques Barzun, in *The Energies of Art,*[6] re-creates the atmosphere of that somber period and the impact of the conflict on the brilliant artistic world of Paris.

The war shattered it, flung its men into the trenches, visibly destroyed that nursery of living culture. Work ceased, conversation dulled, relatives and friends vanished. Some returned only as strangers in uniform, others were heard of as dead, wounded or doing inex-plicable things: why should Glèizes, whose business obviously was to paint, be peeling potatoes day after day near Toul? Why was Apollinaire strutting in high boots and wearing a perforated leather patch over one temple? Poor M———, always so gay and fond of roughhousing, now had a perpetual shake of the head and dropped frightening irrational remarks. Nowhere, in fact, did continuity subsist. Zeppelin raids, instant rousing followed by dreary hours in cellars . . . and the ceaseless wondering "what news?" left nothing sure but the rhythmic tread of anxiety. As season followed season, apprehension itself was dimmed by more slogans, more Red Cross collections, more drudgery and less food. Toward the end of the four years, pointlessness was the controlling emotion, and when the war was over, suddenly, it broke upon one that the self had been permanently loosened from the love of life.

In this atmosphere of despair, Isadora became the symbol of bleeding, enduring, and unconquerable humanity. Because suffering had only increased her compassion, people dared to expose their anguish before her. For many conscripts, not the least of their miseries was a sense of revulsion at the brutalities they were forced to commit. The writer, Georges Denis, wrote to her from the trenches:[7]

Friend,
   I am very unhappy. Come to my help. Write me a few words, and the frightful life I lead will become less hard. Please destroy this note. I've never spoken of my moral distress to anyone. I am ashamed of it. But you, all beautiful and all good, most perfect friend, it seems to me that next to you I could weep—I who used to mock! Tell me that you will be in Paris during my next leave, that I can see you and receive in you all that is beautiful and worth living for.
   Friend, write to the most wretched of soldiers and the most faithful of your friends.

Georges Denis
II/ B. 67
Belgian Army

Easter Day, 1916 On the Yser, in the mud and _____[8]

Back in the army, after his leave, with his memory of her healing presence still strong in him, he contrived to send her a message:

Friend:
   One of my machine gunners on leave brings you this, written

these last nights in the trenches. When he comes back our period of rest will be finished, and I'll return to the Yser.

May a word from you accompany him! Accompany me there. I also want your picture and a little of your perfume, even should it be only a scarf worn by you. Formerly knights thus wore the colors of the lady of their thoughts.

Your knight begs you to see in the enclosed poem[9] the reflection, the memory of what he said to you.

My machine gunner has been ordered to wait for your reply.

Are you going to America? Will you be in Paris in June?

My hands which are your admirers, my eyes filled with your beauty, think of you.

Georges Denis

Midnight Thursday

Denis's question to Isadora about America indicates that the dancer had probably confided in him her intention of signing a contract to tour South America. Although she might have preferred to remain in Paris ("It's sad but it suits my mood"), she needed the money; she had not only the expense of her open houses to meet but also the bills for the schooling of her pupils in Switzerland.[10]

Meanwhile, she was planning to dance at a war charity benefit concert on April 9, 1916, and Dumesnil had agreed to act as her accompanist. This occasion would do nothing to alleviate her financial woes, since the custom in France was for the artist to contribute all of his share of the profits (not half, as in the United States) and even to pay for the incidentals, such as taxi fares.[11]

Besides Isadora and Dumesnil, the organizer, Baron Estournelles de Constant, had also enlisted the aid of the Orchestre des Concerts du Conservatoire, which was to be augmented by musicians from the Opéra. Public interest in the benefit was immense. She had not performed in public in France (except at soirees in her home) since her bereavement. Admiration, spurred by curiosity, produced a tremendous rush for tickets to the benefit.

It should be understood that in Paris Isadora was more than a dancer; she was a beloved public figure. The loss of her children had sent a shock of horror and sympathy throughout the country, and her services to the nation in entertaining soldiers and in donating Bellevue as a war hospital were widely appreciated. She herself tells us that earlier, when she was travelling through the French war zone, her name had served as a safe conduct ("It is Isadora: let her pass"),[12] and the unverified incident is in keeping with what we know about her. The poet Fernand Divoire saw no incongruity in addressing a wartime choral drama, *Exhortation to Victory,* to Isadora. In it, the dancer is seen as the symbol of strength and beauty brought low by tragedy. She is urged to raise herself again and dance for victory.[13]

Isadora could not have chosen a better program for her return to the public eye. All three of her works were new compositions— *The Redemption* (to music of César Franck), Tchaikovsky's *Pathétique* (of which she had danced the second movement in her previous New York season), and *The Marseillaise.* All dealt in different ways with the assault by fate on the human spirit and the latter's ultimate triumph. All three were among her greatest works and would form part of her permanent repertoire. But on that emotionally charged occasion, when German and French forces were locked in a death struggle at Verdun and the Kaiser's army was within a few miles of Paris, it was *The Marseillaise* that roused the spectators to a frenzy. Before a distinguished audience which included the Minister of War, Painlevé, members of the government, and virtually everyone of prominence in France's social, artistic, and intellectual circles, Isadora danced with mounting intensity to the four stanzas of Rouget de Lisle's stirring revolutionary anthem. Noble, resolute, and avenging, clad in a fiery tunic, beaten to the ground to rise with superhuman strength, she seemed a whole nation at arms, and, when in a final gesture of defiance, she faced the enemy with bared breast, the people rose, tears coursing down their cheeks, and shouted until the walls rang.

Carl Van Vechten later wrote of this work:

In a robe the color of blood she stands enfolded; she sees the enemy advance; she feels the enemy as it grasps her by the throat;

Dancing the *Marseillaise*, photograph by Arnold Genthe, 1916 (*New York Public Library and the Museum of the City of New York*).

she kisses her flag; she tastes blood; she is all but crushed under the weight of the attack; and then she rises triumphant with the terrible cry, *Aux armes citoyens!* Part of her effect is gained by gesture, part by the massing of her body, but the greater part by facial expression. In her anguished appeal she does not make a sound beyond that made by the orchestra, but the hideous din of a hundred raucous voices seems to ring in our ears. We see Felicien Rops's "Vengeance" come to life; we see the sans-culottes following the carts of the aristocrats on the way to execution. . . . At times, legs, arms, a leg or an arm, the throat, or the exposed breast assume an importance above that of the rest of the mass, suggesting the unfinished sculpture of Michael Angelo, an aposiopesis which, of course, served as Rodin's inspiration.[14]

It was with a sense of relief and thanksgiving that her friend Divoire reported the occasion for the newspaper *L'Intransigéant,* for which he was a correspondent.

> Paris yesterday showed to Isadora Duncan, during the mati-nee . . . for the benefit of L'Amoire Lorraine, that it knew how to recognize those who have shared its hopes and sufferings. Isadora Duncan has found the heart of Paris again.
>
> There was something other than a theatrical triumph in the acclaim of that packed house which remained for more than an hour after the performance to shout encores and applaud, in the patience of those hundreds of spectators who waited for a long time on the Place du Trocadéro to see the car of the artist pass, and to share her flowers.
>
> These dances of which each is a tragedy, this art, unencumbered by any artifice, and in which one finds the immense simplicity of the human soul, was judged by Paris to be worthy of spreading its hands with a pure gesture above the dead; this woman who took the part of the Marseillaise was judged to be worthy of lending her body to the Marseillaise.
>
> It will be among us, her heart in agreement with ours, that Isadora Duncan will return to stay after the long journey which she is about to undertake, to devote herself to that school which is the aim of her life and where she will be happy to gather our orphans.

He sent the article to her with a little note:

> How happy I am, Big One,[15] about your beautiful victory yesterday, a real victory because it was a day which will be important for the future. I feel a child's joy . . . I am so glad, Isadora, that you have given me a little of your friendship. . . .

The success of this concert was so great that she was asked to repeat it on Sunday April 29. The Grand Théâtre in Geneva was also anxious to present her, and, since this would give her a chance to see her pupils who were nearby in a boarding school, she arranged to go to Switzerland before her second Paris concert.

Her older students appeared with her in the Geneva recital, and she had the pleasure of knowing that her friend, the Swiss composer Ernest Bloch, was among the spectators. In other respects, the audience left something to be desired. The neutral Swiss greeted her with a stolidity which she found disheartening after the enthusiasm of embattled Paris. This left her depressed and when she went back to her hotel she drank too much, but by the next morning she seemed to have recovered her cheerfulness.

She then went to the girls' boarding school, where she learned that the receipts of the Geneva concert would have to be turned over to the school for settlement of the children's bills, "leaving not even enough for traveling expenses."[16] Nevertheless she was happy at the thought of going back to France, whose patriotic fervor was more in harmony with her own mood.

She arrived home to find a notice from her landlord informing her that he would attach all her possessions except her clothes unless her rent was paid immediately. Dumesnil noted with surprise that Isadora did not seem greatly alarmed. "I've had a long career already, and there never was a moment when I wasn't worried financially. . . . We must be confident that things can be arranged. They always arrange themselves."[17]

Nevertheless, there seemed to be no means of paying the rent, so she decided to salvage five paintings by Eugène Carrière. For Carrière's art she felt a tender, almost religious, veneration. One of his pictures showing "a mother gathering to her breast the spirits of her lost children . . . Isadora cherished . . . more than any possession she had."[18] But how was she to get them out of the building under the landlord's eye? While Dumesnil posted himself at the window, Divoire and the poet René Fauchois smuggled two trunks of clothing and the five paintings into a waiting taxi.[19] If the policemen on the beat saw the unorthodox moving procedure, they took no notice, being well disposed toward Isadora, who had often sent them coffee on cold nights.

What is striking in this incident is that it should have been the paintings that Isadora chose to rescue—not her silver or furniture. Isadora felt a profound respect for all art; it was, in truth, what mattered most to her.

Shortly after her trunks and paintings had been spirited away, the landlord took possession of the house and all its furnishings, and Isadora moved back into the Hotel Meurice.

Her costumes and curtains, fortunately, were stored at the Trocadéro, in readiness for her performance on April 29, so she would be able to take them on her South American tour.

After her second concert at the Trocadéro, she made her preparations to leave France. On May 13, she and Maurice Dumesnil, whom she had appointed her musical director, traveled to Bordeaux, where they embarked on the *Lafayette* for New York.

In New York, Isadora asked her brother Augustin to join them; she needed him to act as her personal manager on her tour. With some reluctance, for he had recently remarried and was not anxious to leave his beautiful young wife, he agreed to come with his sister. Family ties among the Duncans were very strong; he knew of her loneliness and her impatience with business details.

Shortly thereafter, she, Augustin, and Dumesnil crossed over to Brooklyn and sailed on the *Byron* for South America.

❧ 25 ❧
South America
1916

HE voyage of the *Byron* from Brooklyn was leisurely, and Isadora could relax and forget about her creditors in Paris and those in New York, left from the expensive season at the Century the previous year. And relax she did in the company of a group of young boxers "whom Isadora passionately admired for their vitality and animal beauty." Also aboard ship was the Spanish painter Ernesto Valls, whose presence added much to her pleasure. She admired the intelligent young artist. "As was often the case she found a 'genius' in him which she was prepared to spread before the world. He on his part thought, as so many artists before him had done, that she was also a genius, a modern goddess. . . ."[1] The boxers would get up early to train and then go swimming in a salt water tank. Isadora "trained with them in the morning and danced for them at night so the voyage was very gay and did not seem at all long."[2]

Nevertheless, there were signs of trouble. The electrician who was supposed to take charge of lighting Isadora's performances on tour had come aboard as a fellow passenger. He proved not to be a professional electrician at all, but rather a press agent—in fact, a friend of Walter Mocchi, Isadora's South American impresario. This boded ill for the rest of Señor Mocchi's arrangements for the dancer.[3]

Then there was the matter of the champagne. The Marquis de Polignac, Singer's nephew, had sent Isadora and her party a case of Pomméry as a farewell present. When this ran out she had it replaced at the various South American ports at which they docked on the way to Rio.[4] She was drinking too much. These purchases worried Augustin who was trying to keep an eye on his sister's funds and welfare.

The dancer's various shipboard affairs were an indication of inner disquiet. True, they gave her an opportunity to exercise her charm; perhaps because of Singer's withdrawal she needed to prove that she was still desirable. But her vivacity had taken on an undertone of desperation. Away from the sustaining devotion of her many close friends in France, she needed admiration and warmth to fight off the despair that had hounded her since the death of her children. Openhearted, she apparently needed the relief of giving love as well as the reassurance of receiving it. Her emotional involvements were a cry for comfort.

When the ship docked in Buenos Aires at the beginning of July, Isadora learned with dismay that her stage hangings and carpet had not arrived. As she was scheduled to appear at the Colisseo Theatre on July 12,[5] there was no alternative but to order new curtains. The cost was approximately $4000, and, since she did not have the cash for this unexpected expense, she arranged to pay on credit. The orchestral scores of her programs were also still en route from France, but they were easily replaced through the help of the director of the Buenos Aires Conservatory, who loaned her the scores from the conservatory library.

Meanwhile, she stayed at the luxurious Plaza Hotel, and, between making preparations for her concerts, she set about seeing the city. With friends she visited not only the fashionable districts but also went slumming in La Boca, the center of the town's flashy nightlife.

Her first concert was coolly received. The public, accustomed to ballet, thought she had no technique.

On the eve of her second concert, she went with a group of intimates to a nightclub where, impelled by the conviviality of the moment, she had the unlucky inspiration of dancing to the Argentine national anthem. This dance in such a setting shocked many of the on-lookers, though it delighted others. Word of the incident enraged the manager of the Colisseo Theatre, who claimed that she had broken her contract with him by this impromptu performance. He threatened to cancel her next concert, and it took all of Dumesnil's tact, and his reminder that the tickets were already sold, to restore peace.[6]

Isadora wanted to devote her third program to Wagner. Here, however, Dumesnil refused his cooperation. He was on leave from the French army, and he felt that it would provoke censure if he took part during wartime in a program playing the works of the German master. Another conductor was therefore engaged for the evening. This Wagner program alienated many of her admirers (as those who were pro-German had been alienated previously by her dancing of *The Marseillaise*). Dumesnil reflected: "Of course I knew it would be like that, and had tried to make it plain to her. . . . Sometimes she acted as if she were anxious to be contradictory at all cost. She wanted to be on the side of the opposition."[7]

These disagreements, first between Isadora and her manager and then between her and her pianist, set the stage for what was to happen next.

During the Wagner program, there was talking in the auditorium. Isadora stopped dancing, then, as the noise continued, she announced that she had been warned that South Americans would understand nothing of art. They were all savages. "Vous n'êtes que des Nègres!"[8] Her intemperate speech not only resulted in the cancelling of her Colisseo engagement by its manager, Renato Salvati, but it also frightened away other impresarios. Eventually, she accepted a con-tract from Cesare Giulietti to give performances in Uruguay and Brazil for a percentage of the profits. It was a smaller percentage than Salvati had offered, but she was now in no position to be choosy.

These arrangements completed, Isadora insisted on visiting a nightclub to celebrate, or possibly to cheer herself up. Dumesnil, who had seen her drink heavily only once before—in Europe, on the night in Geneva when her dancing had been stolidly received—noted that she had been drinking more than usual since they had arrived in Buenos Aires.

Augustin, meanwhile, had returned to the United States. The dancer's next engagement was to be in Montevideo, but before she could leave Buenos Aires she had to settle her bill at the Plaza. Dumesnil, who had been paying for his hotel room himself, though he had yet to be paid, owed money for only two weeks; Isadora's bill covered the whole period of her Argentine stay. She was therefore forced to put up her emerald pendant and ermine coat (both gifts from Singer) as security. The new curtains, too, had to be left behind.[9]

In Montevideo, she scored an immense triumph. Tchaikovsky's *Pathétique* elicited volleys of applause, and, after *The Marseillaise,* the finale of her program, the audience poured on stage, cheering wildly. But the box-office returns for this performance remained surprisingly small. Though the theater had been packed, the sum turned over to Isadora after all the expenses had been paid was only $300. Giulietti explained his bookkeeping methods to the incredulous Dumesnil. "We split sixty-forty with the theatre. What remains we split fifty-fifty with the benefit society which sponsored the concert. Out of our share, I take my commission of fifteen percent."[10]

Giulietti had other ways of increasing his share of the proceeds. He had not bothered to have handbills made. On the leftover posters of some ballerina, he had thriftily pasted announcements of Isadora's appearances. The orchestra was hired for only one rehearsal before each performance. When Dumesnil complained, a local conductor told him: "If you have three rehearsals you get different musicians each time. . . . They send substitutes. So even a second rehearsal would be a waste of money!"[11]

Despite these handicaps, Isadora continued to arouse the enthusiasm of the Montevideans. When, after her second concert, the "receipts showed a profit of hardly over two-hundred dollars,"

Dumesnil felt sure they were being bilked. The third concert was also packed, but their profits were even less. Giulietti explained this phenomenon by saying that he had had to paper the house. Dumesnil investigated and learned that this was far from the case, but, when he confided his suspicions to Isadora, she brushed them aside. She liked Giulietti because he treated her with gallantry instead of browbeating her as the Buenos Aires manager had done. Furthermore, the financial insecurity of her childhood had left her with a positive horror of arguments over money. Rather than make a scene, she preferred to be cheated.

It was a choice she could ill afford. Each package of mail from Europe brought fresh cause for worry. As usual, she was contributing to the care or support of a number of people. A friend, her former business manager Maurice Magnus, forwarded a letter which he had received from Penelope Sikelianos Duncan, Raymond's wife, who was now in a Swiss sanatorium, having contracted tuberculosis while working among the refugees in Albania.

> I had yesterday the visit of the director of the sanatorium. He informed me that the notes (bills) of the sanatorium have not been payed [sic] for some time and that the money owed amounts now to 3,000 frs. He begged me to write to Isidora [sic] and see what was the matter. . . . I was heartbroken and it made me feel deeper than ever what trouble I am giving to that dear Isidora. . . . Tell me please what you think yourself is it possible that Isidora left perhaps for America and the secretary neglects? . . .[12]

In Montevideo, Isadora received word that her pupils had been dispersed. As there were no funds to pay their boarding school, the younger children had been sent back to their families. Since she had undertaken the South American tour precisely in order to support the school, its dissolution was particularly painful.

When Isadora and Dumesnil arrived in Rio de Janeiro after their Montevideo success, their finances were so precarious that Isadora substituted an all-Chopin program for the announced *Iphigenias,* since the latter required the services of an orchestra. (Dumesnil, in fact, had so little cash that he could not afford streetcar fare and had to walk to the theater. Isadora, however, characteristically hired an automobile on credit and stayed at one of the fashionable hotels.) The mood of her program was primarily martial, heroic, and tragic. She gave a series of preludes to which she had appended subtitles, such as "Ecstasy" or "Belgium During the War," to indicate the themes of her dances.[13] She concluded the first half of the program with the *Polonaises* in C minor and A major ("Poland Chained" and "The Resurrection of Poland"). This group of dances was received with a faint scattering of applause. She had no time for brooding, however: her costume had to be changed and her spirits composed for the second, lighter part of the program, which concluded with the *Valse Brillante*.

A tremendous ovation at the final curtain made clear the reason for the audience's previous silence: its members had been too deeply moved to applaud. Now people wept and kissed one another, and she was nearly mobbed by enthusiastic crowds. She was able to make her getaway from the theater only by tossing the wreath of roses she had worn to the waiting throngs who tore the flowers to bits to keep pieces as relics. The next day her reviews pushed the war news off the front page, and the morning paper *O Paiz* devoted its first three columns to "Isadora the divine."[14]

Before the concert, Dumesnil had taken the precaution of stationing a friend at the box office, and, although the house had been only one-third full, this time Isadora's net profit rose to $600. The following day, tickets for all subsequent performances were sold out, and Isadora was able to pay off her bills at the Plaza in Buenos Aires.

The press gave a dinner in her honor, and John do Rio, Chief Editor of *O Paiz,* paid her a great deal of attention.

During her second Rio concert, after her performance of Chopin's Sonata in B flat minor, a young man in the top gallery was moved to make an impromptu speech: "Isadora, you have come to us like a messenger from the Gods. . . . You will never realize what this art has meant to us of the younger generation. It has been the great revelation of truth. . . ."

Isadora wept and answered, "I know you understand me . . . and I love you all. Thank you—thank you."

Fired by the audience's warmth, she then danced even better than before. Dumesnil noted: "On that occasion, and even more than ever, I could see how dependent Isadora was upon the sympathy of her audience. . . . Should [their reaction] be negative, her spontaneity would shrink and turn into an antagonistic disposition. But if it happened to be as decidedly positive as it was in Rio, she would . . . behave like an adorable creature whose charm made everybody kneel at her shrine."[15]

On this night, she was so stimulated by the crowd's responsiveness that after the performance she wanted to continue dancing, so she went to the Copacabana beach, exchanged her dress for a short tunic, and danced at the edge of the waves for a dozen or so friends.

Later, as rumor transformed this impromptu performance, it was said that Isadora had danced on the beach naked. By this time, however, she was such a popular favorite that "Those who had [believed the story] thought it was decidedly original, artistic and 'truly Parisian'!"[16]

At her third Rio concert *(Iphigenia),* the secretary, who had previously insisted that the orchestra be paid in advance, now refused to accept money until after the performance. By this time, Isadora had made enough money to pay her debts in Buenos Aires, and she was hopeful for the return of her ermine coat and emerald pendant.

In Rio, Dumesnil witnessed an astonishing instance of Isadora's method of rehearsal. She was scheduled to dance Beethoven's *Pathétique Sonata* which she had not previously danced with him. She came to the rehearsal in her street clothes and asked Dumesnil to play the sonata for her. She heard it through three times, "listening in an attitude of thoughtful concentration," and, at the end of the third time, she said, "Thank you. This time I have it." At the concert, Dumesnil played for her in a state of amazement. Her performance, without any danced rehearsal, left him baffled. It was as good as anything she had ever done.[17]

Incidents like this, taken with Isadora's statement that she "improvised" the *Marseillaise*[18] at the Metropolitan Opera House, lend credence to the myth that her dances were invented on the spur of the moment. But for all their air of spontaneity, her dances were carefully composed and their general outlines remained fixed, even though, like other choreographers, she might polish or revise. She herself wrote of her work: "Some people explained it all by saying 'See, it is natural dancing!' But with its freedom, its accordance with natural movement there was always design, too,—even in nature you find sure, even rigid design.—'Natural' dancing should mean only that the dancer never goes against nature, not anything is left to chance."[19] The only time she seems to have improvised a dance in public that became part of her repertoire was her performance of the *Marche Funèbre* in Kiev, after visualizing it the night before in all its details.[20]

The audiences of São Paulo were much less enthusiastic than had been those of Rio, but now it no longer mattered greatly; their tour of South America had drawn to a close. Isadora was eager to have Dumesnil return with her to New York and, with her, tour the United States. But Dumesnil was reluctant to accompany the dancer; he had not been paid in four months, and he had also received some tempting offers of engagements in South America. Unable to make her see his point, he privately went to their manager, Sẽnor Giulietti, who withdrew the pianist's share of the profits and paid him separately—in front of Isadora. Furious at what she considered Dumesnil's disloyalty in applying to Giulietti, the dancer denounced both men and had to resign herself to travelling back to the United States alone.[21]

She had the memory of overwhelming triumphs to cheer her departure and the comforting knowledge that by her successes in Montevideo and Rio she had recouped her earlier losses. But her chief purpose, that of raising money for the school, remained unachieved. If she could not find money immediately, the older girls would have to follow the younger girls back to their families, and the school, which had received so many accolades and endured so many vicissitudes, would have to be dissolved.

❧ 26 ❧

Break with Lohengrin
1916–1918

SADORA arrived, unannounced, in New York on the *Vestris* on September 27, 1916,[1] called up her friend Arnold Genthe from the dock, and was delighted to hear Singer answer the telephone. He had not seen her for some time and on learning that she was alone at the pier he at once offered to meet her. Isadora was overjoyed. "When I saw his tall, commanding figure again I had a curious feeling of confidence and safety, and I was delighted to see him as he was to see me. . . . I have always been faithful to my loves, and in fact would probably never have left any of them if they had been faithful to me. For just as I loved them once, I love them still and forever."[2]

As for Singer, Isadora and her concerns were seldom a matter of indifference to him. He "was in one of his kindest and most generous moods."[3] Learning of her anxiety about the school, he at once cabled funds to pay the bills that had accumulated at the children's boarding school. By this time, unfortunately, most of the pupils had been dispersed to their homes, but the six oldest girls remained and Augustin was dispatched to Switzerland to bring them back.

Isadora and Singer assumed their familiar life almost as if they had never been separated, seeing one another constantly, taking trips together, and entertaining their circle at handsome receptions or small elegant dinners. One of these was a party that Singer gave for Isadora at Sherry's on Fifth Avenue. Arnold Genthe, who was one of the guests, remembers: "I have never seen her in better form than she was during the dinner. To please Singer, she wore an exquisite white chiffon frock and diamond necklace which he had just given her. All went well until the dancing began."[4] Isadora wanted to dance the tango with a young man characterized as "the most famous tango dancer in the Argentine," and she asked Genthe to bring him over to the table.

"They proceeded to dance a tango that astonished the guests by something more than mere grace and rhythm."[5] The tango, Isadora believed, was meant to be a sensual and alluring dance "based on sexual desire and the right of possession,"[6] and she was determined to dance it in the authentic sultry Argentine fashion. Out of the corner of her eye, she could probably see Singer nervously raising his shoulders, as he did when he felt impatient or disapproving— a habit that irritated her.[7] He "stood watching them, a giant of fury—he was six feet six—until they were half through. Then he strode into the middle of the floor, took the Argentine by the scruff of the neck and slithered him out of the room."

"Isadora turned pale, and with the air of a prima donna, she called out, 'if you treat my friends like that, I won't wear your jewelry.' She tore the necklace from her throat and the diamonds scattered on the floor. As she swept from the room, I was standing in the doorway. Without looking at me she whispered, 'Pick them up.' "[8]

Their quarrel did not last long, however, and on November 21, 1916, Singer hired the Metropolitan Opera House so that Isadora could give a free gala concert for their friends. Admission was by invitation only. "When we reached the day of the performance,"

Whether it was this notion that upset the dancer, or whether, as another writer[14] stated, Isadora was angry because Singer had objected to her association with Kid McCoy, the fact remains that the course of the dinner Singer later gave at the Plaza Hotel in New York, for the purpose of announcing his plans for Isadora's school, did not go as intended.

> Among those there, [wrote Genthe] were Augustin and Margherita Duncan, Isadora's sister Elizabeth, Mary Desti, George Gray Barnard and myself.
> "Do you mean to tell me," asked Isadora, "that you expect me to direct a school in Madison Square Garden? I suppose you want me to advertise prizefights with my dancing."
> Singer turned absolutely livid. His lips were quivering and his hands were shaking. He got up from the table without saying a word and left the room.
> "Do you realize what you have done?" we asked in a chorus of dismay.
> "He'll come back," she said serenely. "He always does."
> He never did.[15]

After scores of quarrels and reconciliations, separations and joyful reunions, she had at last managed to deal Singer a rebuff which he could not overlook.

The poet, Witter Bynner, in a conversation with the author, cast some light on the background of Singer's offer to Isadora. In Bynner's presence, Singer had chided the dancer for some provocative action. Isadora had said to Singer challengingly, "What did you think of my performance?" Singer replied, "I liked *half* of it very much. And if you could only keep your behavior to the level of the first half, and cease making these public scandals, there's nothing I wouldn't give you!"

"What would you give me?" Isadora asked, half-jokingly.

"—Madison Square Garden," said Singer.

"What are your conditions?"

"That you always behave yourself with dignity in public."

"I'm not sure that I can meet your conditions," Isadora replied, teasingly. The Palm Beach trip followed. And when Singer made a public announcement of his gift, Isadora reacted as we have seen.

But what were the underlying motives that induced Isadora to rebuff Singer? There are striking similarities between this quarrel and previous ones which had occurred between Singer and Isadora. When he proposed to marry her and take her away from the stage, she fell in love with the pianist André Capelet. When he offered to build a theater for her, she flirted with Henry Bataille. When he gave her Bellevue, she loaned it to the French government for a hospital. When he presented her with a diamond necklace, she danced a provocative tango with another man. When he took an option on Madison Square Garden, she publicly ridiculed his gift.

In short, each time Singer gave or offered her something he considered valuable, she refused it or picked a quarrel, as if to demonstrate: "You may be rich, but don't imagine that you can buy me!"

As in her dealings with Otto Kahn and Mayor Mitchell, Isadora often antagonized the very people whose patronage she sought. But with Paris Singer, whom she loved, this compulsion became more pronounced. She mentions several times that he was a commanding person, someone accustomed to getting his own way. While this quality made her feel confident and safe, at the same time she resented it and felt a need to show her independence. Knowing his jealous streak, she would behave in ways that could only provoke his suspicions, even when the object of his jealousy was (like the tango dancer) someone for whom she entertained no special feeling. She resented Singer's wealth; to her, financiers—indeed, all the rich—were insensitive to human values. Throughout her life she would have it known that she considered business morality subservient to artistic morality. Indeed, she had a dislike amounting to dread of business affairs. It is possible that she unconsciously identified Singer with her banker father, who, by his bank's failure and his desertion of his family,* had left the Duncans to fend for them-

---

*Not his *financial* desertion. He helped his family as soon as he was financially able to do so, but his fortunes were subject to extreme ups and downs.

selves. If so, it would explain why she was so anxious for Singer's love and yet had such a drive to test that love and to punish him by rejecting his gifts. This is purely a guess; psychoanalysis at long distance, though stimulating, can lay no claim to authority.

But what of Singer? For all their quarrels and Isadora's rejection of his gifts, he kept returning to her. What was her hold over him? Isadora once asked him this question, and he answered after some thought: "You've got a good skin, and you've *never* bored me."[16]

This remark, for all its superficiality, is telling. Isadora was very different from the fashionable people among whom Singer moved. Clearly, she was unconventional. Though he was a member of high society, too rich, powerful, and well-connected by his sisters' marriages to be snubbed, a sense of his father's humble origins and gaudy domestic arrangements may have made him wonder on occasion to what extent he was truly accepted. Like the dancer, he was aware of old family scandals that must be lived down. Isadora, however, was outside of society and had apparent indifference to society's opinion that he must have found both troubling and stimulating.

Besides, her life had a purpose. She was a "doer." Singer, though a man of taste, intelligence, and ambition, was energetic only by fits and starts, a beginner and dropper of projects.[17] Being rich, he lacked the usual incentives for work. He liked to think of himself as an architect, but he could always cancel his commitments and sail off on his yacht. Only intermittently did he exhibit his dominating and violent father's compulsion to make money.[18]

Yet he was willful, and, like Isadora he was impatient of obstacles, a seer of things on a grand scale. Isadora offered him a hundred ways in which to employ his energies, and by helping her with her projects he could feel that he was making a contribution to the arts. Furthermore, she was never at a loss for ways to spend money, whether it was founding schools, building theaters, adopting children, feeding refugees, or even giving parties. "I had always thought how marvelous a fête one could give if only one had enough money," she wrote, adding pityingly: "It seems to me that rich people never know how to amuse themselves."[19] She was, like Singer himself, both lavish and generous.

And though she accepted presents from him, as an empress might accept presents from a tributary king, she felt bound to demonstrate that she answered to no one but herself. Her independence may initially have reassured him that she did not love him for his money,[20] for she defied it whenever she could. In the end, of course, he found this trait to be infuriating.

But many other traits were permanently endearing. He had been greatly attached to his mother,[21] and Isadora, when she was not battling him, was both gentle and maternal. Thus Singer and Isadora each found in the other qualities which they needed, as well as characteristics which would always anger them.

Isadora's hasty refusal of Singer's gift caused him the loss of $100,000[22] when he sold the option on Madison Square Garden. More than that, it cost her the love of the father of her adored, vanished Patrick, the man on whom she had come to depend in so many ways, both material and emotional. Profoundly wounded, as well as furious, Paris refused all attempts at a reconciliation. His withdrawal left the improvident Isadora with a large hotel bill and bills for the support of her pupils still outstanding. Fortunately, she had the emerald pendant, diamond necklace, and ermine coat, all gifts from Singer, so she sold these and took a house for the summer at Long Beach. Here she gathered her pupils and invited many old and new friends, among them the violinist Ysaye and the playwright Mercedes de Acosta. With pupils and house guests, the hot months passed quickly and pleasantly, and by the time autumn came her funds were nearly exhausted.

It was necessary to work, and so she accepted a contract to tour California. This was the first time she had seen her native San Francisco since leaving it twenty-two years before as an obscure young dancer of seventeen. She was now thirty-nine. Whatever excitement she might have felt at her arrival was dampened by the news from France of the death of her close friend Rodin. Her reunion with her mother, who had returned to California to live, became an occasion for stocktaking. "She looked very old and careworn

... seeing our two selves in a mirror I could not help contrasting my sad face and the haggard looks of my mother with the two adventurous spirits who had set out ... with such high hopes to seek fame and fortune. Both had been found—why was the result so tragic?" In a mood of sad reminiscence, she hired a car and toured the city, looking for the various modest houses where the Duncans had lived between evictions when she was a child. It took her almost an entire day to find them all.[23]

But presently her spirits rose. Her concerts were well received, and the San Franciscans turned out in numbers to welcome their most famous daughter. And as always when she had the chance, she attended the concerts of other artists. On one of these occasions, after she had listened to the playing of Harold Bauer, her friend Ysaye brought her backstage to meet the pianist. To her surprise, Bauer greeted her with: "Miss Duncan, I must tell you the story of my life because you are certainly unaware that you have had a greater influence on it than anyone else." Years before, he explained, when he was still a music student, he had seen an obscure dancer perform in a private salon in Paris. He was then having trouble with his piano technique, and, watching the young entertainer, whose name he had not caught, he suddenly saw a way around his difficulty. "Her movements fascinated me with their beauty and rhythm. . . . As I watched her carefully the idea crept into my mind that this process might conceivably be . . . a reversible one. . . . As long as a loud tone apparently brought forth a vigorous gesture, and a soft tone a delicate gesture, why in playing the piano should not a vigorous gesture bring forth a loud tone and a delicate gesture a soft tone? The fact that this was precisely what had always taken place (in piano playing) did not occur to me." Bauer then delighted her by proposing that they give a recital together.[24]

During the long hours while they rehearsed together, they discovered that they had many friends, attitudes,[25] and interests in common. "Unlike most musicians his scope was not limited to music alone, but embraced a fine appreciation of all art and a wide intellectual knowledge of poetry . . . and philosophy."[26] Their musical dialogues seemed to employ a kind of clairvoyant shorthand in which one would compete or illustrate the other's unspoken thought; they learned from each other about the meaning of phrases not hitherto understood. Each felt the stimulation of working with such a partner. Isadora called him her "musical twin."

Some of Isadora's ideas at first startled Bauer. One of the pieces she was to dance was Chopin's Étude in A flat, Op. 25, no. 1 "in the course of which the melody rises to a dramatic climax and then appears to diminish to the end of the phrase. As we were rehearsing, Isadora said to me, 'You are playing that wrong. The crescendo must continue until the very end of the phrase, and you can soften it later.' I was somewhat nettled and replied that the music clearly indicated the phrasing which I had employed. 'I can't help that,' she retorted with superb egotism. 'The music *must* go that way, otherwise there would be nothing to do with my arms. Besides,' she added obstinately, 'you are quite mistaken' . . . the end of the story is that I have played the piece her way ever since, for I discovered that Chopin's manuscript bore the precise dynamic curve which she had instinctively sensed and which had been subsequently altered."[27]

On January 3, 1918 Isadora and Bauer gave a Chopin program at the Columbia Theatre which the dancer considered one of the happiest events of her career—although the impetus for the recital was far from happy. Isadora's manager had just absconded with the receipts from her performances, leaving her with a bill to be paid at the expensive St. Francis Hotel.[28] Bauer had at once volunteered to give his services for her benefit, and their joint Chopin recital was the result. " 'Isadora Duncan's splendor did not manifest itself alone in her dancing,' reported the San Francisco Bulletin. 'She did a splendidly spontaneous thing when flushed with [success] she . . . retrieved a chaplet of roses and [placed it on] the piano in acknowledgement of the praise that was due her fellow artist.' "[29]

Shortly thereafter, on her return from one of his concerts, we find her writing on the stationery of her San Francisco hotel: "How can I write of this Holy Hour we spent today with the Beethoven Sonatas—how describe those? The public stood like a band of pilgrims come to some holy shrine for revelation, sat with bowed heads and throbbing hearts. Looking over those transformed extatic [sic] faces I realized that Great Art is the highest and most dependable religion we have today and the message of a Beethoven through the Soul of Harold Bauer a thousand times more conducing towards divine living than the dogma of any religion."[30] She was in love.[31] Having formed a close friendship with the music critic Redfern Mason with his permission Isadora wrote a eulogy of Bauer over Redfern's signature.[32] Bauer, however, was a married man, and their association was of necessity short-lived. Isadora says tersely: "Our collaboration ended with a forced and dramatic separation."[33]

After Bauer's departure, Redfern did his best to console Isadora, not unsuccessfully, as will be seen by a note from her, now in the Redfern Mason papers at the Bancroft Library.[34]

> Aren't you glad that I can still dance a Bacchanal and that some-times in a quiet landscape I wish for a Fawn to part the bushes and leap forth to seize a not unwilling Nymph.
>
> Most lovingly,
> Isadora.

Somewhat comforted for Bauer's loss, Isadora left San Francisco and returned to New York.

❧ 27 ❧

Encounter with an Archangel
1918–1921

ACK in New York once more, Isadora considered returning to France. She was emotionally at loose ends
and, as usual, was pressed for funds. In Paris, she
might be able to realize some money on her property.
Thanks to the help of Mary Desti's friend, Gordon Selfridge (the
owner of Selfridge's department store in London), who bought
Isadora a steamship ticket, she was able to sail for England, and
from there an acquaintance from the French embassy brought her
back to Paris.[1]

Here, in the city where her children had died, a city whose
exhausted inhabitants were jolted into consciousness before dawn
each morning by the booming of "Big Bertha" to face a long day
of monotonous anxiety varied only by word of fresh losses, Isadora
tried to get back to work, but she found it an effort.

One day her secretary, Christine Dalliès, brought the pianist
Walter Rummel to see her.[2] Isadora likened his entrance into her
life to a song by Wagner in which a soul sitting in darkness and

sadness is comforted by an angel. She named him "the Archangel."
Rummel played for her and introduced her to Liszt's *Thoughts of
God in the Wilderness* and once again she felt inspired to work.

Walter Morse Rummel was a distinguished pianist. Through his
father, the British pianist Franz Rummel, he was descended from a
German family of musicians. Through his American mother, he was
the grandson of Samuel F. B. Morse, the painter and inventor of
the telegraph. The younger Rummel had made a name for himself
with his interpretations of Bach and the Romantics and his advocacy
of contemporary composers, particularly Debussy, in whose "inner
circle" he belonged. He was also a composer, whose works "combined the charm of Debussy with the romantic dreaminess of Schumann and a strong influence of Wagner and César Franck."[3]

At the time of their meeting, he was a tall man of thirty-one
whose appearance reminded Isadora strongly of that of the young
Franz Liszt. He had great charm and his gentleness of manner and
magnanimity were qualities that must have especially appealed to
Isadora. The musician Sacha Votichenko gave an example of Rummel's generosity toward other artists. Before Votichenko's London
debut, Rummel took the trouble to introduce the Russian musician
to the powerful critic Ernest Newman, with the result that Newman
himself wrote a review of Votichenko's concert—only four days
before Rummel himself was slated to give a concert.[4] Now he
characteristically put aside the demands of his own career in order
to work with Isadora. Thus began a peaceful, productive period in
the dancer's life. As always, Isadora was happiest when she could
collaborate with someone she loved—and she and Rummel, despite
the ten years' difference in their ages, had fallen in love. He was
both a salve and a tonic to her torn spirit: he gave her the serenity
needed to create and the will to extend her art to its farthest limits.

The two moved to Cap Ferrat on the French Riviera where they
lived very quietly. She wrote to her pupils who were touring in
America with the pianist George Copeland, ". . . Music has been in
all my life the great Inspiration and will be perhaps someday the
Consolation, for I have gone through such terrible years. No one
has understood since I lost Deirdre and Patrick how pain has caused

me at times to live almost in a delirium. In fact my poor brain has been more crazed than anyone can know. Sometimes quite recently I feel as if I were awakening from a long fever. . . ."[5] Occasionally she and Rummel visited their neighbors, but they spent most of their time composing and rehearsing in their studio converted from a garage which the Grand Hotel had put at their disposal.[6] During this period, Isadora created dances to Liszt's *Les Funerailles* and *Bénédiction de Dieu dans la Solitude,* enlarged her Wagner repertory, and rearranged some of her already composed Chopin pieces into a Suite: *Poland Tragic, Poland Heroic,* and *Poland Langorous and Gay.*[7]

Sometimes they would emerge from their retreat to tour or give a concert for the wounded, with Rummel accompanying Isadora. The communion that existed between musician and dancer was almost telepathic, as Votichenko recalled. Neither performer tried to upstage the other; instead, each was inspired to surpass his or her own best efforts. Isadora, in any case, was always modest, even humble, with other artists. Her relation to Rummel seems to have been free of the power struggles that marred her relation to Singer. Rummel was a musician and therefore, by definition, a kindred spirit, and his sweetness of manner would in all events have posed no threat to her independence. A glimpse of Rummel as he had been at nineteen is provided by one of his youthful notebooks now preserved in the Duncan Collection of the New York Public Library. How this book came to be found among Isadora's possessions— whether he accidentally left it behind, or had loaned it to the dancer—is not known. It shows the young musician to have been sensitive, introspective, idealistic, melancholy, and rather consciously literary. Though the years had given him more assurance, he remained introspective and idealistic.

After the Armistice was signed, the couple moved back to Paris, where Isadora intended to revive her school. She found the great pavilion at Bellevue a shambles after four years of use, first as a military hospital and then as an educational center for American troops. She spent several weeks in the Herculean task of trying to raise funds to set the place to rights, before Rummel finally convinced her that it would be wiser to sell the building to the French government. Had she received what the property was worth and invested the money, notes Alan Ross Macdougall, she might have been able to live the rest of her life in affluence.[8]

With the proceeds of this sale, Isadora bought a house in the Rue de la Pompe, Passy, a fashionable residential district of Paris. The house contained a small theater, formerly known as the Salle Beethoven, which Isadora felt would be suitable for rehearsals and performances by herself and her school.

This done, Isadora, Rummel, and Christine Dalliès set off for a month's tour of North Africa.[9] From Biskra, on October 29, 1919, Rummel sent a postcard to the poet Fernand Divoire:

> In the sun at last—a marvelous chance to open the School here, many Negro pupils, government backing with a big subsidy and a splendid site offered by the native government. Isadora enthusiastic. Sees the future of the dance in Africa. Cordially, Walter Rummel.[10]

To which Christine added:

> Pronounced sympathetic movement among the "native swallows."
> Ch. Dalliès.

And Isadora, too, signed her name.

Why this scheme fell through is not known. At the end of 1919, they returned to France by way of Italy[11] and Isadora made plans for the coming year.

In March and April of 1920 the dancer, with the assistance of the conductor Georges Rabani, presented a series of recitals to orchestral music at the Trocadéro. She gave a second series of performances in the first half of June, with Walter Rummel acting as her musical partner for their Chopin festival and Rabani and the orchestra accompanying her in performances devoted to symphonic works. In the printed program[12] for these concerts, Isadora speaks with nostalgic pride of her six adult pupils—"deprived of my guidance by the harshness of war"—who were then successfully appearing in America. Eager to reconstitute her school, Isadora now asked them to come, and, although it meant the sacrifice of a profitable American contract, conscious of their debt to her, they hurried to rejoin her.[13]

It was Isadora's plan to go with Rummel and the six girls to Greece. The photographer Edward Steichen, tempted by the thought of photographing the group against the columns of the Parthenon, traveled with them. His camera was to make more than a record of an Aegean holiday; it would provide a clue to what happened that unlucky summer.

In Athens, Eleuthérios Venizélos, the Greek diplomat and friend of Isadora who was sponsoring their visit, put the Zappeion at their disposal. Here Isadora and her young group of dancers rehearsed each morning.

> Every day we went to the Acropolis, and remembering my first visit there in 1904[14] it was for me an intensely touching sight to see the youthful forms of my pupils now in their dance realizing a part, at least, of the dream I had there sixteen years before. . . . We found Kopanos a ruin, inhabited by shepherds and their flocks of mountain goats, but nothing daunted I decided soon to clear the ground and rebuild the house. . . . The accumulated rubbish of years was cleared away and a young architect undertook the task of putting in doors and windows and a roof. . . . Here, every afternoon with the . . . sun setting behind the Acropolis and diffusing soft purple and golden rays over the sea, my Archangel played to us magnificent and inspired music. . . .

A dream realized—as dreams so often are in life, with the vision accomplished, but the results unforeseen. Steichen's photographs, the details clear in the bright Mediterranean light, foretell what happened next. We see the six girls, returned from their American tour, "young, pretty, successful," each seemingly an emanation of the youthful Isadora, and Isadora herself, careworn and matronly, her eager spirit disguised under the too, too solid flesh her body had assumed. Now forty-three, she was ten years older than Rummel; she appears nearly twice that. Taught by the dancer to cherish a certain kind of beauty, it is not astonishing that Rummel should have found it in Anna, one of the six pupils.

The situation soon became impossible for all three. Each was bound to the other two by ties of shared work, common purpose, and deep affection. The couple was reluctant to break up the group. Though she was tortured with jealousy, Isadora did not want to send away her musical collaborator, whom she still loved, nor did she feel she could expel her pupil-rival, who since early childhood had made the school her home. Nor was Isadora, as an exponent of freedom, in a reasonable position to object to their love. But object she did. The violence of her feelings frightened her. In the restlessness of despair, she appears to have wandered into an Orthodox church, where the face of a suffering Christ made a profound impression on her. She sought to lose herself in work, to teach her pupils "Beauty, Calm, Philosophy and Harmony" while she was "inwardly . . . writhing in torment." Her only resource was to assume an "exaggerated gaiety and try to drown my sufferings in the heady wines of Greece."[15]

Their painful sojourn was put to an end by the death of the young king of Greece and the subsequent fall of Venizélos who had invited them to Athens. In her memoirs, Isadora gives the impression that Rummel and Anna left the group shortly after their return to Paris, but, in life, matters seldom arrange themselves as swiftly or tidily as they do in books.

The truth is that Rummel, Anna, and Isadora each made every effort to avoid breaking up the school. Once, moved by the beauty of Anna's dancing to *The March to the Grail,* Isadora told her that beside that achievement their personal differences faded into insignificance.[16] Again, Isadora was torn with jealousy, and the couple's presence or absence would be equally bitter to her.

As late as the second week of January 1921, Isadora and Rummel were in fact giving concerts together in Holland, and the following week, Isadora and four of her pupils, including Anna, danced together at the Théâtre des Champs Elysées in Paris. *La Liberté* (January 27) said of Isadora's dancing of Isolde: "She made her too grief stricken and prostrated, she did not give her the frenetic exaltation

In Paris, 1920 (*Archives for the Performing Arts, San Francisco*).

which is in the music." This tells us something of Isadora's inner state and suggests that a break with Rummel had occurred during the course of this engagement, a suggestion that is strengthened by a letter of Rummel written to Isadora from Monte Carlo on February 21. In this letter, he says that he has not seen Isadora for several weeks, having left because of her unhappiness and her refusal to see him. At the same time, he expresses his concern for the young pupil, whom he did not want to separate from her work or from Isadora. His sense of responsibility toward both women is very evident, as is his devotion. He would try to remake his life away from France and "all that is Duncan." He closes, begging Isadora not to despair: "The great ones that hover over you will always be with you, never forget *that*. . . . There is another world that is *within*. Dionysos has left and has been replaced within, he is above, without— Christ is within and he is building up the shattered temple within you." Apparently this expression of concern at first struck Isadora as pious hypocrisy, for in her bitterness she scrawled on a scrap of paper, later found in her effects, "Dionysus—hier/Christos— aujourd'hui/après demain Bacchus—Enfin!"[17] But on rereading the letter, the suffering and the sincerity of the writer were so apparent that she evidently relented and allowed a reconciliation, for we read that Isadora and Rummel gave a Chopin festival at the Théâtre du Parc in Brussels on May 2, 1921,[18] a concert that was one of the most successful of their joint careers. Shortly before this, Isadora and Walter Rummel had appeared together in a series of concerts in London,[19] where they were so well received that they came back for an extended engagement which presumably lasted through May 29.[20]

But despite their shared successes, the relationship had apparently been too strained by all that had gone before. It could not resume its former closeness, and Rummel again withdrew, not, however, soon enough to avert the break that he had feared between Isadora and her pupil. Anna left the group.[21] The difficulty in ascertaining precisely when or in what sequence these departures took place suggests a cycle of reconciliations after estrangements—suggests, in short, the reluctance that each felt at making an absolute break with the others. On May 31, Rummel wrote sadly to his friend Dolly Votichenko,[22]

> I have not seen [Isadora] since Belgium and I am not going to see her again till she feels she can see me as a friend. Everybody has been doing *all* they can to keep the school together, . . . it is impossible. . . .

The final departure of Rummel and Anna[23] reawoke Isadora's anguish. Each love affair after the death of her children had been an attempt to regain her equilibrium, to give her life meaning, and to make it possible for her to work. Each failure, subsequently, plunged her further into despair. In every loss, she felt the ache of all previous losses as if for the first time. Her relations with her former pupil and her former lover had been made unnatural by a sense of received and inflicted pain. Heartsick, she found it difficult to resume a life of composing and giving concerts alone. Formerly, work had been her refuge, but now her school was scattered. She must resort to heroic measures if she were to continue dancing.

Isadora was not equipped to bear pain passively. A lifetime of surmounting the odds had taught her the necessity of exerting her will through action. It was her creed that something could always be done and that it was up to her to do it, not to do without it. Whenever she had suffered a blow, her first reaction had been to try to forget her suffering by doing something for others. And as she had worked for the refugees at Santa Quaranta after the death of Patrick and Deirdre, and as she had given Bellevue for a war hospital after the loss of her third child, now she thought of founding a new school where it would be most needed.

In the summer of 1920, before her departure for Greece, she had made several appeals to the French government to underwrite her school. Her friend Christine Dalliès took notes on one of these impromptu speeches made from the stage after a concert. Among other things, the dancer said:

> Today I propose my school to France, but France, in the person of the amiable Minister of Fine Arts, gives me a smile. I cannot nourish

the children in my school on a smile. . . . Help me get my school. If not, I will go to Russia with the Bolshevists. I know nothing about their politics. I am not a politician. But I will say to their leaders: "Give me your children, and I will teach them to dance like Gods, or—assassinate me." . . . For if I do not have my school I would far rather be killed. . . .[24]

In the spring of 1921, apparently after her final break with Rummel, she returned to this theme. To reporters she denied a rumor that she had been invited to found a school in Soviet Russia, but she made clear her willingness to accept such an invitation if it should be made.[25] In fact an invitation already *had* been made, but so far it was unofficial. It had originated with Leonid Krassine, the head of the Soviet Trade Commission, who had been very much moved by seeing her dance the *Marche Slave* in London.

The *Marche Slave,* composed in the United States in 1917, celebrated the overthrow of the Russian monarchy and the freeing of the serfs. Carl Van Vechten wrote about this dance:

> With her hands bound behind her back, groping, stumbling, head bowed, knees bent, she struggles forward, clad only in a short red garment that barely covers her thighs. With furtive glances of extreme despair she peers above and ahead. When the strains of *God Save the Czar* are first heard in the orchestra she falls to her knees and you see the peasant shuddering under the blows of the Knout. . . . Finally comes the moment of release, and here Isadora makes one of her great effects. She does not spread her arms apart with a wide gesture. She brings them forward slowly and we observe with horror that they have practically forgotten how to move at all. They are crushed, these hands, crushed and bleeding after their long serfdom; they are not hands at all but claws, broken, twisted, piteous claws! The expression of frightened, almost uncomprehending joy with which Isadora concludes the march is another stroke of her vivid imaginative genius.[26]

Greatly stirred, Krassine came backstage after the performance and offered to try to get her a contract with the Soviet government to found a school. Though pleased, Isadora rejected the idea of a contract that would turn her project into a money-making scheme. Instead, at Krassine's suggestion, she wrote to the People's Commissioner of Education, Anatole Lunacharsky, setting forth her own conditions:

> I shall never hear of money in exchange for my work. I want a studio-workshop, a house for myself and pupils, simple food, simple tunics, and the opportunity to give our best work. . . . I want to dance for the masses, for the working people who need my art and have never had the money to come and see me. And I want to dance for them for nothing. . . . If you accept me on these terms I will come and work for the future of the Russian Republic and its children.[27]

This done, she returned to Paris, where, immediately after issuing her disclaimer, she received a telegram from Lunacharsky:

> Come to Moscow. We will give you your school and a thousand children. You may carry out your idea on a big scale.

Isadora replied:

> Accept your invitation. Will be ready to sail from London July first.[28]

Thus, two days after the rumor had appeared in the newspapers, *Le Figaro* and *Le Petit Parisien* confirmed on May 28 that Mme. Isadora Duncan was going to Soviet Russia to found a school.

She would leave the old bourgeois world of luxuries and self-indulgence, where she had met with so many misfortunes, and devote herself to the necessities of a new world. Her school would help bring it into being, to shape the character of its young citizens, to develop "the free spirit which will inhabit the body of new woman . . . the highest intelligence in the freest body!"[29] Full of revived hope and determination, she crossed over to London, to take the steamer which would carry her on the first stage of her journey to the Soviet Union.

❧ 28 ❧

To Revolutionary Russia
1921

INCE the deaths of her son and daughter, Isadora's life had become a search—for love to replace the love she had lost, for some way to establish the school that would perpetuate her dance, and for the money she needed to carry out her plans. The school had always seemed the most effective way of transmitting her message to succeeding generations. Now it would be her only surviving child, her only hope of immortality. As the body which was her instrument of expression grew older, a sense of the urgency of her mission increased: there *must* be young dancers to ensure the continuation of her art when she was no longer able to perform. It was this sense of urgency that prompted Isadora to go to Russia. She was not repelled by the fact that the country was in turmoil and that she had heard terrible tales of violence from her émigré friends. She had never been sympathetic to the czarist regime, with its institution of serfdom; indeed, she had rejoiced at its overthrow. Like many of the people of the 1920s, she was hopeful that communism would abolish the old abuses and lead the way to a better society.

In London, she gave a final series of concerts with her pupils Irma, Lisa, and Thérèse (Margot was not well enough to dance) at Queen's Hall. They were accompanied by the London Symphony Orchestra, conducted by Désiré Defauw.[1] She also took the opportunity to say farewell to several old friends before leaving for Russia, among them Ellen Terry, grandmother of Deirdre, and Kathleen Bruce, now the widow of the explorer Robert Scott. It was at Lady Scott's house that Isadora for the only time in her life met George Bernard Shaw. This encounter is worth mentioning if only because of the well-known anecdote which describes Isadora as writing to Shaw, urging him, for eugenic purposes, to father her next child: the baby would surely be perfect, with "your brains and my body."

Shaw is supposed to have replied: "But suppose it inherited *my* body and *your* brains?!"

Shaw did receive such an offer but not, he declared, from Isadora.[2] He would not in any case have spoken disparagingly about the dancer's intelligence, for he afterwards wrote, "Isadora was no nonentity either, as I found out, when I met her."[3]

On July 12, 1921, Isadora, her maid Jeanne, and Irma Duncan, who was to help Isadora teach at the new school, embarked on the *S.S. Baltanic* for Reval, the first stage of the long trip to Russia. Isadora was then forty-four. Two of the other girls were to have come with them, but Thérèse was engaged to be married and Lisa was in love,[4] so at the last moment they changed their minds. There was no question of Margot's coming, since her health was too frail. The journey took eleven days in all, six from London to Reval, and five more from Reval to Moscow.

When the tired travelers finally descended from the train on July 24 at 4 o'clock in the morning, they were disconcerted to find no representative of the Soviet government to meet them. After a brief stay in a bleak hotel room, they returned to the train to wait the opening of the government offices.[5]

The situation improved that afternoon, however, when word of their arrival finally reached the Commissar for Education, Luna-charsky, who made the apartment of the ballerina Geltzer, then on tour, available to them. It was the best he was able to do on short notice. He later explained to the American journalist Joseph Kaye that Isadora had arrived in Moscow before she was expected.[6] Whether this was the case, or whether, as Irma Duncan supposed, he had really not counted on Isadora's coming to Russia, believing that her proposed school was simply a whim, it is certain that no preparations had been made to receive her. Now that she was actually in Moscow, he was anxious to make amends, and he promised that he would waste no time in finding a building to house her school.

Lunacharsky also dispatched a man who spoke German to help her and act as her interpreter. He was Ilya Ilyich Schneider, who had worked for the press department of the People's Commissariat for Foreign Affairs and had also taught the history and aesthetics of the dance at the School of Ballet. He had last seen Isadora in 1908, when he admired her slender grace. Now she unexpectedly looked monumental, and she had short dyed red hair. (Her hair had turned white after the death of her children.) When he addressed her as Miss Duncan, she frowned. He later discovered that she had expected to be addressed as Comrade Duncan.

From the moment of her arrival on Russian soil, Isadora found herself confronted with unforeseen social situations. Irma related that Isadora, as a guest at an official party, was dismayed to find herself in the ornate mansion of a one-time sugar king, where Communist functionaries in evening clothes were listening to a fashionably dressed singer warble chansonettes. Never one to mince words in the presence of the powerful, she exclaimed: "Here you all are sitting as they used to do in this place full of bad art . . . listening to the same insipid music they used to listen to. . . . You are not revolutionists. *You are bourgeois in disguise.*"[7] Fortunately, once they had recovered from the initial shock of this declaration, her hosts decided to take her outburst in good humor.

The novelty of life in the Soviet capital did not distract Isadora from the realization that her purpose in coming to Russia seemed no closer to fulfillment. One day, in a restless mood, she and Irma had made a trip to Varabiovy Gory (Sparrow Hills, now Lenin Hills), a wooded rise overlooking Moscow, where by chance they met a person for whom Isadora developed an immediate and lasting regard. This was Comrade Podvowsky, the People's Commissar for Physical Education, who was directing the construction of a sports stadium in the vicinity.

This idealistic and energetic man, who in the first days of the revolution had organized the Red Army, made a profound impression on Isadora.[8] He in turn was impressed by Isadora's ideas on the use of dance for the physical and emotional training of future Soviet citizens. He became a valuable friend who, according to Schneider, helped in the search for a place to house her school and who, for many years, would be connected with both the school and its offshoot, the Duncan Theatre Studio.[9]

At Podvowsky's suggestion (he had teased Isadora about having become too dependent on material comforts), Isadora and Irma took a log cabin in the Sparrow Hills woods. This hut had only two rooms and no sanitary facilities, and after a week of "roughing it" the two women were delighted to return to Moscow.

Their return was prompted by the fact that Lunacharsky had finally found a building suitable for their school—a mansion which before the revolution had belonged to Ushkoff, a wealthy tea plantation owner, and his wife, the ballerina Balachova. For the second time, Isadora had been assigned to the former home of an absent ballet dancer, and she saw the incident as a lucky omen for her work. Eventually her dance would replace the ballet in Soviet Russia.

The house was located at 20 Pretchistenka Street, in czarist days a fashionable neighborhood. One entered this ornate dwelling through a hallway that had rosewood columns ornamented with gold molding. Murals covered the ceilings and walls, and two ballrooms displaying huge paintings of Napoleon on the battlefield opened into the hall. An imposing marble staircase led to a balustrade on the second floor. Isadora took in the imperial grandeur of this scene, then burst out laughing.

Her amusement was prompted by the fact that Balachova had been interested in renting Isadora's house on the Rue de la Pompe

Undated autographed portrait (*Mme. Mario Meunier—Christine Dalliès Collection*).

in Paris: the ballerina had eventually turned it down because there was no proper dining room. Now, by a quirk of fate, Isadora found herself living in Balachova's house in Moscow.[10]

However, Isadora and Irma did not have the house to themselves. They were assigned the master bedroom and the mirrored boudoir for their own private use, while the various homeless families that had been quartered in the other bedrooms were slowly relocated. Little by little the house was put in order to receive Isadora's pupils.[11]

After Balachova and her husband had fled, the mansion had been pillaged of all movable furnishings (the best, it was said, appropriated for Bela Kun's[12] apartment in Moscow). Isadora slept in a camp bed that looked incongruously out of place under the immense eagle-crowned canopy in the master bedroom. The Commissariat of Education shortly assigned to the school a staff of some sixty people—secretaries, typists, maids, and cooks.

Isadora, meanwhile, languished from inactivity. She had come to Russia for a purpose—to teach. Fortunately, among the people sent to her by the government was a young pianist, Pierre Luboshitz, who would later make a name for himself in America as half of the piano team of Luboshitz and Nemenoff. Isadora always insisted on working with good musicians, whom she treated with respect. When she danced with a pianist, she would arrange to have him play on stage in full view of the audience to emphasize that he was a fellow artist, not merely an accompanist. Furthermore, says Schneider, when she listened to a pianist with a view to working with him, "she skillfully avoid[ed] any hint of an official audition."[13] With Luboshitz acting as their musical partner, Isadora and Irma were able to practice their repertoire.

During this waiting period, Isadora also composed two new dances to études of Scriabin, dances charged with pity and terror. They were prompted by the famine then devastating the Volga region[14] and belong to the large number of the dancer's works that deal with social or political themes (among the others being, of course, the *Marseillaise* and the *Marche Slave*).

With the 1917 *Marche Slave*, Isadora had, in fact, created the dance of social protest. The *Marche Slave* and the work dances of her final period (such as *Dubinushka* or *The Blacksmith,* in which she utilized the movements of laborers) were widely shown in the United States in 1929 and had a profound effect on the American choreography of the 1930s. Martha Graham's 1927 *Revolt* was only the first of the many spiritual children of the *Marche Slave* (Doris Humphrey's *Inquest* being another). This point needs to be stressed, for Isadora's art is often equated with the lyrical dances of her early period, and it is said to have all vanished without a trace. (Her early work has, of course, left its mark too on Fokine and others.)

Isadora's scope as a choreographer was indeed extremely wide. Besides the lyrical dances of her youth (joyful, sad, yearning, fiery, playful) and her meditative and religious dances, she created the heroic dances of her mature period (these usually, though not always, political or social in content) and the work dances just mentioned. Her dances were sometimes inspired by ancient Greece (as in the *Dance Idylls, Orpheus,* and the two *Iphigenias*), sometimes by the Renaissance (the *Primavera* and the *Angel with the Violin*), but most often they were simply expressive of the human spirit in all its range.

By mid-October, almost three months after she had arrived in Russia, the school was ready to open its doors. From the hundreds of children who applied, Isadora selected fifty of the most talented.[15] She would have liked more pupils and it was a bitter disappointment to her that the government's goals had dwindled so far from the 1000 pupils it had originally promised. However, she reluctantly agreed with Lunacharsky that even a small beginning was better than none.

Despite his regard for her work, Lunacharsky was beset by economic and political necessity and found himself in the uncomfortable position of having less and less to offer Isadora in the way of assistance. As her friend, therefore, he must have been gratified to bring her the Soviet government's invitation to give a gala concert at the Bolshoi Theatre on November 7. Admission was to be free, so Isadora hoped to dance before an audience of ordinary working people, those who, in the past, could not afford to see her. As matters turned out, the audience was largely made up of high-ranking party members to whom most of the tickets had been allotted.[16] Her program included two Tchaikovsky works—the *Pathétique* and the *Marche Slave*. Lenin, who was in the audience, was so moved by the latter that he stood up, shouting, "Bravo, bravo, Miss Duncan!"[17] For her third number, Isadora had composed a *pièce d'occasion*—the *Internationale*. After she had mimed the first stanza, Irma led from the wings a little child "who was followed by another and another—a hundred little children in red tunics, each with the right hand held high clasping fraternally the hand of the one before . . . surrounding with childish arms outstretched . . . the figure of their . . . teacher."[18]

The occasion of the concert was the fourth anniversary of the Russian Revolution, and it was a mark of official favor for Isadora to have been singled out to perform. Nevertheless, the men in power seemed unable to do anything for her school other than honor its founder. The fuel allotments that were needed to heat the building took days to arrive, and, in the interim, lessons had to be suspended. Food, too, was hard to get. About a month after the opening, Commissar Lunacharsky had the unpleasant duty of telling Isadora that the government could no longer afford to support the school. He explained that under the New Economic Policy (NEP) she would be permitted to give paying concerts to meet expenses. Perhaps later, in better times, the government could resume its assistance.[19]

Lunacharsky seems to have arrived at his decision reluctantly, and probably under considerable pressure from his colleagues, for years later he was to write in his memoirs, with an irony which the official tone cannot disguise:

> In a word, that which had seemed almost compulsory in the hungry and cold period of revolutionary enthusiasm, started to appear extravagant when we went over to a policy of economics, planning and so forth. . . . We could only platonically thank [Isadora], give her paltry aid, and in the end, sadly shrug our shoulders, to tell her that our time was too harsh for such problems.

Thus, Isadora found herself with the alternatives of either abandoning her work or continuing it under the very conditions that had disgusted her with the capitalist world. She did not relinquish her claim to government help without a struggle. Characteristically, in fact, she sought support for two *new* projects, as well as her already founded school. In an article[20] for *Isvestia* dated November 23, 1921, Isadora pleaded that the workers' children be sent to her and suggested that the Bolshoi Theatre be thrown open on Monday nights for free performances so all could see and hear symphonic creations expressing

> Heroism, Strength and Light. . . . What you give the people at present sometimes seems ironical. . . . Is not the one act of a ballet *(Raymonda)* I have seen the other day here in Moscow a glorification of the Czar? The subject of the ballet had nothing to do with the rhythm and mood of our present life. It was EROTIC without Heroism. It is sufficient to watch the part the man is taking in our contemporary ballets. He is not natural but effeminate[21] and only an element of support and background for the ballerina. Whereas man should first of all express courage in his dancing . . .
>
> With these children—independently of my school—I shall practice daily, and in the spring on the first of May we shall give them in the open air a real holiday of Joy! . . . . The children of Communists . . . receive just an ordinary bourgeois education . . . you have ruined the Old; now give the children the New. . . .
>
> I am expecting soon an answer—can the Government give a sum of money for the organization of these "Mondays" in the Big Theatre? I have left Europe and Art that was too tightly bound with commercialism and it will be against all my convictions and desires if I shall have to give again paid performances for the bourgeois public. For the realization of my Ideas of teaching masses of children—I need only a big and warm hall. About feeding and clothing the children I have already received a promise from the A.R.A. (American Relief Association).
>
> Isadora Duncan

(There is a certain comic charm in the spectacle of the American dancer's exhorting the Russian Communists to be more revolutionary, and, on failing to win their support, in enlisting the aid of the American Relief Association for her revolutionary program.)

The government, however, had decided it could not continue to underwrite the school, much less support two new projects, so Isadora was faced with the choice of either abandoning the school and returning to western Europe, or of raising the money for the school herself by going on tour. The decision was clear.

She had, in any case, another reason for wishing to remain in Russia. In November at the house of the artist and stage designer Georgy Yakulov she had met the young and handsome poet Sergei Esenin. Though he was twenty-seven and she was forty-three, he had at once been disturbingly aware of her sexual magnetism. She, on her side, was overpoweringly attracted to him. Coming over to the couch where she was sitting, he had immediately cast himself at her feet, and she, running her fingers through his hair, surprised the onlookers by saying "solotaia golova" (golden head)! At this time she knew barely a dozen Russian words.[22] When she finally left the party at dawn, Esenin jumped into her cab and insisted on driving home with her. Shortly thereafter, he moved himself and his belongings into 20 Pretchistenka Street.

❦ 29 ❦

Sergei Esenin
1921–1922

 am the son of a peasant. I was born on September 21, 1895,"[1] wrote Sergei Esenin in a biographical sketch. "Because of my father's poverty and the size of our family, when I was two years old I was sent to my rather well-to-do maternal grandfather for my upbringing. This grandfather was a miller." His grandparents loved the child and set about ensuring the boy's future: his grandfather by teaching him how to fight, and his grandmother by indulging him and making him go to church. His family intended Sergei to be a rural school-master, and so he was enrolled in the parish school for teachers, but, on graduating, at sixteen, he announced his intention of becoming a poet. The next year he left for Moscow where he took night courses at the university and joined a literary-revolutionary society while supporting himself at a series of jobs.[2] On one of these jobs, while a proofreader at the Sytin Printing Press, he fell in love with Anna Izryadnova, a fellow worker by whom his son Yury

Izryadnova would be born at the end of 1914 or the beginning of 1915. This liaison would break up some two months later when he left for St. Petersburg to seek his literary fortune, though he would return briefly to Moscow in 1915 and 1916 to visit Anna and their son.[3]

"At eighteen, I was surprised, after sending my verses to magazines, that they were not printed, and I suddenly burst forth in St. Petersburg."[4]

"There I was received very cordially. The first person I saw was Blok, the second Gorodetski. When I looked at Blok sweat dropped from me, because it was the first time I had seen a live poet." Gorodetski introduced him to Klyuev, the peasant poet, who became Esenin's friend and literary sponsor.

Another friend, Riurik Ivnev, describes Esenin as he was when he first appeared in St. Petersburg. Ivnev had gone to a poetry reading.

During the intermission a youth approached me, almost a boy, modestly dressed. . . .

I looked at the youth; he was thin, frail, indeed tender. Yes, he seemed to me to be tender from that first moment. "I am Esenin," he said. "I also write poetry". . . .

[Reluctantly] I asked him to recite a poem. . . . Perhaps because I expected dull, weak and poor lines I was shocked—in the full meaning of the term—by his grassy freshness which I could smell through that stuffy hall. . . .

I began to look over Esenin attentively. I wanted to determine whether he knew what a great talent he had. He had a very modest calm mien. . . . It seemed as if he did not value himself. But it only seemed this way until you noticed his eyes. It was worth it to meet him eye to eye, for his secret was revealed: in his eyes little devils jumped about. His nostrils dilated. The glorious steed was intoxicated by the smell of glory and was already tearing ahead into the lead. And his modesty was a fine cover under which beat a greedy, unsatiated striving to conquer everyone with his poems, to subjugate, to trample.[5]

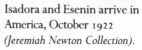
Isadora and Esenin arrive in America, October 1922 (*Jeremiah Newton Collection*).

Ivnev elsewhere recalled Esenin's innocent, disarming smile which made it almost impossible for his friends to retain their seriousness when rebuking him for singing bawdy songs at the top of his lungs ("Well, all right. But may I sing the same thing in a lower voice?"). Other friends speak of his boyish good looks and his "cornflower" blue eyes. Few indeed remained untouched by his combination of youth, charm, and immense talent.

He was just twenty-one in 1916, when his first book of poems, *Radunitsa,* was published. At this point, the pace of his life increased rapidly. The same year he was called up for military service, and, while in the army, he came to the attention of the czarina, for whom he read his poems. Despite this honor, he loathed army life, deserted as soon as possible, and was caught and sent to a disciplinary batallion at the front. At the outbreak of the revolution in 1917, he deserted again and joined the revolutionaries. Soon afterwards in 1917 he married Zinaida Raikh; he separated from her in March 1918, and later the two were divorced.[6] At the end of 1918, he and the writer Mariengof founded the Imaginist movement in poetry. To propagate their ideas they opened a publishing house and a bookstore where they printed and sold their own works and those by other Imaginists, such as Chernichevitch and Koussikov.

The years of war and revolution had left their mark on Esenin. At seventeen he had, for religious reasons, become a vegetarian and a teetotaler. In the army he developed a taste for carousing, and, although he seems to have abstained during his brief marriage, after his separation from his wife he began to drink heavily again.[7]

Esenin's drinking was associated with his periods of depression. He was an ambitious man, overflowing with ideas and vitality, but at times everything seemed pointless and worthless to him. He had achieved his dream of becoming a writer, but at the cost of separation from the parents and sisters he loved and from the country life with which his nature was imprinted. In liquor he found a temporary respite from the despair to which he would be subject all his life.

Outwardly his material circumstances were good. His publishing house was doing well, and he enjoyed playing to the hilt the role of successful businessman. Yet even as his reputation flourished in

Russia, he became very touchy about other writers. He, who had broken into a sweat on first being introduced to a "live poet," could not bear to hear another poet lauded; it was as if any praise given to another man diminished him, Esenin, by that much.

Riurik Ivnev, who after an absence of a year and a half saw Sergei again in 1920, felt that he had somehow changed.

> We fell on each other, embraced . . . but at that very moment I felt as if the former Esenin was not there. Some kind of thin window glass separated us from each other.
>
> And later, in subsequent meetings, my first impression was con- firmed. He was too occupied with himself, with his affairs—plans— this was a period of the most concern with his creative "I". . . .
>
> Before me stood a strong, businesslike, thrifty man, externally almost unchanged, but internally—a completely different person. Even his costume had changed. At this time living was difficult for everyone, everyone dressed every which way and dragged out a miserable existence. Against the background of this poverty, [his] good suits and the dandyism of a poseur seemed out of place and ridiculous. All this was of course simple mischief but he loved to sport the best cut clothes with some sort of unusual boots purchased God knows where.[8]

During that winter of 1920 to 1921, Ivnev, though not an Imaginist, rejoined Esenin's circle of writers, and though the two poets now saw much of one another, Ivnev's impression that Sergei had changed persisted. Beneath their superficial cordiality, he wrote, "our rela- tions were completely devoid of feeling. I did not understand Esenin. Internally he was distant to me."

Despite this apparent change in Esenin, the period was one of the most fruitful in the poet's creative life "and as he finished each piece he gave it to the press."

This, then, was the background and career of the already famous young poet whom Isadora had just met.

She was touched by his beauty, his look of vulnerability, and his pride in his work. His compatriots assured her of Esenin's genius, and she recognized its marks. His air of being a young unarmored

David bravely setting forth to do battle with the Philistine Goliath possibly reminded her of herself at the start of her campaign. As an older campaigner who had suffered fearful blows, she felt her heart go out to him.

He, for his part, despite the heaviness of her body and the difference in their ages, was strongly attracted to Isadora. The fact that she was famous increased her interest for him. "He, who [was] jealous of every man who [seemed] worth more than himself, [did] not suffer from that feeling before a famous woman, because there always [remained] a sense of masculine superiority," shrewdly remarked Francisca de Graaff. At the time of their meeting, Isadora was, in any case, too admiring and sympathetic toward his interests to arouse in him any sense of competition. Since they had no language in common, she decided that she must learn Russian. ("He just read me his verses," Isadora told Schneider. "I didn't understand a thing, but I listened; it's music!")⁹ At her second lesson she disconcerted the elderly woman who was teaching her by explaining that she felt no pressing need to learn phrases about "the red pencil on the desk." Instead, "You'd better teach me what I ought to say to a beautiful young man when I want to kiss him—and things like that."¹⁰

Some of the poet's friends, though they were surprised at Esenin's unexpectedly strong feelings for Isadora, could see a reason for them. Riurik Ivnev, who visited Esenin at Pretchistenka, said, "she was an intelligent and exceptional woman. She was unusually attractive. Quite apart from her art, she was a profoundly talented person."¹¹ And M. Babenchikov wrote, "Duncan understood the poet, and in her own . . . way attempted to ease his . . . despair."¹² Also, Esenin just then was feeling excluded by the recent marriage of his close friend Mariengof. By devoting his time and attention to Isadora, he not only indulged his attraction to her, but he also succeeded in making Mariengof jealous.¹³

But Esenin's feelings for Isadora were subject to rapid fluctuations. "At times he seemed to love her as much as he could, never leaving her side for a moment," noted another of Esenin's friends, Ivan Startsev.¹⁴ "At other times he would stay by himself, turning to her from time to time, cruelly, coarsely, even striking her and cursing her with the most vile street language. At such moments, Isadora would be especially patient and tender, attempting to calm Esenin by any means."

Once when Esenin had been away from Pretchistenka for three days without letting Isadora know where he was, Isadora sent Startsev a note, translated into Russian by Schneider, telling Startsev how worried she had been, and closing: "Don't think that an amorous wench is writing to you, no—this is a mother's devotion and anxious concern."[15] At times the sensation of being enveloped in maternal solicitude must have been infuriating to Esenin, who had always been independent and, indeed, something of a loner.

However, his abrupt changes of feeling were caused not only by her overprotectiveness, but also by his drinking. His friends, too, experienced his sudden shifts of mood. Valentin Volpin,[16] another friend, wrote:

His relations with people when he was sober were always full, warm, his close friends he kissed at meeting, firmly pressed their hands, and strengthened his love by his smile, pure as a child's. . . . On the other hand when he was drunk, he changed sharply, there appeared about him a kind of evil, unquenchable fervor, and in such a state he spoke sharply, was completely intolerant, rather inappropriately praised only his own talent, and would not stand for any objections. Sometimes this mood over a long period of time gave way to a melancholy sentimentalism accompanied by laments over fate and failure which he felt to be persecuting him.

Yet he would cling to the good opinion of others.

He . . . forgave all insults, material damage, injuries, crimes, as long as he knew that the perpetrator of the act, in the depths of his soul, thought a great deal of him.[17]

Politically, though he was a revolutionary, Esenin was not a Communist. In the first of his autobiographical sketches, he wrote: "I never joined the Russian Communist Party because I felt further left." He was, in fact, too individualistic to be a member of any party. At the same time, he felt there was a conflict between the industrialization which the new Russia was fostering and the traditional village life which he feared the new Russia would destroy. He expressed this conflict in his poem *Sorokoust* (1920), with his touching image of the little colt racing vainly with a train. He wrote to a friend about the incident that had inspired the poem:

> During this trip a little colt galloped with all his strength behind our train, galloping so hard it was evident he wanted to pass us. He galloped this way a very long time, then exhausted, he let himself be passed. This episode, which would have been devoid of importance to many people, had considerable significance for me. The steel horse had vanquished the living horse, and this young colt is for me the concrete, moving and intimate image of the extinction, the death of the village. . . . In our revolution the village so greatly resembles this colt, for there, too, living strength measures itself against the strength of steel. It is very painful for me to see that history is living through a period so weighed down with the destruction of living personality. It's that the coming socialism is not at all the one I was thinking of, but a socialism which is deterministic, rigid, and willed, a sort of St. Helena Island without glory and without dreams. A living being feels cramped there.[18]

Not all the poet's friends felt happy at his liaison with Isadora. Whether they disapproved of her because she was so much older and spoke little Russian, or whether they simply feared that she would interfere with their convivial life with Sergei, there were those who did their best to entice him from her. Once, to get him away from her, they persuaded him to take an impromptu trip to Rostov-on-the-Don with his friend Kobalov. But apparently Sergei grew bored, for within a few days he was back in Moscow.[19]

Now that he was living at 20 Pretchistenka, Esenin's poet and artist friends began appearing at the house at all hours, sometimes bursting in when Isadora and Irma were dancing. Esenin's feelings were divided about these visits. He enjoyed entertaining at Isadora's home and dispensing her lavish hospitality, but it interfered with his writing. In one of his letters he reported, "I live somehow, in bivouac fashion, without shelter, because various loafers . . . have started coming to the house and annoying me. I don't know how to break off from such stupid bungling but I'm becoming ashamed and sad at my dissipation."[20]

At the same time, he longed for male society and the freedom of his bachelor days. Mariengof remembers, "Often he came to our house with a little packet [of clothing] in his hand. He said, 'This time, it's definite. I said to her: Isadora, goodbye.'

"Several hours later Isadora would appear smiling tenderly, her blue eyes still shining with tears. She would speak to him caressingly and Esenin would return with her. And so scenes of love and felicity were generally followed by drunken scenes and truancies from Pretchistenka."[21]

One evening when Sergei was out with friends, Isadora, to pass the time, began to play with the Ouija board. The letters spelled out the name Dora, and she was seized with a premonition that her mother, Dora Gray Duncan, whom she knew to be ill at her brother Raymond's home in Paris, was dead. The dancer spent a sleepless night, and Irma records that on the next morning a telegram arrived which confirmed Isadora's fears.

After her mother's death, Isadora became increasingly restless and eager to travel the world outside Russia. Now that she was faced with the necessity of supporting the Russian school, she hoped that she could not only be able to raise funds by giving concerts abroad but also interest wealthy art lovers in backing her work. She therefore got in touch with Sol Hurok, her American agent, and asked him to book a tour for her. The tour would also provide Esenin with a chance to see foreign countries—very important, she believed, for the development of a poet. Even more important, he would have a chance to consult foreign specialists about his health. The hardships of war and revolution and the dissipations of the chaotic postwar period had left their marks upon Sergei's once sturdy frame. Besides the ravages caused by exhaustion and alcohol, he may have suffered from epilepsy. Gordon McVay says[22] that Sergei told his friend

Veniamin Levin that he, Sergei, had epilepsy which he had inherited from his grandfather. And in Paris in 1923, following an arrest for disturbing the peace, "he was booked, 'as suffering from epileptic attacks, he had drunk too much.' " Yet, cautions McVay, the certainty of his epilepsy may be in doubt. No Soviet memoir mentions this disease, nor does his medical report of December 5, 1925.

But to stay in hotels in the United States with Esenin without being married to him would present immense difficulties. Isadora had not forgotten (as she wrote in *My Life*) how "poor Gorky and his mistress of seventeen years standing were hounded from pillar to post, and their lives made a torment to them." True, she had been able to travel with Paris Singer in America but that case, as she noted dryly, was not the same: "Of course when one is so very rich these little disagreeablenesses are all smoothed away." If she were not to leave Esenin behind in Russia, it appeared that she would have to forsake her principles and become his wife. Fortunately the Soviet ideal of marriage at this period was not so different from her own: the contract implied no financial responsibility of either partner for the other and it could be annulled at the pleasure of either. "Such a marriage is the only convention to which any free-minded woman could consent, and is the only form of marriage to which I have ever subscribed."

Yet Isadora herself subsequently told Victor Seroff, whom she had come to know very well, that these were not the paramount considerations that decided her on marriage to Esenin. According to Seroff's account, Commissar Lunacharsky had expressed his concern over her taking the valued poet Esenin to the anti-Soviet west. "Who is there to protect him? . . . . We are not even recognized by some countries, including America; we have no embassies. . . ." He suggested that she marry Esenin. "You are a world-famous artist. Your name would be his protection—that is, if he were Isadora Duncan's husband."[23]

Isadora was under no illusions as to Esenin's condition, or the probable amount of happiness in store for her, but she loved Sergei and revered his genius, and that was enough.

Esenin's feelings for Isadora seem to have been more contradictory. Often, soothed by her gentleness, he felt desire and tenderness for her; yet the sense of being smothered by her care made him resentful and violent. Fearful of being possessed, still he wanted to possess her. For him, not the least of her charms was the gratification of his vanity at having won the love of a famous woman, a *grande amoureuse,* as he believed. To one of his friends, Georgi Ustinov, who disapproved of his marriage, he exclaimed: "You don't understand. She's had more than a thousand husbands, and I'll be the last!"[24]

In all events, they wished to marry. Therefore, on May 2, 1922, she and Sergei had their names entered as man and wife in the Moscow Registry of Civil Statistics. Each chose the double surname, Duncan-Esenin.[25]

Early the next morning, they drove to Trotsky Airport where the chartered Fokker was waiting to take them to Berlin on the first leg of their journey to the United States.

Air service had only recently been instituted; their flight would be the first passenger trip between Moscow and Germany. Persuaded by her friends that she should make a will, Isadora asked for Schneider's notebook and in it she wrote:[26]

This is my last will and testament. In case of my death I leave my entire properties and effects to my husband Sergei Essenine. In case of our simultaneous death then such properties go to my Brother, Augustin Duncan.

Written in clear conscience.

Isadora Essenine-Duncan

Witnessed by

I. I. Schneider
Irma Duncan

May Ninth, 1922, Moscow.

Shortly before nine o'clock the two passengers climbed into their seats. The doors were shut. The motors started and Isadora waved to the children of her school as the plane taxied down the field. Unexpectedly, the plane slowed down. Someone flung open the door and shouted frantically for the lunch basket, which had been left behind. With the basket loaded aboard, the plane took off again. Soon, in the eyes of her friends and school children, it had dwindled to the size of a bird flying in the distance.

Drawing by Christine Dalliès, 1920 (*Christine Dalliès Collection*).

30

To Western Europe with Esenin

1922

N Berlin, the couple installed themselves comfortably in the Hotel Adlon, and Esenin lost no time in getting in touch with the city's large Russian colony. Since the revolution, White Russian refugees had been pouring into the German capital, and this Russian-speaking population was augmented by Soviet citizens living abroad, among them the writers Ilya Ehrenburg and the great Maxim Gorky. Many of these expatriates already knew Esenin's work, and his electric public readings of his poems created such widespread interest that it was decided to publish a volume of his poetry in Berlin. A little later, Isadora had a selection of his works translated into French by the Belgian poet Franz Hellens and brought out in Paris at her own expense.[1]

Gorky described Esenin as he was at this time and discussed his work. Esenin, he believed, was the greatest Russian poet since Pushkin. Gorky was not happy about Esenin's marriage to Isadora, feeling that she was incapable of understanding Russian poetry.

Gorky was repelled when on one occasion Isadora, drinking vodka, toasted the revolution in her bad Russian. "This lady praises the Revolution in the same way a theatre lover praises the successful premiere of a play. She should not do it." He added: "This famous woman, glorified by thousands of European aesthetes . . . sitting next to the small, boyish, wonderful Ryazan poet, was the perfect personification of all he did not need."

Gorky was not among those who responded to Isadora's art: "But I don't like and I don't appreciate dancing that is an expression of intellect. . . ." And still less did he relish the Apache dance which Isadora danced after dinner to entertain the party. "Her dance seemed to me to depict the struggle between the weight of Duncan's age and the constraint of her body, spoilt by fame and love."[2]

In the same article Gorky describes Isadora as: "Aging, grown heavy, . . . shrouded in a brick colored dress, she wheeled and writhed in the cramped room, clutching a bouquet of . . . faded flowers to her breast, and with a meaningless smile frozen on her fat face. . . . While she was dancing [Esenin] sat at the table drinking wine and frowning as he looked at her out of the corner of his eye. Perhaps it was in these moments that his words of compassion (!) formed the line of poetry: 'You've been fondled and soiled so thoroughly . . .' And one could feel that he regarded his female friend as a nightmare which was already familiar and not frightening, but which all the same oppressed him . . ."[3]

At the same time, Gorky speaks of Isadora's drunken smile, and he, who had first met Esenin in 1914, describes the young man's strikingly altered appearance. "His uneasy glance falls first on one face and then another with a defiant and scornful air, then suddenly he becomes uncertain, troubled and suspicious. Nervous, he gives the impression of a man who is drinking heavily."[4] Sergei had sprung to his feet, putting an end to the evening with the words "Let's go somewhere, where there's noise."

Whether Isadora or Esenin seemed lurid or tragic depended on how well the beholder knew each of them. Thus when Esenin's friends speak of Esenin's looking ill, drinking too much, or wearing powder on his face, they note such things in a tone of concern, and when they speak of Isadora Duncan as having dyed hair, running mascara and smeared lipstick, or of being too fat and too old, or of drinking too much, they note these things with sarcasm or repulsion. Isadora's friends or admirers mention Isadora's weight or drinking with concern, but they give reasons for her drinking, and they emphasize how her art overcomes the impression of weight and poor makeup, while at the same time dwelling on Esenin's drinking, his infidelities, and his violence. Biographers, too, are not immune from partisan reactions. Their knowledge—of the formative pressures, disappointments, triumphs, and tragedies—tends to be weighted on the side of their subject. It is easy to see the spouse as the antagonist, who acts arbitrarily, without reason. Gorky's dislike of Isadora must be seen in the light of his feelings for Esenin.

Esenin refers to his Berlin stay in a letter to Mariengof, written some weeks later at Ostend.

> How I should like to leave this nightmare of a Europe, and return to Russia, to my youthful extravagances, and to all our ardor. Here there is such spleen, such insipidity without talent! At Berlin I naturally made many scandals and much noise. My high hat, and the overcoat made by a Berlin tailor angered everyone. They all think that I've come at expense of the Bolsheviks as a member of the Cheka or as an agitator. All that amuses me and makes me gay. . . .[5]

(Creating scandals was something which Esenin often did consciously, for the sake of publicity. His friend N. Poletaev[6] had once accused Sergei of doing this and he confirmed it, saying that scandals caught the attention of the stupid public. He added, "You know, Shakespeare caused scandals in his youth." But if Esenin made scandals, it was not only because he was little known outside of Russia, whereas Isadora was famous, it was also because he felt he was giving publicity to the revolution. Reluctant to be the tail to Isadora's kite, he saw himself an activist, abroad on a mission. On his return he told Schneider,[7] "Did I raise hell there because I was drunk? Not at all. Was it so bad? Not at all, I raised hell for our Revolution!")

After Berlin, Isadora and Sergei went to Wiesbaden, and from here Sergei wrote to his friend Ilya Schneider, at the Duncan School in Moscow.

Wiesbaden
21 June, 1922

Dear I.I.

Greetings to you and kisses. Forgive me for not having written to you for so long. The Berlin atmosphere has shaken me to pieces. At present, after a nervous breakdown, I can hardly move my leg. Now I am taking a cure at Wiesbaden. I have stopped drinking and have begun to work. If Isadora were not so capricious and would make it possible for me to sit quietly somewhere, I could earn a lot of money. So far I have only received a 100,000 and something in marks, but I have in prospect about 400,000 [inflation marks].

Isadora's business is in an awful state. In Berlin the lawyer sold her house and paid her only 90,000 marks! The same thing may also happen in Paris. Her property—library and furniture—have all been appropriated and carried off in all directions. Now she has sent one of her intimate friends down there in a hurry. The famous Paul-Boncour not only did not help her in any way but even refused his signature for a visa to Paris. This is the state of her business. . . . But she acts as though nothing has happened, jumps into the automobile to go to Lubeck, or to Leipzig, to Frankfurt or to Weimar. I follow in silent resignation* because after each protest I make, hysterics.

. . . For God's sake search for my sister through our bookshop (leave a note for her) and help her to get money with the enclosed check through the A.R.A. [American Relief Association]. She must surely be very hard up. The check for Irma is only a trial. When we know that you have received this, Isadora will send as much as is necessary. If my sister is not in Moscow, send her a letter through Marienhof. Then if you go to London, call her to you and give her an exact address where she can receive money, without which she will die.

*I. I. Schneider has noted in *Moskva* (op.cit.): "This, needless to say, was not at all like him."

... About our Russian friends in Berlin I could tell you wonderful things: especially about a denunciation to the French Police which made it impossible for me to get to Paris. About all this later, for I must take care of my nerves now. . . .

I shake your hand, hoping to see you soon.

Your loving Esenin

To Irma my best regards. Isadora married me for the second time and is now not any more Duncan-Esenin, yes, just Esenin.[8]

With Schneider still in Moscow, the couple needed an interpreter, so in Wiesbaden they hired a young secretary, Lola Kinel, who spoke both Russian and English. In her book of reminiscences, *This Is My Affair,* Miss Kinel remembers her first meeting with her new employers at their hotel.

A fat, middle aged woman in a salmon negligee was reclining gracefully on the couch. . . . When she rose after a while and began to move about the room, I saw that she was not fat or middle aged: she was beautiful, she had an innate, a marvelous grace. . . . This was Isadora. After a while, a young man in white silk pajamas came out of the adjoining bedroom. He looked like a Russian dancer from an American vaudeville show: pale golden curly hair, naive eyes of cornflower blue, and the grace of a very strong, muscular body. . . . This was Esenin. Later I discovered that he was not always naive. He was sly, too, and suspicious, and instinctively clever. And he was very sensitive, just like a child, and full of twists and complexes— a peasant and a poet, both.[9]

The fact that neither husband nor wife spoke the other's language threw their secretary from the very beginning into an odd intimacy with the pair. Esenin, delighted to find someone to whom he could talk in Russian, started to speak to Lola Kinel about his childhood and his early writings. "His voice was soft and his eyes dreamy, and there was that about him which made one think that his soul was like a child's, mysteriously wise, yet utterly tender."[10] This was the inspired, vulnerable self which Isadora loved and protected, and which Esenin customarily guarded behind a smooth wall posted with lookouts—his other self: "The ordinary Esenin . . . bland, non-committal, pretending to be something of a fool but rather secretive, with eyes which had such sly corners to them."[11]

Gratified that Miss Kinel had been greatly moved by his reading of his poems, Esenin asked her to translate them into English.

> I wasn't flattered . . . I was a bit frightened and a bit shocked for young as I was, I knew that it was a sacrilege and an impossibility both. Esenin's poetry is almost purely lyrical: it is music expressed in terms of Russian words, of Russian phonetics, and so could never be rendered into any other language. Even in Russian it was the sort of poetry that is a hundred times more beautiful when read aloud than read in silence, and here I was asked to mutilate it. . . .[12]

But the poet was insistent, so Miss Kinel agreed to do her best, and each day she would set to work on his selection.

> The following morning I would bring the poem over to Isadora's room and read the translation to her aloud. Craftily, hungrily, Esenin would watch Isadora's face, and she with the kindness and delicacy of which she was so capable, would smile and show that she was pleased. Sometimes she tried to help me, for her English was better and more fluent than mine and she had read lots more poetry. . . . And always she tried to conceal her real disappointment. Esenin was very sensitive where his poetry was concerned, and to have hurt him would have been like hurting a child.
> One day I asked him why he so much wanted an English translation of his poems.
> "But don't you see," he replied, surprised that I should put such a question, "how many millions will know me if my poems appear in English? How many people will read me in Russian? Twenty million, perhaps thirty. . . . All our peasants are illiterate. . . . But in English!" He spread his arms and his eyes shone.[13]

To be recognized as a poet by the western world was vitally important to Sergei. He who had been jealous of his fame, even in

Russia, hated being seen as Isadora's young husband—a curiosity, when he knew himself to be an artist.

Once he said to Isadora, asking Lola Kinel to translate:

"A dancer can never become very great because her fame doesn't last. It is gone the moment she dies."

"No," said Isadora, "for a dancer if she is great, can give to the people something that they will carry with them forever. They can never forget it, and it has changed them, though they may not know it."

"You are just a dancer. People may come and admire you—even cry. But after you are dead, no one will remember. Within a few years all your great fame will be gone. . . . No Isadora!"

All this he said in Russian, for me to translate, but the last two words he said in the English intonation, straight into Isadora's face, with a very expressive, mocking motion of his hands, as if he had waved the remnants of the mortal Isadora to the four winds. "But poets live," he continued, still smiling. "I, Esenin, shall leave my poems behind me. And poems live. Poems like mine live forever."

Beneath the obvious mockery and teasing tone there was something extraordinarily cruel. A shadow passed over Isadora's face as I translated what he said. Suddenly she turned to me, her voice very serious:

"Tell him he is wrong, tell him he is wrong. I have given people beauty. I have given them my very soul when I danced. And this beauty did not die. It exists somewhere. . . ." Suddenly she had tears in her eyes and she added in her pitiful, childish Russian: "Krasota nie umiray" (Beauty not dies).

But Esenin, already completely satisfied with the effect of his words—for there seemed in him often a morbid desire to hurt Isadora or to belittle her—became all gentleness. With a characteristic gesture, he pulled Isadora's curly head towards him and patted her on the back saying mockingly, "*Ekh,* Duncan." Isadora smiled. All was forgiven.[14]

Esenin's popularity in Russia as a revolutionary poet had not exempted him from having censorship difficulties with the Soviet government. Smiling broadly, he told Miss Kinel,

"The Bolsheviks have forbidden the use of 'God' in print, you know. They even got out a decree to this effect. Once when I sent in some poems the editor returned them to me requesting that all the 'Gods' be replaced by other words. . . . Other words!"

I laughed and asked him what he did.

"Oh, I just took my gun and went to the fellow and told him that he would have to print the stuff as it was, decree or no decree. He refused, so I asked him whether he had ever had his mug beaten, and then I went in the composing room and reset the type myself. That's all."

Isadora . . . wanted to know what it was all about. I told her briefly. For a moment she said nothing, and then to my surprise she said in Russian:

"But Bolsheviki right. No God. Old. Silly."

Esenin grinned, and said with mock irony, as if talking to a child that was trying to be clever and grown up: "Ekh, Isadora! Why, everything comes from God. All poetry and even your dances."

"No, no," replied Isadora, with great intensity, in English. "Tell him that my gods are Beauty and Love. There are no others. How do you know there is a God? The Greeks knew this a long time ago. People invent Gods to please themselves. There are no others. There is nothing beyond what we know, what we invent or imagine. All Hell is right here on earth. And all Paradise." She was standing upright like a Caryatid, beautiful, magnificent, and fearful. And suddenly she stretched out her arms, and pointing to the bed, she said in Russian with tremendous force: "Vot Bog!" (This is God!)

Slowly her arm came down. She turned and went back to the balcony. Esenin sat in his chair pale, silent and completely annihilated. I ran out on the beach and lay down on the sand and cried, though for the life of me, I could not have told why.[15]

The religious views of Esenin and Isadora were not always so divergent as they appear in this instance. Both were sometimes deists, sometimes agnostics, and sometimes atheists. Neither believed in a conventional church God, although both responded with emotional sympathy to the Christian culture and traditions in which they had been reared. Though in this conversation and in his tender *The Keys of Mary,* Esenin would seem to be a believer, in his three autobiographical sketches (written in 1922; the second undated, but probably 1923; the third in 1925) he describes himself as an atheist.

Isadora's beliefs fluctuated a great deal. The woman who wrote "All art that is not religious is mere merchandise," or, again, "My body moves because my spirit moves it," later stated, "there may be a life after this one, but I know not what we shall find there. This is what I do know: Our riches here on earth are in our will, our inner life."[16] Toward the end of her life, Isadora was an atheist, but an atheist who believed in the spirit. Nor was it, for her, a contradiction to believe in the spirit without believing in God. Although systems of belief depend on logic, belief itself stands outside of logic in the realm of feeling; there is no religion which at some point does not require the leap of faith. And it is not valid to attack people for taking the leap at a different place from yours. One believes what one must, and not what one would like or what would be convenient. All her life Isadora revered Christ as a spiritual teacher, but she could not believe many of the Christian teachings about God and immortality. She could take no comfort in the expectation of being reunited after her death with her beloved lost children. Under the blows of fate, she had replaced God, the all-seeing Father, with the gods of Beauty and Love.

> She dwells with Beauty, Beauty that must die,
> And Joy whose hand is ever at his lips
> Bidding adieu . . .

To one pair of ears, at least, her exclamation: *"This is God!"* has the shattering sound of a cry of despair.

Lola Kinel received her first inkling of the darker side of their unusual ménage when Esenin disappeared and the distraught Isadora apologetically searched the secretary's bedroom. Later, when she had learned something of Esenin's domestic habits, the meaning of this incident became clear to her. Yet she felt sympathy for both her extraordinary employers. She could understand equally Isadora's anxiety about her wayward poet husband and Esenin's need to be free of Isadora's encompassing solicitude. But it was impossible to satisfy them both when, as so often happened, their wills were opposed. And when, in the interests of domestic harmony, one of them decided to back the other's claims, any third person was likely to be sacrificed—as Miss Kinel discovered to her cost. She had refrained from sending some telegrams that Esenin had dictated to her while drunk, thinking them unwise. Shortly afterward, Isadora informed her with regret that she would have to leave, for Esenin no longer trusted her. Isadora spoke with sad resignation, and the secretary could not help feeling sorry for her.

From Wiesbaden, the couple traveled through Germany (stopping at Weimar, where they visited Goethe's house) and on to Ostend and Brussels. From Brussels, Esenin wrote again to Schneider:

> ... If you could see me now you probably would not believe your eyes. Almost a month now since I've taken a drink. On account of a heavy neuritis and neurasthenia, I made a promise not to drink until October, and now they are over.
> ... Saturday, the fifteenth of July we fly to Paris. . . .
> Dear, dear I. I., if the school comes to Europe it will create a furore. We await your arrival impatiently. I await you specially because Isadora knows the devil a thing about practical affairs. It hurt me to see the crowd of bandits that surrounds her. When you come the air will clear up.
> I have a great favor to ask you: for God's sake give some money to my sister when you leave. I have repeated this again and again. . . . That is my greatest wish for she must study. . . .[17]

It had been Isadora's plan to tour the United States with the children of her school, and she had in fact made arrangements for this with her American agent, Sol Hurok, but during the summer she received word from the school in Moscow that permission had been refused to take the children out of the country.[18] She would therefore have to tour without them.

From Paris, the Esenins traveled to Venice, where they installed themselves at the fashionable Hotel Excelsior on the Lido. Here, by chance, they found an old acquaintance, the Russian musician Sacha Votichenko. As a friend of Isadora, Votichenko was as little pleased with Esenin as Gorky had been with the poet's wife. Esenin was then wearing his dandyish clothes, and Votichenko thought they gave his young compatriot an affected and ridiculous air. Then Esenin began to read his poetry in his extraordinary, expressive voice, and the musician at once revised his opinion. "I was moved, more than moved. I was shaken to my roots. What a genius! And to think I had despised him for the cut of his coat! I felt like a fool."[19]

At the end of the summer, the Esenins returned to Paris. Isadora found that her tenant had decamped from the house at the Rue de la Pompe, leaving the rent unpaid. Coming so soon after the meager sum realized on the sale of her Berlin property, she could ill afford this loss of income, but at least the house would provide a rent-free rehearsal studio and a home for herself and Sergei until it was time to sail. That day came at the end of September, when she, Esenin, and their new Russian secretary, Vladimir Vetlugin, boarded the *S.S. Paris* en route for New York.[20]

❧ 31 ❧

Esenin in New York

1922–1923

ON their arrival in New York harbor, on October 1, 1922, the Esenins were politely informed by the United States Immigration Service that they would not be allowed to land. It appeared that Isadora's marriage to Sergei Alexandrovich Esenin, which had made her "respectable" in the eyes of the authorities, had also made her a Soviet citizen, and as a Soviet citizen she was suspected of being a propagandist, possibly even a spy for the Communists. Her indignant manager, Sol Hurok, who had come to the pier to meet them, was required to strip and be searched by the immigration inspectors for "invisible writing"[1] to make sure that he was not carrying away subversive messages to the Esenins' New York comrades. The couple's baggage, including Esenin's poems and the dancer's annotated scores, was inspected. "Miss Duncan was plainly shocked and hurt at the unexpected rebuff she had received."[2] As a final test of their intentions, the Esenins were asked their opinion of the French Revolution. Isadora answered the officials with ironic politeness. Esenin, who had developed his own technique for dealing with Russian censors, and who had prepared a speech of greeting to America, kept silent, as he later wrote, from disdain.

The couple's detention caused widespread shock, and Heywood Broun and Anna Fitziu, the opera singer, were among the many notables who protested.[3]

The reporters who interviewed the Esenins on the pier were, on the whole, friendly. They noted Isadora's enthusiasm when she spoke of her husband's genius and the looks of affection exchanged by the pair. ("Though unable to speak English [Esenin] hung over his wife and smiled approval at everything she said. Both appeared to be in love and took no pains to conceal their mutual adoration.")[4] Of course, there was speculation on the age difference between Isadora and Esenin. To Sergei, who had noted the long newspaper articles with approval, it was disillusioning to find himself identified only as the husband of Isadora Duncan, and it completed the bad impression of America which the immigration officials had made on him. Later he wrote, "there was little [in the newspapers] about Isadora Duncan, about the fact that I was a poet, but there was a great deal about my boots and how I had a beautiful physique, that of a lightweight athlete, and that I would certainly be the best 'sportsman in America.' "[5] Yet these gossipy news stories, contrasted with the obvious extravagance of the inspectors' behavior, increased public sympathy for Isadora and Sergei. The next day the authorities, embarrassed by the uproar, released the Esenins who went to the Waldorf-Astoria Hotel to rest for Isadora's opening recital on October 7.[6]

This brush with the law, far from doing them a disservice, caused a huge and enthusiastic audience to fill Carnegie Hall to the upper reaches. Her second New York appearance was received with equal acclaim. But her reception on landing had made her indignant, and in Boston, at the end of her performance of the *Marche Slave,* irritated by a stolid audience, she seized

a red scarf attached to her costume, incidentally and accidentally revealing more of her person than usual, and waved it over her head.[7]

"This is red! So am I!" she cried. "It is the color of life and vigor. You were once wild here. Don't let them tame you."

"You must read Maxim Gorki," she continued. "He has said that there are three kinds of people: the black, the grey, the red. The black people are like the former Kaiser or the ex-Czar—people who bring terror, who want to command. The red are those who rejoice in Freedom, in the untrammeled progress of the soul."

"The grey people are like those walls, like the hall. Look at these statues overhead. They are not real. Knock them down. I could hardly dance here. Life is not real here. Mr. Franko* was doing his best but he could hardly play here. We are red people, Mr. Franko and I. . . ."[8]

The next day country-wide headlines shouted:

RED DANCER SHOCKS BOSTON
ISADORA'S SPEECH DRIVES MANY FROM BOSTON HALL
DUNCAN IN FLAMING SCARF SAYS SHE'S RED

Immediately thereafter, Mayor Curley issued an order banning Isadora from further appearances in Boston to protect "the decent element." The artist, John Sloan, in a letter to his colleague, Robert Henri, commented sardonically: "Her performance . . . in Boston (the Athens of America, it is called) was stopped by police. (They can't stop bootlegging but they can stop barelegging.)"[9]

At the same time, three departments of the government (one apparently being insufficient to guard the country from the threat posed by Isadora) began an investigation to see whether the artist should be deported:

Officials said that while they were shocked at the eccentric dancer's reported omission of wearing apparel, they had no supervision [!] over it. But if she was spreading red propaganda as alleged, she would find herself at Ellis Island. . . .

The departments of Labor, Justice and State initiated inquiries

*Nathan Franko, the conductor.

when they had been advised that Miss Duncan had divested herself of her sole garment, a red sash, and waving it above her head, shouted "I am Red!"

The State Department, and the Department of Justice . . . are seeking information as to what, if any, connection the dancer has with the Soviet Government in Russia.

. . . If the Boston authorities convict her of an immoral exhibition it was said the Department of Labor could deport without more ado. . . .[10]

Isadora, never one to receive a public attack in silence, compounded her offense by telling the press:

They say I mismanaged my garments. A mere disarrangement of a garment means nothing . . . why should I care what part of my body I reveal? Why is one part more evil than another? Is not all body and soul an instrument through which the artist expresses his inner message of beauty? . . . That is a difference between vulgarity and art, for the artist places his whole being, body, soul and mind, on the throne of art. . . . Many dancers on the stage today are vulgar because they conceal and do not reveal. They would be much less suggestive if they were nude. Yet they are allowed to perform because they satisfy the Puritan instinct for concealed lust. . . . I don't know why this Puritan vulgarity should be confined to Boston, but it seems to be. Other cities are not afflicted with a horror of beauty and a smirking taste for burlesque semi-exposures.[11]

Her statement, besides providing wonderful copy for the reporters, resulted in the cancellation of many engagements. Her worried impresario, Hurok, trying to salvage what remained of her tour, warned her not to make any more speeches on the pain of breaking their contract. Isadora complied—until she made her next appearance, when, in response to the cheering of an enthusiastic audience, she stepped to the footlights and declared: "My manager tells me that if I make any more speeches the tour is dead. Very well, the tour is dead. I will go back to Moscow where there is vodka, music, poetry and dancing. Oh, yes, and Freedom!"[12]

John Sloan, the painter, seems to have seen Isadora in Chicago or shortly thereafter, since about a week after her Boston recital, he wrote in the letter already quoted:

A full house, but none of the swells. She deals such incautious, apparently ingenuous slaps to them they have I suppose gradually found it best to stay away. Or maybe they never came. Last evening she was speaking of millionaires, said: "You see I know about them, I lived with one for 8 years." That has a twist for the Puritan tail in it, hasn't it? I hear it said she lacks "tact." Well, so does God Almighty and many another artist is like His Reverence in that way. . . .[13]

After her Chicago performance, Isadora returned to New York for a few days to catch her breath before setting out on tour. Her respite was short-lived. She and Sergei attended a party in the Bronx given in his honor by the Jewish poet Braginski (an émigré from Russia), who under the name of Mani-Leib had translated some of Esenin's poems into Yiddish, and who with his wife, also a poet, had gained Sergei's friendship. Another friend, Leonid Grebnev (pseudonym of Leonid Feinberg), a fellow Imaginist from Russia, planned to conduct the Esenins to Mani-Leib's sixth-floor walkup in the Bronx, and Sergei persuaded his old comrade Veniamin Levin, who had just arrived in the United States, to come with them. (With Isadora wearing a fur wrap over a pink tulle dress, and Esenin a new suit, Levin remembered feeling that his work clothes were too informal for the party. Sergei told him that only a few friends would be there, and so they were all surprised when their host opened the door and they found themselves in a room packed full of people.) There was much to drink and Esenin drank enthusiastically. In response to the crowd's urging, Esenin recited some of his poetry, a monologue from *Pugachov* and the dialogue of Chekistov and Zamarishin from the *Country of Scoundrels*. In the latter, Esenin had Zamarishin say to Chekistov: "I know you are a Zhid [Yid]," instead of "I know you are a Jew," which appears in the printed text. This made a very unpleasant impression on the audience.

Esenin was in a bad mood. Isadora noticed this and was trying to free herself from the hands of several men leaning against her. She moved towards Esenin. But he was already inflamed by the wine. And the huge, unexpected crowd which had come to stare at them, and the impossibility of expressing what he wanted, and the free attentions of these men to his Isadora, and similar attentions of the women to him, but the main thing, wine, wine: and suddenly he who had been staring persistently at Isadora's light dress, grabbed her so that he ripped the cloth, and cursing her violently, would not let her go.[14]

Levin grabbed Esenin by both arms, and other guests hurried Isadora into the next room. "Where's Isadora?" Esenin began shouting, and evidently believing that Isadora had left, he bolted down the stairs, with Mani-Leib, Levin, and some of the guests pursuing. He was captured, and brought back to the party (Levin did not return, preferring to go home instead).

In a few minutes Esenin burst out in a fresh attack of rage, insulted his hosts, and tried to climb down the fire escape. Again he was forcibly restrained; eventually he was accompanied back to the hotel.

The next day, Saturday, the scandal hit the newspapers. Esenin was stigmatized as a Bolshevik and an anti-Semite. Unluckily, Mani-Leib had also asked some journalist friends to the party, and the brawl made copy that was too lively not to use.

The following morning, Sunday, Isadora telephoned Levin and asked him to visit Esenin who was sick in bed. They had moved from the Waldorf, presumably to avoid reporters, and were now staying at the Great Northern Hotel on West 57th Street. Levin arrived, and Isadora tactfully withdrew, leaving the two old friends alone.

Esenin was somewhat paler than usual, and very tender and courteous. And he said that he had had an epileptic fit. I had never heard this before. Then he told me that he had inherited epilepsy from his grandfather. Once when he was in the stable with his grandfather, he had had an attack. I was shocked. Now his conduct at Mani-

Leib's was clarified for me, it was the evening preceding an attack; he was therefore gloomy and nervous. We conversed calmly and in a friendly way. He was very much annoyed by the newspaper calling him an "anti-Semite and Bolshevik." "I have children by a Jewess, and they accuse me of anti-Semitism," he said angrily.[15]

(And in fact in *Iron Mirgorod,* written in 1923, Esenin speaks of the Jewish community in New York as one of the few cultural centers in America. "The Jews were drawn there mainly because they had to flee pogroms. . . . We have several names of world renown in their literature. In poetry, now world-famous, there is the very talented Mani-Leib. . . . Here [with his poems and Russian translations] lies a core of culture." Esenin was apparently not anti-Semitic when sober, only when drunk.)

Greatly distressed by what had occurred, Esenin wrote a remorseful apology to Mani-Leib.

Dear Mani-Leib!

Yesterday you dropped in on me at the hotel, we talked about something, but about what I do not remember for toward evening I had another attack. Today I lie here beaten morally and physically. Nurses watched over me all night long. The doctor came and gave me morphine.

My dear Mani-Leib! Forgive me for God's sake and don't think that I wanted to do anything bad or insult anyone.

Talk with Vetlugin [his secretary], he will tell you more. I have the very same disease as Edgar Poe and Musset. Edgar Poe smashed whole houses during his fits.

What can I do my dear Mani-Leib, my darling Mani-Leib! My heart is not guilty of this act, but my conscience which was awakened today subjected me to bitter tears, my good Mani-Leib! Speak to your wife so that she will not think evil of me. May you try to understand and to forgive me. I beg you to have just a little pity for me.

> Affectionately yours,
> S. Esenin

Give Grebnev all my best wishes. Indeed, we are all brother poets. Our soul is one, but, sometimes it becomes ill in one of us. Don't think that I want to insult anyone. When you receive my letter, tell everyone of my appeal for forgiveness.[16]

After her tumultuous times in the eastern states, Isadora must have been glad to leave for the presumably placid skies of the Middle West.

By now, reporters' interest in her tour was irrevocably fixed, not on the quality of her performances, but on whether she would have trouble with her husband, her garments, or the local police.

In Indianapolis four detectives were stationed in the wings of the stage, by order of Mayor Lew Shanks, to make sure she would not divest herself of her tunic. In Louisville, the shoulder strap of her dress broke, and the fact was duly noted under the headline, "Isadora Smirches Art."[17] In another city the mayor confiscated some of her costumes to prevent her from performing any revolutionary dances. Isadora took care of this situation (and its instigator) by gently announcing to the audience: "I'm sorry I cannot dance the second part of the program as it has been arranged. It is not my fault. It is because your Mayor loves red so much. He loves it so much that he took away my red tunics even without my permission." She continued in the same style, developing a vein of sarcasm and irony that put the audience in sympathy with her and brought on laughter and derision for the mayor. The aftermath was that the executive had to leave the city for three days to avoid questioning and let the affair blow over.[18]

In Toledo, the critic of *The Toledo Blade* wrote of Isadora in two Liszt works, *Les Funérailles* and *Bénédiction de Dieu dans la Solitude:*

"Her ghastly white countenance was a mask of tragedy, her eyes at times were glassy . . . [her] facial contortions and gestures were alternations of horror, suffering and despair, although . . . there were moments of spirit, exaltation and yearning to uplift others to the same heights." He and the audience preferred the latter, lighter part of the program: three études, and *Sonata Number Four* by Scriabin. Performing these somber rhapsodies must have given Isadora a needed sense of release, for throughout the tour she was tormented by worries about her young husband whose drinking and black depressions were increasing.

Relations between Isadora and Sergei had worsened. Beginning with their reception on landing, the trip to the United States had been a series of rebuffs and disappointments. Now he found himself in the heartland of a strange country whose language he did not know and where he himself was unknown. He remembered how the pleasure he had felt at seeing a photograph of himself in a magazine had turned into bitter disillusionment when someone translated the caption for him: "Sergei Esenin, Russian poet, husband of the famous dancer, Isadora Duncan."[19] He was remarkable only as a famous dancer's young husband—a freak, whose poetry might as well not exist. Sometimes he must have wondered whether he *was* a poet, since the pressures of being on tour robbed him of the time and the quiet necessary for writing. He unburdened his resentment of Isadora to her Russian-speaking accompanist, Max Rabinovitch, describing her in terms of coarse and angry contempt. Frequently his frustration erupted in violence, and more than once the pianist had to interpose himself between him and Isadora in order to protect her.[20] Magically—despite his lack of English, and no matter where they were—he never seemed to have any trouble finding bootleggers to supply him with bad whiskey.

It was not only his separation from Russia, his inability to work, and his status as second fiddle to Isadora that made trouble for Esenin. In all his love relationships with women, Esenin felt a deep conflict. This conflict arose, suggests Simon Karlinsky, from ambivalence about his own sexual preferences. In a review of Gordon McVay's fine biography, *Esenin: A Life,* Professor Karlinsky praises Dr. McVay for bringing up the subject of Esenin's "latent bisexuality" but says that McVay does not go far enough. "Nor is there anything 'latent' about the love letters and poems Esenin and Klyuev exchanged. . . . Esenin's alternating attraction to homosexuality and his revulsion against it . . . may well have contributed to his alcoholism. . . . His battered and abandoned wives and mistresses seem to have been the principal victims of this poet's inability to come to terms with his bisexuality."[21]

If bisexual feelings contributed to Esenin's unhappiness, Isadora evidently did not suspect it. Her husband had reasons enough for feelings of homesickness and depression.

Gradually their itinerary brought them back east, and, on Christmas night, Isadora and Max Rabinovitch were scheduled to perform at the Brooklyn Academy of Music. By now, however, the strain of the last months was telling on Isadora. Hearing the news that Sarah Bernhardt was dying, Isadora suddenly announced that she would dance *Les Funérailles* in honor of the great actress. The audience and press were startled by this premature memorial service. Their bafflement grew as the program continued its impromptu course. At the end of the next dance, a Scriabin sonata, Isadora and Rabinovitch took a bow holding hands. Abruptly, he snatched his hand away and walked off. The dancer, recalled for an encore, signaled for her accompanist but he had vanished. Isadora tried dancing as she herself sang the Brahms *Waltz in A flat,* then evidently decided that this looked too odd and waltzed off stage. Minutes later, Esenin hurried from the wings, frantically searching for Isadora who had also disappeared.

Some years later, Rabinovitch gave his account of the incident to writer Joseph Kaye. In the second part of the program, the pianist noticed that Isadora, instead of dancing the movements that she had planned, was wandering dreamily around the stage. Her improvisations increased during the Scriabin sonata and her languishing glances at Rabinovitch grew increasingly embarrassing.

When they took their bow, Isadora would not release her grip on his hand, and Rabinovitch, convinced that the audience had noticed his attempts to get free and was snickering, pulled his hand away, ran off, and locked himself in the washroom.

When he saw Isadora the next day he expected her to be outraged, but instead she asked him almost timidly whether he was angry with her, and apologized, saying that something she had drunk during the intermission had made her giddy and irresponsible.[22]

Much has been written about Isadora's drinking. Just how heavy was it? Irma Duncan wrote in her autobiography:

Outside of an occasional cocktail before meals, none of us girls, nor Isadora ever indulged in drinking or especially craving hard liquor. Our European tastes were conditioned to wines. Only in her late forties, after her marriage to a Russian and under his malign influence, did she acquire a habit for stronger stuff. But no one could ever honestly accuse her of becoming an alcoholic in her last years. That to my certain knowledge represents a gross calumny.[23]

Victor Seroff, who knew Isadora very well during the last years of her life, said:[24]

I never saw Isadora drunk,[25] and in fact having heard about her drinking I was rather surprised by proof to the contrary when we arrived in Nice at the end of 1926. . . . I, looking for a book, opened a wall cabinet which I had taken for a book cupboard. To my surprise, all the shelves were filled with liquor of every description. Although Isadora knew about it, she never "helped herself," because, she said, since I did not drink, she would not drink by herself. And that is hardly a drinking person's philosophy.

Mrs. William A. Bradley (the widow of Isadora's literary agent, who eventually sold her memoirs), who became a good friend during Isadora's last year, wrote in answer to a letter of Francis Steegmuller:

I do not think that one can speak of alcoholism in Isadora's case. It was after the loss of her children and her separation from Singer that she began to seek occasional consolation in the vague forgetfulness that comes with drinking. But she did not drink when she was happy, and when she was dancing. She certainly liked Goebler champagne and drank it when she could, particularly during her last years, when, no longer dancing, she was unhappy and felt herself somewhat forgotten. Alcohol was for her a remedy, a pleasant remedy, and she so considered it: she refused, for example, to allow any to be given to the young piano-accompanist, Yasha, whom she had brought back with her from Russia, saying that he was not unhappy and had no need of it.[26]

However, Isadora usually drank as a matter of course. Minna Besser Geddes, who worked for a while as Isadora's literary secretary when the latter was writing her memoirs, stated: "I've seen her drink, but never to excess."[27]

Yet, from all accounts, Isadora did drink too much on her South American trip (after her children's death, when she was away from the sustaining presence of friends) and while touring with Esenin and vacationing with him in Germany. The evidence suggests that she drank more when she was lonely or under stress than when she was working, teaching, or happy in love. And both she and Esenin were apt to drink more as a challenge to people they considered reproving or hostile.

Her last New York concerts were given on January 13 and 15, 1923, at Carnegie Hall.[28] Because of canceled bookings after the Boston episode, her tour had not made money, and her manager might reasonably have provided only a piano for her final performance. "But Hurok felt he could not let Isadora take her leave of America in this penurious manner,"[29] so he provided a full orchestra under the direction of Modeste Altschuler. Before a full house Isadora danced Wagner—*The Ride of the Valkyries,* the *Valhalla Processional* from *Götterdämmerung,* the *Liebestod,* and the *Tannhäuser Bacchanale*— as well as waltzes and the Schubert *Marche Militaire.*

At the end of January, Isadora and Esenin boarded the *George Washington* for France.[30] Far from having made any money to send back to the Moscow school, Isadora's funds were by this time so depleted that she had been forced to borrow the price of their passage from the open-handed and forebearing Paris Singer.[31]

The departure was not without incident. Joseph Kaye tells us, "When she left America she waved a red flag from the boat in obvious defiance of bourgeois Philistines. When she was later asked abroad if that didn't indicate her Bolshevist sympathies, she replied, 'No, I waved that flag only to make them mad.' "[32]

This story, though probably apocryphal (I have been unable to find any references to the flag in newspaper accounts of her sailing), certainly sounds like Isadora. Earlier, in the midst of the uproar over admitting her to the United States, she had told a friendly reporter, "I can give you clues to follow in writing of me. I am sensitive. I like a sympathetic atmosphere—that is why it was so terrible to be treated as if I had committed a crime, when I landed here."[33] This self-sketch is born out by Dumesnil's observation on her South American tour: "I could see how dependent Isadora was on the sympathy of her audience. Should [it] be negative, her spontaneity would shrink and turn into an antagonistic disposition. But if it happened . . . to be . . . positive . . . she would open up . . . like a flower."[34] Though her initial reaction to rebuffs was usually one of hurt, once aroused she would display "a frenzy of opposition"[35] to those she considered her attackers. At that point, she *enjoyed* making people angry.

Whether or not she flew the Communist banner from the ship hardly matters; it would have been superfluous after the verbal red flag she waved at reporters who came to see her off. In a final attempt to set the record straight about her politics she said:

"I am not an anarchist or a Bolshevist. My husband and I are revolutionists. All geniuses worthy of the name are. . . . Goodbye America. I shall never see you again."[36]

Drawing by Lucien Jacques, dancing to *Orpheus* by Gluck (*Christine Dalliès Collection*).

Isadora at Pompeii (*Mme. Mario Meunier—Christine Dalliès Collection*).

Isadora at Cape Ferrat, 1920 (*Mme. Mario Meunier—Christine Dalliès Collection*).

Isadora wearing heavy material probably woven by her brother Raymond, Cape Ferrat, 1920 (*Mme. Mario Meunier–Christine Dalliès Collection*).

Isadora Duncan Pointing, Edward Steichen, 1921 (*Collection, The Museum of Modern Art, New York*).

A view of Kopanos, the Duncan house facing the Acropolis in Athens (*Jeremiah Newton*).

Isadora dancing at the Erechtheion with Anna and Thérèse, photograph by Steichen (*Mme. Mario Meunier—Christine Dalliès Collection*).

Isadora outside her dacha in Moscow, 1922 (*New York Public Library*).

Isadora's school in Moscow (1921–1928) (*New York Public Library*).

Gordon Craig at Bordighera, March 16, 1953 (*Mme. Mario Meunier—Christine Dalliès Collection*).

Elizabeth Duncan, Isadora's sister
(*Jeremiah Newton Collection*).

Isadora's brother Raymond, circa 1977, standing beside one of the figures from the vault of his father's bank (*Archives for the Performing Arts, San Francisco*).

Drawing by José Clarà, dated September 19, 1927. The inscription reads: "To my dear friend, Fernand Divoire, in memory of his touching words spoken during the cremation of our great and gentle friend, *Isadora.*" (*Blair Collection*).

Isadora at a sidewalk cafe in Nice, 1927, the year she died (*New York Public Library*).

❧ 32 ❧

Return to Russia
1923–1924

N their arrival in France, the Esenins were met in Paris
by Isadora's old friend Mary Desti, now Mrs. Howard
Perch, who had come over that very morning from
London in response to an urgent cable from Isadora.
The dancer, descending from the train alone, had just time to
warn Mary in answer to the latter's anxious inquiries, "Don't try
to understand anything. I will explain later. Only, whatever you do,
forget I'm the great artist. I'm just a nice intelligent person who
appreciates the great genius of Sergei Esenin. He is the artist, he,
the great poet. . . . You will understand later, I assure you."[1]

Then Sergei was helped from the coach and, on being introduced
to "my dearest friend," lifted Mary in a wild bear hug. Isadora
beamed. "She was never sure how Sergei would receive anyone . . . a
scene had been averted."[2]

Isadora insisted that Mary accompany them to the Crillon, where
she and the Esenins booked adjoining rooms. Dinner, which was
served privately in the Esenins' suite, began cheerfully. Sergei, in

an ebullient mood, threw himself affectionately at his wife's feet and recited some of his poems for Mary. But his high spirits became increasingly infected with restlessness. "Every few minutes [he] would dash down the hall, once for cigarettes, again for matches. . . . Each time he returned he looked a bit paler, and Isadora more nervous. . . . The last time he didn't come back . . . so Isadora rang for her maid.

"The maid then told us he had come several times to her room and ordered champagne, but now he had gone out . . . a look of melancholy settled on Isadora's face."[3]

On Esenin's uproarious return to the Crillon several hours later, Isadora barely had time to lock herself in Mary's room when she heard the familiar sounds of shattering glass and splintering wood. Her husband next door was smashing the hotel furniture. The management sent for the police, who escorted Sergei to the police station. Isadora returned to her own room, and tried to decide how she would ever manage to reimburse the Crillon for the breakage.

Once Isadora had paid the damages, she set about trying to get the charges against Esenin dropped. His release was obtained only with the aid of influential friends, and, according to Mary, only on condition that he leave the country immediately.

It was agreed that the stalwart maid Jeanne would travel with him to Berlin, where a large Russian colony would make his exile more bearable, and he would wait there until the scandal blew over. Isadora and Mary later joined him only to discover that Sergei, far from languishing in solitude, was in the center of a coterie of poets and roisterers. Once again there were night-long parties and shattered glassware. After one such occasion, the dancer disappeared, and Mary, who had dropped off to sleep, was wakened by Sergei "sobbing piteously, explaining . . . that Isadora was gone, gone forever, perhaps a suicide."

"I told Sergei not to worry, and to stop crying . . . and that I would go out and look for Isadora. . . . In these after spells he was just like a pathetic little child, until your heart ached with pity for him."[4]

Isadora had in fact fled the hotel, and presently she sent Mary a message asking her to bring her some clothes and toilet articles, and not to disclose her whereabouts to Sergei. She told Mary that Sergei had said something "so brutal about her children that she simply had to leave."[5] Sergei was intensely jealous of his wife's love for her dead son and daughter, and more than once he had made scenes when Isadora talked about them,[6] although he sometimes spoke to her of his own children by other women.

All this being so, why did Isadora put up with Esenin? Even though her marital requirements were not the usual ones, such as sobriety or financial responsibility, how could she remain in love with a man who behaved scandalously in public, who threatened her, who was unfaithful, and who insulted the memory of her children?

There were many reasons for her attachment to Sergei and her determination to excuse his faults. She admired him for his gifts and was touched by his youth and beauty. She told Mary that she thought he looked like her son Patrick. (What if Patrick were ill, and had no one to take care of him?) As for Isadora's tolerance for his fits of violence, "I do believe," wrote Mary, with sudden insight, "that if he had not attacked her, she would never have resented these spells as they were so in keeping with the awful inner torment from which she never ceased to suffer. They had the same soothing effect on her as a mad racing auto or an airplane. The utter disregard for everything conventional and for all life that had so brutally destroyed her, seemed to give her some respite from sorrow."[7] They were a release from her anguish. She could understand Sergei's urge to destroy because she identified with it.

His drinking, too, though it worried her, did not repel her as much as it would have if she herself did not enjoy good wines and liquors. After the death of her children, in periods of anxiety Isadora drank heavily to deaden her own pain, and so she could sympathize with Sergei's need. In periods of happiness, when she felt loved, she drank less. But married to the poet, she would have turned to drink as much for relief from his frenetic conviviality as from his black moods. (And, in turn, Sergei's marriage to Isadora, which interrupted his work and uprooted him from his country, gave him an incentive to drink.) Although sometimes in her public statements she had attributed his disorderly behavior to shell shock (which may have contributed to his condition), Isadora did not conceal from herself the nature of his illness. But she excused it, believing that weaknesses and emotional disturbances usually accompanied the greater sensitivity of genius. Esenin's conduct was a consequence, perhaps even a proof, of his gifts. And although he caused her much grief, she believed that tragedy was the human lot. "I remember all through my childhood a distinct feeling of the general unpleasantness of life as being a normal condition," she wrote in an early draft of her memoirs. Poverty, dunning landlords, her anxious mother and her absent father had given her that conviction. "The state in which we lived, continually hunted [by creditors and bailiffs] had seemed to me the normal thing."[8] This is doubtless part of the reason why she put up with Esenin and other impossible conditions for so long— because she thought they were part of the natural unpleasantness of life and that it was futile, infantile, to try to rebel against things that could not be changed; better to accept the defects of the person one loves, as one also accepts the good qualities. And Isadora had a terrible need for love—a need which had grown overpowering since the death of her children. She was committed to Esenin. Now, hearing from Mary of his panic at her disappearance, she could not resist telephoning Sergei, and he was so penitent that she promised to return to him.

But the scandal of the previous night had made it obvious that the experiment of taking Sergei out of Russia had been a failure. Since his malady had not yielded to treatment, there seemed to be no alternative other than to bring him back to his country and his friends. In order to finance the trip, she returned to Paris, where she intended to rent her house and sell her furniture. Perhaps she could also make some money on the two recitals she was scheduled to give on May 27 and June 3.[9] Esenin, though he supposedly had been barred from France, accompanied her.

Back in the French capital, he had another run-in with the authorities. According to Irma Duncan and Allan Ross Macdougall, after Isadora's Trocadéro recital on May 27, during a party that she gave for a few intimates, Sergei got into a fight and hurled a candelabrum at the mirror. A servant called the commissariat, and again Esenin was taken away under police escort. This time Isadora had him transferred to a private sanatorium. Reporters, of course, got wind of these scandals, and Isadora had the unpleasant task of writing to the newspapers to deny that Esenin had beaten her.[10]

As soon as her business in Paris was concluded and Sergei was well enough to travel, the dancer and her husband left for Moscow. With relief Isadora returned to the country that recognized Sergei's genius and made allowances for his malady.

Her school (now being taught by Irma) had moved to Litvino, a village fifty miles outside of Moscow. Isadora decided to motor there with Esenin and with Irma and Schneider, who had come to the city to welcome Isadora. It was evening when they arrived at Litvino, and they were met by the smiling children of Isadora's classes, who ran through the woods carrying torches in their eagerness to greet their teacher. It rained during their stay and, after several days in the country, Isadora and her companions returned to Moscow.[11]

To Sergei, the homecoming must have been a liberation, and he wasted no time in putting the nightmare of everything foreign out of his mind—including Isadora. The day after the group returned to Moscow, he disappeared and was not heard from for three days. On the third day, Isadora decided that she had had enough: she would leave that night with Irma for the Caucasus. The secretary, Schneider, was to follow shortly afterward. Sergei reappeared as she was packing, and she warned him that if he ever went away again without telling her where he was going, all would be over between them. He affected not to believe her. Her words must have made an impression, however, for that evening he materialized at the station, his demeanor affectionate, his state sober. Touched, Isadora urged him to come with them. He would not be persuaded, but he promised to join them later.

After a week or so at Kislavodsk, Isadora's energy had returned, and she decided to make a concert tour of the surrounding region. Her first recital was to be at Kislavodsk itself. She decided to give her Tchaikovsky program: the *Symphonie Pathétique* and the *Marche*

Slave. The morning before the performance, passersby were elec-
trified to hear the strains of the czarist national anthem, which
Tchaikovsky used in the *Marche Slave,* coming from the bandstand
at the Kursaal. Naturally, it was not long before word of this
counterrevolutionary demonstration reached the secret police, and
when Isadora was about to go on stage that evening, two Cheka
men informed her that she would not be allowed to dance the czarist
hymn.

Isadora met the challenge head-on. Calling for an interpreter, she
told the audience that there were members of the police backstage
who had come to arrest her if she attempted to dance the *Marche
Slav* but that she intended to dance it anyway. "After all, the prison
cannot be much worse than my room at the Grand Hotel." Since
most of the audience had also received entertainment at that flea-
bitten establishment, this remark provoked laughter, and the interpreter, a local official, gave Isadora permission to go ahead with her
announced program. The concert was enthusiastically received,
doubtless as much for the novelty of seeing the Tcheka defied as
for Isadora's artistry. In any case, her dance to the *Marche Slave* left
no doubt where she stood on the issue of the czar and serfdom.

The police, however, did not consider the incident closed. Afraid
to attack the dancer directly, the next day they came to arrest her
secretary, Schneider. Isadora, who did not believe in wasting time
with petty officials, demanded to see Trotsky, then War Minister,
who providentially had a villa in the neighborhood, and although
his guards would not let her enter, he read her letter of protest
and issued orders that the dancer's party was not to be molested.
The men withdrew, but not before they had, in the best operatic
style, vowed revenge on Isadora for her insults.[12]

After leaving Kislavodsk, Isadora gave concerts in a number of
Caucasian towns, among them Baku and Tiflis. On the train to Tiflis
a stranger handed Schneider a letter for Isadora. Having heard by
chance that the man would be travelling to the Caucasus, Esenin
had given him a letter, saying "Duncan is somewhere in the Caucasus." (This casual method of sending personal mail was typical of
Esenin, remarked Schneider.)[13] The note read:[14]

Sweet Isadora,

    I could not come to you because I was very busy. I shall come to Yalta. I love you endlessly. Yours Sergei.

    Love to Irma,

Isadora!!![15]

Reassured by his tender words and the thought of their coming reunion, the dancer raised the note to her lips and kissed it.[16]

On the outskirts of Tiflis, Isadora visited a huge relocation camp for homeless Armenian children who were being cared for by the American Near East Relief Association. She entertained the children by performing an impromptu dance.[17]

From Tiflis, Isadora and her little party went to Batoum on the Black Sea and from there, at Isadora's insistence, took the boat to the Crimean peninsula.[18] Since the brief note Esenin had sent her shortly after her departure, she had heard nothing from her husband although she had written to him frequently. At Yalta, the following message was delivered to her:

Moscow, 9, 10, '23

Don't send any more letters telegrams Esenin he is with me and won't join you [you] must count on his not returning to you.

Galina Benislavskaya[19]

Reacting to this missive, Isadora wired to Esenin:

    I've received telegram evidently from your servant Benislavskaya she writes that I should no longer send telegrams to Bogolovsky [Lane] have you changed address I ask you to explain by telegram I love you very very much Isadora.[20]

Galina Benislavskaya, however, was not a servant. She was an old friend of Sergei.[21] According to Galina's memoirs, Esenin told her: "I felt passion, a great passion. This lasted a whole year. . . . My God, how blind I was! . . . I feel nothing now for Duncan." Galina

343

advised him that if he was sure this was so, he had better end everything with Isadora. Consequently he sent a telegram to her at the Hotel Russia in Yalta: "I love another am married and happy Esenin."[22] He was neither married nor in love, but it seemed a sure way to make a conclusive break.

Whether Isadora eventually received this telegram is unclear. According to Ilya Schneider, it had been sent to Yalta on October 13, the day after he, Irma, and Isadora had left for Moscow.[23]

Some time after her return, probably in November 1923, while Isadora was in her room at Pretchistenka with some callers, Esenin arrived to claim the wooden bust which the sculptor Konienkoff had carved of him. He was noisy and insistent. He had evidently been drinking, and he ignored Isadora's request to come back later. Catching sight of the bust, which stood on top of a cabinet, he climbed on top of a chair, reached awkwardly for the bust, and toppled to the floor. Getting to his feet unsteadily, his likeness clutched to his chest, Sergei stormed out of the room, slamming the door behind him.[24] It was the end of his life with Isadora.

Much has been made of the fundamental incompatibility of Esenin and Isadora. Was Isadora the embodiment of all that Esenin did not need, as Gorky believed? Initial sexual attraction aside, how much love and understanding was possible between two sensitive and articulate people who were reduced to conversing in sign language and through interpreters?

Veniamin Levin thought that the fact of their speaking different languages mattered less than one would have supposed.

From my observations they were a very congenial couple. . . . The complications stemmed from the fact that he spoke only Russian, while she spoke English, French, German and only about ten words of Russian. But she was a dancer and she understood him without words, she understood each gesture. And he rejoiced at her dancing, and her gestures and her fantastically kind heart. She did not enter his poetry or his literary life; he lived this part of his life independently. He was already accustomed to this from his home life in the Ryazan province, where his parents only "spit on his poetry," and to them he was "dear like the field and the flesh." [These quotations are from his poetry.] . . . He had almost the same relationship with Isadora. The only real difference was that she knew his poetry in English and French, and she told me that she preferred the French. We discussed them in German, and it turned out that we were speaking the same language since we talked of Esenin and his poetry—everything which derived from him was dear to us, and this quickly brought us very close.[25]

If Isadora understood and appreciated Sergei's poetry far more than Gorky supposed, what were Esenin's feelings about Isadora's dance? We know that he did not care for classical music, which must have been an obstacle to his understanding of her work; nonetheless he saw a kinship between her art and his.

> One day Esenin said to Isadora: "You are an Imagist."
> She knew what he meant but raising her blue eyes to him, asked in broken Russian, "Why?"
> "Because in your art the image (obraz) is the main thing."
> "What is obraz?" she asked, turning to me. [Schneider]
> I translated: "Image." Esenin laughed.
> "Isadora," he said, "Marienhof is not *obraz,* your *Marche Slave* is *obraz* . . . you are an Imagist. But a good one. Understand?"
> She nodded.
> "You are *revolution!* Understand?"[26]

Victor Seroff says that Esenin was proud of Isadora's revolutionary dances and their enthusiastic reception by Russian audiences. According to Seroff, Sergei was profoundly moved on the famous occasion when Isadora was dancing for the crew of the *Aurora* in the Maryinsky Theatre in Leningrad and the lights failed. Isadora held a lantern, her upraised arm unfaltering, while for an hour the sailors sang folk songs and songs of the Revolution. When it was over, Esenin came backstage with his eyes shining and flung his arms around her, saying "Sidora, Sidora," his pet name for Isadora.[27]
Had Esenin been dazzled by Isadora's fame? Were his feelings for

her mere infatuation? His friend Riurik Ivnev thought that Esenin was incapable of "simple, human love."

> He could not love anyone or anything besides his own poems and his own muse. . . . In all the marvelous warmth of his lyrics, his love was without object. All who knew Esenin well know that he never truly loved any one woman.[28]

This may well be true. It is certain that the strain of touring in foreign countries where he could not speak the language, where he could not work, and where he was regarded as merely an exotic member of Isadora's entourage, eroded their marriage. But it is also true that at one time Sergei's feeling for Isadora was intense. He once said to Schneider, "Is not sensuality part of a powerful and real love? Are we walking on clouds and not on the earth?"[29]

Indeed sensuality was part of Esenin's feelings for Isadora, but his sensuality may have been of an ambivalent nature which Schneider did not suspect. The nature of this ambivalence was initially raised by Gordon McVay in his carefully researched, sober biography, *Esenin: A Life,*[30] and further examined by Simon Karlinsky in *The New York Times Book Review* (May 9, 1976) and elsewhere, and by McVay in his subsequent biography, *Isadora and Esenin.*[31] There is evidence to suggest that Esenin was attracted to men as well as to women. He may have been in love with Mariengof as well as Klyuev and other men.

To quote Simon Karlinsky, Professor of Slavic Languages and Literature at the University of California at Berkeley:

> The notion that Esenin and Marienhof might have been lovers first occurred to me when I read Nikritina's memoir in *Esenin i sovremennost'*. She describes the two poets' life together as not very Bohemian: they shared their lodgings, pooled their money, took their meals together at set times and were always identically dressed in white jackets, dark blue slacks and white canvas shoes. This struck me as a typical ménage of a gay male couple. . . . In *Esenin i sovremennost'* there is also a memoir by Esenin's daughter who states that

her father left her mother (Zinaida Raikh) because of his growing closeness to Marienhof. Ordinarily, a husband's closeness with a male friend does not make him lose interest in his wife, unless the man is replacing the wife in the husband's affections.

Re-reading *Roman bez vran'ja* after these two memoirs, I became aware that Marienhof is deliberately signaling the nature of his relationship with Esenin to readers capable of picking up such signals, while at the same time covering up his tracks for the rest. Thus, in the brief Chapter 18, Esenin begs of Marienhof help in getting rid of Raikh in what seems to be a love scene between the two men. At the end of Chapter 21, Esenin is wildly jealous of Marienhof's new girlfriend and takes to drink when Marienhof spends the night with her. Kusikov fans the flames of jealousy by accusing Marienhof of being unfaithful to Esenin (cf. Klyuev's similar jealousy of women, described by Cherniavsky). In Chapter 24, the "poetess" they hire to warm their bed storms out in disgust because the two men show no interest in her naked body but prefer to sleep together. (Here and in *Roman s druz' jami,* Marienhof says that he and Esenin shared the bed because the room was cold. This happens to be a classical homosexual dodge, used to reassure straights that nothing sexual is going on. Studying the literature of the period, one never finds Mayakovsky or Mandelstam sharing the bed with another man, no matter what the temperature. Esenin, however, does it again and again and invariably with the same excuse.)

Chapters 41 to 43 of *Roman bez vran'ja* describe Marienhof's growing involvement with Nikritina. His behavior toward Esenin during that time is that of a guilty, unfaithful lover. Nikritina can't bear to face Esenin, Marienhof "can't look him in the eye while embracing him" and hides from him the fact that he is going to see Nikritina off at the train station. Esenin spies on Marienhof to determine whether he is seeing Nikritina. It is implied in those chapters that Marienhof's relationship with Nikritina is what breaks up his four-year closeness to Esenin. It is also implied that Esenin's involvement with Duncan came about in part as a retaliation for Marienhof's betrayal. From Chapter 46 on, Marienhof is clearly jealous of Duncan and resents her presence in Esenin's life. The two women seem to have been aware of what was going on, to judge from Duncan's remark in fractured Russian quoted in Nikritina's memoir. In *Roman bez vran'ja* and in his letters from abroad, Esenin addresses Marienhof as *jagodka,* a dialectical term for "darling" or "sweetheart." It is used in peasant wedding songs to designate spouses (cf. Stravinsky's *Les Noces*), it can be used by a peasant girl to address her lover or by a mother to address a daughter. But I know of no other instances where it is used between men.

Finally and most importantly, there is "Proscanie s Mariengofom." I know of no other poem by him so powerfully suffused with pure sexual electricity, especially the opening stanza, with its pun on "unbridled happiness" and "naked bodies" in the first line, "convulsions of frenzied emotions," and the "love that melts the body as though it were a candle." "Vozljublennyj moj" in the second stanza is very different from the quasi-ecclesiastical "vozljublennj" (plus Christian name and patronymic) that Klyuev sometimes uses in the salutations of his letters ("My beloved in Christ"). Here it is the "vozljublennyj" of literary usage, i.e. "my lover." I could go through the rest of the poem in this manner, but I'm sure you see what I mean.

So, if you ask me whether I have any proof that Esenin and Marienhof were sexually intimate, I will have to admit I have none. But I do believe that they were lovers in the full sense of the term and that the information outlined above is not mere speculation, as you put it. What is interesting about the relationship from the literary point of view is its emotional impact on Esenin. The important question is whether the realization of the nature of the relationship brings new understanding to our reading of "Proscanie s Mariengofom" and possibly of other poems. I believe that it does.[32]

If Karlinsky is correct, to what extent was Isadora aware of Esenin's bisexuality? Initially, not at all. Later, to judge from a remark of her's to Anna Nikritina, Mariengof's wife, she recognized the strength of Sergei's feeling for Mariengof and his sense of exclusion at Mariengof's marriage. Just before Isadora and Esenin were to leave for Europe and America, they invited the newly married Mariengof and Nikritina for dinner. Isadora made the first toast to Esenin and Mariengof's friendship. "She was, after all, a very perceptive woman," Nikritina observed. "Later she said to me: 'I and you is trifles, but Esenin and Mariengof is everything, is friendship.'

I for one, knew that I was certainly 'Trifles.' "[33] Years later, Nikritina, commenting on this passage to biographer Gordon McVay, wrote:

> Duncan was a wonderful, intelligent woman! She understood perfectly well that for Seryozha [Esenin] she represented a passionate infatuation and nothing more, and that his real life lay elsewhere. Whenever they visited us and she sat down on our broken bed, she would say, "Here there is something genuine, here there is love." . . . And yet at the same time she thought that the principal and most important thing for them [Mariengof and Esenin] was their art and not women.[34]

Nikritina found Karlinsky's suggestion that Mariengof and Esenin were homosexuals ridiculous, though not offensive. Their closeness was the closeness of friends. Moreover, she knew that Mariengof and Esenin had had many affairs with women.

As for Isadora, she was well aware that Esenin was attracted to other women, and she must have sensed that he now found her a burden. The possibility that he may also have been attracted to men probably did not enter her mind.

In summing up, McVay comments:

> Esenin's seeming bisexuality is a legitimate topic for discussion; it may help to clarify certain aspects of his psychology and his poetry. . . . It is too easy to dismiss this whole topic as idle "speculation" or "sensation seeking." At present it may be impossible to reach a definite conclusion. Some facts may have been suppressed and all opinions can be questioned.[35]

Isadora suffered at Sergei's departure, yet, with him gone, she found it easier to carry on with her work. She had once expressed to a party official her belief that if religious rituals were banned, the state would still need rites to solemnize the naming of infants or the formalities surrounding marriage and burial. (Though an unbeliever when it came to dogma, Isadora was far from hostile to the religious impulse.) As a result of this comment, she was invited to dance for the first Octobrina christening, which would take place in November 1923. Unorthodox in her response to atheism as to everything else, Isadora decided to perform a composition already in her repertoire, the *Ave Maria,* to Schubert's music. She had choreographed two versions of this work—a solo, with herself dancing the role of Mary, and a group work in which her pupils took the parts of adoring angels. Fortunately, the officials in Moscow were less nervous about counterrevolutionary music than were their colleagues of the provinces, and Isadora's solo was enthusiastically received.[36]

In the beginning of 1924, Lenin died. Isadora, though she had never met the Russian leader, was struck by the sight of hundreds of sorrowing people standing in the intense cold of Red Square, waiting to file past his bier. She transformed her impressions into two funeral marches which she later danced with great success during her Ukrainian tour that spring. This tour was in every way a happy one. In Kiev, she managed to pack the theater for eighteen consecutive nights, a feat which most soloists would have difficulty in equaling, and an unusual one for a dancer of forty-seven.

Her foray from Leningrad to Witebsk and back at the end of May[37] included an experience of a different kind. On her return from the latter town, as she careened along country lanes in an ancient automobile, the car broke in two.[38] Isadora was more shaken than surprised, for as she later told a friend, she had always expected to be killed in an automobile accident. There was nothing uncanny about this premonition. Since her children's death, closed cars gave her claustrophobia. She avoided them. And the cars she did ride, because of her insistence on driving at top speed, must have been a constant temptation to fate.

Despite the hazards of transportation, Isadora found herself under increasing financial pressure to tour. No rent was coming in from the house on the Rue de la Pompe, and she had instructed her Paris lawyer, Maître Thorel, to find out whether her tenant, Leonid Gordieff, was still there.[39] Meanwhile the costs of the Moscow school continued to mount. She wrote to an American newspaper correspondent:[40]

The Soviet Government has completely abandoned the school since one year—not sent one paicock [rations to which they had formerly been entitled] or any aid whatever. The A.R.A. [American Relief Association] from whom we received some help have also since a year left Moscow. We are forced to pay very dear for electric light, fuel and even *water*. Food and clothes and all cost[s] of the school, teachers, musicians comes [sic] now only from the public performances we are able to give; and as you can imagine, the financial state of Moscou [sic] at present makes these performances very rare—for instance, from one performance for which we receive 50 Chervonetz, or $250., I have bought wood for the winter, and with a second performance, flour, potatoes, etc.

The children are at present in splendid health and working with enthousiasm [sic] and they are most of them so talented that it will be a thousand pities if this two years['] work, sacrifice and effort is to be lost. My only hope at present is to recieve [sic] help from our friends in America. If the school is helped for the next few years, I am confident that it will then be self-supporting. . . .

Since returning here I have completely severed all relationship with Sergei Esenin whose actions and declarations have become more and more incomprehensible and demented. There is no way to account for them except by except on [sic; this repetition suggests how greatly the subject upset her] the explanation of temporary insanity.

It will be most kind . . . if you will write to me as I recieve [sic] no news from America.

With many good wishes—remembrances—

A tour, then, was imperative. Remembering her enthusiastic reception in Kiev that spring, she decided to begin her new tour there in June. But after two weeks in the ancient Ukrainian capital, performing with Irma, fifteen pupils, and a symphony orchestra, it became evident that the expense of the musicians and of hotel accommodations was swallowing up the profits. She therefore decided to send the others back to Moscow and continue the tour with only her pianist, Mark Meichik, and her manager, Zinoviev.

They resumed their reduced tour at Samara in the Volga district. Almost at once everything began to go wrong. Curtains did not arrive, audiences were stolid, accommodations were grim, and the heat was overpowering. The dancer's letters to Irma in Moscow are a vivid record of this disastrous tour. They have been reproduced with only a few minor omissions in Irma's book about Isadora,[41] as well as in the later biography by Allan Ross Macdougall,[42] and thus will be quoted only briefly here.[43]

Tashkent, July 10, 1924

. . . Again no hotel. Spent two days; wandering the streets very hungry. Zeno [Zinoviev, her manager] and Metchnik [the pianist] slept in the theatre. I, next door in a little house without water or toilet. Finally we found rooms in this fearful hotel over-run with vermin. We are so bitten as to appear to have some sort of illness . . .

Tashkent, July 19

Received your telegram to-day only to find that Yashenka is in Moscow!!! For God's sake find him and make him telegraph us money to return. We came here because Zeno has an idiot for an advance man who telegraphed us that prospects were "brilliant." He must have been hired by the ballet to bring us to ruin . . .

Ekaterinburg, 4-8-24

You have no idea what a living nightmare is until you see this town. . . . Our two performances were a *four noire*, and as usual we are stranded and don't know where to go. There is no restaurant here, only "common eating houses," and no coiffeur. The only remaining fossil of that name, while burning my hair off with trembling fingers, assured me that there was not one *dama* [lady] left here—they shot 'em all.

We saw the house and the cellar where they shot a *certain* family. Its psychosis seems to pervade the atmosphere. You can't imagine anything more fearful.

Vyatka, August 12

We did not make expenses; and arrived here without a kopeck. This is a village with an awful hotel. Bed bugs, mice and other agreements. . . . I haven't had a bottle of eau de cologne, no soap nor tooth paste since a month. The beds are made of *boards,* and populated.

Throughout this appalling tour, her hardships could not prevent her from noticing either the beauty of the countryside or the comic aspects of their situation. ("I keep on making jokes which are not appreciated, but it's my Irish way.") No matter how tired she was, the sight of children to be helped always had the power to revive her. "I am almost at the last gasp," a characteristic entry reads. "Today I visited the children's colony and gave them a dancing lesson. Their life and enthusiasm is touching—all orphans."[44] And while she bombarded Irma, in Moscow, with requests and injunctions ("No news of curtains. Telegraph and inquire for them . . ."),[45] she also took the time to try to cheer her harried colleagues—and herself: "Courage, it's a long way, but light is ahead. . . . These red tuniced kids [the pupils] are the future. So it is fine to work for them. Plough the ground, sow the seed, and prepare for the new generation that will express the new world. What else is there to do? . . . with you I see the Future. It is *there*—and we will dance the *Ninth Symphony* yet."[46]

Isadora returned to Moscow at the end of August, exhausted from the long trip and happy to be home. All summer, with the sponsorship of her friend, Comrade Podvowsky, the Commissar of Physical Education, the children from her school had been giving dancing classes in the Sparrow Hills Stadium to the children of workers. Now, hearing that Isadora had returned, child-teachers and pupils together, some 500 strong, dressed in their red tunics, gathered beneath her balcony at 20 Pretchistenka Street, cheering and waving. "Then the band struck up the *Internationale* and all the children danced past the balcony, each one holding high the hand of the comrade in front. Isadora wept to see them."[47]

They were proof that, despite the hardships and disasters of the last months, her coming to Moscow had not been in vain. She found the happiness and enthusiasm of these children boundlessly touching. Here was the vision that had brought her to Russia at last on the point of accomplishment: the massed free movements of 500 eager children, who moved in joy, their natural element, with the careless assurance of birds winging through air.

Dancing to the *Marche Slave* by Tschaikovsky, photograph by Arnold Genthe (*Museum of the City of New York*).

⚜ 33 ⚜

The Invisible Banner

1924

NCE back in Moscow, Isadora settled down to creating new dances for her young pupils. One day, in a burst of inspiration, she composed a group of dances to seven revolutionary songs.[1]

> *With Courage Comrades, March in Step*
> *One, Two, Three*
> *The Young Guard*
> *The Blacksmith*
> *Dubinushka*
> *The Warshavianka* ("In Memory of 1905")
> *The Young Pioneers*

Because these are her last works, and because they mark a further development in her style, these compositions must be discussed in some detail.

Fernand Divoire, who later saw these dances in a concert given on July 3, 1929 when the pupils of the Moscow school were on tour in Paris, wrote of them:

> It must be said, one remains overwhelmed.
>
> *Warshavianka:* Irma, savage, her face contorted by heroic fury, brandishes a flag. She falls. A young Amazon leaps above her, brandishes the flag and also falls. And another. And another. And still others, while the song continues without faltering. And finally all raise themselves up still singing. It is magnificent. And the faces of the young warriors must be seen. . . .
>
> *Dubinushka* (a work song): In horizontal lighting which falls only on the arms, the singers haul a rope. Ah, the splendid rhythm of those arms:
>
> *The Blacksmith:* All the girls are lying down. Led by the wide energetic gestures of the Blacksmith (Irma), they raise themselves up and unchain themselves, fists held forth, hair swinging to the refrain.
>
> *One, Two, Three:* a sort of stylization of a Cossack dance.[2]

It would be quite easy for one who has never seen any of Isadora's choreography to assume from this description that both her choreographic ideas and her symbolism were simple to the point of banality, and that, if Divoire found these dances "overwhelming," he must have been either easily overwhelmed or influenced by friendship for Isadora. But such an assumption would fail to explain why the dances produced on critics and audiences elsewhere an effect similar to the one he reported.

Reports of Isadora's triumphs remain baffling for those who have not seen her work. Two critics, unable from descriptions to account on artistic grounds for the reaction which she produced on the public, concluded that she must have achieved her success by arousing emotions fundamentally extraneous to the dance. The writer Rayner Heppenstall believed that audiences responded to Isadora's personal magnetism. "They were in love with her. I am half in love with her myself." And the dance historian Margaret Lloyd wrote: "One has only to read Carl Van Vechten's early reviews . . . to wonder if the *Marseillaise* and the *Marche Slave* wouldn't seem like ham-dancing today. They sound terribly overwrought and self-expressional in spite of their impersonal radiations. They were really propaganda in pantomime . . . shackles were taken from torn wrists and patriotism glorified. . . . Such dances belong to the past. History had better be careful about repeating itself here."[3]

Curiously enough, Margaret Lloyd approves of Doris Humphrey's *Inquest* (1944), the story of a cobbler who died of starvation, and of the social impact of his death. "The people rose in the streets in a swelling outbreak against their oppressors who caused such things to be. In stormy cross currents their angry twisted bodies and violent gestures bespoke their wrath and despair. . . . In a street that was no street, where no doors were [the cobbler's wife] knocked in vain. . . . For this was not stunning group choreography or theatrical hokum. This was suffering 'out of the hurt heart' of humanity."[4]

Fortunately, as in the example of Doris Humphrey above, one choreographer can seize a hint given by another and elaborate on it so creatively that the resultant work has artistic validity independent of its social message. As Margaret Lloyd understood so clearly in the case of *Inquest*, which she had *seen*, the factual inspiration, literary occasion, or program of a dance does not automatically make it "theatrical hokum," any more than it makes it important. Of course the war-inspired *Marseillaise* was "patriotism glorified." But had it referred to the First Punic War instead of that of 1914, it would still have been a great dance which would have produced a tremendous emotional impact on those who saw it, because the emotions expressed in it were authentic, not stereotypes, and because the form of the work was aesthetically satisfying.

As for Rayner Heppenstall's belief that Isadora made her impression through personal magnetism, it must be said that Isadora's choreography remained effective even when she was not dancing it. The power of the *Ave Maria* or of the scherzo from the *Pathétique* is still evident when performed by amateurs in a bare studio. This is not to say that these dances are equally effective regardless of the training of the performers. Of course, the better the performance, the more moving they become. Isadora's compositions are no different from those of other choreographers in this respect. And as with other choreographers, the Duncan compositions that require the widest range of gifts, or gifts of an unusual type, in their interpreter are those that lose the most when performed in a routine, or standard, manner. Thus, Fokine was never satisfied with other dancers in roles that he had choreographed for Nijinsky.[5] That does not mean that Fokine's choreography was weak, needing to be carried by Nijinsky's personality. It does mean that Fokine's choreography was designed to take advantage of Nijinsky's particular strengths. Isadora's lyric dances retained their freshness and beauty when danced by her pupils, and such stirring compositions as *The Warshavianka* (danced by Irma, in the review just quoted) or *The Furies* (danced by Anna at the Lewisohn Stadium) continued to create their powerful effect.

In contrast to Margaret Lloyd's serious doubts about Isadora's work, the dance critic and scholar Arlene Croce, writing in *The New Yorker*[6] of a four-day symposium on historic modern dance, found the works by Isadora far more satisfying than those of her immediate successors, which included—and Croce assures us they were all well performed—*Variations and Conclusions* from Humphrey's *New Dance,* Charles Weidman's *Lynchtown,* and Helen Tamiris's *Negro Spirituals.* The Duncan dances, executed at the symposium by Annabelle Gamson, included Scriabin studies from Isadora's late Russian period and—perhaps surprisingly, since it is an early work that might seem too limited in its technical means to delight a contemporary critic—*The Blue Danube.* Croce called this performance a "masterpiece of Duncanism . . . not so much a portrait of Isadora" as an evocation of her. ". . . [Gamson's] dancing is in a similar impressionistic vein. In *The Blue Danube,* the inflections of her line through a series of rhapsodic poses, her gradations of attack and recoveries of impetus were the best dancing of the evening." Of course, the more recent past always looks more out of date than the older past, which assumes classical status. Does this appreciation of Croce's mean that Isadora's art has at last emerged from the limbo of the old-fashioned, and can be judged on its own merits? One hopes so.

That Isadora's successes had artistic validity we have the testimony of no less a witness than Fokine, who could not tolerate Isadora's imitators (neither, of course, could she) and whose remarks on the Californian also provide us with a clue to her power.

> Duncan has reminded us of the beauty of simple movement. . . .
> I wish to talk about Isadora Duncan in some detail. She was the greatest American gift to the art of dance. Duncan proved that all the primitive, plain, natural movements—a simple step, run, turn on both feet, small jump on one foot—are far better than all the richness of the ballet technique, if to this technique must be sacrificed grace, expressiveness and beauty . . .

In all the arts, Fokine continues, "The pursuit of perfection should not lead to complication of form, overlooking the purpose for which the art form exists." Isadora, by simplifying the dance, by cutting away all extraneous matters, such as technical virtuosity for its own sake, and the like, was able to focus our attention on the meaning of each work and the grace and appropriateness of the movements used to express that meaning.

Duncan reminded us: "Do not forget that beauty and expressiveness are of the greatest importance."[7] Granting this, the question remains of how she was able to create great works when the technical means at her disposal—"the plain natural movements" which Fokine cited—were so restricted.

An analogy from two of the other arts may suggest an answer. The poems of Wordsworth and Péguy, and many of those of Blake and Hardy, are deliberately simple in language; in some cases the tone is intentionally conversational and flat. In every case, the simplicity is used to heighten the effect of what the poet is saying; no rhetorical flourishes are interposed between us and the reception of the poet's truth; he seems to speak to us directly, without artifice, from an overflowing heart. We are moved even as we wonder how he achieves his effects in a manner so apparently artless. Similarly, the melody of *An Ode to Joy* is simple enough, but how moving, how emotionally true, and how overpowering the clear affirmation of all those massed voices!

In a like manner, Isadora could take a very simple visual idea, for example, the carrying of a flag, and with repetition, variation, beauty of line, and psychological truth of movement, build these elements into a dance that had tremendous emotional impact. I have not seen *The Warshavianka,* but I know the blood-stirring results she achieved with a kindred flag-bearing motif in the *Pathétique.*

Concerning these two compositions, Ilya Schneider remembers saying to Isadora:

> "How was it that you yourself held a banner with such a heavy pole, in the third part of the *Sixth Symphony?*"
>
> She looked at me in surprise, and I broke off my tirade, having remembered that in reality there was nothing in her hands. But the force of her art was so great that I was not alone in seeing the heavy pole of a great flag in her hands.[8]

André Levinson and other critics also noted her ability to make immaterial objects visible and tangible to the beholder by the vividness of her miming.

Simplicity has, of course, its own pitfalls. Any confusion of thought or lack of meaning becomes immediately obvious. Furthermore, the artist cannot count on holding our interest by displaying and surmounting technical difficulties. The technical difficulties have been overcome offstage, so to speak, in the preliminary sketches of the work. We see only the final result which aims at clarity and immediacy. The artist who would hold us must interest us in what he is saying. If what is said does not strike us as particularly fresh or important, monotony is almost sure to result.

This is a charge that Isadora does not always escape. André Levinson, the distinguished French critic, cites *The Dances of the Furies* in *Orpheus* as an example (one among many) of Isadora's failing to make the most of her subject because the technical means at her disposal were limited.

... her dance, as such fails because of the irreparable poverty of its means of locomotion. This dance, unacquainted with the resources of the leap and of movement on points, is reduced to using variants of the run and the step. The vertical projection of the knee, around which the light tunic billows, the throwing back or rearing back of the leg, displacing the folds of the chiton, return incessantly.[9]

Levinson's argument is convincing and I can imagine myself agreeing with him—did I not know the choreography for *The Furies*. I have discussed the two *Furies* dances earlier and I shall say here only that to me their lack of technical display is more than made up for by their drama, which springs from Isadora's ideas about the Furies' nature. This idea—that the Furies are at once Eumenides and lost souls who dimly regret their humanity and want to destroy Orpheus out of envy, for they are monsters made so through their inability to love—makes them both terrifying and poignant. It is the sharpness of Isadora's psychological insights, the beauty of her movements, and the grandeur of her conceptions which give her works their power.

Her gestures, like her ideas, too, have a monumental quality: one is reminded of the gestures in Michelangelo's *The Last Judgment*.[10] Christ's raising his arm to damn, the humble turning aside of the Virgin, the multitudes ascending, falling headlong, or staring ahead in anguish—all are movements of great power and expressiveness and yet all are within the realm of natural movement. Performing them does not require a ballet dancer's virtuosity.* What they do require is the mind of a master for their conception. What makes Isadora a master is the scale of her ideas, a sure sense of form, and a range of feeling which, like that of Berlioz, can encompass without strain the innocent, the roistering, the lyrical, the heroic, the blessed, and the damned.

I would agree with Levinson, however, that because of the lack of variety in the kinds of movement used, Duncan technique, when used by a lesser artist than Isadora, may not succeed in sustaining

---

*They would, however, require *good* dancing—not imitation Duncan dancing, student Duncan dancing, or poor dancing of any kind.

the viewer's interest.[11] Duncan technique does not rely on virtuoso display to cover weaknesses of composition. The ballet choreographer, on the other hand, can say less and still say it interestingly by using technical display to cover lack of content. (In fact, if the display is good enough, it *becomes* content.)

There are, however, certain technical satisfactions in the Duncan dance, undeveloped in other forms of dance before the advent of Isadora. There is the visual satisfaction of seeing a long movement unfold with fluid variations. There is the sense of muscular release in watching continued movement, comparable to the sense of release one experiences in watching the apparent suspension of gravity in ballet.[12]

Moreover, even if the excitement of virtuoso display is missing from Duncan technique, Isadora was a master of providing another kind of excitement—the sort of visceral excitement produced by massed choral groups, a cavalry charge, or the sudden blare of trumpets in the *St. Matthew Passion*. There is a critical assumption in some circles that artists are coarse if they use these effects, that composers who want fortes, volume, as well as pianissimos, are somehow not "pure" musicians, "as if," in the words of Jacques Barzun,[13] Bach were "an austere intellectualist who would just as soon have had his ears cut off." Isadora was not vulgar in wanting mass effects and visceral excitement. Let it be noted that she sometimes used a startling economy to achieve such powerful expression. In the *Marseillaise* she could convey the impact of an entire nation at arms, dancing *alone*. In the scherzo of the *Pathétique,* when the warriors advance toward you, your hair stands on end—yet this part was danced sometimes as a solo and sometimes by six girls at most. In short, Isadora's effects were produced by *art* and not by the sheer weight of numbers, although she used all the dancers she could get and in some compositions wanted more for maximum impact.[14]

To summarize, visceral excitement in art is no more base than the excitement generated by virtuosity. Nor is absence of virtuosity inherently virtuous, as Duncan followers too often assume. Both virtuosity and visceral excitement are a part of art if they are placed at the service of art; if not used for artistic purposes, they become simply stunts. It was Isadora's art that Divoire and other critics responded to when they found *The Warshavianka* "overwhelming."

With *Dubinushka, The Warshavianka, The Blacksmith,* and the other dances to revolutionary songs, Isadora was continuing to explore the vein of political comment and social protest which she had opened in 1917 with the *Marseillaise* and the *Marche Slave.* These later dances, making use of work movements (hammering at a forge, hauling a rope), were reported in Europe and America. And they reinforced the message of her earlier political dances. And in America their message was not lost.[15] In 1927, Martha Graham performed her *Revolt,* pointing the way for the procession of proletarian and social protest dances that would follow in the 1930s.

Undated drawing by Christine Dalliès (*Christine Dalliès Collection*).

❧ 34 ❧
Farewell to Russia
1924

UCH as Isadora would have liked to devote her time
to composing and teaching, the problem of feeding
the children remained as pressing as ever. She saw
that she would have to go on tour, and, with the
amenities of small-town Slavic hotels vivid in her mind, she opened
negotiations with a German manager.

Meanwhile she made plans for a series of eight farewell concerts[1]
to be given in September with her pupils at the Kamerny Theatre,
a final attempt to awaken the government's interest in her teaching.
These would include a Scriabin-Liszt program, a Chopin program,
and—most important for enlisting official and popular support—
an evening of revolutionary dances. She opened the revolutionary[2]
program with a mimed dance to *The Wearing O' the Green,* followed
by the children in an arrangement of a jig and a reel. She next
performed her great *Marseillaise,* then she and the children danced
a fiery *Carmagnole.* After this came the *Rakoczy March* which she had
first given in 1902 in Budapest when she was in love with Beregi.

The second part of her program was devoted to her Russian dances—most of them presented on the stage for the first time. The *Internationale,* in which the pupils of the school were joined by the 500 children whom they had coached all summer at the stadium, made a rousing finale to the program.[3]

Her second recital, on September 21, a solo performance accompanied by the pianist Mark Meichik, comprised Liszt's *Les Funérailles* and *The Legend of St. Francis of Assisi,* and Scriabin's *Fourth Sonata.*[4] Her next concert was an all-Chopin program.[5]

At her eighth concert, on September 28,[6] before the children were to dance Schubert, Gluck, and Strauss, Isadora made a long speech in German which was translated into Russian by Schneider. She spoke of her childhood, summarized her educational theories, and appealed for support for her school. "The same necessity which brought me, as a four-year-old child, on the stage, brings the children of our school before the public."[7]

After the last concert, Mme. Kalenina, wife of the president of the U.S.S.R., who had been greatly moved by the revolutionary dances, came backstage to ask what she could do to help Isadora. The latter replied that she would like to show the work of the school to party leaders. But it would have to be done immediately: she was about to leave Russia. Mme. Kalenina promised to arrange an evening for her at the Bolshoi Theatre the next night. She was as good as her word, and Isadora had the satisfaction of receiving a tremendous ovation from an audience of top-ranking communists, and of hearing her former sponsor, Commissar Lunacharsky, praise her as a force for the training of youth.[8]

With this breach finally made in the wall of official consciousness, it seemed as if Isadora were at last in sight of her goal. Unfortunately, she could not stay to follow up her advantage. She had to leave for Germany the next morning, and she could do no more than instruct Irma to fan official interest and keep her informed of the outcome. At dawn on September 30, the dancer said good-bye to her friends and associates and boarded the plane for Berlin.

❧ 35 ❧

Stranded in Berlin
1924

T the end of September 1924 Isadora Duncan arrived in Berlin, the first stop on her concert tour of Germany. Anxious to raise money for her struggling Russian school, she had signed an agreement with a manager she had never seen, and the relation was proving unhappy. She wrote to Irma in Moscow: "He . . . says that I have broken the contract because I was not here eight days beforehand, and wants to bring lawsuit *against me* although I danced two evenings *without receiving a penny*. I must have the contracts and telegrams at once to refute his presumptions."[1]

This was not the only time that Isadora had been stranded. But in the past she had always been able to joke about her hardships, and now her reserves of strength were exhausted. Her letter continues: "Altogether it is Hell!!! And I spend my time wondering which sort of poison doesn't hurt the most. I don't want to take any of the fearful kind." She had apparently approached her sister Elizabeth for aid, for she says in the same note, "Elizabeth is sweet, but has not a pfennig." Through her letters, like a sad refrain, run references to her brother and sister in Europe. Her relations with them steadily worsen as her appeals to them increase: "Elizabeth cannot help as she is very busy and has not a sou." "I have telegraphed Raymond but he is in Nice, and apparently *can't* or *won't* do anything." "Elizabeth has deserted me and gone to visit a rich friend in Vienna. Her school in Potsdam won't even let me in."[2] Their lack of response to her pleas is understandable. The impossibility of keeping her finances on a stable basis must have proved disheartening to anyone wishing to help her. Nonetheless, they were her family and had taken help from Isadora again and again in the past. Augustin, in America, eventually arranged to send her funds monthly for as long as his money should hold out.[3]

Augustin was the member of Isadora's family to whom she felt closest. Yet whatever the individual differences between them, should an outsider attack the family, it was the "Clan Duncan" against the world. (The suit that Raymond Duncan had begun against Isadora's pupils for using the name "Duncan" at a time of strained relations between Isadora and the girls had been out of family feeling.) Augustin was particularly sensitive to Isadora's claims on her family. He had repeatedly interrupted his own career to come to Isadora's rescue when she needed him. Yet such was his fairness that whatever the strains between Isadora and her pupils, or Isadora and his brother or Elizabeth, he and his wife Margherita always remained on good terms with them all. Isadora deeply appreciated Augustin's generosity; to a friend, Bernardine Szold Fritz,[4] she called him a saint. Gus had recently gone blind and was experiencing difficulties in his profession, so his offer of help at this time must have represented a considerable sacrifice on his part.

Isadora's letters to Irma from Germany sound far more despairing than did those she wrote during her disastrous tour through Turkestan. There, at least, she had had the companionship of her manager and her pianist Meichik and a hope of breaking ground for the school. Evidently, she found material hardships easier to bear than a sense of spiritual isolation and an inability to work, for she wrote from Berlin: "I am nearly on the verge of suicide . . . I feel

Undated photograph, probably taken at Cape Ferrat (*Mme. Mario Meunier—Christine Dalliès Collection*).

very lonely and would like to be back in that 'awful room' in Pretchistenka."[5]

Teaching had always been Isadora's consolation. She needed to love and to give, and teaching was one way of giving, of sharing the things she loved with children or with people she cared for. In her family, teaching had always been a means of showing love. Her mother had taught her children music and literature; the young Duncans had learned from their father's art objects. And whenever Isadora had been in love the need to teach and to learn from her beloved became very strong in her. She and Craig always showed their literary and artistic treasures to one another, pointing out their merits and learning from one another's ideas. The sharing of books, paintings, scenery, poems, and music was a very important part of their love. So it was also with Rummel and with Bauer. And with Esenin she had longed to introduce him to the beauties of Europe and America and, most of all, teach the world about Esenin's poetry.

In her life she often felt a conflict between love and art—as when, for her art's sake, she made a tour that took her away from the person she loved. When Isadora was teaching, however, love and art worked in harmony. When she was teaching, she was able to withstand her lover's (Esenin's) desertion with more equanimity than usual because she was using her capacity for loving. Later she told Schneider that her stay in Russia had been the happiest period of her life. In Germany, she was separated from her work, the responsiveness of the children, and the companionship of her colleagues, and she was faced with unresponsive or hostile audiences.

A sympathetic but unsparing observer who attended her concert at the Blüthner Saal provides several clues to her cool reception in Berlin. Fred Hildebrandt, in the *Berliner Tageblatt* of October 4, wrote that the recital began late after an announcement "that the expected conductor was missing, that another would replace him, and that the dancer had not been able to rehearse."

> After a considerable delay, a woman with made-up face, heavy, big, running to flesh, began to come and go while swaying slowly,

silently, to the rhythm, then going faster, arms wide open, holding them high. . . .

But . . . it must be recognized that there emanated from this woman always more strongly something noble and enchanting . . . one followed with a glance . . . with unequalled astonishment the light rhythm of that heavy woman . . . and all those who, today . . . have written beautiful chapters in the history of the modern dance . . . who are they all? Heirs of this woman . . . who is capable of having preserved all the brilliance of the dance in her most touching and moving gestures.

After the concert she spoke:

She admitted simply, childishly, with a touching naiveté, the faults of which she had been accused. Yes, Germany had given a lot to her.—Yes, she had danced against Germany. Yes, after the war she had danced against France—yes, she had found in Moscow the song of the whole world. . . .

It was probably unfortunate that she felt compelled to discuss her various political allegiances instead of retaining a diplomatic silence, but the subject had already been broached by the newspapers. In any case, she had to speak of her Moscow school, for whose benefit she had undertaken this German tour.

Meanwhile her business affairs continued their disastrous course. The tenant of her house at the Rue de la Pompe, Gordieff, continued to owe her rent. Her dealings with managers grew increasingly unhappy. In one of the letters already quoted,[6] she gave Irma some of the details:

I am here stranded in this awful city. I have signed three contracts and have been swindled three times. The last for Hanover. When the time came, the agent didn't have the money for the R.R. ticket. They are all swindlers.

I cannot move from here! Since four weeks the hotel will serve no more food. An American friend brings me a slice of roast beef a day, but he has no money either.

One reason why agents felt emboldened to cheat Isadora was that she had, by her wartime espousal of the Allied cause as well as by her Russian stay, made herself politically *persona non grata*.[7] Her permit to remain in Germany had nearly expired, and the Russian embassy, inexplicably, would not give her a Russian passport.[8] Pressed for time, she had to accept whatever contracts were offered to her, aware that in the event of a dispute it would do her little good to complain to the hostile authorities. In spite of her despair, Isadora characteristically did not fail to appreciate the ironies of her situation. "Every country has refused me visa on account of my 'political connections.' What are my political connections? Where are my political connections, I would like to know?" And in another letter, "I am living from hand to mouth. . . . The joke of the whole thing is that it is current gossip that I receive vast sums from the Soviets."

While she was existing in this limbo, she was approached by two American journalists, George Seldes of the *Chicago Tribune* and Sam Spiwak of the *New York World*,[9] who wanted the dancer to write her memoirs for serialization in their newspapers. According to Seldes,[10] when he arrived at Isadora's hotel she was in a state of deep depression and would not talk about writing her memoirs until he had brought her something to drink. Seldes, who remembered his fervent admiration of her as a young dancer, was shocked at her appearance—her air of lassitude, her unkempt hair, her heavy body. She was forty-seven and looked much older.

She said that she was at the end of her rope. She must get to France to sell her house, but the French refused to give her an entry visa, claiming that she was a Bolshevik. So she would have to sell her love letters—they were all she possessed. Their sale might "ruin a lot of fat reputations," but why should she care? Since starting her Russian school and her last American tour, she had come to the conclusion that she hadn't a friend left in the world.

Perhaps she would publish the letters in a book. A book would be worth writing if it helped other people. "I want to tell the truth about my loves and my art because the whole world is absolutely brought up on lies."

Art, she said, was not necessary for people. Only love was truly necessary—to be able to love as Christ and Buddha loved. Lenin, too, loved humanity. But most people loved only themselves, their ideas, power, and wealth. Her book would be worth writing if it showed people that they didn't know how to love. Unselfish love was very rare. Even mother love "is like loving your own arms and legs; it is simply loving a part of yourself."

Many men had loved her, but she now knew that the feelings they called "love" were the feelings they would have had for a bottle of whiskey. They simply wanted to possess her.

In Moscow, she had seen little children sleeping in doorways. Could people treat children like that if there was love in the world? She had taken them into her school, but after Lenin's death the government would no longer allow it. And on the East End of London, too, she had seen children living under dreadful conditions. As long as there were children suffering anywhere, true love did not exist in the world.

Men had loved her, but her only real love had been children. Seldes should have seen the children dance after they had been at her school for a year.

Of course, that love may have been egotistical too. It had made her feel like a god to inspire children, to shape their lives, to hear the audiences cheering them, and to know that they were giving the public the love and the ecstasy which the world needs.

She was not a dancer, Isadora told her visitors. "All I see in what people call dancing is merely a useless agitation of the arms and legs." She wanted to express a new form of life, to give children a purpose in life, and to teach them to live harmoniously. It was almost impossible to accomplish any ideal on earth, yet was anything else worth living for?

Seldes, who was pressing Isadora to sign a contract with the *Chicago Tribune,* returned for a second visit to settle the matter, and discovered that Isadora had developed qualms about the wisdom of the project. He had already published a story about Isadora's intention of selling her love letters, and apparently she had received some distressing telegrams. She told Seldes: "I'll phone you if I decide to go on with it."[11]

She did not phone, however, so in a day or two he called on her and was met by an Isadora who seemed to have nothing in common with the listless, despairing woman of his initial visit. The dancer was brisk and energetic. She had stopped drinking. She was going to reduce her weight. She planned to spend the winter in Nice where she would have her own theater, and she invited him to come to her first performance.

"And your book—and the letters—?"

"Oh, that's all finished. Publish my memoirs, now? What do you think I am? An old woman?"

The volte-face was explained to Seldes's satisfaction when a friend told him that the newspaper paragraph which Seldes had written saying that Isadora was considering selling her love letters had been seen by a man who had telegraphed her "that she was foolish because it would ruin her career; that she had better return to her art. [He] would get her a studio if she wished. And so everything has been fine for her ever since."[12]

Seldes evidently believed that one of Isadora's lovers—a rich man, presumably Singer—had offered to pay Isadora's debts and underwrite her next recital if she would agree not to sell her love letters.

This explanation leaves many loose ends. If Singer, or some other wealthy former lover, were sufficiently worried to help Isadora in return for guarantees to withhold her letters, he would hardly have haggled over the price, and, if he had given Isadora a sizable settlement, it would have been reflected immediately in her standard of living. Thrift was not a trait of either Isadora or Singer.[13]

Still less was blackmail characteristic of her. It is possible that in her bitterness and despair, feeling that she had been abandoned by friends, family, and lovers, she may have talked of publishing her love letters and taken pleasure in imagining the dire consequences of her act (the ruin of "a lot of fat reputations"), but that she ever soberly considered selling her love letters is difficult to believe— she who cared so little for money that, when in severe financial difficulties later, she refused the royalties from Esenin's estate, saying that his mother and sister needed the money more than did she.

Furthermore, it is questionable whether anyone would pay to have the letters suppressed and yet leave them in Isadora's hands; we are told the papers were still in her possession when the actress Lottie Yorska called on her in 1925.[14]

This is not only incredible. It is not what happened. During this period in Berlin when Seldes had been negotiating with the dancer for the rights to her memoirs, she had met another American newspaper correspondent, Isaac Don Levine.

Levine was one of the few of her acquaintances in Berlin who visited Isadora to keep up her morale while she was waiting for some country to give her an entry permit. (Lacking a passport, and unable to get papers from the Russian embassy, she had had to dance at the police station in order to establish her identity.)[15] Levine tried to distract her from her worries by introducing her to people in whom she had expressed an interest, among them the revolutionists Alexander Berkman and Emma Goldman. He urged her to work on her memoirs and listened while she spoke at length about her Moscow experiences, her life, and the men she had loved. Her great loves, she told him, were Craig, Singer, and Harold Bauer. Curiously enough, she did not include Rummel or Esenin, though later she named the two, with Craig and Singer, to Mary Desti, as the men she had loved most deeply.[16] Perhaps, in 1924, the breaks with Rummel and Esenin were still too recent and painful for her to be willing to mention them. Of the others she said, "They may have loved me but they always went back to their wives."

Her loneliness, recalled Levine, had made her very possessive, and he could understand why any man might feel he must get away from her. And yet, despite her possessiveness and her profound discouragement, he recognized in her a goodness and an invincible innocence that he found very touching.[17]

Distressed at her hand-to-mouth existence, and convinced that her career was at a dead end in Germany, Levine appealed to the French Socialist deputy, Jean Longuet, a grandson of Karl Marx, who at length obtained permission for Isadora to return to France.[18]

Before she could leave Berlin, her debts had to be settled, however, so Levine paid Isadora's accumulated hotel bills and accompanied her to Paris. There she installed herself in an unpretentious hotel near the Étoile, where she set about renewing contacts with old friends, meanwhile thinking of ways to raise money for her school in Moscow.

At Cape Ferrat, 1920 (*Mme. Mario Meunier–Christine Dalliès Collection*).

❧ 36 ❧

Treading Water
1925 – 1927

HEN news came out of Berlin that Isadora was writing her memoirs, newspapers began clamoring for the serial rights to her life story. In January 1925, therefore, shortly after her return to Paris, Isadora for the first time in several years had the prospect of realizing a substantial sum. But, as it turned out, the newspapers had their own idea of what her life story should be like. They wanted to publish her love letters and her reminiscences of the men who had written them; they were not interested in her ideas about the dance. Indignant, she denied that she had ever intended making her love letters public, and to all offers to buy them she answered with an obdurate, "No." She was rewarded by seeing all the old scandals and gossip once more spread forth for the benefit of the Sunday supplement readers.

Such treatment no longer had the power to surprise her and, in any case, she was preoccupied with graver worries. On February 2, 1925, she wrote to Irma from Paris:

Dearest Irma:

I have not had the courage to write, I have been going through sad, fearful experiences. . . .

I was offered by the Chicago Tribune a sum for my "memoirs" but afterwards it all turned to *blackmail,* and they wrote fearful articles by way of revenge.

For three months they refused me a visa to come to Paris. At last, here I am. For Heaven's sake write to me. . . . Tell me what hope is there for the school? . . . Is anything stable or is it a quicksand? My only hope of funds at this moment is in the Memoirs. I have now met a good friend who will occupy himself with the book, but I need all the *letters and documents necessary,* which are in my trunk in Moscow. Will you give them only to whoever comes to you from the part of Isaac Don Levine?

If I receive the $20,000 promised, I will either come to Moscow in the spring with *money,* or if you think Moscow hopeless, you can join me in London with sixteen pupils. . . .

I am much worried about Margot, who, I have just heard by telephone, is in a hospital here very ill. I will go and see her tomorrow, but Christine should have told me this sooner. . . .

Dearest Irma, I was just writing the above when they suddenly telephoned me that Margot was dying. I took a taxi and rushed to the hospital but *too late.* It all seems so unhappy and miserable. I am ill but will write soon. Love,

Isadora[1]

The death of Margot [presumably due to grippe], one of the five girls to whom Isadora had given legal permission to take her name and whom she had reared from childhood,* came as a profound shock to Isadora. It had the power to awaken all the terrible emotions she had felt at the loss of her children, a loss whose sudden rec-ollection could still stab her afresh with anguish, twelve years after the accident. Heartsick, she was glad to leave the scene of these

---

*According to Anna Duncan, Erica Lohmann, the sixth Isadorable, was still a minor when the five older girls took the name of Duncan, and therefore she did not change her name.

events, and to accept her brother Raymond's invitation to visit him in Nice.

Levine, who had made several tries[2] to get Isadora started on her book, gave up the attempt to help her with her memoirs and went back to Berlin.

From Raymond's studio on March 12, 1925, she wrote:

Dearest Irma:

I have suffered a nervous prostration and could not put pen to paper. All the different hardships and calamities of the past year have been a bit too much. However I am resting here with Raymond, and hope soon to begin the battle again. . . . Love to all the children, love to you, and hope through everything. My motto: *Sans Limites,*

Isadora[3]

After some time in the Riviera sun, she began to feel restless (a sign of returning health) and to wish that the accommodations in Raymond's Greek arts-and-crafts style studio were a little less authentically Spartan. Her old friend, George Maurevert, was able to get her a room at the Hotel Negresco at a reduced rate, and another friend rented a small theater for her, in which Isadora hoped to give lessons and concerts.

On March 30, she wrote from Nice to Irma:

Nobody realized it, but poor little Margot's death was the finishing touch. I simply almost gave up entirely. I am only just recovering from the ghastly cruelty and terror of the whole thing. I confess— I can't understand—the whole scheme of things is too unbearable.[4]

Meanwhile she was trying to raise money by selling articles on the dance, but there was no discernible interest on the part of the magazines. Her memoirs had a better chance of finding a publisher, yet she was having a hard time getting started. Her friends accused her of being lazy. But the problem was not laziness. The hardships and sorrows she had been through had left her will temporarily paralyzed. Her career seemed to have reached a standstill. She was no longer a novelty whose recitals were mandatory for the fashionable. Nor could she still appeal to those who simply enjoyed watching a pretty young girl. She had, moreover, alienated a large part of her audience by her statements hailing the Soviet Union as the hope of humanity. Had she been willing to represent herself as disgusted with communism, a repentant prodigal daughter returned to the capitalist fold, she might have regained a measure of popular favor. But, although her feelings about communism were by now ambivalent (enthusiasm for its ideals, dissillusionment about its lack of support for her work), her school was in Russia, and she had no wish to threaten its already uncertain existence by making remarks that might be interpreted as hostile by the Soviet government.

She wrote Irma, in the letter already quoted:

> Any reports that I have spoken against the Soviet government are *absolutely* false and unfounded. On the contrary, it is because I speak only well of them that I meet with a *universal persecution.* My dancing the *Internationale* . . . in Berlin was the starting point of a . . . libellous newspaper campaign against me, universally undertaken by the world's press. . . .
>
> I tried through the Soviet Embassy in Paris to have the school brought [here] but without success. Have you been to Tovarish Kalenina? Can nothing be done?[5]

She was not doing creative work. That would have taken a greater reserve of strength than Isadora had just then. Worn out by grief and material worries, and her plans blocked at every turn, she spent her baffled energies in unproductive ways: on the one hand, in spasmodic attempts to get help for the Moscow school while also trying to organize a new school in France; and, on the other hand, in dissipating what small funds she had. Whatever money her friends managed to send her would vanish in a few days, usually through acts of compulsive generosity. The pianist Victor Seroff remembered an incident in a restaurant when Isadora rewarded a musician who had offered to play whatever she liked. "She took from her pocketbook all the money she had just received [from a friend], and gave it to the musician, explaining to her astonished friends: 'He plays so badly! And you know, once he probably thought he would be a Paderewski!' "[6]

Meanwhile she exhausted herself in Herculean efforts to find sponsors for her school. She refused to imagine the possibility of failure. She still lived by the creed she had voiced after meeting Mme. Miroski: "I could not understand . . . why she had not gone to him. . . . For I have never waited to do as I wished. This has frequently brought me to disaster and calamity, but at least I have had the satisfaction of getting my own way."[7] The more her appeals were rejected, the more grandiose her plans became. Now she pursued fruitless negotiations with members of the French Communist party, urging that they sponsor classes to be taught by her, for 1000 proletarian children. In the back of her mind was the hope that a successful school in France would shed luster on the sister establishment in Moscow and persuade the Soviet government that such a cultural showcase deserved their support.

She was still preoccupied with these plans when she received grim news,[8] word of the suicide of her husband, Sergei Esenin. On the night of December 27, 1925, he hanged himself in the very room of the Hotel Angleterre in Leningrad where he and Isadora had gone on their first love trip together. He left behind a poem written in his blood, addressed to an unnamed friend.[9] The Paris newspapers naturally sensationalized the story, enlivening it with accounts of Esenin's encounters with the police and his domestic difficulties, real and imagined, with Isadora. With a heavy spirit his widow sent out a statement to the press, eulogizing Esenin's genius, and declaring: "I protest strongly against the frivolous and inexact statements printed in the American press out of Paris. There was never between Esenin and myself any quarrel or divorce. I weep his death with anguish and despair."[10]

To Irma, she opened her heart more fully: "I was terribly shocked about Sergei's death, but I [had] wept and sobbed so many hours about him that it seems he had already exhausted any human capacity for suffering."[11]

Although Isadora had thought it was no longer possible for her to feel anything further on Sergei's account, apparently she had underestimated the effect of his death on her, for on April 1 she wrote to Irma: "I spent the entire month of March ill in bed.... The doctor said something-itis. But I think it was a congestion of despair. I am up again, but weak, and I'm celebrating Good Friday with a performance of sacred music and dance in the studio."[12]

After this Good Friday concert (which was an artistic success, but brought in only enough money to pay expenses), the Riviera season was over, and Isadora longed to be back in Paris. Lacking the cash for a train ticket, she hired a car (her usual approach to deficits), which she continued to use in Paris. This time she installed herself at the Lutétia, a large hotel on the Boulevard Raspail.

Though on the left bank, the Lutétia was hardly cheap. One evening, when an acquaintance from New York, the American-Spanish playwright Mercedes de Acosta, impulsively called on the dancer, she found that Isadora had gone the whole day without eating and owed the management several months' arrears. Isadora, overjoyed at Mercedes' sudden appearance, exclaimed, "I think you are an archangel. I shall always call you that from now on. How did you find me?" This lucky encounter was the beginning of a new friendship for Isadora. Mercedes at once ordered dinner sent in, and the next day she withdrew enough money from her bank to settle Isadora's account at the Lutétia. Mercedes also encouraged her to get back to work on her memoirs and promised, if she did so, to find her a publisher.

Mercedes was later to assert, in her own autobiography, *Here Lies the Heart*,[13] that she had not only found a publisher for Isadora, but that she, Mercedes, had been responsible for keeping Isadora at work on her manuscript. "How she struggled and suffered over the book! Many days I locked her in her room, and only let her out when she slid a number of finished pages under the door." Victor Seroff and Mme. Jenny Bradley, widow of Isadora's literary agent, William Bradley, disputed both of these statements, Seroff commenting,[14] "I never read a sillier lie." In fact, it was William Bradley who sold the book. Mme. Bradley assured her long-time acquaintance Liliane Ziegel[15] that Mercedes de Acosta did not influence Isadora in anything, nor was the playwright, who moved chiefly in the circle surrounding Gertrude Stein, a particularly close friend of Isadora.

Although skeptical of Isadora's supposed submissiveness in writing her memoirs to order, Seroff apparently believes that Mercedes did edit Isadora's manuscript after her death. But Mme. Bradley maintains that Isadora and Isadora *alone* wrote *My Life*. According to her, the editors made few changes in Isadora's original text and those changes were insignificant. "If certain of her statements were too extravagant, Boni [her publisher] may have softened them."[16] William Bradley, too, had gone over Isadora's manuscript with her and helped her to make a few corrections of style, but Mme. Bradley insists, "The editors say that Isadora alone wrote her text, and it's true." This point is worth settling because Seroff and Gordon Craig both believed that Isadora's manuscript had been altered after her death.

Shortly before Mercedes returned to America, another friend from the United States, Ruth Mitchell, arrived in Paris. A generous woman of moderate means, Ruth, shocked by the bill being run up for Isadora's rented automobile, bought a car and offered to drive Isadora wherever she wanted to go. The latter suggested that since living in Paris was so expensive, they might travel about France, stopping at little out-of-the-way inns and restaurants. Like all of Isadora's schemes for saving money, this one proved more costly than the alternative it replaced. The little inns turned out to be famous for their chefs and their cellars, and Isadora always insisted on their trying the *specialité de la maison,* accompanied by the proper wines. Ruth, who was underwriting this jaunt, was appalled at the bills, and she accepted with alacrity when Isadora proposed that they wind up the tour at her studio in Nice.

It seems likely that Isadora took Ruth to expensive places on purpose—at least Mary Desti, who described the trip, thought so. Hurok[17] and other business associates and friends reported similar instances of being stuck with large restaurant bills, or of inviting Isadora to dine out and having her arrive with several extra guests. This habit, which grew pronounced in her later years, seems to assort oddly with Isadora's real kindness. Perhaps it was a way of paying back her acquaintances for their homilies on her extravagance, of testing the love of her remaining friends, and of working off, on them, the hurts that the world had inflicted on her. As her means diminished, her need to bestow gifts and to entertain lavishly grew. One guesses that her "cavalier" attitude toward money was partly defiance and partly suppressed panic, a way of saying, "I will not accept the want and the corner-cutting I had to put up with in my childhood. I have earned a right to better treatment from life than that."

She and Ruth spent the summer pleasantly in Nice, where Isadora gave two or possibly three recitals, among them a Liszt program on September 10, and on September 14 a combined concert and poetry reading with the collaboration of Jean Cocteau and Marcel Herrand.[18]

Of these recitals, Janet Flanner wrote in *The New Yorker:*

. . . her art was seen to have changed. She treads the boards but little now. She stands almost immobile or in slow splendid steps with slow splendid arms, moves to music, seeking, hunting, finding. Across her face, tilting this way and that, flee the mortal looks of tragedy, knowledge, love, scorn, pain. Posing through the works of Wagner, through the touching legend of St. Francis feeding crumbs and wisdom to his birds, Isadora is still great. By an economy (her first) she has arrived at elimination.[19]

When the time came for her friend to leave for America, Isadora's restlessness prompted her to drive back to Paris with Ruth and two other friends, Walter Shaw and Marcel Herrand. There Ruth left the car with Isadora for safekeeping.

It was during this or an earlier stay in Paris that Isadora met, at the Montmartre studio of a Mrs. Marvine,[20] the young Russian pianist, Victor Seroff. Vitya Seroff presently became her friend and lover.

Seroff entered her life at a crucial moment. Besides their common love of music, he was one of the few sympathetic and understanding people with whom she could discuss her Russian experiences. Like her, he had experienced life in revolutionary Russia, and because Russian was his native tongue and he appreciated literature, Esenin was to him more than the curiosity and maker of scandals that he was to many of Isadora's western friends. Indeed, the fact that Seroff was so much younger than Isadora made him particularly aware of the awkwardness of Esenin's position,[21] married to a woman eighteen years his senior. To Vitya, Isadora confided many things about her marriage that she would not have told to anyone else. She even told him of a painful incident when Esenin's reading of a poem convinced her that their marriage was at an end. Esenin read *The Song of the Dog* to Isadora, a poem about a bitch whose seven newborn puppies have been drowned by her master. Isadora wept, and when he finished she asked him timidly what he would think of a woman to whom the same thing had happened.

"To a woman?" he frowned, covering up the tears he himself had shed in reciting the poem. "A woman?" he repeated. He suddenly spat on the floor. "A woman is a piece of shit."

"I never knew why he chose to read this poem to me," Isadora told Seroff. "I am sure it was not intentional. He was in an excited state, he needed an appreciative audience, and he was sure that at least this poem was one of the few that I knew. But—you may think I am unreasonable—from that moment on I knew that I could never live with him. . . . I am sure it never occurred to him how much he had hurt me. . . . That is when I decided to take him back to Russia and leave him forever."[22] (Actually, however, as we have seen, the final rupture took place some time after her return to Moscow.)

Isadora had never recovered from the loss of Deirdre and Patrick. For many years, it was acutely painful for her even to see children, particularly very young ones. An incident told me independently by three witnesses springs to mind. It happened at the Lido where Isadora and her six young dancers were sunning themselves shortly before they and Walter Rummel would leave for Greece. They had been joined on the beach by their friends Sacha and Dolly Votichenko and the pianist George Copeland. Sacha's and Dolly's little boy, Taras, saw them and came skipping up to join the group.

Swimming at Cape Ferrat, circa 1920 (*Mme. Mario Meunier—Christine Dalliès Collection*).

Isadora and Christine Dalliès at Cape Ferrat (*Mme. Mario Meunier—Christine Dalliès Collection*).

At his approach, Isadora suddenly rose to her feet and fled. Copeland never forgot the stricken movement with which she raised her
hand to her face before she ran down the beach like a wounded
animal.

Anna later told me, "All of Isadora's friends had been warned to
keep children away from Isadora at that time—the sight of them
was more than she could bear. But of course it didn't occur to
Sacha that the request applied to his son."

As for Taras,* he could not imagine what had happened to Isadora.
He had thought she was his friend. Was she angry at him? Had he
done something wrong? His childish feeling of bewilderment and
hurt still remains fresh in his memory.

Vitya's conversations with Isadora were by no means always serious. Sometimes he cheered her up by joking with her or teasing
her. She had need of cheering, for she was now beset by fresh
worries. Her Neuilly house, which held so many memories of her
children, her last remaining property of any value, was to be sold
by court order to pay a debt that had grown with the years and
bailiff's fees that had accumulated from 300 francs in 1922 to over
10,000 francs in 1926. Her friends hoped to raise funds to save the
house, but time was short.

On November 24, 1926, the day before the sale was to take place,
Isadora was notified by the Moscow court that, as Esenin's legal
widow, she was entitled to the royalties from his poems, now
approximately 400,000 francs. Since his separation from Isadora,
Esenin had remarried,[23] but as he had neglected to divorce the
dancer, she, rather than his third wife, Sophia Tolstoy, the writer's
granddaughter, was adjudged to be his widow. Isadora would not
accept money. Perhaps she felt she had no right to it, no matter
what the law decreed, because of the estrangement between her
and Sergei. (She held that marriage ceased as soon as love vanished.)
Instead she directed that Vitya telegraph the High Court in Moscow,
disclaiming all right to the estate and expressing the wish that it
be divided between Esenin's mother and sisters, who were in greater

*Today the author's brother-in-law.

need than she.[24] The next day the Neuilly property, which perhaps could have been saved had she accepted Esenin's money, was sold for 310,000 francs.[25]

Where finances were concerned, Isadora was extravagant, but according to her own standards, principled. No matter how desperate her circumstances, she would never consider raising money by any means she thought dubious. She would never consent to cheapen her art, either by altering a program to make it more popular, or by accepting contracts to appear in music halls. She would present her dance unexpurgated in dignified (even if makeshift) surroundings or not at all. Though unusually outspoken, she would not write popular articles about her romances for magazines. She would not sell her love letters. Her giving away Esenin's money (which she could have taken with a clear conscience, quite apart from marital right, in fair repayment of the bills she had paid for him) may have been an unconscious rebuke to the people who called her "spendthrift"—a way of proving that she was financially more scrupulous than they.

Her generosity was not only heroic, it was also ill-timed, for she had by then run up a large hotel bill, and though she was anxious to drive to the Riviera with Vitya, she could not leave until she had settled her account. Fortunately, Lottie Yorska, the actress, heard of her friend's plight and came to the rescue as she had many times before.[26] Thus Isadora and Vitya were able to drive to the Riviera with untroubled minds. Once in Nice, however, Isadora ran out of money again. The Negresco, which had hitherto been patient with its distinguished guest, suddenly demanded payment,[27] and Isadora escaped eviction only by explaining that she planned to go to Paris the next day to collect the proceeds (!) from the sale of her house. In view of her assets—she pointed out that she had at that very moment an automobile in the hotel garage—it was absurd to bother her about so trivial a sum. The management allowed itself to be mollified, but not before it had attached her trunks and the car— Ruth's car—as security for her debt.

Back in Paris, perforce, Isadora found that a group of friends and admirers had organized themselves into a committee to buy back the Neuilly house. The members, to whom she was beholden for many kindnesses, were Mme. Cécile Sartoris, Mme. Yorska, and Messrs. André Arnyvelde, Alfredo Sidès, and Georges Denis. But, despite their concern for their friend, differences almost immediately developed among the several members of the committee, and between the committee and Isadora, as to how they could best help the dancer.[28]

The initial plan had been to buy back the house and present it to Isadora as a home for herself and her students. At her death, the property would be turned over to the French government for it to manage as the Isadora Duncan Memorial School. But the money the committee collected was to be used exclusively for the repurchase of the Neuilly house and the operating costs of the school. What was Isadora to live on meanwhile? She had reduced her rent by moving to a studio hotel, but her bills continued to accumulate, and her creditors were starting to threaten. The committee refused to advance her any of the funds that had been earmarked for the school, saying that they had no authority to do so. This decision was logical in view of the way francs and dollars ran through Isadora's fingers, but it left her actually needy and with a feeling of desperation. Even worse than her terror of poverty was the sense of being abandoned by old friends. Yet in reality they had not abandoned her. Many of them, including her former lovers Singer and Craig,[29] as well as Divoire, José Clara, and Georges Denis,[30] kept a watchful eye on her from afar and did what they could, usually secretly, to alleviate her material wants. Once, recalls Mary Desti,[31] when the periodic payment of Isadora's debt to the government was due and her house was about to be seized for lack of 12,000 francs (this despite the committee's previous payments), Georges Denis, her close friend from wartime days, had contributed the needed sum from his own limited funds. "On hearing this, Isadora wept like a child"—less at the relief of reprieve than at learning that Denis still cared for her. Still, whatever funds her friends were able to provide for her were soon swallowed by her compulsive spending. The hotel cut off her credit at their restaurant, so she ate at other restaurants—at twice the cost. Mary Desti said shrewdly: "I believe creating these daily difficulties were [sic] what made life possible; it kept her shattered thoughts from the one great sorrow eating at her heart night and day."[32] This sorrow was, of course, the loss of her children. Perhaps the less fulfillment her life offered her, the more this terrible memory came back to haunt her. Her original pupils were dispersed, and she had no assurance that the Moscow school or any other work would survive her. She was furious on learning that Irma, Schneider, and her Russian school had made a tour of China without consulting her. On hearing of this tour in a letter from Irma written at the end of 1926, Isadora wrote in protest to Soviet officials, complaining that it was the first word of her school she had had in six months.

> When it comes to the exploitation of my work by a private organization without so much as asking my advice—I must protest! This is an exploitation of my art which I would not have expected, considering the primary object of my visit to Russia was to escape from just such exploitation of Art, which Soviet Russia condemned Europe for in 1921.
>
> The Camerade Lunacharsky wrote of my school: "Isadora Duncan wanted to give a natural and beautiful education to every child. The Bourgeois Society, however, did not understand this, and put her pupils on the stage to exploit them for money. We will know how to act differently!"
>
> *I ask when?*[33]

(According to Irma, she did not learn of Isadora's official letter of protest until much later.)[34]

Lacking certainty about her school's future and financially insecure, Isadora was also without a continuing, stable love. Though she had Vitya's affection, she was now fifty and he was only twenty-five.[35] She could not entertain illusions as to the permanence of their relation.

On one occasion, in Nice, her uncertainty about Vitya's affection nearly had serious consequences. As Seroff tells it, Isadora had invited several guests to dinner: Countess Linda de Monici and her friend Captain Patterson, a retired English officer, a young couple known only as Mary and John, Alice Spicer, an American girl, and Alice's love, Ivan. Alice had known Vitya for a long time, and possibly this made Isadora jealous. At any rate, Isadora told Alice that she was drinking too little and kept refilling the younger woman's glass. Seroff soon saw that if Alice drank any more she would be sick. He led the young woman to his bedroom, where he made her lie down. Then he returned to their guests to find that Isadora, who had perhaps become tipsy in drinking with Miss Spicer, had left the table in a fit of despondency and walked into the sea in an attempt at suicide. She had been rescued by Captain Patterson, who brought her home, where Seroff insisted that she get into some dry clothes and go to bed.

Unfortunately, the next day an account of the suicide attempt appeared in the newspapers, with the result that the Paris Committee stopped its work for Isadora's school and refused to send her any more money. Without funds, Isadora was unable to pay what she owed at the pension, and she soon found herself evicted. She moved back into the Hotel Negresco and advised Seroff to return to Paris to see the committee and urge them to reconsider their stand. After Seroff had been in Paris for ten days, Isadora wired him that she was joining him there. This time she took an apartment in the Studio Hotel at the Rue Délambre, in Montparnasse.

At this time, Irma was summoned to Germany by her mother's death to settle her affairs and she took the opportunity to travel to Paris to see Isadora. Their reunion was happy, although Isadora chided Irma for not seeking her approval before taking the school to China. Irma replied that she could not ask Isadora's permission "every time I want to dance with my pupils (for they are mine, too, you must know). . . . I told her I had earned the right to an equal partnership and would tolerate no more nonsense about who was exploiting whom. . . . She took it all very amiably and was in complete accord with my views."[36] Whatever Isadora's reservations may have been,[37] this conversation apparently cleared the air, for Irma saw Isadora several more times before she returned to Russia, and they parted on friendly terms.

Meanwhile, Cécile Sartoris of the committee had been making

arrangements for Isadora to give a recital at the Mogador Theatre, and Isadora had been dieting and rehearsing intensively to appear before an audience that had not seen her for several years. The performance took place on July 8, 1927. As if she had divined that it was to be her farewell performance, she performed only serious works: César Franck's *Redemption,* Schubert's grave and tender *Ave Maria,* the tragic second movement of his *Unfinished Symphony,* the *Tannhäuser Overture,* and the *Love-Death of Isolde,* dancing to a hushed, then weeping, wildly applauding audience.

Shortly after the concert, Alice Spicer, who was driving to the Riviera with a friend, offered to take Isadora and Mary Desti along. Isadora accepted with alacrity. Knowing the members of the party and foreseeing trouble, Seroff arranged to travel to Nice independently. On the second day, however, friction developed between Alice and Isadora, and the party split up,[38] Isadora and Mary continuing their journey to Nice alone. They arrived at their destination not only penniless but in debt. Because Isadora had refused on principle to travel by train second-class, which was all their funds would permit, they had instead hired an automobile on credit. At Nice, they were joined by Vitya, who had traveled by train. Isadora needed a place to live in Nice. Her studio, unluckily, was out of the question, as it lacked bedrooms and running water. So she took rooms in an expensive hotel, but it was obvious that the party must find some better long-range solution.

At this juncture, Vitya decided to go back to Paris to see what he could do about raising funds. According to Mary, he chafed at his inability to help Isadora. He himself says he found it particularly galling to see her wasting her time and means in entertaining friends at the Negresco who might possibly "do something" for her. Entertaining would improve their credit at the hotel, explained Mary: "People mustn't think we have no money." To Vitya, this was an absurd way of dealing with a serious situation, and he felt he could be more useful in Paris. After several discussions with Isadora, she reluctantly agreed that he should go.

On the night he left, Isadora, lonely and unable to settle down, proposed to Mary that they walk to Port Juan where there was a seaside café. As the friends were eating, Isadora's attention was caught by a good-looking man at the next table. After a few minutes the man, a garage keeper, got up to leave. Still depressed, she waved at the young man, and he bowed before driving off in his Bugatti.

The day after Seroff's departure, Mary and Isadora moved to an inexpensive little hotel near her studio. This proved an unfortunate decision, for soon afterward the hotel notified the two women that they would have to leave unless the rent were paid by Sunday. Isadora had not yet managed to sell the American serial rights to her now completed memoirs, and Mary's long awaited remittance from home had been swallowed up almost immediately by their daily expenses, so once again they were penniless. Isadora, in desperation, suggested that Mary approach Paris Singer, who was now at St. Jean Cap Ferrat, not far from them.

Mary felt friendship for both people and shrank from exposing Isadora's plight to her former lover. Nevertheless, she hired a car (again on credit) and, with dismay, drove to Singer's imposing villa and had herself announced. Singer greeted Mary kindly but refused to give any money to Isadora—he said she would only run through it in a few days.

When Mary told Isadora the result of the interview, the dancer made no complaint, but her face grew pale and a line formed about her nostrils—with her, a sign of suffering. She had never ceased to care for Singer, and she felt the humiliation of his refusal. The next morning, however, there was a knock at the door, and Singer stood on the threshold. Mary wrote: "I suppose he felt sorry after I left. He always felt sorry for Isadora, but no one could cope with her extravagance. There were no explanations, no questions, simply love and tender greetings. . . . Earthly love or desire had no part in this marvelous meeting. Just pity and tenderness on one side, and happiness that one was still loved on the other." When Mary, who had left them alone, returned after Singer's departure, Isadora exclaimed: "He is a lovely, lovely being and I love him. I believe he is the only one I ever loved."[39]

" 'How can you say that, Isadora? Tell me now the absolute truth. Whom above all did you really love the best? . . .' "

" 'Well, to tell you the real truth, Mary, I don't know. I seemed to love each one of them to the uttermost limits of love, and if Ted, Lohengrin, the Archangel and Sergei stood before me, I wouldn't know which one to choose. I loved, and still love them all. . . .' "

This recalls what Isadora wrote in her memoirs about her lovers: "Just as I once loved them, I love them still and forever."[40] Gordon Craig has marked this sentence in his copy of *My Life,* commenting in the margin: "This is well said, and true." Perhaps, for him too, that was the nature of all loving.

Singer, too, could not feel unconcerned about Isadora. Out of his old regard for her and his admiration for her dance, he had offered not only to take care of Isadora's immediate needs, but to underwrite her expenses until she had a new program ready to be presented. His kindness, and the evidence of his continuing friendship made Isadora very happy.

Seroff has remarked:

> It is most unfortunate that in her book, *The Untold Story,* Mary Desti let herself be carried away into the most fantastic fiction in giving an account of what took place during the eight days after my departure from Nice. . . . I will mention here only three of Mary Desti's stories which apparently made Macdougall remark at this point in his book, "Things, it seemed, were going to brighten up." According to Mary Desti, she had gone to see Paris Singer . . . and Singer had promised financial assistance to Isadora. This fiction was followed by another—a gay luncheon with Robert Winthrop Chandler, an American painter . . . at which the forthcoming marriage of Isadora to Chandler had been announced. Finally, if this was not enough to fill a week, Isadora was supposed to have planned a new amorous adventure with a young Italian who owned a Bugatti car.[41]

Unluckily for Seroff's view of the situation, despite Mary's slapdash writing style, two of these incidents did take place. The third, Isadora's intentions toward the Bugatti's driver, remains open to conjecture. Seroff apparently bases his conviction of Mary's errors on a letter he received from Isadora dated Sunday, September 11, in which she wrote: "We have nothing to eat and no way of getting out unless I sell the furniture here—so I can't very well wish you here under such deplorable circumstances."

But there is no contradiction between the letter and Mary's account. On the same day that Isadora wrote to Vitya, Mary went to Singer to ask for help and was turned down. Apparently, the following day, Monday (at first, p. 253, Mary writes, "one day"), Lohengrin walked in. But then she says (p. 257), "He said he wouldn't be able to see her the next day, Tuesday but Wednesday he would come at four o'clock." So Lohengrin must have come to see Isadora on Monday. Hence there would be no conflict between Isadora's note to Seroff and Singer's offer of help on Monday.

In any case, Macdougall knew Singer well enough to verify Mary's account of his reconciliation with Isadora. A letter dated October 12, 1927 from Macdougall to Mary Fanton Roberts reinforces that account. "Her death was a great blow to him [Paris]. Isadora was so touched by their making up that she decided to cut out of her memoirs all the nasty unkind references to Joan [Singer's second wife] and also hand back to Paris his love letters."[42] This letter was written before both Mary Desti's *The Untold Story* and Irma Duncan's and Macdougall's *Isadora Duncan's Russian Days* (both published in 1929), so it does not find its source in either book.

The second incident, the luncheon at which Chandler and Isadora jokingly announced their engagement to the press, also can be verified. A newspaper account reporting the engagement exists in the Newspaper Collection of the New York Public Library.[43] Furthermore, Bernardine Szold Fritz, who was a member of the party, recalls: "Bob [Chandler] arranged a bouillabaise party down on the edge of the harbor in the adorable old town of Antibes. . . . There must have been twenty of us there. The names of some I don't remember, but beside Isadora and Desti there were Glenway [Wescott], Monroe [Wheeler], Varèse and his wife Louise. . . . We'd been at lunch for hours when Isadora had . . . an impish idea. She thought how funny it would sound to pretend she was engaged to Bob. . . . We all went on making nonsensical jokes about it until finally someone said, 'Let's make it a hoax, and wire the New York papers.' It took a bit to send a straight cable to New York . . . but we each dug up something and two of the party, scarcely able to walk at the thought of the commotion it would arouse, dashed over to the telegraph office." [Copy of Mrs. Fritz's manuscript in the author's possession.]

As to Mary's third assertion, that Isadora was planning "a new amorous adventure" with the driver of the Bugatti, who can say?

According to Seroff, some days before Mary's appeal to Singer, Isadora had pointed out the Bugatti, saying, "I would love to have a ride in a car like that."[44] Vitya told her that this could be arranged very simply: all she had to do was go to the garage and tell the owner that she was interested in buying the car. And after Vitya had gone, Isadora apparently did just that. On learning that the driver, Bénoit Falchetto, was agent for the car, she made an appointment with him to show her how it performed. However, he came to the hotel when Isadora was resting and Mary sent him away. When the dancer heard what Mary had done, she became upset.

Isadora made a new appointment with Falchetto on September 14 and arranged that Singer, who wanted to discuss business with her, should come an hour earlier. But Singer was detained and arrived to find Isadora gaily conversing with the young driver about her art and his life (she had discovered that he also piloted airplanes). Displeased, her former lover said to her, "I see you haven't changed." Isadora explained with embarrassment that Mary was shopping for a Bugatti. But Singer well knew the state of Mary's finances and, discounting the excuse, he rose, saying he would return the next morning to complete Isadora's business arrangements. The driver meanwhile was dismissed with instructions to come back at nine that night.

After the two men had left, Isadora was fearful that she would never see either one again: her behavior must certainly have offended both. She, Mary, and Ivan (Alice Spicer's friend who had dropped by to see Mary) then decided to have dinner at Henri's, the restaurant across the street. On the way there, Isadora's spirits soared. She told Mary: "If you could have seen Lohengrin's face when he saw Bugatti [the name she gave the driver], you'd know he still loves me. Oh, I am so happy. . . ."

Mary was far from sharing her elation. Her friend's excitement only made her uneasy. Less disapproving than unaccountably anxious, she said: "Please, Isadora, don't go in that auto. My nerves are terribly unstrung; I'm afraid something might happen to you."

But lightheaded with relief and full of anticipation, Isadora was heedless of Mary's warnings. Indeed, they only served to increase her eagerness. "My dear, I would go for this ride tonight even if I were sure it would be my last. Even then, I would go quicker."

Back in her hotel room, Isadora saw the Bugatti waiting below, and flinging her red shawl around her, she started for the door.

She refused both Mary's offer of a cloak and the driver's proffered leather coat—her shawl, they said, would not be warm enough. Seated in the car, she turned to wave to Mary and Ivan, calling out, "Adieu, mes amis, je vais à la gloire."

The automobile leapt forward, then jerked to a stop, and the watchers saw that Isadora's head had slumped against the rim of the door. Even before they could take in the implications of this fact, the driver began to scream. Still dazed, unable to connect his cries with disaster, they ran to the automobile.

Isadora's scarf had wound itself around the axle of the wheel, crushing her larynx and breaking her neck. Frantic, Mary hailed a cab and drove with the motionless dancer to L'Hôpital de St. Roch. There the surgeon told her what she had feared to hear, that Isadora Duncan was dead.

Paris Singer was notified, and he helped Mary to do whatever remained be done. They had no need to consult one another. They knew, from the funeral of Isadora's children—Singer's son— what her wishes would have been. While Mary was greeting the stream of mourners who filed past the flower-strewn couch, a telegram was handed to her, announcing the sale of Isadora's memoirs to the Bell syndicate: the money was waiting for the dancer in a Paris bank.

Vitya had returned to Nice, and, on September 16, he, Mary, and

Raymond Duncan traveled back to Paris in the train that carried Isadora's casket. They were met by Elizabeth Duncan, Lisa Duncan (the only one of Isadora's original pupils then in Paris), and her friends Fernand Divoire, Christine Dalliès, Dougie, Marcel Herrand, and Alfredo Sidès. Isadora's body was brought to Raymond's studio in Auteuil, which had been hung with her blue curtains to receive her. Two days later, on the morning of September 19, her friends gathered at the studio to escort her body to the crematorium at Père Lachaise. Mary had thrown a purple robe over the coffin (it was the mantle Isadora wore when she danced *The Resurrection*), and now Raymond draped the American flag over one end of the casket. Then the hearse started off, followed immediately by Raymond and Elizabeth, he with his head high and lips compressed, she with her eyes down and face composed, both remembering their little sister and the high hopes with which they had long ago embarked for Europe. Behind them walked Mary Desti, supported by Victor Seroff and Christine Dalliès, Vitya's face a mask of concentration and grief. After them came Lisa Duncan, Macdougall, Fernand Divoire, José Clara, Mercedes de Acosta, Albert Wolff (the conductor of Isadora's final concert), Lottie Yorska, Marcel Herrand, Thalia Rosalès, Alfredo Sidès, and many other friends, old and new.

There was an American Legion parade that day, and so the funeral cortège was forced to stay on the left bank of the Seine until it reached the Pont Royal. Mary Desti noticed that some Legionnaires on the way to their parade saw the American flag and asked, "What American was passing?" How appropriate it was, thought Mary, that the Stars and Stripes should be flying from the pinnacle of the Trocadéro (site of the legionnaire's convention), where Isadora had so often appeared, as if in memory of America's greatest dancer. Members of a detachment of Chasseurs Alpins, on their way to protect the American Legion procession from sympathizers of the recently executed Sacco and Vanzetti, lowered their tricolors in a salute as they passed the hearse—and Seroff reflected that this gesture would have amused Isadora, who had demonstrated for the release of Sacco and Vanzetti.

As the mourners slowly neared the grounds of Père Lachaise,

Mary remembered the last two occasions on which she had been there—the funeral of Isadora's mother and earlier when she and Isadora had accompanied the bodies of Isadora's children and their nurse. Mary must have remembered many other things: her meeting with the eager, slender girl, years ago, and their shared confidences and laughter; Isadora standing with arms outstretched acknowledging thunderous applause; Isadora turning her head away, with pitiful face and empty arms after the death of her ill-fated third baby.

It had begun to drizzle. Nonetheless, at the gates of Père Lachaise there was a huge crowd waiting, some 4000 people, young and old, rich and poor, obscure and famous. As the hearse passed between the mourners, a low murmur broke from the expectant crowd: people crossed themselves and whispered: "Pauvre Isadora!"

Inside the chapel, Ralph Lawton, who had accompanied Isadora in Brussels and Paris, played *Les Funérailles* of Liszt. The Calvet Quartet performed a Beethoven Andante, and Bach's *Air for the G String,* and Garcia Marsellac sang Schubert's *Ave Maria.* Then Isadora's old friend, the poet Fernand Divoire, read the funeral oration. Moving as his tribute to the dead woman was, the imperishable Isadora is captured for us in words he wrote earlier, about the living dancer:

> She knows that . . . each time she becomes the young girl, the Amazon, the Bacchante, the crowd will shout, will cry out her name amid wild bravos.
>
> She makes no concession. She is not there for applause.
>
> She is there to lead that crowd which she had awakened, and acquainted with joy, still farther on. . . .
>
> Thus, having known sorrow, she has brought the pure tears of sorrow to our hearts, having felt pity, she has given us the strength to bear with other men the weight of the cloak of shadow. . . .
>
> What she is has a name in all human languages, because she is the very life of the human soul: beauty, calm, sure of itself; the only sister to Samothrace, the presence of the soul in tears, of the being in tears who knows how to add to the word "sorrow" all it contains of resignation, of love, of self-pity, of the nobility of the man unjustly

struck down, and the abandonment of him who remains alone with hands empty. Dionysos in mourning.[45]

Divoire had finished speaking.

Outside a thin plume of smoke rose from the crematory chimney. At the sight, a sound of regret, of release, swelled from the waiting throngs.

In the chapel, Garcia Marsellac sang Beethoven's *In Questa Tomba Oscura,* Duse's favorite song, which she had sung to comfort Isadora in Viareggio. After Lawton had closed with a Chopin nocturn, family and friends filed out of the chapel to witness the urn containing Isadora's ashes placed in the columbarium wall next to the sealed niches that sheltered the ashes of Deirdre and Patrick. A fine mist was still falling: monuments and shrubs gleamed wet in the veiled September light. On the grounds of Père Lachaise, the crowds slowly began to disperse.

❧ 37 ❧

Isadora's Legacy

HAT of Isadora's work still remains today? Can anything of a dancer's art be said to endure, once her limbs are stilled? Isadora's liberating influence on customs, costume, and women's moral standards has been discussed many times. So, too, has her influence on education. The widespread acceptance of dancing as physically healthful and intellectually respectable is directly traceable to Isadora.

She joined Gordon Craig (and his contemporary, Adolph Appia) in the campaign to abolish the literal, the fuzzy, and the superfluous from the theater and to replace them with the evocative, the selective, and the expressive.

Her celebration of the body and the life of the emotions and her preaching against hypocrisy form part of the movement for freedom in the arts and in social relationships so characteristic of the beginning of the twentieth century, a movement whose momentum is not spent today. But what of her influence on the dance itself?

The categorical answer must be that her influence was tremendous, although not in the way that she would have foreseen. Very few of today's dancers have had Duncan training, yet Isadora has left her mark on both modern dance and ballet.

Her influence on ballet, particularly in her creation of plotless or "pure" dances and her use of great music, has been transmitted through Fokine to many of the major ballet choreographers working today. The line of descent from Isadora's Chopin waltzes to *Chopiniana* (1907) and *Les Sylphides* (1908) is clear, as is that from the *Seventh Symphony* (Beethoven) choreographed by Isadora, to the *Seventh* of Massine, or to the *Symphony in C* or *Serenade* of Balanchine. Fokine is the direct ancestor, but Isadora is the founder of the line. (It must be remarked in passing that Balanchine once saw Isadora dance when she was overweight and in her forties, and he disliked her intensely.)

The English choreographers Anthony Tudor and Frederick Ashton are both descendants of Isadora through Fokine, Tudor through his use of music and of gesture that aims at psychological truth, and Ashton in the "extraordinarily beautiful tilt of the head" and the softly curved arms of his ballerinas which he remembered as characteristic of Isadora. In *Ondine,* he deliberately evoked Isadora's wavelike movements,[1] and in his *Five Brahms Waltzes in the Manner of Isadora Duncan,* he sought to evoke Isadora herself in both technique and essence.

But among the choreographers of the modern dance, Isadora's influence has been greater. In her use of movements expressing weightiness and ugliness she created new possibilities for the dancer. In *The Dance of the Furies,* portraying the damned, she appeared to be lifting great weights; she rose laboriously from the floor in a way that would be used later by the German Expressionist dancer, Mary Wigman and whole generations of modern American dancers. Her arms grew twisted, contorted; her fingers became claws. She moved rapidly across the stage in a series of prowling, crouching, and turning leaps. Her head was bowed with despair; her hair swept the floor. Martha Graham is sometimes spoken of as the dancer who "discovered the floor"—a claim which can also be made for Mary Wigman. But the discovery goes back to Isadora, with her insistence that the ballet was wrong to try to create the illusion that gravity did not exist. Isadora fell heavily to the floor; she writhed on it. Dancing to Tchaikovsky's *Pathétique,* she spent an entire movement of the symphony in simply rising from a prone to a standing position. Yet her eloquence stunned the dancer Helen Tamiris; according to Tamiris, it was to have a profound influence on her own choreography and teaching.

Isadora was the first to use ugliness as an important element in the dance. *The Dance of the Furies* (Gluck) showed how powerful ugliness could be as a means of expressing emotion in the dance. *The Dance of the Furies* was composed in 1911 but she had already introduced ugliness as an element in *Death and the Maiden,* which she was performing in 1903. For her, the criteria of a movement were: Is it natural? Is it truthful (not literal, but truthful)? Is it expressive?

Beginning in the years of World War I, Isadora composed dances on political and social themes, such as the *Marseillaise* (about the war) and the *Marche Slave* (about the Russian Revolution). The use of such subjects for dances influenced Mary Wigman in *Todentanz,* and Kurt Joos in *The Green Table.* (The Standard Bearer in *The Green Table* is prefigured in both the *Symphonie Pathétique* and the *Warshavianka* of Isadora.) When Isadora had her school for child dancers in Soviet Russia, she composed a whole series of dances based on the theme of labor and revolution that influenced Graham, Holm, Humphrey, Limon, Tamiris, and Sokolow, among others. The dances on social themes of the 1930s and 1940s are thus lineal descendants of the *Marche Slave* and Isadora's other revolutionary dances. The use of performers who dance to folk songs which they or their fellow performers sing, so successfully employed by the Moiseyev folk ballet, originated in Isadora's Russian dances.

Though the modern dance in the United States seems to descend from Isadora's pioneering contemporaries, Ruth St. Denis and Ted Shawn, through their pupils, Martha Graham, Charles Weidman, and Doris Humphrey, and, in turn, through the choreographer-pupils of Graham (Paul Butler, Merce Cunningham, Eric Hawkins, Jean Erdman, and Yuriko, to name a few), or through the pupils of Weidman and Humphrey (particularly José Limon and the members of his group), we have seen that a number of these dancers followed hints given them by Isadora in her performances or her writings. Graham used both Greek mythology and contemporary social themes for her dances. Doris Humphrey, in her use of music, of long movements, each one developing flowingly from the one before, and of veils to extend the gesture (something Isadora herself learned from Loie Fuller), shows how well she had absorbed what Isadora had to offer her. Humphrey's composition to Bach's *Air for the G String* is very Isadorian in both spirit and appearance.

José Limon was influenced by Isadora's autobiography, not only in his conception of the dance,[2] but also in the character of his flowing, slowly unrolling, long successive movements.

Even St. Denis and Shawn themselves were influenced by Isadora's use of Greek themes *(Greek Veil Plastique, Adonis)* and by her use of symphonic music. They tell us that it was her music and a sense of what she had *not* attempted that prompted them to create their synchoric orchestra. All the forerunners of the modern dance—Isadora, St. Denis, and Shawn—had the same attitude to their art: the purpose of the dance should be primarily spiritual, dealing with the deepest concerns of humanity.

At present, modern dance is moving through a new phase—where attention is focused on movement—its difficulty, its unexpectedness, its transitions, and its juxtapositions. "Meaning," apart from movement itself, is seen as irrelevant. As Merce Cunningham phrased it to Clive Barnes: "I am first concerned with human activity, ordinary gesture, and making continuity out of human gesture. I do not consider that one gesture is more interesting than another. . . . What I find interesting is when a movement gets difficult, but there are, remember, only six or seven ways in which the human body can move. My work is often said to have something of the feeling of classical ballet about it. This is, I think, because I regard physical action as important in itself."[3]

This view would seem to be directly contrary to the teaching of Isadora, and it might be thought that for audiences accustomed to Cunningham, to the abstract classicism of Paul Taylor, to the in-

ventive depersonalized shapes and nonhuman cadences of Alwin
Nikolais, or to the offbeat rhythms and deadpan virtuosity of avant-
garde choreographers Twyla Tharp and Meredith Monk, the dance
of Isadora would seem sentimental and irrelevant. Of that, more
will be said in a minute.

Until recently, it was widely supposed that although Isadora
influenced both ballet and modern dance, her own dances had for
all practical purposes vanished without a trace, that is, that they
were mainly performed in Duncan classes by amateurs, mostly middle-
aged, who met once or twice a week, usually under the direction
of some pupil of a pupil of a pupil of Isadora. To judge her choreography from such occasions would be rather like judging *Giselle*
if one had seen it performed only by the beginning students of a
small-town ballet school and had never seen professional ballet at
all. What is remarkable is how much of the force of *The Furies* or
the tenderness of the *Ave Maria* can be glimpsed under such circumstances—although matters improve instantly when the class is
being taught by one of Isadora's original pupils, or even a pupil at
second remove. To see one of Isadora's original pupils dance is to
guess at what Isadora's dancing looked like—although none of them
duplicated her, nor did she intend them to. "Each person must
create his own dances," she said. In New York, two of the original
pupils, Anna Duncan and Maria-Theresa, sought funding about fifteen years ago for documentaries, concerts, or books, but for various
reasons, among them a belief that Isadora's dances were of no
contemporary interest, no funding was available.

In the past few years, however, and particularly since the cele-
brations in connection with Isadora's centennial, the dance public,
for the first time in many decades, has had the opportunity to see
Isadora's work, and the enthusiasm expressed for it has been unexpectedly great.

Anna Kisselgoff wrote:

> That these Duncan dances are popular is indisputable. The Isadora
> Duncan Centenary Dance Company's engagement last spring at Riv-
> erside left many would-be ticket buyers at the door, and just two

months ago, at Agnes de Mille's evening at the Joffrey Ballet, it was Isadora's *Three Graces,* danced by Miss [Hortense] Kooluris, Miss [Gemze] de Lappe and Judith Epstein, that drew some of the strongest applause. Similarly the sensation at a New York Dance Festival in Central Park a few years ago was Miss Gamson's interpretation of a Scriabin Étude derived from Isadora's pro-Bolshevik odes to the oppressed.[4]

Tobi Tobias noted:

Duncan created a dance that was motivated, both physically and emotionally, from the center of the body, as opposed to a peripheral merely decorative operation of arms and legs—"tricks" as she scornfully called them, that could be taught to the feet. At first glance, her vocabulary looks fairly narrow and simple—based as it is on walks, skips and runs, the upper body moving in complement—but its plasticity and rhythms are remarkably subtle (today's virtuoso professionals are regularly defeated by it), and with it, Duncan was able to create a world of emotion. The repertory she left ranges from the sensual lyricism of the *Brahms Waltzes,* to a stark monument to grief, *Mother,* to the brilliant violence of the so-called *Revolutionary Étude,* in which the body seems alternately to give in to the gravity and lassitude that suggest oppression and defiantly rip itself from its fetters; it poses the gentle purity of the *Dance of the Blessed Spirits* (to Gluck) against the overripe wine-madness of the Bacchanale. . . .

[Her] work is enjoying a surge of interest in the present period when modern dance is looking back over its history and consolidating its achievements. Duncan's clear, simple, lucidly constructed dances go back to fundamentals of shape, weight and dynamics that contemporary dance has lost touch with in its pursuit of virtuosity.[5]

In *The New York Times,* Tobias quoted the soloist Annabelle Gamson as saying: "The more I explored Isadora's works the more wonderful I thought they were—minimal dances that manage to say everything with economy and depth." To Tobias's observation that, although the dance vocabulary is elementary, its style is difficult to capture, Gamson explained, "Why? *Because* they're so simple. Simple is hard."[6]

Tobias continued:

A pair of Scriabin études . . . *Mother* and the *Revolutionary* study, are remarkable for their starkness and compression. In the first, a Niobe figure conveys nurturing love and inconsolable loss through images as plain as rocking, a curved torso, an out-stretched arm. The revolutionary figure, fists clenched, mouth wide open in a soundless yell, seems to rip her limbs away from gravity's pull. These dances deal in basic, often literal gestures and primal emotions— elements that might easily lend themselves to the banal or the overwrought—yet their effect is, surprisingly, both abstract and profoundly moving.

About this *Revolutionary Étude,* Anna Kisselgoff wrote:

The same solo is performed by [Julia] Levien, and significantly the differences between hers and Miss Gamson's performances offer a clue as to what we are really seeing. What we are seeing is in fact an outline of choreography that, true to Isadora's principles, does not depend on individual steps. But because of its organic basis, it changes with the way it is filled out by the individual dancer.

Miss Gamson's rendering of the "étude" has a contemporary thrust. The way her shackled peasant rises to one knee and punches a clenched fist through space carries the militancy of the power salute of the 1960's. Miss Levien, who performed as a young girl with Irma Duncan in the 1930's, offers a different power. Her anonymous downtrodden figure digs into the ground, asking "Why?" When she shoots her fist forward, it is not with the triumph of Miss Gamson's dynamism but with the inevitability of rage and frustration breaking through a bond.

Different bodies, different times. Miss Gamson reflects our day. Miss Levien is closer to the heroism of the 1930's. . . .

Today this "economy of movement" is very probably the reason for the new appeal of the Duncan dances. We live in an age of increased virtuosity in both modern dance and ballet. Technique for its own sake was opposed not only by Isadora but Fokine and its reemergence is capable of producing a counter-reaction. The economy of means of the Duncan repertory finds its resonance in another way in the deliberately reduced vocabulary of younger modern-dance choreographers.[7]

Robert Kimball spoke of a different quality which delights audiences now as it delighted them in Isadora's day.

> Each gesture had breadth and amplitude, a lyrical quality that conveys a deceptive lightness, a kind of airiness that is sustained in tandem with the musical phrase. One had the sense, particularly when one watched the Misses [Sylvia] Gold, Kooluris, de Lappe and Levien, that no matter how rooted they were to the earth, they used their bodies to release themselves from travail and tribulation. The sky was not their limit but their goal.[8]

Economy of means, lightness, lyricism, emotional intensity, and the joy of dancing. It seems as though Isadora's art is more durable than critics once thought.

What remains of Isadora's teaching on the wider dance scene is not her technique but her approach to the dance. She made possible the development of free, natural, and expressive dance. The modern dance springs from her principles, and the ballet has been permeated by her emphasis on musicality and psychological truth.

At present, we are experiencing a counterdevelopment in the dance, where movement taken out of its psychological or musical context is used to extend the vocabulary of the dance.[9] But this development is in reaction to the work of Isadora, St. Denis, and their immediate successors, and it, too, is being absorbed. We are not conscious of the extent of Isadora's influence because it has been assimilated.

Finally, as Agnes de Mille wrote, Isadora caused the dance to be considered "important and dignified." Before Duncan, the dance was considered an entertainment. She left it an art.[10] And if her life, like that of heroes of antiquity, was brought low by a tragic flaw, she had heroic stature. "La soeur unique de Samothrace!"[11]

At Bellevue, circa 1917 (*Mme. Mario Meunier—Christine Dalliès Collection*).

Notes

The following abbreviations are used in the notes:

AAJ   *An Amazing Journey,* by Maurice Dumesnil, Washburn, New York, 1932.

CD   Craig-Duncan Collection, The Dance Collection, The Library for the Performing Arts at Lincoln Center, New York.

DC   The Dance Collection, The Library for the Performing Arts at Lincoln Center, New York.

DD   *Duncan Dancer,* by Irma Duncan, Wesleyan University Press, Middletown, Connecticut, 1966.

EAB   *Esenin, A Biography in Memoirs, Letters and Documents,* edited and translated by J. Davies, Ardis, Ann Arbor, 1981.

EAL   *Esenin: A Life,* by Gordon McVay, Ardis, Ann Arbor, 1976.

ET   *Ellen Terry,* by Roger Manvell, Putnam, New York, 1968.

GC   *Gordon Craig,* by Edward [Anthony] Craig, Knopf, New York, 1968.

HLTH   *Here Lies the Heart: A Tale of My Life,* by Mercedes de Acosta, Reynal and Co., New York, 1960.

I   *Impresario: A Memoir,* by S. Hurok and Ruth Goode, Random House, New York, 1946.

IAE   *Isadora and Esenin,* by Gordon McVay, Ardis, Ann Arbor, 1980.

IARIAAL   *Isadora: A Revolutionary in Art and Love,* by Allan Ross Macdougall, Thomas Nelson and Sons, New York, 1960.

ID   *Isadora Duncan,* edited by Paul Magriel, Henry Holt, New York, 1947.

IDAIP   *Isadora Duncan: An Intimate Portrait,* by Sewell Stokes, Brentano, London, 1928.

IDRD   *Isadora Duncan's Russian Days and Her Last Years in France,* by Irma Duncan and Allan Ross Macdougall, Covici-Friede, New York, 1929.

IDTRY   *Isadora Duncan: The Russian Years,* by Ilya Ilyitch Schneider, Macdonald, London, 1968.

ITTSOMD   *Index to the Story of My Days,* by Edward Gordon Craig, Viking, New York, 1957.

LON   *Love or Nothing: The Life and Times of Ellen Terry,* by Tom Prideaux, Scribner, New York, 1975.

ML   *My Life,* by Isadora Duncan, Boni and Liveright, New York, 1927.

SAEM   *Sergei Alexandrovich Esenin: Memoirs* (Sergei Alexandrovich Esenin: Vospominaniia), edited by I. V. Evdokimov, Moscow, 1926.

SE   *Sergei Essénine,* par Sophie Laffitte, Editions Pierre Seghers, Paris, 1959.

SESVESO   *Sergei Esénine: Sa Vie et Son Oeuvre,* par Francisca de Graaff, Leyde, E. J. Brill, 1933.

SPOAA   *Self Portrait of An Artist,* by Lady Kennet, John Murray, London, 1949.

TAOTD   *The Art of the Dance,* by Isadora Duncan, edited by S. Cheney, Theatre Arts, New York, 1928.

TIMA   *This Is My Affair,* by Lola Kinel, Little, Brown, Boston, 1937.

TRI   *The Real Isadora,* by Victor Seroff, Dial, New York, 1971.

TURL-UCLA   The University Research Library: Department of Special Collections, University of California at Los Angeles, Edward Gordon Craig Collection, Collection 1006.

TUS   *The Untold Story,* by Mary Desti, Liveright, New York, 1929.

TWIMC   *To Whom It May Concern: The Story of Victor Ilyitch Seroff,* by M. R. Werner [pseud. V. Seroff], Jonathan Cape and Smith, New York, 1931.

UTA-CA   The Humanities Research Center at the University of Texas (Austin), The Craig Archives.

YI   *Your Isadora: The Love Story of Isadora Duncan and Gordon Craig,* edited by Francis Steegmuller, Random House and the New York Public Library, New York, 1974.

Preface

[1] *The New York Times,* May 22, 1977.
[2] *New York Post,* January 13, 1978.

³IARIAAL, pp. 127–128.

⁴ITTSOMD, pp. 260–262.

<h2 style="text-align:center">1 ◆ Signs and Portents</h2>

¹DC; see also IDRD, p. 229.

²According to Raymond Duncan, it was Henry House, now the Portland Hotel, in Oakland, California.

³Augustin Duncan in the *Herald Tribune,* May 2, 1937.

⁴*San Francisco Evening Bulletin,* October 12, 1977, and October 9, 1977. *Appleton's Cyclopaedia of American Biography,* Appleton, New York, 1877 says he served in the War of 1812 and became adjutant general during 1813–14.   ⁵October 12, 1877.

⁶According to Paul Hertelendy, the *Oakland Tribune,* June 13, 1976, Duncan was born in Philadelphia in August 1819. Mary Isadora Gray was born in St. Louis in 1849. They were married on June 26, 1869. I am indebted to Hertelendy, dance critic of the *Tribune,* for a number of facts concerning Isadora's background and her early life.   ⁷October 8, 1877.

⁸*San Francisco Evening Chronicle,* October 18, 1877, says that William T. Duncan was "an actual creditor of the bank in the sum of $112,240.07."

⁹William T. Duncan was Duncan's son by his first marriage to Eleanor Hill.

¹⁰Macdougall, IARIAAL, p. 23, gives Isadora's name as Dora Angela. According to the Delayed Certificate of Birth signed on January 2, 1947 by Augustine Gray Duncan (Augustin—without the "e"—was his professional name), his sister's name was Angela Isadora Duncan. Moreover, in an interview with Margaret Lloyd, *Christian Science Monitor,* February 16, 1946, Augustin remarked that Isadora had been christened Angela Isadora after her mother, whose baptismal name was Mary Isadora. He added that his sister's initials spelled "AID," which was what she had always given to her family. Isadora, then, was her real name, and not a stage name as some writers, Macdougall among them, have speculated.   ¹¹ML, p. 9.

¹²"What Love Meant to Isadora Duncan," *The Mentor,* February 1930.

¹³*San Francisco Evening Bulletin,* July 3, 1878.

¹⁴IARIAAL, p. 22. Suits against the Pioneer Land and Loan Bank continued as late as September 25, 1912, according to C. W. Calbreath, Clerk of the United States District Court for the Northern District of California, in San Francisco.

¹⁵In "Isadora Reconsidered," *Dancemagazine,* July 1977, Nesta Macdonald writes, "after prolonged trials, he was given a jail sentence." She is mistaken, however. These headlines from California newspapers make clear the course of the trial. "Duncan Arraigned." (*Daily Alta California,* San Francisco, May 12, 1878.) "Trial of Joseph C. Duncan. The long deferred trial of Joseph C. Duncan Commenced yesterday afternoon in Municipal Court. . . ." (*Daily Alta California,* November 30, 1878.) "Supreme Court: Denial of a petition of Joseph C. Duncan for Reduction of Bail." (*Daily Alta California,* December 28, 1878.) "J. C. Duncan's Bail." (*Daily Alta California,* June 27, 1879.) "The Reduction of Duncan's Bail." (*Daily Alta California,* June 21, 1880.)

"Case of J. C. Duncan Dismissed." (*Sacramento Daily Record-Union,* July 27, 1882.) This last news item reads, in its entirety: "The case against J. C. Duncan of the defunct Pioneer Bank was dismissed today, owing to the failure of important evidence relied upon by the prosecution."

2 ♦ A Missing Father

[1]ML, p. 14. [2]ML, p. 12. [3]DC. [4]ML, p. 15. [5]ML, p. 16.

[6]According to the legal deposition of Augustine Duncan. (He would drop the final "e" later.)

[7]Augustin Duncan, *Herald Tribune,* May 2, 1937. [8]ML, p. 19.

[9]Raymond Duncan, speaking in Carnegie Hall, January 28, 1961. [10]DC, Isadora's notebook.

[11]Maria Theresa (Mrs. Stephan Bourgeois, formerly Thérèse Duncan), one of the six original pupils who remained with Isadora from childhood to young adulthood.

[12]Augustin Duncan, *Herald Tribune,* June 24, 1928.

[13]According to the *Oakland Tribune,* March 7, 1976, she was first listed as a dancing teacher in the *Oakland Directory* under the name of Miss A. Dora Duncan in 1892–93. This would make her age fifteen. But she may have taught neighborhood children before this. [14]IARIAAL, pp. 32–33.

[15]Father of the poet, Percy MacKaye, who would become a friend of Isadora.

[16]ITTSOMD, p. 264. [17]"Emotional Expression," *The Director,* March 1898.

[18]*Every Little Movement,* p. 25. [19]Ibid., p. 33.

[20]Delsarte seems to have advocated Greek costume: at least, Mrs. Hovey is described as having "a passion for classic lines and Greek drapery," and Genevieve Stebbins, another teacher of Delsarte, wore a Greek tunic when she lectured.

[21]A practice which lingered on with the "living statues" of the circuses of my childhood. In Paris, in 1930, the Cirque d'Hiver, more artistic, but hardly more up to date, offered "The Loie Fuller Dancers"—presumably held over from 1900.

[22]IARIAAL, p. 81. [23]Ibid., p. 31.

[24]Now the site of the Scottish Rite Hall. See the introduction by Isadora's relative, George H. Cabaniss, Jr. to a memorial exhibition of drawings by Jules Grandjouan at the Palace of the Legion of Honor, November 1956. [25]IARIAAL, p. 29.

[26]ML, pp. 15–16. Mr. George Cabaniss, Jr., a relative of the Duncans, told me that the children used to visit their father at the home of Mrs. Smedberg, their half-sister. He doubted that the young Duncans had not seen their father for as long as Isadora supposes.

[27]Years later, when Raymond returned to California, he was able to show the current owners of the house the passage whose existence they had not suspected. (Raymond Duncan, in conversation with the author.)

[28]Aia Bertrand stated that Augustin's first barn theater had been at their 1365 Eighth Street home in Oakland, where the family had lived from 1886 to 1893.

3 ♦ Apprenticeship in the Theater

[1]IARIAAL, p. 35.   [2]Ibid.   [3]ML, p. 36.

[4]IARIAAL, p. 37.   [5]ML, p. 39.   [6]IARIAAL, p. 37.

[7]Ibid., p. 38. See also *The Director,* issue of October–November, 1898.

[8]*The Director,* issue of October–November, 1898.   [9]Ibid.

[10]"Emotional Expression," *The Director,* March 1898.

[11]IARIAAL, p. 39. Macdougall incorrectly believed that it was her first trip, but that took place in December 1904.

[12]*Musical America,* September 4, 1904.

[13]Vance Thompson later wrote a *Life of Ethelbert Nevin: From His Letters and His Wife's Memories,* Boston Music Company, 1913.

[14]Several years later, Ruth St. Denis faced the same problem. Unable to find a manager or a theater willing to hire her, she was forced to appear in vaudeville, until (in 1906) she raised enough money to present *Radha.*

[15]Mrs. Augustin Duncan was my informant. See also IARIAAL, pp. 38–39 and Margaret Lloyd's interview of Augustin Duncan in *The Christian Science Monitor* on February 16, 1946.   [16]ML, p. 164.

[17]DC, undated clipping.   [18]*The New York Times,* March 19, 1899.

[19]*New York Herald,* March 18, 1899.   [20]Ibid.

[21]Augustin, who had recently married a young actress, decided against accompanying them. (ML, p. 46.)   [22]DC, undated clipping.

[23]Ruth St. Denis, making her formal Broadway debut in 1906, fared no better. Ted Shawn, speaking at an anniversary celebration for his wife at The Museum of the City of New York, recalled that one critic had described her performance as "The greatest navel display since the fleet sailed up the Hudson."

4 ♦ Beginning in London

[1]IARIAAL, p. 52.

[2]Ketti Lanner was a choreographer (*Rose d'Amour, Diana, The Dream of Wealth,* etc.) as well as a dancer. Daughter of the Viennese waltz composer Joseph Lanner, she had appeared at The Vienna Opera House as a child with Fanny Ellsler.

[3]Also known to three generations of children as the author of *The Red Fairy Book* and the other books of that series.   [4]The Hellenic scholar.   [5]DC, clipping in The Irma Duncan Collection.   [6]Ibid.   [7]IARIAAL, p. 55.

[8]ML, p. 141.   [9]ML, p. 55.   [10]ML, p. 57.   [11]ML, p. 59.

5 ♦ Paris

[1]ML, p. 67.   [2]ML, p. 90.   [3]IARIAAL, p. 59.

[4]Ibid., pp. 60–61.   [5]DC, clippings.   [6]Gabriel Fauré, the composer (1845–1924).

[7]Octave Mirbeau, the satiric playwright and novelist (1850–1917).

[8]ML, p. 71.   [9]ML, p. 171.   [10]ML, p. 91.

[11]Preston Sturges, who later became the well-known motion picture director.

[12]In *Dance,* Putnam, New York, 1935, pp. 26–27.   [13]TAOTD, p. 51.

[14]Irma Duncan: *The Technique of Isadora Duncan,* Kamin Publishers, New York, p. 12.

[15]Reprinted in ID.   [16]*The Technique of Isadora Duncan,* p. 15.

[17]Quoted by Walter Terry: *Isadora Duncan: Her Life, Her Art, Her Legacy,* Dodd, Mead & Co., New York, 1963, p. 155.   [18]Remark to the author.

[19]*The Book of the Dance,* Golden Press, New York, 1963, pp. 84–85.

[20]*Dance Index,* reprinted in ID. For Isadora's understanding of the emotional basis of movement, see ML, pp. 75–77.

[21]This compilation was done. See *The Art of the Dance* by Isadora Duncan, which is a book of principles, unlike *The Technique of Isadora Duncan,* by Irma Duncan, which is a book of exercises.

[22]By now, of course, the modern dance has broken into many movements, and such choreographers as Alwin Nikolais, Merce Cunningham, Twyla Tharp, and Meredith Monk seek to take gestures and movement from their everyday contexts.

[23]Isadora Duncan, TAOTD, p. 52.   [24]Ibid., p. 79.

6 ♦ Berlin and Vienna

[1]IARIAAL, p. 59.   [2]ML, pp. 95 and 97.

[3]IARIAAL, p. 66.   [4]ML, p. 66.   [5]ML, p. 95.

[6]Isadora would not, of course, have spoken of herself in these terms. See Chap. 37 for the relationship of Isadora to the modern dance.

[7]Walter Terry, "The Legacy of Isadora Duncan and Ruth St. Denis," *Dance Perspectives* 5, 1960.   [8]ML, p. 97.

[9]Loie Fuller: *Fifteen Years of a Dancer's Life,* Herbert Jenkins, London, 1913. See also IARIAAL, p. 67.   [10]Ibid.   [11]Ibid., p. 231.

7 ♦ Budapest—and Romeo

[1]DC, Isadora's notebook.   [2]*Uz Idök,* April 20, 1902.

[3]DC, Allan Ross Macdougall Collection.   [4]April 20, 1902.

[5]Joseph Kezler in *Magyar Nemzet,* April 23, 1902.

[6]Julius Pekar in *Pesti Naplo,* April 20, 1902.   [7]TAOTD, p. 52.

[8]ML, p. 101.   [9]ML, p. 104.   [10]ML, p. 107.   [11]ML, p. 109.

8 ♦ Convalescence, Success, and a Manifesto

[1]ML, p. 110. Like many raconteurs, Isadora sometimes embellished stories to increase their interest or to make a point.

[2]Allen Monroe Foster, in the *St. Louis Sunday Gazette,* December 26, 1902.

[3]Cléo de Mérode, a dancer and beauty, favorite of the Belgian king.

[4]ML, p. 111.   [5]ML, p. 112.   [6]ML, pp. 113–114.

[7]Which took place shortly before January 11, 1903, according to *The New York Times* of that date.   [8]DC, clipping.

[9]Translated into English by Irma Duncan in her pamphlet, *Isadora Duncan: Pioneer in the Art of Dance,* the New York Public Library, 1958. The rough draft of this letter, with small variations, appears in DC, Isadora's blue notebook, pp. 103–107.

[10]Reprinted in TAOTD, pp. 54–64.

[11]Martha Myers, "Is the Grand Plié Obsolete?" *Dancemagazine,* June 1982, pp. 78–79.

[12]DC, newspaper clipping.   [13]DC, newspaper clipping.

[14]See Antoine Bourdelle: *La Sculpture et Rodin,* Emile-Paul Frères, Paris, 1937. See also Frederick Lawton: *Life and Work of Auguste Rodin.*

[15]SPOAA. Her autobiography, written in 1932, is based in part on her diaries, kept from 1910 until her death (see Introduction, p. 10). The dates in the early years were put in later from memory, and they are frequently wrong.

[16]But see Harold Bauer, p. 278, on her musicality.

[17]SPOAA, p. 44.   [18]ML, pp. 115–116.

9 ♦ Pilgrimage to Greece

[1]ML, p. 120.   [2]ML, p. 116.   [3]ML, p. 123.

[4]SPOAA, p. 73.   [5]SPOAA, p. 165.   [6]DC, clipping.

[7]*New York Press,* Sunday, October 16, 1898. Paul Hertelendy, dance critic of the *Oakland Tribune,* told me that Joseph Duncan, Mary Cuppola Duncan, and their little girl, Rosa, are buried in the Church of St. Keverne, near Falmouth.

[8]ML, p. 128.   [9]IARIAAL, p. 86.   [10]ML, pp. 129–133.   [11]DC, clipping.

10 ♦ Germany—and Bayreuth

[1]Irma Duncan: *Isadora Duncan: Pioneer in the Art of Dance,* New York Public Library, 1958, pp. 7–8.   [2]ML, p. 138.   [3]Ibid.

[4]In his preface "Nach Funf und Zwanzig Jahren" (dated 1928) to *The Dance of the Future,* Jena, 1929. (A German reissue of Isadora's pamphlet, Eugen Diederich's, Leipzig, 1903.) Quotation translated by Irma Duncan in *Isadora Duncan: Pioneer in the Art of Dance.*

[5]ML, p. 141.   [6]IARIAAL, p. 91. Haeckel's birthday was February 16, 1904.

[7]Originals of Isadora's letters are in the Ernst Haeckel archives in Jena, Germany. The Haeckel letter is in DC.

[8]In *The Dance of the Future,* Eugen Diederichs, Leipzig, 1903, p. 19, she had written, "I do not know whether I have the necessary qualities: I may have neither genius

nor talent nor temperament. But, I know that I have a Will; and will and energy sometimes prove greater than either genius or talent or temperament."

[9]Note dated August 3, 1903, IARIAAL, p. 78.

[10]ML, p. 142.   [11]TUS, p. 35.   [12]ML, p. 143.   [13]ML, p. 151.

[14]Ibid., pp. 150–151.   [15]ML, p. 149.   [16]TUS, pp. 42–43.

[17]Lucretia M. Davison, "Bayreuth Revisited," *The Theatre Magazine,* October 2, 1904.

[18]It seems odd that Isadora should have consented to dance in a production which also used ballet dancers. She probably did so because she loved Wagner's music and regarded it as an honor to appear at Bayreuth.   [19]ML, pp. 149–150.

[20]ML, pp. 159–160.   [21]ML, p. 159.   [22]Ibid.

[23]The prospectus for the school says it was founded in December. (In the Mary Fanton Roberts Collection: The Theatre Collection of the Museum of the City of New York.)

[24]Isadora says forty (in ML, pp. 173, 177), but this is an exaggeration or a slip of memory. See DD, p. 17, and IARIAAL, p. 8.   [25]ML, p. 176.   [26]Ibid., p. 57.

11 ◆ Twin Souls

[1]ITTSOMD, p. 165.

[2]Ibid., pp. 178–180. His friend, the artist William Rothenstein, painted him as the Danish prince.

[3]Ibid., pp. 198–201. For a fairer account of his relationship to Jess Dorynne, see GC, p. 19 and Chap. 5.

[4]These were Rosemary, b. 1894; Robin, b. 1895; Philip, b. 1896; and Peter, b. 1897. Edward Craig, in his understanding, yet critical, biography of his father tells us (p. 109) that May Craig was willing to let him visit them at the home of his mother, Ellen Terry, but May did not want them to visit him while Jess Dorynne was there. Gordon Craig apparently found this incomprehensible and cruel.

[5]Who as Edward Carrick pursued a career as a designer for films and the stage. His biography of his father, however, is written under the name of Edward Craig.

[6]ITTSOMD, pp. 244–245.   [7]Ibid.   [8]GC, pp. 181–183.

[9]ML, p. 180.   [10]ITTSOMD, pp. 257–261.

[11]Letter to the author, December 8, 1958, from Vence, France. For the complete text, see Appendix, p. 445.

[12]GC, p. 190.   [13]ML, p. 180.   [14]GC, p. 190.

[15]UTA-CA, Book Topsy.   [16]DC, programs (CD).   [17]ITTSOMD, pp. 261–262.

[18]GC, p. 192.   [19]DC, programs (CD).   [20]ITTSOMD, p. 258.

[21]*Der Berliner Tageblatt,* April 18, 1928.

[22]ML, pp. 182–183. "My love, my self—for we were not two but one, that amazing being of whom Plato tells in the *Phaedrus,* two halves of the same soul."

[23]ITTSOMD, p. 259.   [24]UTA-CA, Book Topsy.   [25]GC, p. 145.

[26]Isadora (ML, p. 183) says that she stayed there for two weeks, but the letters in the Craig-Duncan collection (DC) indicate that she stayed with him from December 17 to the 19.

[27]ITTSOMD, pp. 6–7.   [28]GC, pp. 20–21.

[29]From Watts' deposition in the divorce proceeding, much later in 1877 (ET, p. 52).

[30]ITTSOMD, p. 48.   [31]ML, p. 18.   [32]In Gordon Craig's copy of *My Life*, p. 15.

[33]ITTSOMD, p. 269.   [34]ITTSOMD, p. 164.   [35]GC, pp. 195–196.

[36]GC, p. 197.   [37]CD 5, letter of December 23, 1904.   [38]CD 6, December 23, 1904.

[39]CD 11, December 24, 1904.   [40]He also had a one-room apartment at 6 Siegmundshoff.   [41]CD, DC.

[42]CD 8. Craig has dated this "December 19, 1904, Russian Reckoning: 26th our reckoning." He is mistaken, however. Another letter from Isadora on the stationery of the Grand Hôtel d'Europe, St. Petersburg says, "Just arrived this morning. Christmas morning. Here it is the 12 of December." Therefore she could not have been *on her way* to Russia on December 26.

12 ◆ Introduction to Russia

[1]CD 12 (one of the few times Isadora dates a letter).

[2]CD 13.   [3]Translated by Jane Harris.

[4]Quoted by Francis Steegmuller, YI, pp. 42–44. Translation by Norbert Gateman.

[5]December 19 and 26, Russian calendar; that is, January 2 and 13, 1905. Translation by Jane Harris.

[6]Letter dated "Tuesday." Actually Tuesday, December 27, 1904 (CD 16).

[7]CD 21. Undated (Written December 31, 1904).

[8]CD 23. Written on the train to Dresden, January 15, 1905.

[9]YI, p. 64.   [10]ITTSOMD, p. 270.   [11]CD.

13 ◆ Russia: Signs of Two Revolutions

[1]ITTSOMD, p. 269.

[2]Announcement in *Novoye Vremya,* January 7 (Russian calendar; western calendar, January 20), 1905, p. 1, of her concert scheduled for February 3.   [3]YI, p. 64.

[4]*Novoye Vremya,* January 21, 1905. (Western calendar, February 3.)

[5]Western calendar, February 2.

[6]For a full discussion of this subject, see Chap. 18, "New York: 'Pure' Music and the Dancer."

[7]Exchange of letters between Ziloti and Auer in *The Russian Musical Gazette* 1905, N. 5. CTP. 130, kindly found for me by the Soviet dance scholar Elisabeth Souvitz. See also YI, p. 65.   [8]YI, pp. 65, 379.

[9]Date passed by censor January 25 (Russian calendar; western calendar, February 7), 1905.

[10]Since Vilkina mentions Isadora's dancing to the work of Chopin, Rameau, and Gluck as well as to Beethoven's symphonies, the enthusiastic curtain calls must refer to the earlier concerts. Steegmuller and Elisabeth Souvitz both note the cool critical response to the Beethoven program. Steegmuller describes a cool audience as well.

[11]Andrei Bely, pseudonym of Boris Nikolaevich Bugaev. (Symbolist poet and novelist, 1880–1934.)

[12]Alexander Blok, the Symbolist poet, 1880–1921.

[13]Andrei Bely, *Vospominaniia of Alexandre Bloke.* I am indebted to the historian and journalist Harrison Salisbury for this translation.   [14]ITTSOMD, p. 270.

[15]Constantin Stanislavski: *My Life in Art,* Meridian Books, New York, 1957, p. 505. In this passage, Stanislavski says that he first came to know Isadora in 1908 or 1909. However, he had seen her dance before that, for, on January 24, 1905 (Russian calendar, February 6, 1905), he noted in his diary: "Saw Duncan tonight . . . I am charmed by her pure art and taste." (Natalia Roslavleva, "Stanislavski and the Ballet," *Dance Perspectives* 23, 1965, p. 14.)

[16]IARIAAL, p. 98.   [17]Tamara Karsavina: *Theatre Street,* Dutton, New York, 1930, p. 208.

[18]Quoted by Cyril Beaumont, *Michel Fokine and His Ballets,* Beaumont, London, 1935, p. 23.   [19]IARIAAL, pp. 101–103.

[20]Its only tangible result "was a bulletin instructing singers in the opera no longer to interrupt the action by taking bows after their arias." (John Martin: *The Dance,* Tudor, New York, 1946, p. 53.)

[21]Quoted in IARIAAL, p. 101.   [22]The pseudonym of V. Y. Ivchenko.

[23]V. Svetlov: *Le Ballet Contemporain,* Golicke et Willborg, St. Petersburg, 1912, p. 35.

[24]Ibid., pp. 68, 38.

[25]Tamara Karsavina: *Theatre Street,* Dutton, New York, 1930, pp. 210–211.

[26]"What Music Means to the Interpretive Dancer," *Musical Courier,* 1923 (no month or page given) and interview with the Duncan dancers by Basanta Koomar Roy. The dancers speaking: "Perhaps you do not know that Pavlova and Isadora are great friends . . . each has great love and respect for the other. . . . We never miss a chance to see Pavlova dance." (Clipping in DC.)

[27]She said this to Anna Duncan, who told me. According to Mary Fanton Roberts (writing in *Denishawn Magazine,* Summer, 1925), "Pavlova told me one night when Isadora and I were having supper with her . . . that much she had accomplished beyond the actual ballet she owed to Isadora. 'She came to Russia,' Pavlova said, 'and brought freedom to us all.' "

[28]ITTSOMD, p. 270.   [29]Western time (Russian calendar, February 18).

[30]V. Svetlov: *Le Ballet Contemporain,* Golicke et Willborg, St. Petersburg, 1912, pp. 62, 63, 66, and 84.

Notes

14 ♦ The Birth of Deirdre

[1]ITTSOMD, p. 268.   [2]UTA-CA. See also YI, p. 64.   [3]UTA-CA. See also YI, p. 72.

[4]CD 35.   [5]CD 162.   [6]ITTSOMD, p. 267.   [7]Ibid., p. 271.

[8]ML, p. 188.   [9]ML, p. 186.   [10]Ibid., p. 187.   [11]DC, clipping.

[12]ML, p. 239.   [13]For more about Magnus, see Appendix, p. 446.

[14]UTA-CA. Quoted YI, pp. 69–71.   [15]ML, p. 184.   [16]ITTSOMD, p. 203.

[17]Her notes on *The Art of the Theatre* appear in her 1905 black notebook in the Craig-Duncan Collection (DC).

[18]TAOTD, p. 62 (reprint of her 1903 speech, *The Dance of the Future*).

[19]Adolphe Appia was also working along the same lines as Gordon Craig, but the two did not know about one another until 1914 when they met in Zurich when both were taking part in an exhibition at the Kunstgewerbe Museum. [Denis Bablet: *Edward Gordon Craig*, p. 174.] This seems to be one of those historic cases, like that of Darwin and Wallace, when two men, unknown to each other, independently developed the same idea. According to Edith Rose, Craig later introduced Appia's work to England.

[20]In a review by Dr. Max Osborn in *Der National Zeitung*, October 31, 1905 (quoted in a prospectus of the school), the first concert is spoken of as having taken place on the Sunday previous to his review; however, there must have been an earlier concert, for both Craig [ITTSOMD, p. 274] and Irma Duncan [*Isadora Duncan: Pioneer in the Art of Dance*, p. 2] agree that the first joint concert took place on July 20, 1905.

[21]ITTSOMD, p. 263.   [22]Dr. Max Osborn, *Der National Zeitung*, October 31, 1905.

[23]ITTSOMD, p. 285.   [24]ML, p. 188.

[25]ITTSOMD, p. 285. The complete passage reads:

> Topsy's thoughts were all of baby-clothes. Mine were certainly not—mine were of *The Mask* [the magazine which he would presently publish]. Anyhow, we two—Topsy and I—did not use the *usual* arguments to each other—those of self-interest, used by all the world. I never pointed out the advantage to her and her work of *The Mask*, neither did she ever attempt to show me what advantage to me her world could be.

[26]CD 66.   [27]ML, p. 189.   [28]*Boston Herald*, January 6, 1906.

[29]She appeared in the Ostermalms Theater in Stockholm from May 1 to May 15, 1906. See receipts in the Maurice Magnus–Duncan–Craig Collection. (Maurice Magnus was the assistant to Duncan and Craig between 1905 and 1907. He is described in ITTSOMD, pp. 275–84.)   [30]ML, p. 176.

[31]Noordwijk, June 1906 (misdated by Craig as 1905). CD 76.

[32]GC, p. 215.   [33]CD 82, July 9, 1906.

[34]CD 79, July 6, 1906.   [35]CD 55.

419

³⁶SPOAA, Lady Kennet, p. 61.

³⁷Ibid., p. 63.   ³⁸Ibid., p. 64.   ³⁹CD 77.

⁴⁰Craig was familiar with Isadora's favorite poem—Walt Whitman's *Song of the Open Road*. Their letters are filled with references to "Walt."

⁴¹See pp. 222–223 for the full text of the letter which he wrote to her on the death of the children.

⁴²Letter dated "Noordwijk 1906," from internal evidence apparently written around July 17. CD 86.

⁴³GC, p. 214.   ⁴⁴GC, p. 215.   ⁴⁵SPOAA, p. 64.   ⁴⁶YI, p. 151.

⁴⁷"Why wasn't my dear Mother with me? It was because she had some absurd prejudice that I should be married." [*My Life*, p. 193.] Craig had underlined this passage in his copy and had noted "Exactly." Dr. Grantley Dick, an advocate of "natural" childbirth, noticed that women whom he studied suffered from acute labor pains only when they were giving birth to a child in circumstances disapproved of by society—for example, if they were adulterous or accused of adultery. It seems probable that the same physical reaction would be produced if society condemned the birth on other grounds.

⁴⁸SPOAA, p. 65.

⁴⁹Allan Ross Macdougall, op. cit., p. 122, gives the date as 1905, apparently following the dates in *Self Portrait of an Artist*. These, however, were inserted after the memoirs were written. Deirdre's birth certificate leaves no doubt that she was born in 1906. The dates in Kathleen's *Diary* (quoted in YI, p. 151) are correct.

⁵⁰If Craig's previously quoted statement in ITTSOMD (p. 285) for the year 1905 ("December: In Holland:—Topsy's thoughts were all of baby-clothes.") is taken as an indirect way of saying that Isadora had discovered she was pregnant, then there would have been an additional reason for her difficult delivery, September 22 to 24, 1906: the baby was a month overdue.   ⁵¹ML, p. 196.   ⁵²Ibid., p. 216.

15 ◆ Duse, *Rosmersholm,* and Illness

¹YI, p. 153.   ²ITTSOMD, pp. 290–291.

³ML, p. 199.   ⁴ML, p. 203.

⁵ITTSOMD, p. 291. See also Craig, in an article, "On Sig. Eleonora Duse," in *Life and Letters,* London, September 1928.

⁶Letter in the Maurice Magnus–Duncan–Craig Collection. (Magnus was business assistant to Isadora and Craig from 1905 to 1907. After 1907, his association with Isadora was only occasional.) This collection was on loan to the New York Public Library. I do not know its whereabouts now.

⁷CD 109; December 19, "Hotel Bristol, Varsovie." The persistence of the pain suggests a dying nerve.

⁸CD 105, December 18, 1906.   ⁹CD 108, probably December 30, 1906.

¹⁰CD 278, February 13 or 14, 1908.   ¹¹CD 281, Florence, 1908.

¹²CD 112.   ¹³ML, p. 18.   ¹⁴CD 121, Warsaw, January 1907.

¹⁵CD 132.   ¹⁶CD 164.   ¹⁷CD 129.   ¹⁸CD 130.

¹⁹Draft of a letter to Isadora, CD 266, dated January 23, 1907. All the explanatory insertions were made by Craig in 1944.

²⁰CD 134.   ²¹ML, p. 206.   ²²GC, p. 222.

²³This telegram or another—Duse had sent several (YI, p. 193).   ²⁴ML, p. 207.

²⁵A monthly edited by Desmond MacCarthy, London. (Gordon Craig, "On Sig. Eleonora Duse," September 1928.)   ²⁶GC, p. 222.

²⁷From which, on February 11, he sent a note to his friend Martin Shaw (YI, p. 195).

²⁸CD 137.   ²⁹CD 256, dated by Steegmuller, "Possibly Nice, March 1907."

³⁰GC, p. 227.   ³¹GC, p. 226.   ³²CD 139.

³³TURL-UCLA, Edward Gordon Craig Collection.

³⁴CD 140.   ³⁵GC, p. 231.   ³⁶CD 142.

³⁷CD 141.   ³⁸CD 144.   ³⁹CD 149.   ⁴⁰CD 153.

⁴¹CD 154.   ⁴²CD 159.   ⁴³CD 152.   ⁴⁴CD 156.

16 ◆ On T'Other Side of a River

¹"Nelly" was Craig's nickname for Elena. It is interesting that he gave this name to her and to both of their daughters—Nelly and the first Nellie, who died in infancy—for this was also his nickname for his mother, Ellen Terry.

For those who know Freud's *Oedipus and Hamlet,* Gordon Craig's remark on the latter play in *Index to the Story of My Days* [p. 162] is illuminating:

I too had lost a father. I too saw my mother married to another. I exaggerated these things then and supposed my stepfather might well have poisoned him in his orchard at Harpenden . . . I needed him . . . I sat ashamed alone—ashamed of what? I was always haunted by my father who was, yet was no longer there. . . .

My mother I could see every day . . . and I loved her very much—but strange as it may sound, I loved him more. . . . He never was at hand: and thus it came about that he grew in grandeur and immensity— . . .

Craig indeed showed many of the traits of the Freudian Hamlet, including a belief that his mother was somehow responsible for his father's absence. About Craig and his mother, see also pp. 166–167 and Chap. 17, fn. 14.

²See her letter from Noordwijk of July or August 1906. "If there is anyone you care for very much who feels unhappy and wants to come with you she can have half of my little house with *all my* heart." CD 86.   ³CD 158.

⁴Augustin felt the same way. His former wife, Sarah Whiteford, appeared profes-

sionally with him and Isadora at the Dionysion two years after their divorce. So, too, with Elizabeth, who lived and worked with outward serenity at the Darmstadt School, although her codirector, Max Merz, was now in love with someone else.

[5]Though the resumption of her career hastened the couple's drifting apart, and Godwin's break with Ellen Terry and his abandonment of his children came a year later.

[6]CD 160.   [7]CD 160.   [8]CD 163.

[9]Ibid. As Francis Steegmuller points out, it was Craig who had drawn up her contract with Stumpff. "Her persistence in saying that everything he does is wonderful, and the contrasting moments when she can no longer pretend that this is so are two of the elements that make the letters . . . so touching." YI, p. 218.

[10]CD 169.   [11]CD 178.   [12]CD 183.   [13]CD 183.

[14]CD 184. Summer was always a bad season for engagements and, because of her illness, she had not been able to make bookings early enough.

[15]CD 269.   [16]CD 268.   [17]CD 192.   [18]CD 195.

[19]He had broken his foot. See CD 190. See UTA-CA for the draft of his letter.

[20]Craig has noted, "Mr. Loeser—Whew! What a hope!" He was no longer living in Loeser's villa, having lately moved to a larger house, Il Santuccio, 35 via San Leonardo.   [21]CD 194.

[22]CD 201.   [23]CD 202.   [24]CD 203.   [25]CD 270.

[26]All through his life women found Craig to be magnetic. They cared for him, helped him, and loved him. They also tried to further his work and his concerns, often to the neglect of their own interests.

[27]CD 340. Steegmuller (YI, p. 262, fn. p. 394) gives the Craig Archives, University of Texas, Austin, as the source of this quotation, but it is a slip of memory.

[28]CD 205.   [29]CD 274.   [30]CD 273.

[31]From Craig's notebook. It is in this same long note that he speaks of being "let down by Madam Duncan."

[32]CD 340.   [33]YI, p. 12.   [34]CD 272.

[35]Isadora, by the way, continued to send him money after their break. She wrote to him from St. Petersburg at the beginning of January 1908—Craig has mistakenly dated her letter December 1907—saying, "I don't know if you are in Florence. You wrote saying you might be coming to Berlin. Did you receive the two checks I sent you from the Munich bank?" CD 216.

It should be added that, years later, when Isadora was in serious financial straits and her friends were trying to raise money to save her Neuilly house, Craig sent a generous contribution which he could ill afford.   [36]CD 281.

[37]Years later, in his copy of *My Life,* Craig wrote, "*Were* you jealous, dear? To your

eternal credit I never knew it." To Isadora's credit, he did not remember it, because she struggled with and (partly) overcame her jealousy of Elena. However he also did not remember it because he *chose* not to remember it. Other people's emotional scenes were profoundly upsetting to him, and he fled from them, bodily if he could; if that was impossible, he erased them from his consciousness.

[38]ML, pp. 208–209.

[39]Irma Duncan told Francis Steegmuller that there was a Pim and that "we children" met him once in Neuilly in 1908. "In I.D.'s life he was only a passing fancy..."

[40]TRI, p. 108.

[41]This, of course, was a cry for help to Craig. (Passive suffering was alien to Isadora. Having learned to turn her will into the channel of energy, she had no patience with self-restraint. *Any* action was better than none.) By the passage about her drinking, Craig wrote: "Oh—big fool."

[42]CD 209.   [43]CD 210.   [44]CD 276.

17 ◆ Stanislavski and a London Interlude

[1]He had first seen her dance on February 6, 1905 (January 24, 1905—Russian calendar) and he had written in his diary: "Saw Duncan tonight. It is necessary to write about this. I am charmed by her pure art and taste." (Quoted by Natalia Roslavleva, "Stanislavski and the Ballet," *Dance Perspectives* 23, 1965, p. 14.)

[2]ML, p. 170.

[3]Letter in the Stanislavski Archives at the Moscow Art Theatre, quoted in TRI, pp. 115–116.

[4]Ibid.   [5]Ibid., p. 117.   [6]TRI, p. 118.   [7]CD 214, beginning of 1908.

[8]CD 278. (Steegmuller thinks this letter may have been written in March.)

[9]Letter of April 2 (?), 1908, CD 218.   [10]CD 279, April 1908.

[11]CD 280, July 1, 1908.   [12]CD 222.

[13]*Current Literature,* London, July 11, 1908, "An attempt to waken an art that has slept for two thousand years."

[14]Beside each word that Isadora wrote about his mother's kindness to her, Craig has written, "lies." Apparently he feared that his mother had taken Isadora's side. Later he crossed out these comments.

[15]CD 282, Florence, August 1908.

[16]DC, clipping, July 11, 1908.

[17]Ted Shawn: *Ruth St. Denis: Pioneer and Prophet,* printed for John Howell by John Henry Nash, San Francisco, 1920, pp. 13–14.

[18]She had appeared (though not as a concert artist) in Belasco's production of *Zaza* in London. (Walter Terry, *Dance Perspectives* 5, Winter 1960, p. 26.)

[19]Baird Hastings, "The Denishawn Era" *Dance Index,* June 1942, p. 89. This would

have been the date of one of the previews. Walter Terry: *Miss Ruth,* Dodd, Mead, New York, 1969, p. 48, gives the date of the first regular performance as March 22, 1906.

[20]In "The Legacy of Isadora Duncan and Ruth St. Denis," *Dance Perspectives* 5, Winter 1960, p. 26, Ruth St. Denis is quoted by Walter Terry as saying that she first saw Isadora in 1900 at the Duke of York Theatre, London. However, this seems to be a slip of memory. She could have seen Isadora in 1900 in London at the New Gallery, but this seems unlikely in view of her statement in St. Denis with Buckmaster: *An Unfinished Life,* Harper, New York, 1939, p. 89, that at the time of her (St. Denis's) first German tour in 1906 she had not yet seen Isadora.

[21]If pitifully small, this matinee audience may have been atypical. IARIAAL, p. 117 states that Isadora played to "crowded houses."

[22]Ruth St. Denis, with Henrietta Buckmaster: *An Unfinished Life,* Harper, New York, 1939, pp. 117–118.

[23]*Current Literature,* July 11, 1908, an English publication. Also the *Sun* (New York), September 20, 1908. The *Sun* identifies the mansion as "formerly the home of Jerôme Bonaparte," but evidently one relative of Napoleon was much like another to the reporter of the *Sun.*

[24]For a full account of their stay at La Verrière, see DD Chap. 5. (Irma refers to the mansion as the Château Villegenis, but she says it is a few kilometers south of Paris, not far from Versailles to the west, while the wood of Verrière is to the north. There is no doubt that the Château de la Verrière is the place referred to, because it had belonged to Eugénie de Beauharnais.)

18 ◆ New York: "Pure" Music and the Dancer

[1]*Variety,* August 2, 1908.

[2]The *Sun,* August 21, 1908, "Isadora Duncan at the Criterion."

[3]The Mary Fanton Roberts papers in the Theatre and Music Collection at the Museum of the City of New York.

[4]The *Sun,* August 19, 1908, had written all too prophetically: "There is no doubt that she scored a most artistic success. Whether or not her engagement will draw crowds remains to be seen. . . . Theatrical managers usually provide pretty light entertainment for the summer season—something which doesn't require much intelligence to . . . follow. So when a thorough artist like Miss Duncan appears while the roof garden season is still on there is reason to suppose that perhaps she may fail to be appreciated."   [5]ML, pp. 216, 219.

[6]The *Sun,* January 1, 1909.   [7]The *Sun,* November 15, 1908.   [8]IARIAAL, p. 120.

[9]This seems to be inaccurate. *Musical America,* November 14, 1908, and *Musical Courier,* November 11, 1908, both say of this performance that she danced the second, third, and fourth movements, using the first as a prelude. *Musical America* even mentions her different costumes for each movement. Thus the symphony was played in its entirety.

[10]Basanta Koomar Roy, "What Music Means to the Interpretive Dancer: An Interview with the Duncan Dancers," *The Musical Courier,* 1923. Anna Duncan: "For the ideal mating of the dance with music, we need perfect freedom." Roy: "If you feel so cramped with the music of the great masters, how does Isadora feel about it?" Anna: "She feels the need of a new music even more."

[11]The (Rochester?) *Post*—a word is missing. The day and month are not given, but the year is marked 1908. DC, clipping.

[12]See Harold Bauer, p. 278.   [13]November 19, 1909.

[14]In *The Art of the Theatre,* he excuses the stage designer for making scenery for *Hamlet* on the grounds that the play will be presented on stage—even if it is better left unperformed, and "the duty of the interpreters is to put their best work at its service."   [15]TRI, p. 119.   [16]IARIAAL, p. 170.

[17]Carl Van Vechten, however, would later protest that Isadora had included the chorus of priestesses from *Iphigenia in Taurus.* (*The New York Times,* November 10, 1909; reprinted in ID, p. 19.)

19 ♦ Singer, Stanislavski, and Craig

[1]February 21, 1909.

[2]With Elias Howe. See John Kobler, "Mr. Singer's Money Machine," *The Saturday Evening Post,* July 7, 1951. There had been previous inventors of the sewing machine, among them Charles Weisenthal (1775), Thomas Saint (1790), Barthélémy Thimmonier (two machines—one in 1830, one in 1851), and Walter Hunt (1834). These models lacked the inexpensiveness and convenience of the Singer model. (Ruth Brandon: *A Capitalist Romance: Singer and the Sewing Machine,* Lippincott, Philadelphia, 1977, Chap. 5.)   [3]IARIAAL, p. 125.

[4]John Kobler, "Mr. Singer's Money Machine," *The Saturday Evening Post,* July 7, 1951, p. 59.

[5]John Kobler, "Mr. Singer's Money Machine," *The Saturday Evening Post,* July 14, 1951, p. 22.   [6]Ibid., p. 59.

[7]Ruth Brandon: *A Capitalist Romance: Singer and the Sewing Machine,* Lippincott, 1977, p. 143. (Kobler gives Isabella's age as twenty-one.)

[8]John Kobler, "Mr. Singer's Money Machine," p. 22.

[9]Mrs. Augustin Duncan was my informant. She believed that Singer's architectural experience had been limited to buildings built for him; in short, he was a patron, not a practicing architect.

[10]DD, pp. 101–105.   [11]DD, pp. 141–144.   [12]ML, p. 233.

[13]TRI, p. 146. Victor Seroff believes that, if Singer told Isadora this, it was an excuse; it was completely likely that he would have been welcomed in czarist Russia.

[14]ML, p. 235.   [15]DC, Craig's notebook.

[16]UTA-CA, *Book Topsy,* for an account, in Craig's words, of this incident.

[17]*Musical America,* August 14, 1909.   [18]IARIAAL, p. 130.

[19]*Musical America,* October 2, 1909.   [20]ML, p. 241.

[21]*St. Louis Globe,* November 2, 1909.   [22]November 5, 1909.

[23]Carl Van Vechten, *The New York Times,* November 10, 1909, quoted in ID, p. 19.

[24]*Musical America,* November 20, 1909.   [25]November 17, 1909; ID, p. 20.

[26]ML, pp. 241–242.   [27]*Musical America,* December 11, 1909.

[28]ML, p. 242. They were divorced in 1913. (*New York Tribune,* August 28, 1913.)

[29]*Musical America,* December 18, 1909. See also DC, unidentified clipping dated December 12, 1909.

20 ◆ Life with "Lohengrin"

[1]The Mary Fanton Roberts papers in the Theatre and Music Collection of the Museum of the City of New York.

[2]They did so, the following year, and took the nearly 15-year-old Irma Duncan with them.

[3]Charles Coburn, the actor, and at that time, Isadora's agent. He later had a distinguished stage and screen career.

[4]Isadora and Pavlova were friends and admirers of one another's art. Isadora also admired the dancing of Kschessinskaya and Nijinsky.

[5]ML, pp. 244, 245.   [6]DC, photocopy of Patrick Duncan's birth certificate.

[7]Reprinted in *Der Berliner Tageblatt,* July 22, 1928.

[8]George S. Maurevert: *Art, Life and the Boulevard,* N. Chini, Nice, 1911, pp. 278–280.

[9]The Mary Fanton Roberts papers in the Theatre and Music Collection of the Museum of the City of New York.

[10]ML, pp. 247–248.   [11]ML, p. 248.   [12]ML, p. 250.   [13]ML, p. 251.

[14]Isadora tells us only that the musician was the composer of *The Mirror of Jesus.* Allan Ross Macdougall identifies him as André Capelet. Op. cit., p. 133.

[15]TRI, pp. 170–172.   [16]Arthur Farwell, in *Musical America,* February 25, 1911.

[17]Ibid.   [18]Ibid.

[19]She was assisted by the flutist Georges Barrère, a small chorus, and Florence Mulford, who, stationed in the wings, sang the arias from the opera.

[20]*Le Soleil,* January 18, 1917; also *Le Figaro,* January 18, 1917.

[21]Her schedule (incomplete):
    Boston, Feb. 23 [see *Musical America,* February 25, 1911]
    New York, Thursday, Mar. ? [see *Musical America,* March 11]
    Washington, March 8 [see the *Washington Post,* March 8]
    St. Louis, March 28 [see the *St. Louis Globe,* March 28]
    New York, March 31, Farewell Appearance [see the *New York World,* April 1]

[22]ML, p. 254.   [23]DC (Duncan Collection).

[24]ML, p. 25.   [25]IARIAAL, p. 134.

[26]See article by Louis Sue, "Isadora Duncan: Meteor of Genius," March 3, 1966, in an unidentified Paris newspaper [author's collection]. See also, YI, pp. 314–315, and IARIAAL, p. 135.   [27]ML, p. 273.

[28]Correspondence in the Donald Oenslager–Edward Gordon Craig Collection, the Beinicke Library, Yale University. Plainly, Craig was unfair when he wrote in his notebooks that Isadora never did anything for him, although she was always going to find him a rich backer. She did find him this opportunity, and it was at her urging that Stanislavski invited Craig to produce *Hamlet* at the Moscow Art Theatre. [29]YI, p. 316.

[30]This incident is described by Cleveland Amory in *The Last Resorts,* Harper and Brothers, New York, 1952, p. 354.   [31]ML, pp. 237–238, 244–245.

[32]Paul Poiret, in his autobiography, *King of Fashion,* Lippincott, Philadelphia, 1931, pp. 205–207, remarks that Isadora had already angered Singer by seating Poiret next to her at dinner. Offended, Singer had left the party, and, when he returned, he was told that Isadora had gone to her room to rest. He went to her bedroom and found her, as Poiret says, "in close conversation with M. Henri Bataille." The journalist Paul Pierre Rignaux, in a highly colored account in the *New York American* (datelined Paris, November 16, 1912), says that Bataille was kissing Isadora's foot. However, judging from the misspellings of guests' names and other inaccuracies, this may well be a journalistic invention.

[33]A. R. Macdougall, (IARIAAL, p. 135) attributes the dropping of the plans to build a theater for Isadora on the Champs Elysées to opposition by the Marquis de Dion and other prominent Parisians, who disapproved of the erection of a commercial building in a residential neighborhood. It is possible that Singer, wearied of all the arguments and expenses, was glad to have the opportunity to cancel the project.

[34]ML, p. 262. I have not been able to trace the Bataille letter.

21 ♦ Heartbreak

[1]DC, letter to George Maurevert, summer of 1913.

[2]She says that she improvised *La Marseillaise* in New York (ML, p. 316), but this is not accurate. She had actually composed the work for the benefit concert which she gave for "l'Armoire Lorraine" on April 9, 1915.

[3]DC, letter to George Maurevert.   [4]Letter in the collection of Louis Sue.

[5]DC, letter to George Maurevert.   [6]TUS, p. 50.

[7]The *New York World,* Paris, April 20, 1913.

[8]ML, p. 274. Louis Sue, in an interview with Liliane Ziegel in October 1966 [author's collection], says that he was the one who had to tell Isadora that her children were drowned. Isadora asked him only one question: "Is there any hope?" Sue, who had seen the bodies, answered, "No." Isadora then asked him to break the news as gently as possible to Paris Singer, who had heart trouble. The doctor put Singer under his care and Isadora did not see him until after the funeral. This belated account could, nonetheless, be correct. Isadora would not have liked to write that Singer was not with her in the hour of her bereavement. Macdougall says (p. 134)

that Augustin broke the news to his sister and that Singer hurried from his home to be at Isadora's side. Macdougall, however, was not a witness to these events. It is perhaps to be expected that accounts should differ as to what happened in the confusion and agony following the fruitless rescue attempt.

⁹TUS, pp. 56–57.   ¹⁰See Appendix, p. 447.   ¹¹TUS, p. 58.

¹²CD; quoted by Gordon Craig, in a letter to his mother, Ellen Terry.

¹³Anna Duncan was my informant. See also DD, Chap. 8.

¹⁴CD; letter from Edward Gordon Craig, Florence, Italy, May 13, 1913, to Isadora Duncan, Villa San Stefano, Corfu, Greece.

¹⁵GC, p. 248. Craig had not seen Elena for more than a year at the time of their reunion.

¹⁶DC.   ¹⁷*The New York Times,* April 29, 1913.

¹⁸CD 230. Such was the exchange between two magnanimous and noble women.

¹⁹She must have remembered the death of her father, his third wife, and their daughter in the waves off Falmouth. "Always fire and water and sudden fearful death."

²⁰CD 231.   ²¹ML, p. 278.

²²DC, letter to George Maurevert already quoted in fn. 1.

²³Collection of Louis Sue.   ²⁴ML, p. 279.

²⁵Interview with Liliane Ziegel, October 1966 [author's collection].

²⁶"Duncan Settlement at Santa Quaranta," The *New York Herald,* Paris, August 24, 1913.   ²⁷ML, p. 281.   ²⁸DC, clipping.   ²⁹ML, pp. 282–289.

³⁰Ibid., pp. 288–289.   ³¹Ibid., pp. 290–291.

³²ML, pp. 296–297. She told Louis Sue that the father of her third child did not know that she was pregnant. (Louis Sue, interviewed by Liliane Ziegel, October 1966.)

³³DC, copy of the letter to Lugné-Poë by Duse. (Gift of Allan Ross Macdougall.)

³⁴ML, p. 298.   ³⁵Ibid.   ³⁶ML, p. 299.

³⁷Told to me by Anna Duncan. Concerning the decision of Elizabeth to send Isadora the older girls, see also Irma Duncan, *Duncan Dancer,* pp. 143–144. (Dr. Max Merz, Elizabeth's collaborator, had opposed the girls' departure.)

³⁸ML, p. 303.

³⁹Mary Fanton Roberts, "Isadora the Dancer," *Denishawn Magazine,* Summer 1925.

⁴⁰Ibid.

⁴¹Calmette, editor of *Le Figaro,* was shot on March 16, 1914, by Mme. Joseph Caillaux, wife of the minister of finance, whose husband had been accused by Calmette of financial irregularities.

⁴²ML, p. 309.

22 ◆ Exodus

[1]ML, p. 310.   [2]DC, unidentified newspaper clipping, 1914.

[3]DC, unidentified newspaper clipping, 1914.   [4]IARIAAL, p. 149.

[5]*Musical Courier.*   [6]DC, address on her letter paper.

[7]Arnold Genthe: *As I Remember,* Reynal and Hitchcock, New York, 1936, p. 180.

[8]Mabel Dodge Luhan, "Isadora Duncan," in *Town and Country,* July 1936, p. 180.

[9]Ibid.

[10]Isadora Duncan's letters to the *New York Evening Sun,* quoted by Mary Fanton Roberts in "The Modern School," an article in the Mary Fanton Roberts Collection at the Museum of the City of New York.   [11]SPOAA, p. 44.

23 ◆ The Dionysion in New York

[1]Irma Duncan, in *Duncan Dancer,* p. 151, believed that the girls appeared with Isadora on a rainy November afternoon. I have been unable to find any record of such a performance. Both *The New York Times* and the *Musical Courier* say that Isadora returned to the United States on November 24, 1914. An unidentified clipping in the Duncan Collection says that the girls were to make their New York debut on December 3, "under the direction of the Symphonic Society of New York, and Miss Isadora Duncan."

[2]"Miss Duncan through the Herald sends $268 to War Sufferers."

[3]DC, program of January 12, 1915, at the Century Theatre.

[4]*In Memory of W. B. Yeats,* by W. H. Auden.

[5]These sources included poems by her friend Percy MacKaye and (later in the season) Edgar Allan Poe.

[6]The *Chicago Herald,* February 21, 1915.

[7]Sylvester Rawlings, in the *New York Evening World,* February 26, 1915.

[8]Arnold Genthe: *As I Remember,* Reynal and Hitchcock, New York, 1936.

[9]*New York Evening Mail,* March 3, 1915.   [10]DC, unidentified clipping.

[11]Just how revolutionary this setting was has been recalled by Mary Fanton Roberts, in "Isadora the Dancer," *Denishawn Magazine,* Summer 1925.

> We . . . owe to her, in collaboration with Gordon Craig, our simple modern stage draping. I do not know of any person who ever used one-tone curtains as a background for dancing or drama before Isadora's time . . . the scenery for this play [*Oedipus Rex,* another Duncan production at the Century] consisted of four wide high flights of steps that could be moved and grouped at will and hundreds of yards of blue cheesecloth falling in full folds from the top of the stage to the floor. . . . I have every reason to believe that the idea was her own.

[12]*New York Evening Mail,* DC, undated clipping.

[13]Arnold Genthe: *As I Remember,* Reynal and Hitchcock, New York, 1936, p. 181.

[14]*New York Star,* May 5, 1915; also DC, unidentified newspaper clipping dated April 24, 1915.

[15]Genthe, op. cit., p. 181.   [16]In an interview with the author.

[17]In *Duncan Dancer,* Irma Duncan insists (pp. 167 and 189) that Isadora and George Copeland met for the first time in Venice in August 1920 when Isadora's pupils introduced her to him, the girls having previously toured with him in America in 1918–19. But Irma has forgotten that Isadora had appeared with Copeland at the Century Opera House in March 1915, as the programs make clear.

[18]Maurice Dumesnil: *An Amazing Journey,* Washburn, New York, 1932, p. 287 reports a similar instance of Isadora's dancing after having "rehearsed" only by listening to Dumesnil's playing.

[19]George Copeland, in conversation with the author. Copeland, like Isadora, was a raconteur, so caution should be used in accepting every detail of his stories.

[20]*Musical Concert,* March 6, 1915.

[21]*Toledo Blade,* May 7, 1915; also DC, an article in the *New York Tribune,* May 7, 1915.

[22]DC, unidentified newspaper clipping. (It says that she sailed May 8, but *The Dramatic Mirror*'s date of May 6 is probably correct.)

[23]IARIAAL, p. 153.   [24]ML, p. 318.

[25]*The Dramatic Mirror,* May 26, 1915.   [26]ML, p. 318; TUS, p. 68.

[27]TUS, p. 70. Anna Duncan has confirmed the main points of Mary Desti's account. It also is substantiated by a telegram from Isadora to Augustin: "Toye Turned Traitor!" now in the Duncan Collection, DC.

24 • A Call to Arms: The *Marseillaise*

[1]October 23, 1915.

[2]Letter dated December 5, 1915, in the Mary Fanton Roberts Collection of the Museum of the City of New York.

[3]AAJ, p. 22.   [4]AAJ, p. 28.   [5]AAJ, p. 33.

[6]Jacques Barzun: *The Energies of Art,* Harper, New York, 1956, p. 6.

[7]DC, Georges Denis to Isadora, Easter 1916.

[8]See the comparable letter from John Cowper Powys, Appendix, p. 447. In any kind of trouble, people instinctively turned to Isadora.

[9]DC; the poem referred to is missing.

[10]According to Dumesnil, there were about thirteen girls in the junior school besides her older pupils (AAJ, p. 33).   [11]AAJ, p. 26.   [12]ML, p. 310.

[13]F. Divoire: *Exhortation à la Victoire,* written June 24, 1914, Jouve & Cie, Paris, 1916. "The main character bears a name known to all. I felt that in its grandeur, its eternal Promethean symbol, the subject is equal in value to the royal dramas of antiquity." (Divoire's note.)   [14]ID, pp. 30–31.

[15]A nickname given to Isadora by several of her friends, in contrast to the name "Little Ones" which was used for her six oldest pupils. Both the Divoire note and the newspaper article are in the Duncan Collection, DC.

[16]AAJ, p. 46.   [17]Ibid., p. 47.

[18]Mary Fanton Roberts, "Isadora the Dancer," *Denishawn Magazine,* Summer 1925.

[19]AAJ, pp. 49–51.

25 ◆ South America

[1]IARIAAL, p. 161.   [2]ML, p. 324.   [3]AAJ, pp. 66–67.

[4]AAJ, pp. 79, 94; IARIAAL, pp. 161–162.

[5]AAJ, p. 109.   [6]Ibid., pp. 134–135.   [7]Ibid., p. 148.

[8]It is jarring to hear Isadora insult anyone with a racial epithet. That this angry remark does not represent her complete—or considered—thoughts on the subject of race is shown by her hope of founding a school of dance for the natives in North Africa. See p. 283.

[9]AAJ, pp. 170, 180.   [10]Ibid., p. 199.   [11]Ibid., p. 192.

[12]Penelope Sikelianos Duncan, Sanatorium Schatzalp, Davos, July 24, 1916, to Maurice Magnus in Rome. Letter in the Duncan Collection, DC.

[13]AAJ, p. 243.   [14]Ibid., p. 249.   [15]Ibid., p. 269.

[16]Ibid., p. 273.   [17]Ibid., p. 287.   [18]ML, p. 316.

[19]TAOTD, p. 79.

[20]See her letter to George Maurevert, quoted on p. 218.   [21]AAJ, p. 302.

26 ◆ Break with Lohengrin

[1]IARIAAL, p. 166.   [2]ML, p. 328.   [3]Ibid.

[4]Arnold Genthe: *As I Remember,* Reynal and Hitchcock, New York, 1936, p. 182.

[5]Ibid. Anna Duncan, also a guest, said that the young man was her admirer Billy Hamilton.

[6]Isadora, speaking on the tango to George Seldes, quoted in *What Love Meant to Isadora Duncan.* Isadora disliked many of the then current hip-shaking ballroom dances such as the Charleston and the Black Bottom. "Not because of their indecency but because of their indecent sterility"—the dancers had not the faintest idea of what the movements of their body conveyed. TAOTD, p. 125.

[7]The musician Sacha Votichenko told me of this mannerism.

[8]Genthe, op. cit., p. 183.

[9]Mary Fanton Roberts, from a speech delivered to the Mills School. Mary Fanton Roberts Collection in the Theatre Collection of the Museum of the City of New York.   [10]*New York Sun,* March 7, 1917.

[11]During this engagement, two events of world importance occurred which added

to the fervor of Isadora's audiences. These were the abdication of the czar on March 15, 1917, and the entry of the United States into the war on April 6, 1917. Isadora and her sister-in-law, Margherita Duncan, drove down to Washington to hear the declaration of war, and it was while she was there that the choreography of a dance began to take place in her mind. She worked at white heat, and, before the season had ended, she had added the *Marche Slave* to the great heroic dances in her repertoire.

[12]April, 1917. A copy of this letter was given to me by David Weiss, whose novel, *The Spirit and the Flesh,* Doubleday, New York, 1959, was suggested by the life of Isadora. [13]IARIAAL, p. 169.

[14]Alva Johnson, "Addison Mizener, the Palm Beach Architect," *New Yorker,* November 29, 1952. [15]Genthe, op. cit., p. 186.

[16]Sewell Stokes: *Isadora Duncan: An Intimate Portrait,* Brentano, London, 1928, p. 152. Sometimes, of course, she did bore him. See Appendix, pp. 447–448.

[17]See his plan for his medical institute, in his obituaries in *The New York Times* and *New York Herald Tribune,* June 25, 1932.

[18]John Kobler, "Mr. Singer's Money Machine," *Saturday Evening Post,* July 14, 1951.

[19]ML, p. 246.

[20]For more about Isadora's attitude toward accepting money from him, see Appendix, pp. 447–448. [21]ML, p. 237.

[22]See his obituary, *The New York Times,* June 25, 1932. [23]IARIAAL, pp. 24–25.

[24]Harold Bauer: *Harold Bauer: His Book,* Norton, New York, 1948, pp. 70–71.

[25]If they took time to discuss the war, Isadora must have discovered with pleasure that, like her, he remained an internationalist despite pro-Allied sympathies. He had been outraged by the Red Cross official who had said to him, "You would hardly expect us to take care of the *enemy* wounded, would you?" (*Harold Bauer: His Book,* Norton, New York, 1948, p. 231.) [26]ML, p. 338.

[27]Harold Bauer: *Harold Bauer: His Book,* Norton, New York, 1948, p. 71.

[28]IARIAAL, p. 171. See also Lois Rather: *Lovely Isadora,* The Rather Press, Oakland, California, 1976, p. 82.

[29]*The Musical Courier,* January 17, 1918. [30]DC, Ms. by Isadora.

[31]She later told her friend Isaac Don Levine that Bauer had been one of the four great loves of her life. [32]ML, pp. 338–339.

[33]ML, p. 338. According to Victor Seroff (TRI, p. 242), Mrs. Bauer had threatened a scandal.

[34]Quoted by Lois Rather, op. cit., p. 84.

27 • Encounter with an Archangel

[1]ML, pp. 345–346.

[2]Mme. Mario Meunier (sister of Christine Dalliès) interviewed by Liliane Ziegel.

[3]*Grove's Dictionary of Music and Musicians,* vol. VII, 1955.

⁴This incident was told to me by Votichenko.

⁵Reprinted in TAOTD, p. 107.   ⁶IARIAAL, p. 174.

⁷Ibid., p. 172. The same dances were sometimes presented as *Belgium Tragic, Belgium Heroic, Belgium Langorous and Gay.* See IARIAAL, p. 174.   ⁸Ibid., p. 175.

⁹They were still there in mid-November 1919, as a letter from Vera Tchaikovsky, dated November 17, 1919, requesting their aid for a Russian relief benefit concert, makes clear. (DC)

¹⁰Author's collection.   ¹¹IARIAAL, p. 175.

¹²Preserved in the Bibliothèque de l'Opéra in Paris.

¹³One of the six, Maria-Theresa (Mrs. Stephan Bourgeois), is my informant on this point. See also DD, p. 185.

¹⁴Actually 1903. See the article in *Musical America,* January 26, 1904, which says that Isadora is dancing at the Thalia Theatre in Berlin after five months spent in Greece.

¹⁵ML, p. 355.

¹⁶Anna Duncan told me this incident, and it is borne out by a letter from Anna written in 1920 to Mary Fanton Roberts, now in the Mary Fanton Roberts Collection at the Museum of the City of New York.

¹⁷In *Isadora Duncan: Her Life, Her Art, Her Legacy* (p. 6), Walter Terry, following Irma Duncan, gives a different explanation for this phrase and note. Irma believed that Isadora had written it in answer to a question asked by Arnold Genthe at his studio: "Who are the Gods of today?" Isadora, according to Irma, handed Genthe the paper, saying "Here is your answer." But if Irma is right, this does not explain why the note turned up in Isadora's papers, not Genthe's, nor why she found it necessary to write when she was in Genthe's presence.

¹⁸*Le Soir,* Brussels, May 2, 1921.

¹⁹See the enthusiastic review by Ernest Newman in *The Sunday Times,* April 17, 1921. See also the review in *The London Telegraph,* April 13, 1921.

²⁰*The Globe,* Boston, May 29, 1921.

²¹Erica had already left several months before, in order to study painting with Wienold Reiss. (Reiss had previously painted portraits of the six girls for the fashionable Crillon Restaurant in New York.)

²²Wife of musician Sacha Votichenko [author's collection].

²³That Anna had behaved with as much restraint as was possible under the difficult circumstances is suggested by the fact that Augustin Duncan remained her friend.

²⁴IDRD, pp. 7–8.   ²⁵*L'Avenir,* May 26, 1921.   ²⁶ID, *The New Isadora,* p. 31.

²⁷IDRD, pp. 12–13.   ²⁸IDRD, p. 13.

²⁹Isadora Duncan: *The Dance of the Future,* Eugen Diederichs, Leipzig, 1903; reprinted in TAOTD.

28 ✦ To Revolutionary Russia

[1]IDRD, p. 18.

[2]See the article "Duncan Revelation: GBS Tells More Life Secrets," *Daily Express,* Toronto, March 6, 1930. Also note to Joseph Kaye in the April 1929 *Dance Magazine* from Shaw's secretary: "Mr. Bernard Shaw desires me to say that the story is true, but the lady was not Isadora Duncan."

[3]Interview with Shaw by W. G. Bishop, *The New York Times,* November 24, 1931. Reprinted in *Shaw on Theatre,* Hill and Wang, New York, 1958, p. 207.

[4]Anna Duncan was my informant.   [5]IDRD, pp. 18–36.

[6]"The Last Chapters of Isadora Duncan's Life," *The Dance Magazine,* May 1929.

[7]IDRD, p. 47.   [8]Ibid., p. 55.

[9]IDTRY, p. 43. See also I. I. Schneider, "Isadora Duncan," *Moscow Today,* translated by Peter Golden, 1961.

[10]I. I. Schneider, "Isadora Duncan," *Moscow Today,* translated by Peter Golden, 1961. See also IDTRY, pp. 47–48.

[11]IDRD, p. 73.   [12]Ibid.   [13]IDTRY, p. 54.

[14]IDRD, p. 79.   [15]Ibid.   [16]Ibid., pp. 91–93.

[17]IDTRY, p. 74.   [18]IDRD, p. 96.   [19]IDRD, pp. 97–98.

[20]The typescript of this article, with corrections in Isadora's hand, has been preserved in the Duncan Collection (DC).

[21]Needless to say, this remark outraged those in ballet circles. The Soviet dance historian, Natalia Roslavleva, by no means unsympathetic to Duncan, comments in *Dance Perspectives* 64, Winter 1975, p. 47: "And she said this of the Bolshoi, which has produced male dancers that were the personification of manliness."

[22]Mariengof, *A Novel Without Lies,* quoted in IDTRY, p. 88. Schneider, who brought her to Yakulov's party, says that this is the only truthful episode in the novel (IDTRY, p. 56). For another account of her first meeting with Esenin, see Appendix, p. 448.

29 ✦ Sergei Esenin

[1]Russian calendar dates; on the western calendar he was born October 4, 1895. *Pamyatka O Sergee Esenin,* Segodnia, Moskva, 1926.

[2]SESVESO.   [3]EAL, pp. 48–49.

[4]Sergei Esenin, *About Myself.* In his second autobiographical sketch (he wrote three), he says he went to St. Petersburg at age nineteen. *Pamyatka O Sergee Esenin,* Segodnia, Moskva, 1926.

[5]Riurik Ivnev, "About Esenin," from SAEM.

[6]She subsequently became "the celebrated actress-wife of Meyerhold," SESVESO.

[7]Ibid.   [8]Ivnev, SAEM.

[9]I. I. Schneider, in *Moscow Today,* 1961.   [10]IDRD, pp. 107–109.

[11]Ivnev, SAEM.   [12]M. Babenchikov, SAEM.

[13]Simon Karlinsky, professor of Slavic languages and literature at the University of California, Berkeley, in a letter of August 31, 1976, to Dr. Gordon McVay, author of *Esenin: A Life,* Ardis, Ann Arbor, Michigan, 1976.

[14]Ivan Startsev, SAEM.   [15]Ibid.

[16]Valentin Volpin, SAEM. (A female relative of Volpin, Nadezhda Volpina, had a son by Sergei. He is Esenin-Volpin, a well-known mathematician and poet, who has been in and out of Soviet prisons as a political dissident.)

[17]Ivan Gruzinov, SAEM.

[18]Letter to Genia X, Summer 1920, quoted SE, p. 44.   [19]IDRD, pp. 97–98.

[20]Letter quoted by I. I. Schneider, "Isadora Duncan," in *Moscow Today,* translated by Peter Golden. It was not only at Pretchistenka that he had allowed his work to be interrupted by friends. He had complained of this before he knew Isadora, according to Michael Murachev, SAEM.

[21]Mariengof, *A Novel Without Lies,* quoted IDRD, pp. 114–115.

[22]EAL, pp. 200–201.   [23]TRI, p. 307.

[24]Georgi Ustinov, SAEM.

[25]IDTRY, p. 100. See also, I. I. Schneider, "Isadora Duncan," in *Moscow Today.*

[26]IDRD, pp. 126–127.

30 ♦ To Western Europe with Esenin

[1]IDRD, pp. 131–133.   [2]TRI, pp. 314–315.

[3]Translated by Gordon McVay, IAE, p. 66.   [4]Gorky, quoted SESVESO, p. 36.

[5]Esenin, quoted SESVESO, p. 38.   [6]N. Poletaev, SAEM.

[7]IDTRY, p. 110; TRI, p. 312.   [8]IDRD, pp. 134–136.

[9]TIMA, p. 230.   [10]Ibid., p. 244.   [11]Ibid., p. 245.   [12]Ibid., p. 246.

[13]Ibid., p. 249.   [14]Ibid., pp. 251–252.   [15]Ibid., pp. 253–254.

[16]TAOTD, p. 141.   [17]IDRD, pp. 137–138.

[18]IDTRY, p. 117. Schneider says that it would have cost too much for the children to travel to the United States, since the trip's purpose was to raise money for the school.

[19]Votichenko, in a statement to the author.

[20]IDRD, pp. 141–143.

31 ♦ Esenin in New York

[1]*Musical America,* October 7, 1922.   [2]*New York Globe,* October 2, 1922.

[3]IDRD, pp. 146–149.

[4]*The Philadelphia Inquirer,* October 2, 1922. See also the *New York Evening Journal,* October 4, 1922.

⁵S. Esenin, "Iron Mirgorod," *Izvestia,* August 22 (September 16—western calendar), 1923. Mirgorod was Gogol's name for an imaginary complacent provincial town in one of his satires.   ⁶IARIAAL, p. 215.

⁷"What Isadora Meant When She Shocked the Staid Folks of Boston"—clipping in Isadora's scrapbook, DC. See also IDRD, pp. 152–153.

⁸IDRD, pp. 152–153.

⁹Quoted by Robert Henri in a letter to Mary Fanton Roberts, November 25, 1922. Letter in the Mary Fanton Roberts Collection, The Theatre Collection of the Museum of the City of New York.

¹⁰"Ready to Deport Her if Guilty," *The Boston American,* October 24, 1922.

¹¹IDRD, pp. 155–157.   ¹²IDRD, p. 159.

¹³John Sloan to Robert Henri, quoted by Robert Henri in a letter of November 25, 1922, to Mary Fanton Roberts, Mary Fanton Roberts Collection, Museum of the City of New York.

¹⁴Veniamin Levin, "Esenin in America," *Novoye Russkoye Slovo,* August 12, 1953.

¹⁵Ibid., August 9 (August 13, western calendar), 1953.

¹⁶Avram Yarmolinsky, "Esenin in New York," *Novyi Zhurnal,* 1957, book 51.

¹⁷*Louisville Courier,* November 25, 1922.

¹⁸Joseph Kaye, "The Last Chapters of Isadora's Life," *The Dance Magazine,* June 1929.

¹⁹SE.   ²⁰Joseph Kaye, "Last Chapters," op. cit., June 1929.

²¹*The New York Times Book Review,* May 9, 1976. For a more complete discussion of this important subject, see Appendix, pp. 448–449.

²²Joseph Kaye, op. cit.   ²³DD, p. 200.   ²⁴TRI, p. 411.

²⁵It is, however, Seroff who suggests (TRI, pp. 402–403) that Isadora might have had too much to drink on that night in Nice when she walked into the sea in a suicide attempt. See p. 390.

²⁶YI, p. 273.   ²⁷*Dancemagazine,* January 1978.

²⁸IARIAAL, p. 220.   ²⁹Joseph Kaye, op. cit.

³⁰IARIAAL, p. 220.   ³¹IDRD, p. 165.

³²*The Dance Magazine,* June 1929.

³³Julia McCarthy, *New York Evening Journal,* October 4, 1922.

³⁴AAJ, p. 268.   ³⁵Ibid., p. 178.   ³⁶IDRD, pp. 166–167.

32 ◆ Return to Russia

¹TUS, p. 120.   ²Ibid., p. 121.

³Ibid., pp. 122–123.   ⁴Ibid., pp. 147–148.

⁵Ibid. Concerning Mary, Victor Seroff remarks (TRI, pp. 333–335), "Mary Desti was the least suited [of Isadora's friends] for the role of confidante to the couple.

The very sight of this . . . middle aged woman repelled Esenin . . . her role of policeman only incited him to an almost routine violence."

[6]According to Irma Duncan, in 1922, when Isadora and Esenin had first arrived in
Berlin, Sergei, on finding Isadora weeping over the photographs of her dead children,
had in a rage flung the album into the fire. (IDRD, p. 135.) Irma, however, was
not in Berlin. Did she hear this account from Isadora or Mary Desti?

[7]TUS, p. 143.

[8]DC. An early draft of her memoirs, written in Moscow, around 1924. (Quoted in
IDRD, pp. 229–233.)

[9]IDRD, pp. 181, 185.   [10]Ibid., pp. 182–185.   [11]IDTRY, p. 146.

[12]IDRD, pp. 198–205. See also IDTRY, pp. 153–156. He says that the president of
the Kislavodsk Executive Committee called on them to offer his apologies. Schneider
does not mention Trotsky.   [13]IDTRY, p. 161.

[14]Ibid. I. I. Schneider gives the text of a different note:

Dear Isadora,
    I am very busy with publishing matters and cannot come. I often remember
you with all my gratitude to you. From Prechistenka I moved first to Kolobova
and now I have moved again to another apartment which Marienhof and I are
buying.
    My affairs are excellent
    I never expected a great deal
    I am given a lot of money for my publishing business.
    I wish you success and health and less drinking.
    Regard to Ilya Ilyich.
    Love, S. Esenin
    29. VIII. Moscow

But it is plain that this must be an earlier letter because, Schneider says, "In
the letter, Esenin . . . concluded by promising to go to the Crimea if Isadora
went there. . . . The word 'Crimea' [actually 'Yalta'] stuck in her [Isadora's]
mind, and emerged unexpectedly, introducing a sudden change in our itinerary."
Since there is no mention of the Crimea, or any Crimean town, in the note of
29. VIII, the note received on the train must have been the message about Yalta.
In his earlier version of this incident in *Moscow Today,* Schneider does not quote
the text of the letter, but he again states that in it Esenin promised to go to
the Crimea if Isadora would be there.

[15]Note in the Duncan Collection (DC).

[16]Years later, on seeing the faint imprint of Isadora's mouth, and already knowing
what Esenin's next message to his wife would say, the author found that her hands
were shaking.   [17]IDRD, pp. 216–219.

[18]Isadora had canceled her concerts at Novorossysk and Krasnodar in order to meet
Esenin in Yalta. IDTRY, p. 170.   [19]IDRD, p. 224. See also IDTRY, p. 171.

[20]Russian text of Isadora's telegram translated by Gordon McVay, IAE, pp. 215, 298,

fn. 54. Photocopies of this and Esenin's subsequent telegram (and its rough drafts), preserved in the Institute of World Literature, are reproduced in McVay's book.

[21] In love with Esenin, Galina Benislavskaya selflessly took care of his literary business with publishers, even though she knew that he did not return her love. He had written to her bluntly, "Dear Galya! You are close to me as a friend, but I do not love you one jot as a woman." Later, on March 21, 1925, he wrote to Mariengof (quoted EAB, p. 186), "Dear Anatoly! Galya is my wife." Their affair was short, and, according to Sophia Vinogradskaya (EAB, p. 188), his estrangement from Galya impelled him to marry Sophia Tolstoy, the granddaughter of Leo Tolstoy. A year after Esenin's suicide, Galya killed herself on his grave.

[22] IAE, pp. 215–216; p. 298, ffn. 56, 57.   [23] IDTRY, p. 173.

[24] IDRD, pp. 226–227; IDTRY, p. 183. Schneider says that Esenin came to Pretchistenka a few times after that without disclosing where he was living, but presently his visits stopped.

[25] Veniamin Levin, "Esenin in America," *Novoye Russkoye Slavo,* August 9, 10, 11, 12, and 13, 1953.   [26] IDTRY, pp. 75–76.

[27] TRI, pp. 302–303. Neither Schneider nor Irma says anything about Esenin's presence at this concert.

[28] SAEM   [29] IDTRY, p. 175.   [30] EAL.   [31] IAE.

[32] Letter from Simon Karlinsky to Gordon McVay, August 31, 1976.

[33] Anna Nikritina, "Esenin and Marienhof," in *Esenin i sovremennost* [*Esenin and Our Time*], Moscow, 1975, pp. 382–383, brought to my attention by Simon Karlinsky.

[34] Letter from Anna Nikritina to Gordon McVay, December 1, 1976, quoted in IAE, pp. 58, 268.

[35] IAE, pp. 31, 257–259. Other evidence subject to varying interpretations includes a letter from a man who states, "To tell you the truth, he [Esenin] made me the gift of his love."   [36] IDRD, p. 228.

[37] Ibid., p. 243.   [38] Ibid., p. 240.

[39] Letters of January 15 and January 20, 1924, from Isadora to Maître Thorel, DC.

[40] Constance Drexel of Philadelphia. The letter, dated December 14, was reproduced in the *Washington Post,* January 27, 1924.

[41] IDRD.   [42] IARIAAL.   [43] These letters are now in DC.

[44] Mark Meichik, according to McVay, IAE, p. 224.   [45] Letter to Irma from Orenburg, June 24, 1924.

[46] Letter to Irma from Tashkent, July 10, 1924.   [47] IDRD, p. 258.

33 ♦ The Invisible Banner

[1]IDRD, p. 263.   [2]*Gringoire,* Paris, 1929. Month not given. DC.   [3]Margaret Lloyd: *The Borzoi Book of Modern Dance,* Knopf, New York, 1949, p. 6.

[4]Ibid., pp. 120–121.

[5]Michel Fokine: *Memoirs of a Ballet Master,* Little, Brown and Co., Boston, 1961, pp. 155–156.   [6]May 4, 1981.

[7]His italics. Fokine, *Memoirs,* op. cit., p. 256. The passage, which also takes appreciative note of the contributions of Ruth St. Denis and Loie Fuller, has been reprinted more fully in the Appendix. Fokine adds a word of caution about the virtues of simple movements. (See Appendix p. 450.)

[8]I. I. Schneider, "Isadora Duncan," in *Moscow Today.*

[9]André Levinson, "The Apogee of Isadora Duncan," in *Comoedia,* Paris, September 14, 1928.

[10]This is no accident. Isadora studied the masters of the Renaissance as carefully as she did the Greeks. Yet her movements, for all their classic familiarity, are constantly illuminated by unexpected touches of her own, such as the "expression of frightened, almost uncomprehending joy" (in Carl Van Vechten's phrase) at the end of the *Marche Slave.*

[11]Noel Carroll, in his criticism of "Dancers for Isadora," *Dancemagazine,* May 1981, notes: "It is one thing to reconstruct dances from the past and another to make new dances in their image." His point is that Isadora's simplicity was a revolt against a particular dance establishment, that we understand her dances in their historical context, but that new dances imitating her manner look childish. Nonetheless, he believes that broad aspects of her style—her commitment to the natural, and the unity of the physical and the spiritual—can still inspire contemporary dancers.

[12]Isadora's long, continuous movement reappears in the work of more recent choreographers, such as Graham, Humphrey, and Limon, to name but a few, and is one of the chief delights of such a post-Duncan, post-Fokine ballet as Ashton's *Ondine.* Ashton, by the way, said he was influenced by Isadora. See Walter Terry: *Isadora Duncan: Her Life, Her Art, Her Legacy,* New York, Dodd, Mead, 1963, p. 152.

[13]*Berlioz and the Romantic Century,* vol. I, Atlantic, Little, Brown, Boston, 1950, p. 76.

[14]As we have seen, one of her dreams was to dance Beethoven's *Ninth Symphony* with a vast chorus of dancers. After her death, at the request of Walter Damrosch, Irma Duncan composed choreography for the last movement of the Ninth, which the conductor and Irma presented jointly with full orchestra and about fifty dancers. (Interview with Irma Duncan by Suzanne E. Noble in *The Chatham Courier,* August 16, 1962.)

[15]They were also seen and noted in Europe. Irma Duncan, in a conversation with the author, expressed the opinion that the composing of art dances to folk and revolutionary songs, later employed so successfully by the Moiseyev and other companies, dates from the Russian tours made by the pupils of the Moscow Duncan School.

34 ◆ Farewell to Russia

[1]IAE, pp. 223–224, 229, fn. 14.   [2]IDRD, pp. 265–266.

[3]Ibid. See also Appendix, p. 450.

[4]Her notes about the meaning of this music appear in IDRD, pp. 226–228.

[5]IDRD, p. 268; IAE, pp. 224 and 299, fn. 14.

[6]IAE, pp. 224 and 299, ffn. 14 and 17. McVay points out that there were eight performances, not four, as a reading of IDRD, pp. 265–276, might lead one to assume, but each of the programs was performed twice, which accounts for the possible misconception. McVay also states that the eighth performance took place on *Sunday,* September 28, not *Saturday* as Irma has it (p. 276).

[7]This speech, which contains some interesting sidelights on her life and her teaching philosophy, has been preserved in IDRD (pp. 269–276). Isadora was older than four when she began to appear regularly in public, but I have not been able to determine the age at which she made her first professional appearance. Her accounts vary, as do those of her brothers.   [8]IDRD, pp. 276–278.

35 ◆ Stranded in Berlin

[1]DC, quoted in IDRD, pp. 285–286.

[2]IDRD, p. 289. Mary Desti, TUS, p. 177, says that Max Merz, superintendent of the school, turned Isadora away. As Mary was not in Berlin at the time, she may have heard this from Isadora.   [3]TUS, p. 178.

[4]From a manuscript by Bernardine Szold Fritz, in her possession. (I have a copy.)

[5]DC, undated letter to Irma Duncan, reprinted in IDRD, pp. 283–285. Macdougall has dated it "end of September 1926," but from Isadora's reference to her concert at the Blüthner Saal, it must have been written at the beginning of October 1926.

[6]DC; IDRD, p. 288–289. Letter of November 27, 1924. The Central Hotel, on whose paper Isadora wrote this letter, must have been a dreadful place to which to owe money. It had printed on the bottom of its stationery, apparently as an ordinary precaution, "Absender is nicht das Central-Hotel." [The Sender is not the Central Hotel.] What suspicious people! The routine use of this phrase on stationery also suggests the financial demoralization then prevalent in Germany which prompted such precautions.

[7]The fact that she had divided receipts from her wartime relief concerts between the French and German Red Cross was forgotten.

[8]December 16, 1925, Central Hotel, Berlin

Dear Irma:

Why don't you answer my telegrams and letters? Since six weeks I am without any word from you, although I repeatedly sent *luftpost* letters and telegrams. I am frightfully anxious. Are you ill? Does the school still exist? I can obtain no passport here from the Russian Embassy. Please do whatever is necessary to obtain this passport for me, and also a divorce from Sergei Alexandrovitch— God bless him, but he's no good for a husband.

mother and sisters needed the money more (TUS, p. 180)—is "sheer fantasy," though he agrees that Isadora had written him that she would never have claimed Esenin's estate because it should go to his sisters and mother. The fantasy, then, relates to the amount of money in Esenin's estate. IDRD may be correct in saying that by November 24, 1926, when the Moscow Court ruled that Isadora as Esenin's widow was his legal heir, his estate had grown to 400,000 francs from "the royalties on the fantastic sale of his poetry all over Russia after his death." An article in *The New York Times,* September 4, 1926, headed "Bar Isadora Duncan as Esenin's Heir," estimated that Esenin left copyrights worth $10,000 or more. However much money Esenin left, the fact remains that Isadora refused his estate in favor of Esenin's mother and sisters at a time when she herself was in financial difficulties.

²⁶IDRD, p. 328.

²⁷Ibid., pp. 328–329. Macdougall, the young English writer Sewell Stokes, the caricaturist Gabriel Atkin, and Isadora's secretary Ruth Nickson, to whom she was dictating her memoirs, all were with Isadora when the hotel delivered its ultimatum. Stokes, though he does not mention the Negresco's eviction threat, nor the presence of Macdougall, gives some lively impressions of what was apparently the same evening in *Isadora Duncan: An Intimate Portrait,* Brentano, London, 1928, pp. 122–135.

²⁸The committee, which was soon expanded to include Gabriel Alphand, Antoine Bourdelle, Paul Boncour, Albert Besnard, Fernand Divoire, Georges Duhamel, Andre Messager, and Theodore Reinach, sponsored a benefit organized by Mme. Yorska on April 28, 1927, at the Salle Comoedia, at which a statue donated by Bourdelle was to be sold and eminent artists and writers would deliver tributes to Isadora. (Program: *Hommage à Isadora Duncan.* An original program is in the possession of Jeremiah Newton, who kindly supplied me with a copy.)

²⁹See Craig's account of writing to Singer, asking him to help Isadora financially, and Singer's reply, May 12, 1925. Craig also sent a generous sum to the committee to save her house but received no acknowledgment from her, though his name was published in the newspapers as a donor. (DC).

³⁰Concerning Divoire, Denis, and Clara, Mary Desti comments: "It was their deep love for Isadora which kept them away, as it did many others, seeing her ride to destruction." (TUS, p. 184.) ³¹TUS, p. 183. ³²TUS, p. 204.

³³Reprinted in TAOTD, pp. 114–115. When Isadora speaks of the exploitation of her work, she means touring for money, as she herself had had to tour, to raise funds for the Moscow School. And in fact, it had been risky to take the school to China at a time of civil war there. ³⁴DD, pp. 283, 310.

³⁵He was born in 1902. See TWIMC, p. 3. ³⁶DD, pp. 311–312.

³⁷Mary Desti believed that the Chinese trip had left Isadora suspicious of Irma. (TUS, p. 207.)

³⁸The account of this trip (Desti, TUS, pp. 232–239) makes painful reading. It shows how greatly Isadora's native disposition—which, in 1903, her old friend Kathleen Bruce described (SPOAA, p. 44) as being "Open-handed, sweet tempered, pliable

and easy-going . . . [she] was a simple-living, hard working artist"—had been affected by her prolonged disappointments and sorrows.

³⁹TUS, pp. 253–254.

⁴⁰ML, p. 328.   ⁴¹TRI, p. 428.

⁴²In the Mary Fanton Roberts Collection of the Museum of the City of New York. The letter is signed "Mac," not "Dougie," Macdougall's usual nickname; however, that it is by him is made clear by references to two articles which he was writing for Mary Fanton Roberts's magazine, *Arts and Decoration*.

⁴³*Daily Mirror*, New York, Wednesday, September 14, 1927. On the front page, with the heading, "TO WED AGAIN," a picture of Isadora accompanied an item reading, "A cable yesterday announced the forthcoming marriage of Isadora Duncan . . . to Robert Winthrop Chandler."   ⁴⁴TRI, p. 431.

⁴⁵"Danses d'Isadora," *Découvertes Sur la Danse*, Les Editions G. Crès et Cie, Paris, 1924, p. 80 and p. 79 (with drawings by Bourdelle). I have placed the first paragraph last because it seems to sum up Isadora's life.

37 ◆ Isadora's Legacy

¹Walter Terry: *Isadora Duncan: Her Life, Her Art, Her Legacy,* Dodd, Mead, New York, 1964, p. 152.   ²Ibid., p. 159.

³Clive Barnes, "The Cold War in Modern Dance," *The New York Times Magazine,* July 28, 1968.   ⁴*The New York Times,* January 8, 1978.

⁵*The New York Times,* May 22, 1977.   ⁶*The New York Times,* November 14, 1976.

⁷*The New York Times,* January 8, 1978.   ⁸*New York Post,* January 6, 1978.

⁹See Merce Cunningham, Alwin Nikolais, Twyla Tharp, and Meredith Monk, among others.

¹⁰*The New York Times Magazine,* September 14, 1952, pp. 14, 15, 60, 61, 62.

¹¹Fernand Divoire: see p. 398.

Appendix

p. 94 (Chap. 11, fn. 11). I had written to Edward Gordon Craig on December 3, 1958:

> What I am wondering is whether Isadora might not have felt she was saying something essentially (though not literally) true when she depicts you as surprised at seeing her embody your ideas, dance before your curtains. "I invented you"— did you ever say anything like this at another time? Your view of the essential truth of that situation is that you would not have been rude enough to argue with her or even tire her out with conversation after she had just finished dancing, whereas her view of the essential truth of the situation may have been that you felt surprise and recognition at seeing that your ideas were independently held by her. . . . Do you think there is a possibility that Isadora could have written that doubtful passage?

He answered in a December 8, 1958, letter:

> 1st question: *"Isadora might have written that passage."* Well, she *might,* since we all do forget this and that often—but I very much doubt whether she forgot about our first meeting . . . Now for, "she depicts you (me) as surprised at seeing her embody your (my) ideas"—"dance before your (my) curtains"—I never saw her embody my "ideas" at any time—I never saw any of "my curtains" in Berlin. (They were brought out only a year or so *later in Paris*—a Mr. Magnus possibly thought it clever to have 20 feet high curtains (à la EGC) in place of

445

the 5 or 6 feet high bits used till then—(Magnus & Lugné Poë & others)—
Not I (me).

To explain a bit why and how

Although my tendency was always to design *tall* sceneries—& I used tall 20–
25 feet curtains in LONDON in *1900*—*1901*—& *1902* in 3 lovely musical pieces,
Dido & Aeneas, Acis & Galatea, The Masque of Love—I rather hugged these tall
scenes (& all my designs) to myself—never once suggested to Isadora that I-
I-I should push myself forward and exploit my particular peculiarities in the
scenic line in any way around her—Together we were (& by chance our work
was by nature) *akin*. Yes, but that was in our natures, in our hearts & life—
not in business—*not*, I felt, possible ever to be united—the *2 works*. Can't
explain here properly. (She sometimes did say in our 1000 talks that she and I
might . . . together . . . [These are his dots.] What? I merely remained silent
whenever that little talk began—Do you understand??) (I suppose I helped her
a bit. I hope so. She inspired me—not by her talk—just by the grace of
God—)
Now do you ask (how can you?) if I ever said to her "I invented you." That
or anything at all like that would have been & is impossible. You see I loved
her & it—what she did—*it* was recognizable by me as by all others as being
a thing of genius . . . The dear darling never gave two thoughts about all this
stuff & nonsense which people would push into her mouth to speak now she
is not here. She loved what I do—my ideas too, she didn't mind them—&
had no need (*no thought,* even) to take from each other anything but what the
heart gives.
I'm so glad to hear you are at work on a biography of her. Be careful dear,
be so careful & be bold.
If only I could write of her I would—but I have no command of verse—&
prose *from me to her* is not enough. What silly lives we 2 have lived—somehow—
but we never yet pulled down our flags—Hers was hers—mine is mine—&
I do believe we *both* gave to this damn grey world some LIGHT which will
never be put out.
Can't write more today—Am tired—but so happy to know of you . . .

p. 123 (Chap. 14, fn. 14). The American Maurice Magnus, Craig's and Isadora's
manager and secretary, was a promoter with much outward assurance who moved
in artistic and literary circles. At one time connected with the English language
newspaper, *The Roman Review,* Magnus lived beyond his means, and he left large bills
for his friends to settle. When his creditors would no longer wait, he committed
suicide. At his death, it was discovered that he was an illegitimate grandson of Kaiser
Friederich III. Magnus's posthumous *Memoirs of the Foreign Legion,* published in 1925
with an introduction by D. H. Lawrence, precipitated a feud between Lawrence and
Norman Douglas, author of *South Wind,* which became one of the famous literary
vendettas of the 1920s. (See Robert Lucas: *Frieda Lawrence: The Story of Frieda Von
Richthofen and D. H. Lawrence,* Viking, New York, 1973, pp. 161–173.)

p. 221 (Chap. 21, fn. 10). Undated draft in the possession of Mme. Mario Meunier (whose husband was the secretary of Isadora Duncan). The chauffeur was released as a result of this letter.

68 rue Chauveau
Neuilly

Monsieur Lescouvé
Public Prosecutor
Paris

Dear Sir:

For my peace of mind, allow me to intercede for the unfortunate man who was the cause of the misfortune which was struck me, to ask you to set him free immediately.

I wish to assure you that I do not bear him ill will. He is a father, and I need to know that he has been released to his family before I can regain some measure of calm.

Please accept, dear sir, the assurance of my profound gratitude.

Isadora Duncan

p. 254 (Chap. 24, fn. 8). Letter in CD. Georges Denis was not the only person to find a source of strength in Isadora's compassion. Friends, acquaintances, and complete strangers wrote to her, confident that she would help them in their needs and understand their griefs. Characteristic of the letters she received is this message from John Cowper Powys (written probably in May or June 1915) as he was recuperating from an operation. She admired his poetry, was attracted to him, and danced for him in the hospital. A poem in *Mandragora* was inspired by her. His letter reads:

I am still seized with that sort of whoreson lethargy . . . which seems like an insane terror of having to undertake the struggle of life again. In the effort not to yield to this weakness I keep making use of your friendship, I keep an almost fierce hold on your hand. I seem to see you always with a secret of courage and of some wonderful terrible kind of ecstasy that is able to defy everything and springs from the very depths. This is your genius and there is none like you in this.

p. 275 (Chap. 26, fn. 16) and Notes, p. 432. In a letter to Paris Singer (now in the Donald Oenslager–Edward Gordon Craig Collection, the Beinicke Library, Yale University), Isadora writes (from 68 rue Chauveau, Neuilly):

Please if I really bore you as you say, if you are tired of me, or if there is anyone else that you would rather take to Greece please dear tell me now— I am far too proud to care to stay with you if you do not want me—I love and adore you and I love little Patrick—the same, perhaps even more, when he cries as when he is amusing. Please tell me the truth if you do not care for me any longer—if there is anyone else—it would be much kinder to say so—

I find it too humiliating to take everything from you and have you say that in return I only annoy you. There is still time for me to cable to America and accept their offer. The idea that you may continue to see me from a sense of duty and not from love makes me quite sick & desperate. You know I never accepted anything from anyone before I met you—and I cannot bear the idea of taking things from you unless you love me. Answer me the truth—

Isadora

Francis Steegmuller: YI, p. 397, has dated this letter "probably summer, 1912."

p. 434 (Chap. 28, fn. 22). George Ivanov, in "Esenin's Fate," *St. Petersburg Winters,* Paris, 1928, gives a different version of Isadora's and Esenin's meeting. According to Ivanov, Isadora first saw Sergei at a banquet in her honor, given after her first performance at the Bolshoi Theatre, and elated by her enthusiastic reception, she kissed him on the mouth. Esenin, who was drunk, pushed her away with an insult, but Isadora, who did not understand his coarse remark, kissed him again, at which, he slapped her. She cried out, and Esenin, sobered, kissed her hands, tried to calm her, and entreated her forgiveness. "And so their love began."

This, however, unlike Ivanov's sketch of Isadora and Esenin in Berlin which follows in his book, is presumably a second-hand account, for Ivanov speaks of Isadora in her Bolshoi debut, breathing heavily and running on stage with a red flag. Isadora's program for her Bolshoi performance on November 7, 1921 (the fourth anniversary of the Russian Revolution) consisted of the Tchaikovsky *Sixth (Pathétique) Symphony,* the *Marche Slave,* and the *Internationale,* which she danced surrounded by the children of her school. It seems highly improbable that there was a red flag in any of her dances. Certainly Irma, in IDRD, pp. 91–96, makes no mention of one. It is true that in the *Marche Slave* the dancer waves an imaginary banner, but in none of her dances did Isadora use props because she felt that the movements of the dance itself should express wings, flags, trumpets, swords, etc.

p. 436 (Chap. 31, fn. 21). Simon Karlinsky, in reviewing *Esenin: A Life,* by Gordon McVay (EAL) for *The New York Times Book Review,* May 9, 1976, wrote:

An archetypal instance of the violent, alcoholic doomed poet, Esenin was driven by a series of irreconcilable love-hate conflicts that pervaded all areas of his life and consciousness: his confused feelings about the Revolution which he had hailed and whose results he came to loathe; his ambiguous sexuality; his mixed attraction to and detestation of the Jews; and his sense of having betrayed his peasant heritage and his later sophisticated and decadent poetry. . . .

To his credit, Gordon McVay's book takes up an important theme until now avoided by Esenin's biographers: his sexual ambivalence. McVay examines Esenin's relationship with Kluyev and concludes that Esenin "may have succumbed to the pressure of the milieu and discovered in himself a latent bisexuality."

This points in the right direction but it does not begin to cover the subject. There is nothing "latent" about the 17-year-old Esenin confessing to Maria Balzamova, a young woman infatuated with him, that the great love of his life might turn out to be either a man or a woman; nor is there anything "latent" about the love letters and poems Esenin and Kluyev exchanged. "Pressure of the milieu" cannot account for Esenin's recurrent close relationships with men who were either homosexual or had bisexual episodes in their lives (Gorodetsky, Ivnev, and Leonid Kannegiser, to name a few) or for his widely attested habit of sharing his bed with his male friends. Esenin's alternating attraction to homosexuality and his revulsion against it (strikingly illustrated in Nicolas Nabokov's recent memoir "Bagazh") may well have contributed to his alcoholism and suicide. His battered and abandoned wives and mistresses seem to have been the principal victims of the poet's inability to come to terms with his bisexuality.

McVay fails to notice that this entire complex is a key to understanding a number of Esenin's more significant poems, such as "The Day Departed" (1916), where the poet sends his shadow to make love to other men in his stead; "Farewell to Marienhof" (1922) with its homoerotic imagery; the opening section of "Prayers for the Dead" ("Sorokoust") where the poet's self-disgust bursts forth in the deliberately shocking images of oral and anal sex with animals and objects; and finally, Esenin's famous suicide poem which is also a love letter to the young man who spent the night with him a few days earlier (McVay's discussion of this poem is handicapped by his failure to convey the grammatical gender of the addressee, unequivocally stated in the second line of the Russian original. . . .)

To this review, McVay comments: "As for Esenin and homosexuality/bisexuality, this also has to be a sphere of (informed) conjecture. I raised the matter, and am pleased that Karlinsky wrote further about it. I think Karlinsky is basically correct, although he exaggerates at times. Esenin's farewell poem is certainly addressed to a man (I don't dispute that), but I do dispute whether this should be called a "love poem." Also the confession to Maria Balzamova seems fairly harmless and innocent. But I don't basically disagree with Karlinsky's other points. (Letter from Gordon McVay to the author, May 29, 1977.)

It is also possible that the harshness with which Esenin treated the women who loved him may not have been caused by latent—nor outright—bisexuality, but because in his depressed state he could only feel their love as a demand on his emotions, and as something which he was incapable of returning. In his last days he compared himself to "God's flute"—hollowed out and emptied of all feeling—as a reed is hollowed to make music. (See EAB, p. 201.) In such a state, evidence of love for him is seen as a *demand* for love, and so a threat, a drain on his dwindling life force.

As for the issue of bisexuality, McVay concludes in IAE, p. 31, "At present it may be impossible to reach a definite conclusion. Some facts may have been suppressed and all opinions can be questioned." For more contradictory opinions and evidence on this subject, see IAE, pp. 32–33.

p. 359 (Chap. 33, fn. 7). Michel Fokine: *Memoirs of a Ballet Master,* translated by Vitale Fokine, A. Chujoy, ed., Little, Brown, Boston, 1961, p. 256. The passage reads:

I consider the greatest manifestations of recent times to be the separate and so dissimilar achievements of Isadora Duncan, Loie Fuller and Ruth St. Denis.

Duncan has reminded us of the beauty of simple movements. Loie Fuller introduced the effect of lights and shadows, of the combination of the dance with floating veils. Ruth St. Denis has acquainted us with the dances of the East.

I wish to talk about Isadora Duncan in some detail. She was the greatest American gift to the art of the dance. Duncan proved that all the primitive, plain, natural movements—a simple step, run, turn on both feet, small jump on one foot—are far better than all the richness of ballet technique, if to this technique must be sacrificed grace, expressiveness and beauty. . . .

It is true that one should not sacrifice beauty or grace to the execution of technical difficulties. The error is in the supposition that technical difficulties could not be executed with grace, as if beauty and expressiveness may be associated only with simple movements.

Not only in the dance, but in all art forms, the pursuit of perfection should not lead to complication of form, overlooking the purpose for which the art form exists. One must be reminded of this. Duncan reminded us: *Do not forget that beauty and expressiveness are of the greatest importance.*

p. 440 (Chap. 34, fn. 3). At least one critic did not enjoy Isadora's performance. Amshinskii, a writer in an unidentified Russian newspaper whose review has been preserved in the Duncan Collection of the New York Public Library, thought that Isadora danced both *The Wearing O' the Green* and *The Marseillaise* badly because of "her venerable age." But he found Irma and the children of the school "a magnificent spectacle," though he wanted his readers to understand that their "movements . . . cannot be called *dances.* This is a new type of physical culture which helps to develop the body. . . . these gay, beautiful children, full of the joy of life, truly children of the revolution, are completely unlike those urchins which we are accustomed to see around barracks . . . without doubt the workers . . . will want their children to become as gay, healthy, and full of the joy of life as the children of the Duncan School. This new understanding must be supported by all means. . . ." (Review captioned, in Russian, "Dances of the Revolution," CD.)

p. 441 (Chap. 36, fn. 8). The improbable bearer of these bad tidings was James Thurber, then a young journalist in Paris, who had been sent by the *Paris Tribune* to get a statement from the bereaved dancer. (Burton Bernstein: *Thurber: A Biography,* Dodd, Mead, New York, 1975, p. 145.)

Bibliography

Allan, Tony. *Americans in Paris.* Chicago: Contemporary Books, 1977.

Amory, Cleveland. *The Last Resorts.* New York: Harper and Brothers, 1952.

Ashton, Sir Frederick. "Unforgettable Isadora Duncan." *The Reader's Digest,* September 1948.

Aveline, Claude and Dufet, Michel. *Bourdelle and the Dance: Isadora and Nijinsky.* Paris: Arted, Editions d'Art, 1969.

Bablet, Denis. *Edward Gordon Craig.* Translated by Daphne Woodward. New York: Theatre Arts Books, 1966.

Barnes, Clive. "The Cold War in Modern Dance." *The New York Times Magazine,* July 28, 1968.

Bauer, Harold. *Harold Bauer: His Book.* New York: Norton, 1948.

Beaumont, Cyril. *Michel Fokine and His Ballets.* London: C. W. Beaumont, 1935.

Bibliothèque Nationale, Paris. *Gordon Craig et Le Renouvellement du Théâtre.* Catalogue of the Gordon Craig Exhibit, 1962.

Bolitho, William. *Twelve Against the Gods.* New York: Simon & Schuster, 1929.

Brandon, Ruth. *A Capitalist Romance: Singer and the Sewing Machine.* New York and Philadelphia: Lippincott, 1977.

Cheney, Sheldon. "Gordon Craig: The Theatre's Chief Revolutionary." *Theatre Arts Monthly,* July 1927.

Bibliography

Combe, Jean. *La Vie et l'Oeuvre de Mario Meunier: Le Secretaire d'Auguste Rodin et d'Isadora Duncan.* Paris: Bibliothèque National Imp. 16° Ln 27, 88880.

Craig, Edward Anthony. *Gordon Craig.* New York: Knopf, 1968.

Craig, Edward Gordon. *The Art of the Theatre.* Edinburgh and London: T. N. Foulis, 1905.

Craig, Edward Gordon. "The Artists of the Theatre of the Future." *The Mask,* vol. 1, no. 1.

Craig, Edward Gordon. *Ellen Terry and Her Secret Self, Together with a Plea for G.B.S.* New York: Dutton, 1932.

Craig, Edward Gordon. *Henry Irving—Ellen Terry: A Book of Portraits.* (Woodcuts and Posters) Chicago: The Lakeside Press, 1899.

Craig, Edward Gordon. *Index to the Story of My Days.* New York: Viking, 1957.

Craig, Edward Gordon. "A Letter from Ellen Terry to her Son, Gordon Craig." *The Mask,* vol. 1, no. 1.

Craig, Edward Gordon. "On Sig. Eleonora Duse." *Life and Letters,* September 1928.

Craig, Edward Gordon. "To Mme. Eleonora Duse." *The Mask,* vol. 1, no. 1.

Craig, Edward Gordon. *Towards a New Theatre.* London: J. M. Dent & Sons, 1913.

Croce, Arlene. *After Images.* New York: Knopf, 1977.

Davies, J. *Esenin, a Biography in Memoirs, Letters and Documents.* Edited and Translated by J. Davies. Ann Arbor: Ardis, 1981.

de Acosta, Mercedes. *Here Lies the Heart: A Tale of My Life.* New York: Reynal and Co., 1960.

de Acosta, Mercedes. "Isadora Duncan: A Paradox." *Speaking of the Famous: An Anthology of Spoken Esteem.* London: Macmillan and Co., 1962.

de Graaff, Francisca. *Serge Esénine, 1895–1925: Sa Vie et Son Oeuvre.* Leyde: E. J. Brill, 1933.

de Gramont, E. *Les Marronniers en Fleurs.* Paris: Bernard Grasset, 1929.

Dell, Floyd. "Olive Schriner and Isadora Duncan." *Women as World Builders.* Chicago: Forbes, 1913.

deMille, Agnes. *The Book of the Dance.* New York: Golden Press, 1963.

deMille, Agnes. Article about Isadora Duncan. *The New York Times Magazine,* New York: September 14, 1952.

de Segonzac, André Dunoyer. *Dessins sur les Danses d'Isadora Duncan.* Précédés de *La Danseuse de Diane.* Glose de Fernand Divoire. Paris: La Belle Edition, 1910.

Desti, Mary. *The Untold Story.* New York: Liveright, 1929.

The Director: Dancing, Deportment, Etiquette, Aesthetics, Physical Training. vol. 1, no. 4. Portland, Maine: Melvin Ballon Gilbert, March 1898. (Reviews of Isadora Duncan's dances) September 1898; Mrs. Richard Hovey (Teacher of Delsarte's

Theories), October; and November 1898, "Narcissus and Other Scenes done into Dance by Isadora Duncan."

Divoire, Fernand. *Découvertes sur la Danse*. (Illustrations by Bourdelle.) Paris: Les Editions, G. Cres et Cie, 1924.

Divoire, Fernand. *Exhortation à la Victoire*. (Written June 24, 1914.) Paris: Jouve et Cie, 1916.

Divoire, Fernand. *Isadora Duncan, Fille de Prométhée*. (Illustrations by Bourdelle.) Paris: Editions des Muses Françaises, 1919.

Divoire, Fernand. *Pour la Danse*. Saxe, Paris: Editions de la Danse.

Dumesnil, Maurice. *An Amazing Journey*. New York: Washburn, 1932.

Duncan, Anna. "Isadora and Vanessa: Anna Duncan Talks to Parker Tyler." *Ballet Review*, vol. 3, no. 1, 1969.

Duncan, Irma. "Follow Me." *Dance Perspectives*, nos. 1 and 22, 1965. Republished in expanded form as Duncan, Irma. *Duncan Dancer*. Middletown, Connecticut: Wesleyan, 1966.

Duncan, Irma. *Isadora Duncan: Pioneer in the Art of the Dance*. New York: the New York Public Library, 1958.

Duncan, Irma, and Macdougall, Allan Ross. *Isadora Duncan's Russian Days and Her Last Years in France*. New York: Covici-Friede, 1929.

Duncan, Irma. *The Technique of Isadora Duncan*. New York: Kamin, undated.

Duncan, Isadora. *The Art of the Dance*. Edited by Sheldon Cheney. New York: Theatre Arts, 1928.

Duncan, Isadora. *The Dance of the Future*. Introduction by Karl Federn. Leipzig: Eugen Diederichs, 1903.

Duncan, Isadora. *My Life*. New York: Boni and Liveright, 1927.

Eastman, Max. "Heroism Plus Heroics: Difficulties in Worshiping Isadora Duncan." *Heroes I Have Known*. New York: Simon & Schuster, 1942.

Esenin, Sergei. "Iron Mirogorod." *Isvestia*. August 22, 1923 [September 16, 1923, western calendar].

Esenin, Sergei. *Pamyatka O Sergee Esenin*. Moskva: Segodnia, 1926.

Esenin, Sergei. *Sergei Alexandrovich Esenin: Memoirs*. Edited by I. V. Evdokimov. Moscow: 1926. Containing articles by Riurik Ivnev ("About Esenin"), M. Babenchikov ("Esenin"), Ivan Startsev ("My Encounter with Esenin"), N. Poltaev and Valentin Volpin ("About Sergei Esenin"), Ivan Gruzinov ("Esenin"), Michael Murachev ("Sergei Esenin in Petrograd"), Georgi Ustinov ("My Memoirs of Esenin"), E. Ustinova ("Four Days of Sergei Alexandrovich Esenin"), L. Fainshtein, V. Kirillov, N. Assev, and I. Evdokimov.

Flanner, Janet [Genêt]. *Paris Was Yesterday: 1925–1939*. New York: Viking, 1972.

Fokine, Michel. *Memoirs of a Ballet Master*. Translated by Vitale Fokine. Edited by A. Chujoy. Boston: Little, Brown, 1961.

Bibliography

Fuller, Loie. *Fifteen Years of a Dancer's Life.* Introduction by Anatole France. Herbert Jenkins, London, 1913.

Genthe, Arnold. *As I Remember.* New York: Reynal and Hitchcock, 1936.

Genthe, Arnold. *The Book of the Dance.* Boston: International Publishers, 1916.

Godwin, Edward W., F.S.A. "The Architecture and Costume of the Merchant of Venice." *The Mask,* vol. 1, no. 5, July 1908.

Gordon, Lady Duff. *Discretions and Indiscretions.* New York: Jarrold, Norwich, Eng, and Stokes, 1932.

Harbron, Dudley. *The Conscious Stone: The Life of Edward William Godwin.* London: Latimer House, 1949.

Hellens, Franz. *Documents Secrets: Histoire Sentimentale de Mes Livres et de Quelques Amitiés.* Paris: Editions Albin Michel, 1958.

Huddleston, Sisley. "The Tragedy of a Dancer." *Paris Salons, Cafes, Studios.* Philadelphia: Lippincott, 1928.

Hurok, S., and Goode, Ruth. *Impresario: A Memoir.* New York: Random House, 1946.

Ivanov, Georgy. "Esenin's Fate." *St. Petersburg Winters.* Paris: 1928. Republished in *In the Bitter Air of Exile.* Translated by Brant Bassett. Edited by Simon Karlinsky and Alfred Appel, Jr. Berkeley: University of California Press, 1977.

Joel, Lydia. "Finding Isadora: Notes from the Editor's Desk." *Dancemagazine,* June 1969.

Johnson, Alva. "Addison Mizener, the Palm Beach Architect." *The New Yorker,* November 29, 1952.

Karlinsky, Simon. "Isadora Had a Taste for Russian Love," review of *Esenin: A Life,* by Gordon McVay. *The New York Times Book Review,* May 9, 1976.

Karlinsky, Simon. Letter to Professor Gordon McVay, August 31, 1976.

Karsavina, Tamara. *Theatre Street.* New York: E. P. Dutton, 1930.

Kaye, Joseph. "The Last Chapters of Isadora's Life." *The Dance Magazine,* April, May, and June, 1929.

Kennet, Lady. *Self Portrait of an Artist: From the Diaries and Memoirs of Lady Kennet.* London: John Murray, 1949.

Kinel, Lola. *This Is My Affair.* Boston: Little, Brown, 1937.

Kirstein, Lincoln. *Dance.* New York: Putnam, 1935.

Kobler, John. "Mr. Singer's Money Machine." *Saturday Evening Post,* July 7 and July 14, 1951.

Laffitte, Sophie. *Serge Essénine.* Paris: Editions Pierre Seghers, 1959.

Lavrin, Janko. "Sergey Esenin." *From Pushkin to Mayakovsky.* Richmond, Virginia: Sylvan Press, 1948.

Leeper, Janet. *Edward Gordon Craig: Designs for the Theatre.* Harmondsworth, England: Penguin, 1948.

Bibliography

LeGallienne, Eva. *The Mystic in the Theatre: Eleonora Duse.* New York: Farrar, Straus and Giroux, 1965.

Lenoir, Jacqueline. "Cécile Sorel: Idole de la IIIe République." *Jours de France.* September 30, 1967.

Levin, Veniamin. "Esenin in America." *Novoe Russkoe Slovo.* New York: August 11, 12, and 13, 1953.

Levinson, André. "L'Apogée d'Isadora Duncan" (Pour l'Anniversaire de Sa Mort). *Comoedia.* September 14, 1928.

Lloyd, Margaret. *The Borzoi Book of Modern Dance.* New York: Borzoi, 1949.

Lowenthal, Lillian. "Isadora Duncan in the Netherlands." *Dance Chronicle.* vol. 3, no. 3, 1979–1980.

Luhan, Mabel Dodge. "Isadora Duncan." *Town and Country,* July 1936.

Macdonald, Nesta. "Isadora Reexamined: Lesser Known Aspects of the Great Dancer's Life." *Dance Magazine.* July through December, 1977. Excerpts from *Isadora Duncan,* to be published by Alfred Knopf.

Macdougall, Allan Ross. *Isadora: A Revolutionary in Art and Love.* New York: Thomas Nelson and Sons, 1960.

Magriel, Paul, ed. *Isadora Duncan.* New York: Henry Holt, 1947. Containing: "Isadora Duncan and Basic Dance," by John Martin; "Duncan Concerts in New York" and "The New Isadora," by Carl Van Vechten; "Isadora Duncan and the Artists," by Allan Ross Macdougall; "Isadora Duncan: Studies for Six Dance Movements," by Edward Gordon Craig; Chronology; Bibliography of Isadora Duncan; Albums and books of drawings of Isadora Duncan.

Manvell, Roger. *Ellen Terry.* New York: Putnam, 1968.

Martin, John. *The Dance.* New York: Tudor, 1965.

Maurevert, Georges S. *Art, Life and the Boulevard.* Nice: N. Chini, 1911.

McAlmon, Robert, and Boyle, Kay. *Being Geniuses Together.* New York: Doubleday, 1968.

McVay, Gordon. *Esenin: A Life.* Ann Arbor: Ardis, 1976.

McVay, Gordon. *Isadora and Esenin.* Ann Arbor: Ardis, 1980.

Meryman, Richard. *Mank: The Wit, World and Life of Herman Mankiewicz.* New York: Morrow, 1978.

Nabokov, Nicolas. *Bagàzh: Memoirs of a Russian Cosmopolitan.* New York: Atheneum, 1975.

Nikritina, Anna. "Esenin and Marienhof." *Esenin i Sovremennost* [Esenin and Our Time]. Moscow, 1975.

Ostrom, Nicki Nowlin. "The Gordon Craig–Isadora Duncan Collection: A Register." *Bulletin of the New York Public Library,* vol. 76. Includes biographical indications.

Poiret, Paul. *King of Fashion: The Autobiography of Paul Poiret.* Philadelphia: Lippincott, 1931.

Bibliography

Prideaux, Tom. *Love or Nothing: The Life and Times of Ellen Terry.* New York: Scribner, 1975.

Rather, Lois. *Lovely Isadora.* Oakland, California: The Rather Press, 1976.

Reavey, George. *Soviet Literature Today.* London: Lindsay Drummond, 1946.

Roberts, Mary Fanton. "The Dance of the Future as Created by Isadora Duncan." In the collection of Mme. Mario Meunier. (My copy gives neither the publisher nor the publication date, which was probably at the time of Isadora's first return to New York after the founding of the school.)

Roberts, Mary Fanton. "Isadora, the Dancer." *Denishawn Magazine,* Summer 1925.

Rood, Arnold. *Edward Gordon Craig: Artist of the Theatre, 1872–1966.* Catalogue of a Memorial Exhibition. Introduction by Donald Oenslager. New York: the New York Public Library, 1967.

Rose, Enid. *Gordon Craig and the Theatre.* London: Samson Low, Marston and Co., 1931.

Schneider, Ilya Ilyitch. *Isadora Duncan: The Russian Years.* London: Macdonald, 1968.

Seldes, George. "What Love Meant to Isadora Duncan." *The Mentor.* Springfield, Ohio: 1930.

Seroff, Victor. *The Real Isadora.* New York: Dial, 1971.

Shaw, Martin. *Up to Now.* Oxford University Press, 1929.

Shawn, Ted. *Dance We Must.* The Peabody Lecture Series 1, from June 13 to July 2, 1938. Published in 1940.

Shawn, Ted. *Every Little Movement.* Pittsfield, Mass.: Eagle Printing and Binding Company, 1954. Copyright 1910 by M. Witmark & Sons. Copyright 1954 by Ted Shawn. (A book about François Delsarte.)

Shawn, Ted. *Ruth St. Denis: Pioneer and Prophet.* San Francisco: Printed for John Howell by John Henry Nash, 1920.

Slonim, Mark. *Modern Soviet Literature.* New York: Oxford University Press, 1953.

Stanislavski, Constantin. *My Life in Art.* Translated by J. J. Robbins. New York: Meridian Books, 1957. (Copyright 1924 by Little, Brown.)

St. Denis, Ruth, and Buckmaster, Henrietta. *An Unfinished Life.* New York: Harper, 1939.

Steegmuller, Francis. *Your Isadora: The Love Story of Isadora Duncan and Gordon Craig, told through letters and diaries never before published.* Edited, with a connecting text by Francis Steegmuller. New York: Random House and the New York Public Library, 1974.

Stokes, Sewell. *Isadora Duncan: An Intimate Portrait.* London: Brentano, 1928.

Stokes, Sewell. "Listening to Isadora Duncan." *The Listener.* June 27, 1957.

Svetlov, Valerian. "Isadora Duncan." *The Dancing Times,* December 1927.

Svetlov, Valerian [V. Y. Ivchenko]. *Le Ballet Contemporain.* St. Petersburg: Golike et Willborg, 1912.

Terry, Ellen. *Memoirs.* With a preface, notes, and an index by Edith Craig and Christopher St. John, and a letter from G. B. Shaw about the Shaw–Craig controversy over Ellen Terry's letters. London: Gollancz, 1933.

Terry, Walter. *Isadora Duncan: Her Life, Her Art, Her Legacy.* New York: Dodd, Mead, 1963.

Terry, Walter. "The Legacy of Isadora Duncan and Ruth St. Denis." *Dance Perspectives,* no. 5, Winter 1969.

Weiss, David. *The Spirit and the Flesh.* New York: Doubleday, 1959. (A novel inspired by the life of Isadora Duncan.)

Werner, M. R. *To Whom It May Concern: The Story of Victor Ilyitch Seroff.* New York: Jonathan Cape and Smith, 1931.

Wigman, Mary. *The Language of Dance.* Middletown, Conn.: Wesleyan University, 1966.

Yarmolinsky, Avram. "Esenin in New York." *Novyi Zhurnal,* Book 51, 1959.

Yeats, John Butler. "On Isadora Dancing." Ms. letter from John Butler Yeats to John Quinn, November 1, 1908. From *Abroad in America: Visitors to the New Nation, 1776–1914.* Edited by Marc Pachter and Frances Wein. Washington, D.C. and Reading, Mass.: National Portrait Gallery and Addison Wesley Publishing Company.

Index

Index

Index

Duncan, Isadora (*cont.*):

death and funeral, 396–399

and death of her children, 219–235, 236, 255–256, 262, 280, 281–282, 288, 291, 293, 321, 334, 335, 339, 350, 377, 384–386, 389, 396, 399

debut before a large public, 56–58

and Delsarte, 16–18

drinking, 333–335, 339

early life, 1–2, 9–20, 76, 122, 154, 195–197, 241, 265, 274–275, 340, 383

school, 10, 11–12, 13

engagement to Miroski, 23–24, 25, 36–37, 90, 240

and Esenin (*see* Esenin, Sergei Aleksandrovich)

and her father, 12–13, 19–20, 76, 100, 101, 153–154, 197, 241, 274–275

feminism, 84–85, 122, 140, 290

in Germany, 50–51, 62–69, 71, 79–90, 108, 110, 111, 118, 119, 126, 155–161, 163, 313–323, 365–376, 379

Bayreuth, 83–90

in Greece, 71–78, 250–252, 284–285

Greek inspiration, xvi, 1–2, 30, 35, 39, 40, 46, 56, 58, 66–67, 73, 76, 81, 82, 116, 117, 180, 188, 244–246, 249, 297, 320, 403

in Holland, 141–145, 146, 152–155

illness, 142–151

intellectual nature, 36, 41, 64, 77, 81–84, 88, 103, 201, 209

study of dance, 44–49

in Italy, 63–64, 136–137, 141

last performance, 391

and "Lohengrin" (*see* Singer, Paris Eugene)

in London, 33–38, 179–180

Love and Art, 123, 369

and music, relation to dance, 139–140, 184–193, 249, 403

on music-drama, 85, 87

musical culture, 190

My Life, xi, xvi, 1–2, 12, 25, 29, 33, 50–51, 65, 90, 94–95, 97, 101, 110–111, 143, 167, 168, 171–172, 200, 201, 210, 232, 310, 376–377, 378, 381–382, 392, 393, 396

in New York and the U.S.A., 180–193, 201–204, 211–213, 238–250, 256, 261, 269–290, 324–336

notebook, 55–56

parents, 2–8

in Paris and France, 38–49, 69–70, 194–195, 210–211, 215, 252–260, 280, 282–290, 323, 337–341, 374–399

and "Pim," 167–168

in Poland, 137–138, 141

prenatal influence on, 2, 7

rehearsal methods, 267–268

religious inspiration of her art, 21, 67, 69, 81, 83, 124, 127, 186, 226–227, 243, 279, 320, 321, 327, 349–350, 372, 403

revolutionary dances, 355–363

her "Romeo" (*see* Beregi, Oscar)

in Russia, 28, 103–118, 168, 171–176, 199–201, 218–219, 289–312, 341–365, 369

her school, 90, 108, 119, 122, 123, 125, 135, 137, 161, 164, 176, 179, 180–181, 183–184, 193, 195, 198, 203, 215, 222, 235, 236, 237–238, 239, 240, 252, 255, 258–259, 265, 268, 269–270, 282, 283, 285, 288–290, 291–300, 309, 312, 322, 335, 341, 350–351, 353–354, 364–354, 366, 367, 370, 371, 372, 375, 379, 380, 388, 389, 390, 402, 448, 450

and Seroff, 383–384, 386, 387, 389–390, 391–392, 393–394

significance and legacy, xi–xvi, 400–409

in South America, 255, 260–268, 335, 336

and Stanislawski, 171–174

suicide attempts, 130, 390

on Swedish gymnastics, 127

a symbol during the war, 254–259

theatrical beginnings, 21–32

her third child, 233–236, 237, 398

and Thode, 87–90, 132

in Vienna, 51–53, 60

writings about the dance, 48, 49, 65–69, 116, 118, 124, 212–213, 268, 378

Duncan, Joseph Charles (Isadora's father), 2–8, 12–13, 19–20, 76, 100, 101, 153, 154, 197, 241, 274–275, 369

Duncan, Ligoa, xii

Duncan, Lisa, xiii, 242, 292, 397

Duncan, Margherita Sargent (Augustin's wife), 237, 245, 260, 273, 367, 431–432n11

Duncan, Margo (Gretel), 242, 292, 377, 378

Duncan, Maria-Theresa, xii, xiii–xiv, xvi, 47, 242, 292, 404, 433n13

Index

Index

Index